saturn
apartments 1

Trav

HISAE IWAOKA

saturn apartments 1

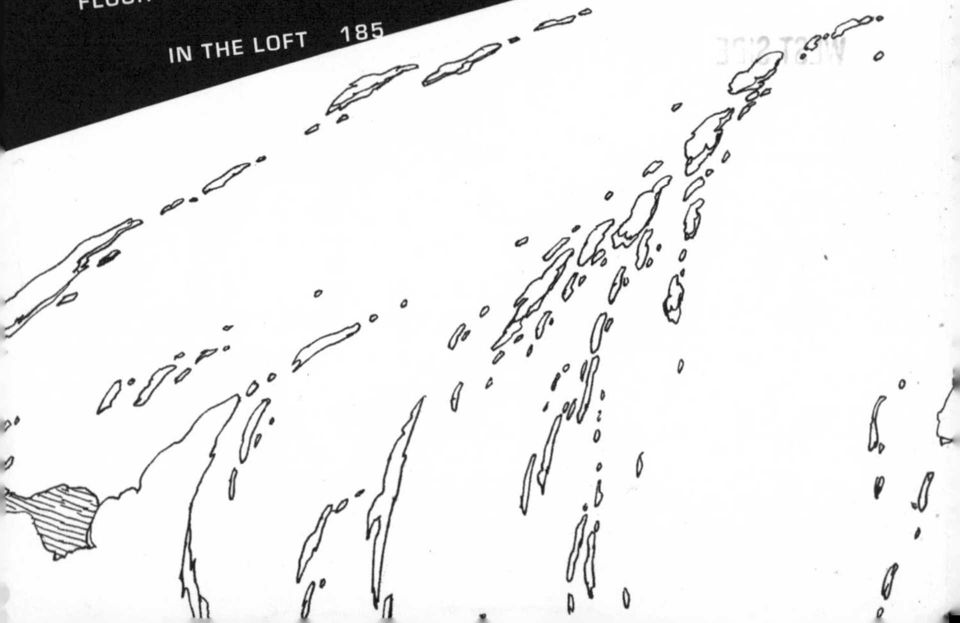

floor 1. earth

I'VE FINISHED CLEANING THIS WINDOW.
RIGHT. NEXT ONE.

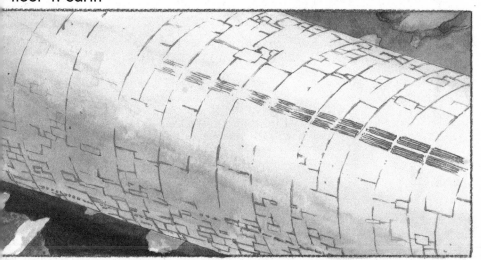

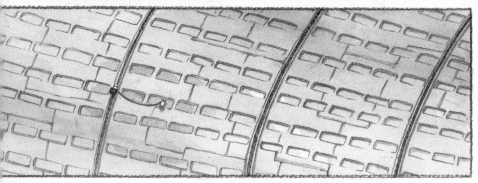

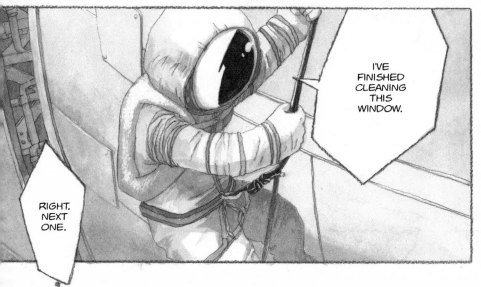

floor 1. earth

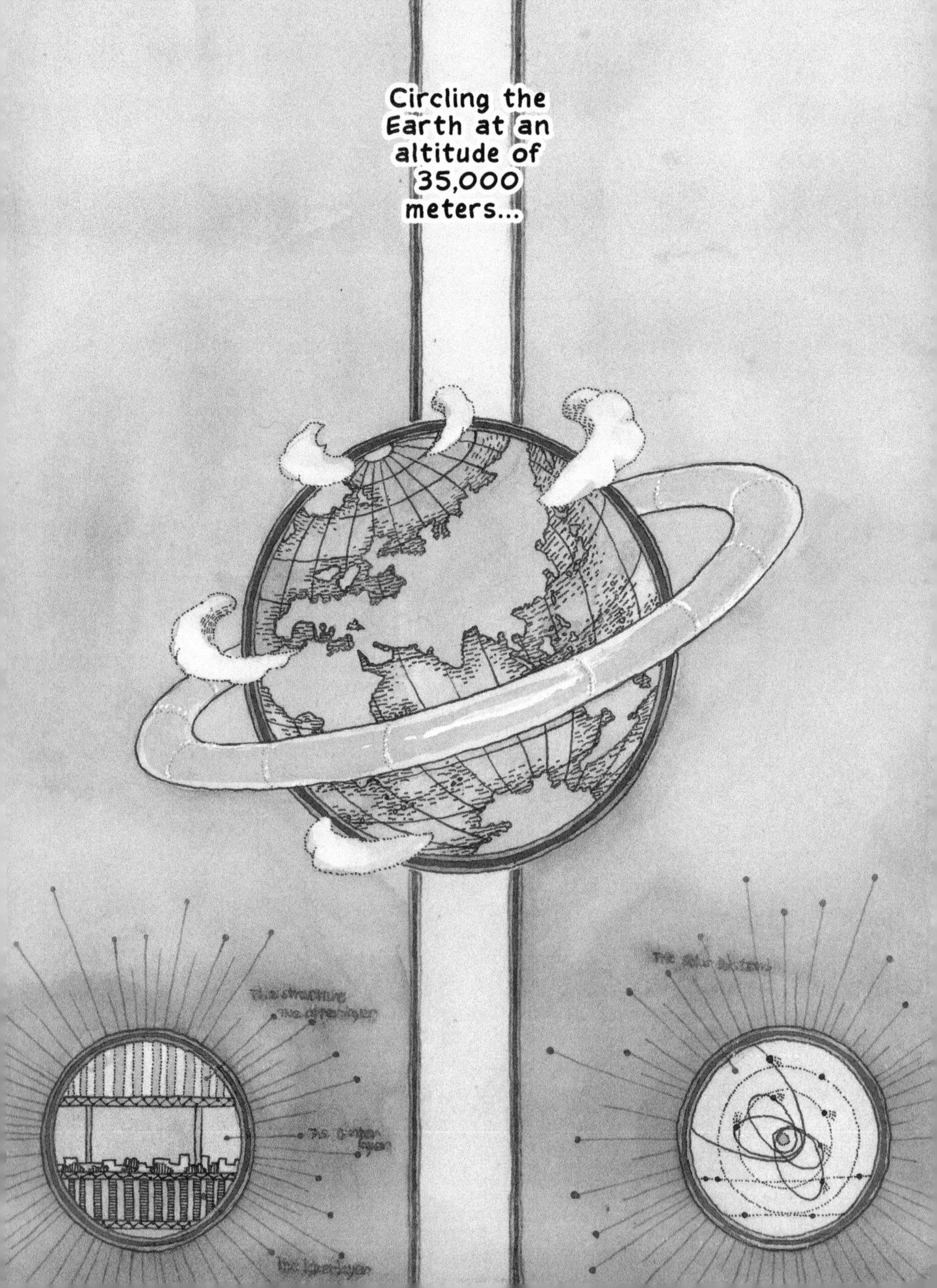
Circling the Earth at an altitude of 35,000 meters...

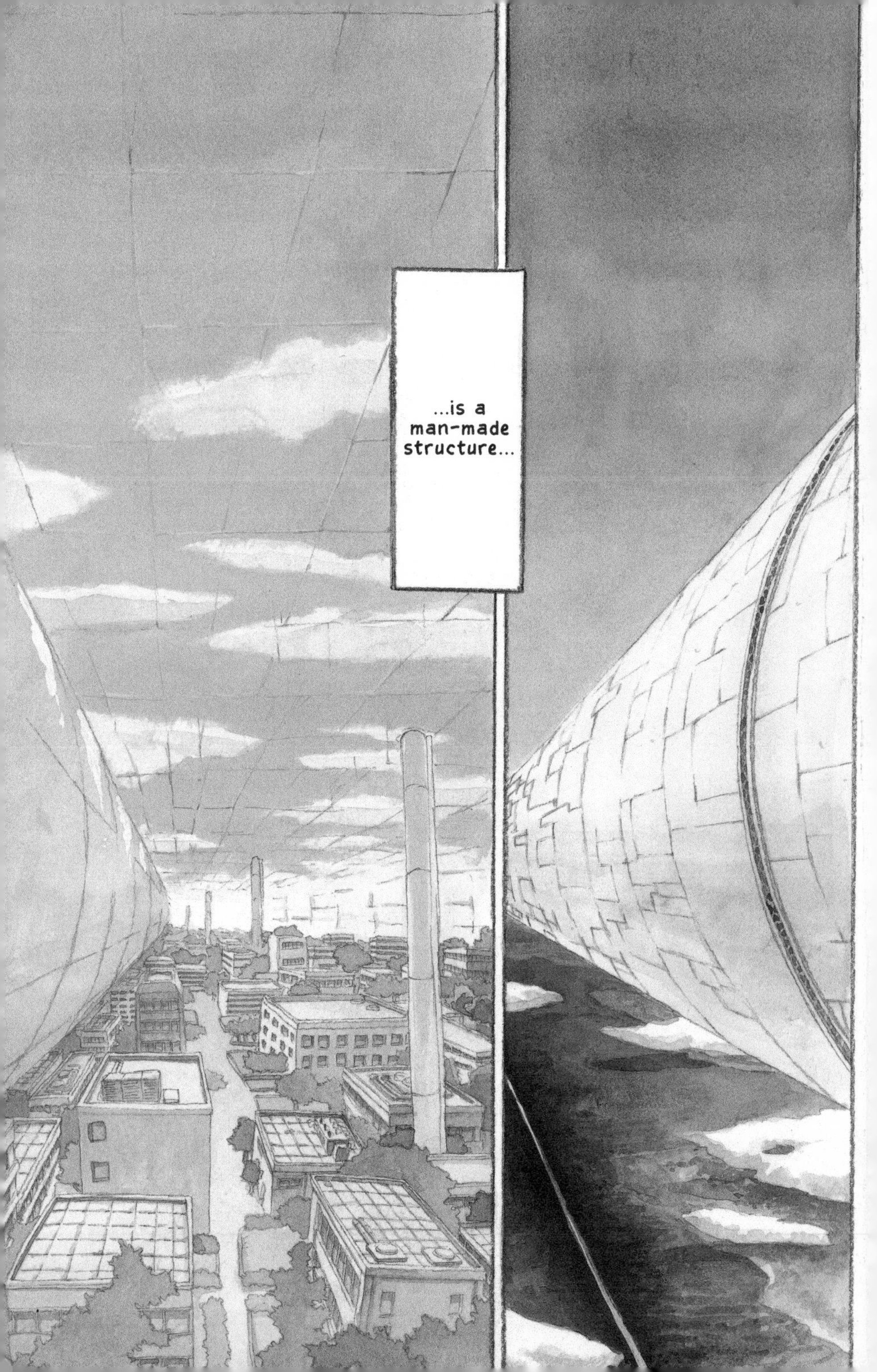
...is a man-made structure...

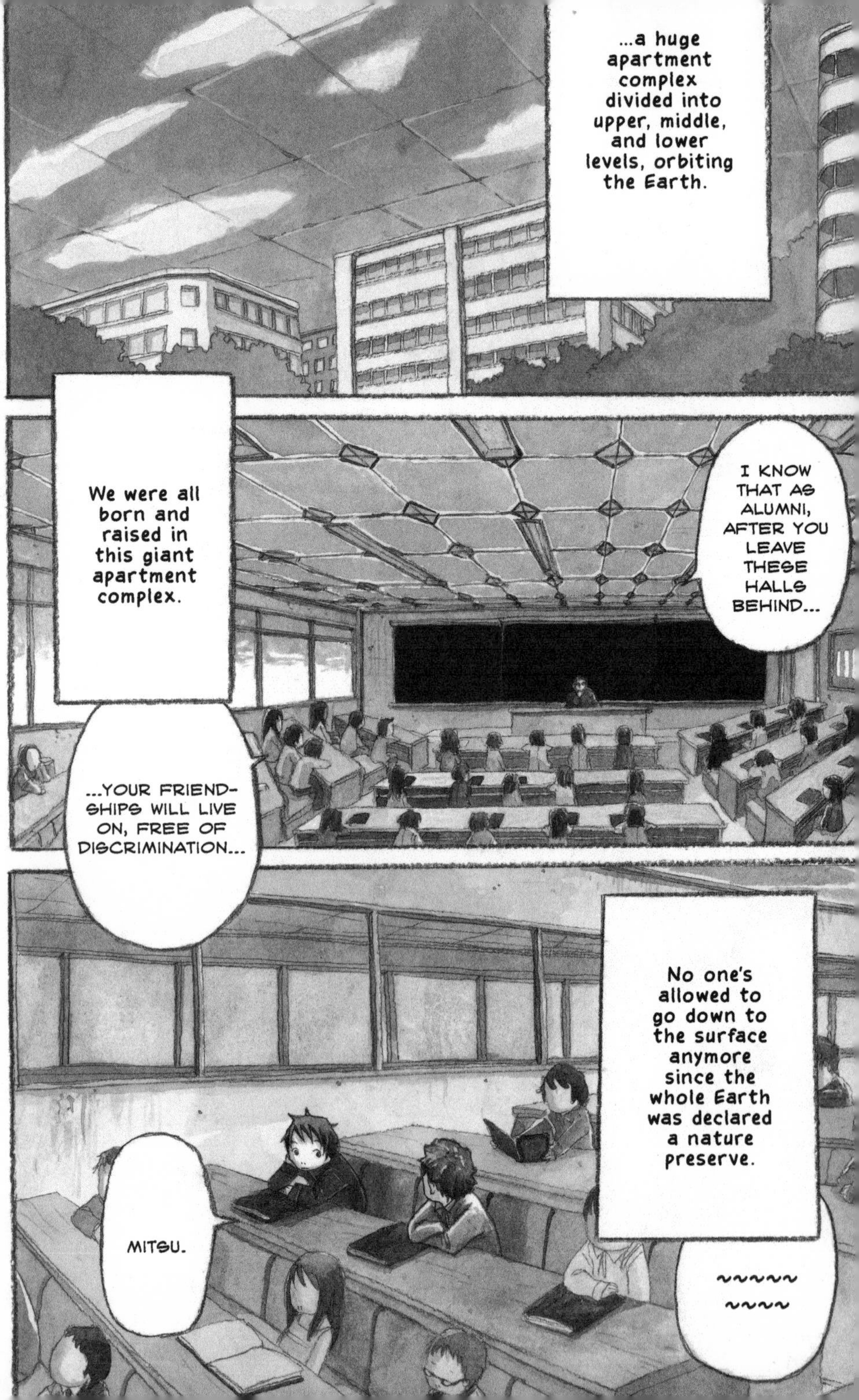
...a huge apartment complex divided into upper, middle, and lower levels, orbiting the Earth.
I KNOW THAT AS ALUMNI, AFTER YOU LEAVE THESE HALLS BEHIND...
We were all born and raised in this giant apartment complex.
...YOUR FRIEND-SHIPS WILL LIVE ON, FREE OF DISCRIMINATION...
No one's allowed to go down to the surface anymore since the whole Earth was declared a nature preserve.
~~~~~ ~~~~
MITSU.
~~~~~

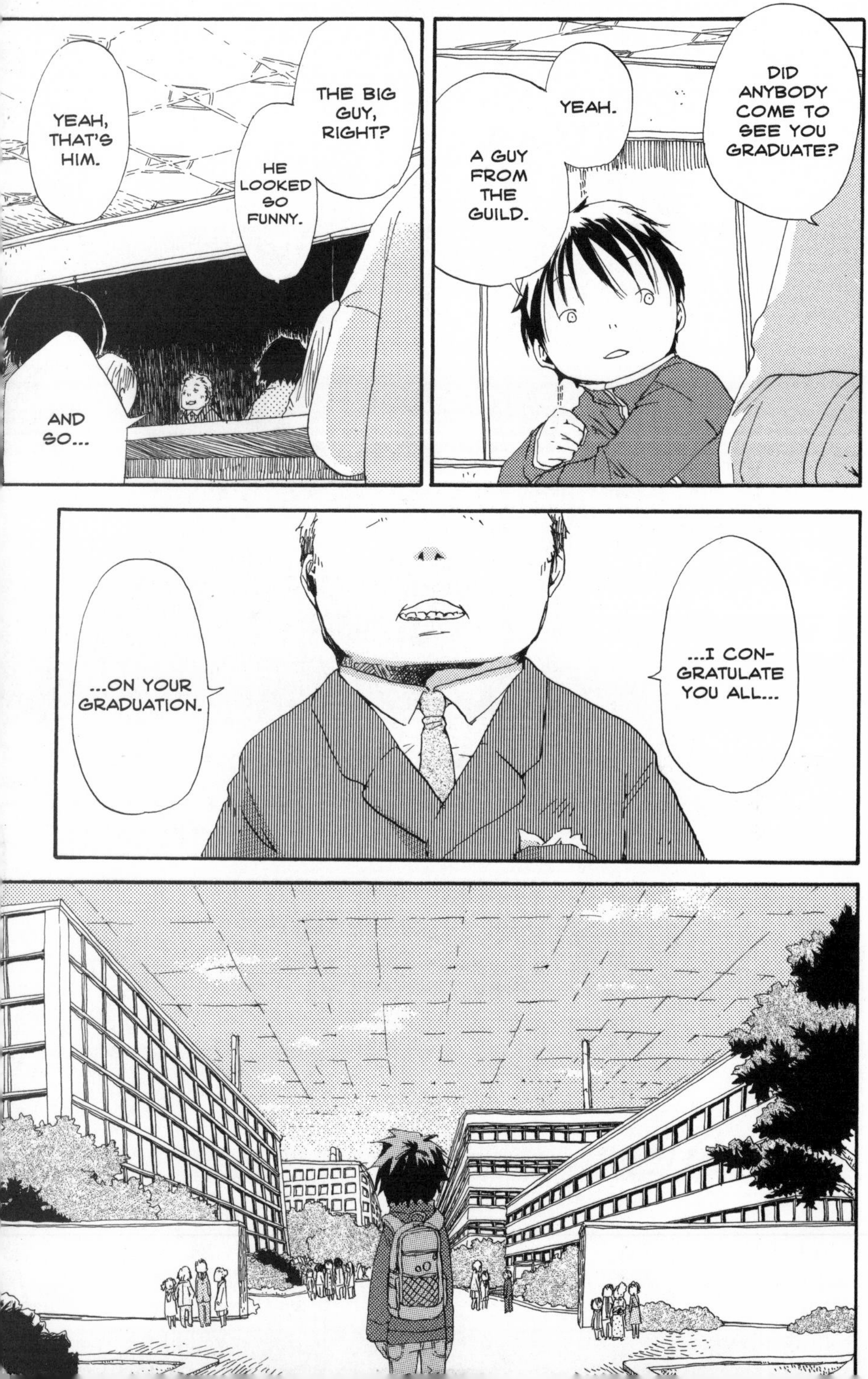
DID ANYBODY COME TO SEE YOU GRADUATE?
YEAH.
A GUY FROM THE GUILD.
THE BIG GUY, RIGHT?
HE LOOKED SO FUNNY.
YEAH, THAT'S HIM.
AND SO...
...I CON-GRATULATE YOU ALL...
...ON YOUR GRADUATION.

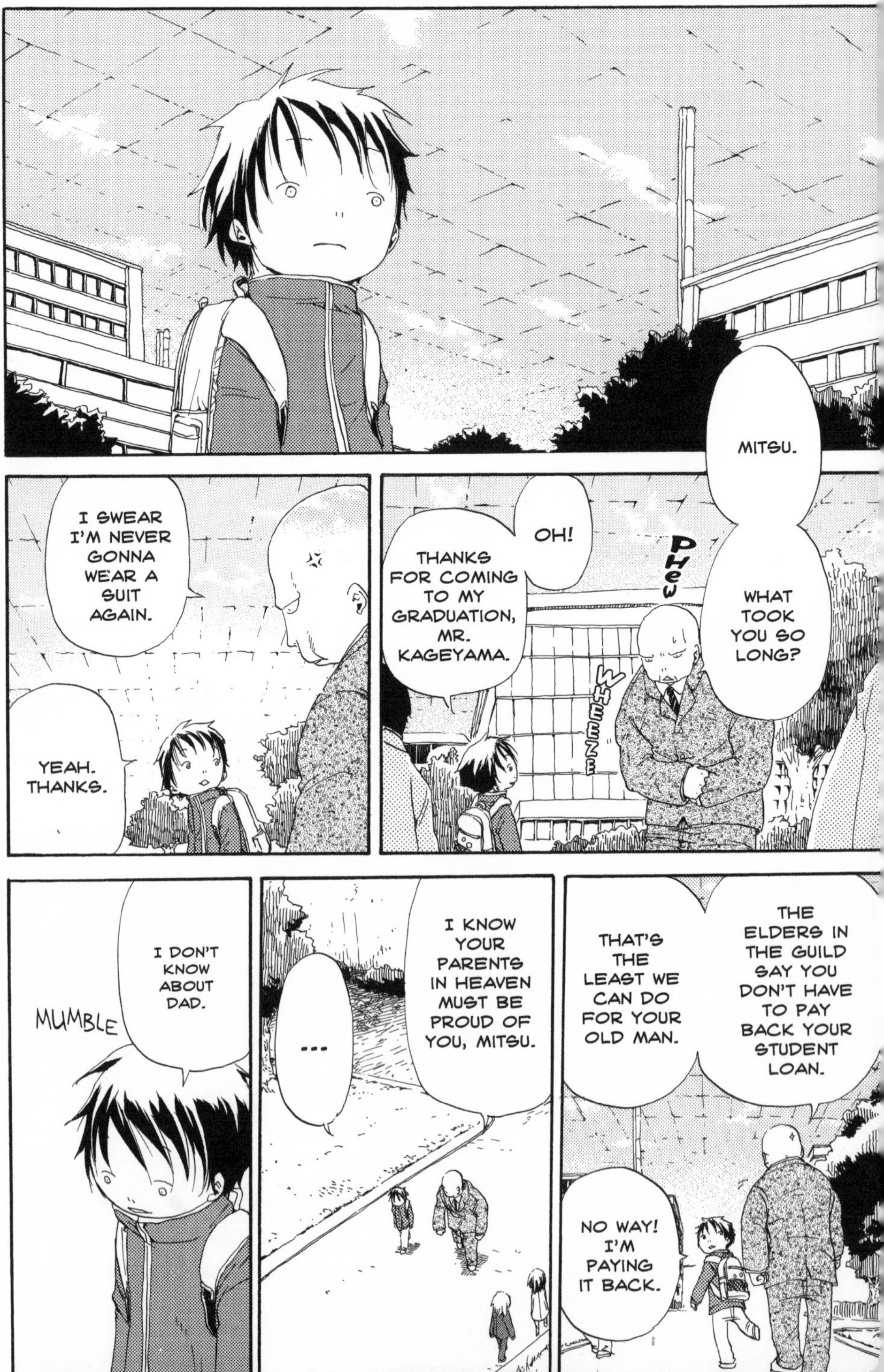
MITSU.
WHAT TOOK YOU SO LONG?
PHEW
WHEEZE
OH!
THANKS FOR COMING TO MY GRADUATION, MR. KAGEYAMA.
I SWEAR I'M NEVER GONNA WEAR A SUIT AGAIN.
YEAH. THANKS.
THE ELDERS IN THE GUILD SAY YOU DON'T HAVE TO PAY BACK YOUR STUDENT LOAN.
THAT'S THE LEAST WE CAN DO FOR YOUR OLD MAN.
NO WAY! I'M PAYING IT BACK.
I KNOW YOUR PARENTS IN HEAVEN MUST BE PROUD OF YOU, MITSU.
...
I DON'T KNOW ABOUT DAD.
MUMBLE

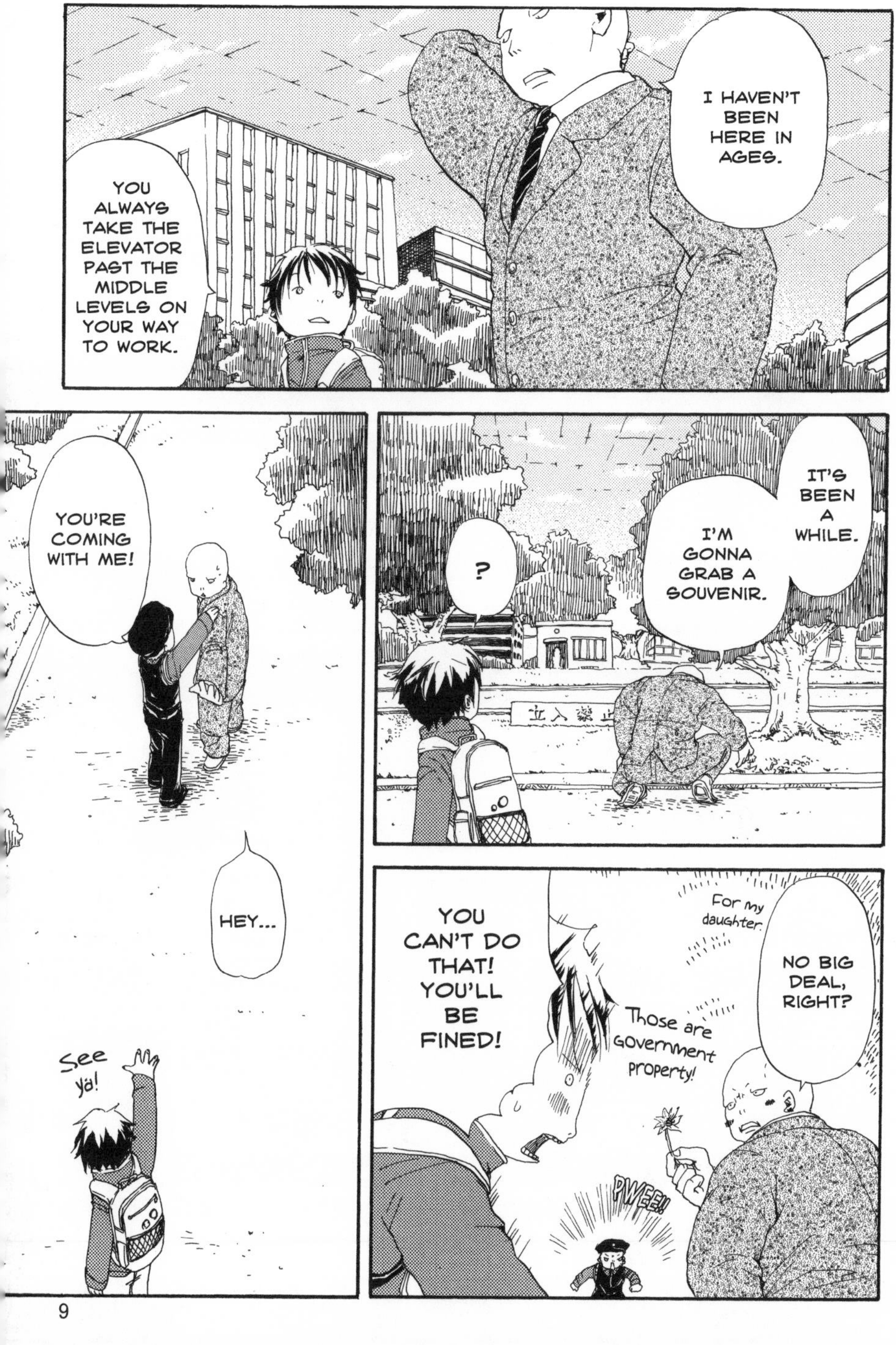
I HAVEN'T BEEN HERE IN AGES.
YOU ALWAYS TAKE THE ELEVATOR PAST THE MIDDLE LEVELS ON YOUR WAY TO WORK.
IT'S BEEN A WHILE.
I'M GONNA GRAB A SOUVENIR.
?
NO BIG DEAL, RIGHT?
For my daughter.
YOU CAN'T DO THAT! YOU'LL BE FINED!
Those are government property!
PWEE!!
YOU'RE COMING WITH ME!
HEY...
See ya!

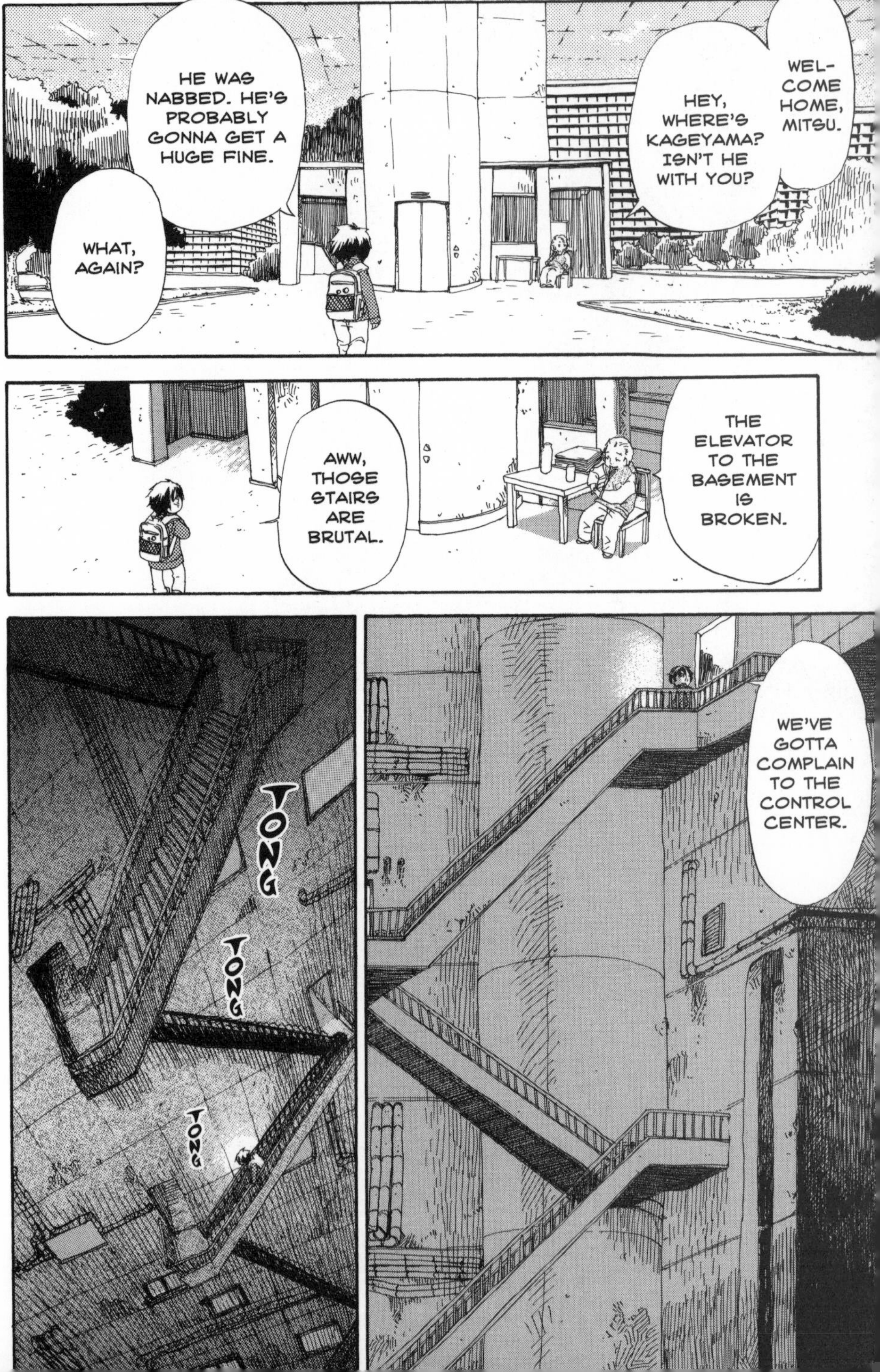
WEL-COME HOME, MITSU.
HEY, WHERE'S KAGEYAMA? ISN'T HE WITH YOU?
HE WAS NABBED. HE'S PROBABLY GONNA GET A HUGE FINE.
WHAT, AGAIN?
THE ELEVATOR TO THE BASEMENT IS BROKEN.
AWW, THOSE STAIRS ARE BRUTAL.
WE'VE GOTTA COMPLAIN TO THE CONTROL CENTER.
TONG
TONG
TONG

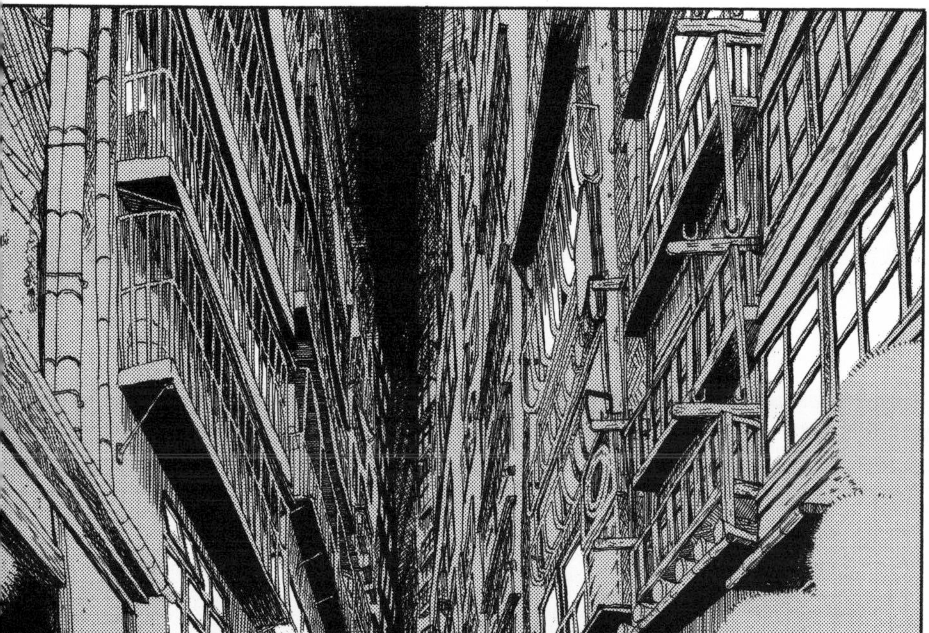

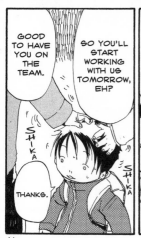

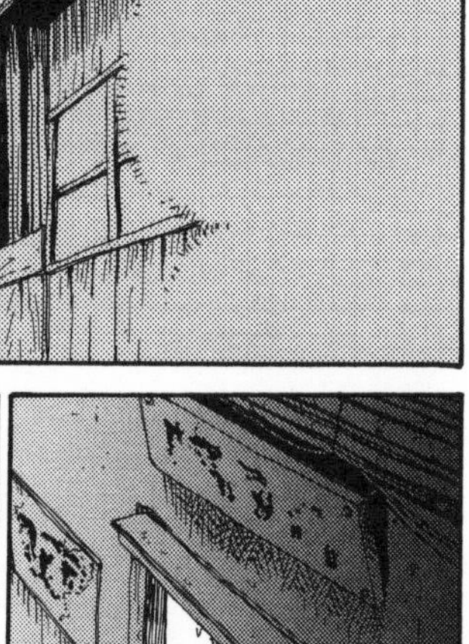
HELLO.

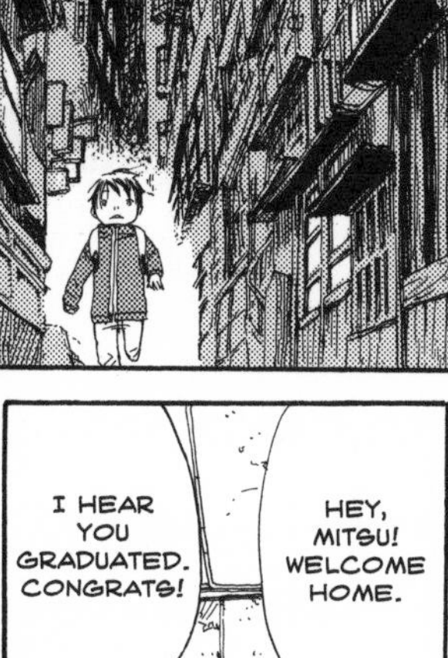
HEY, MITSU! WELCOME HOME.
I HEAR YOU GRADUATED. CONGRATS!
WOW.

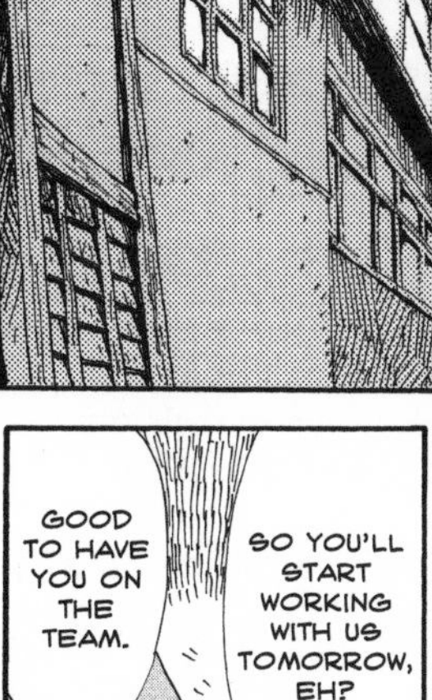
SO YOU'LL START WORKING WITH US TOMORROW, EH?
GOOD TO HAVE YOU ON THE TEAM.
SHIKA
SHIKA
THANKS.

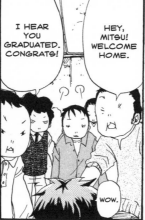

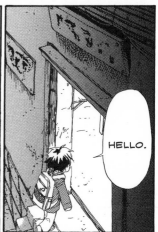

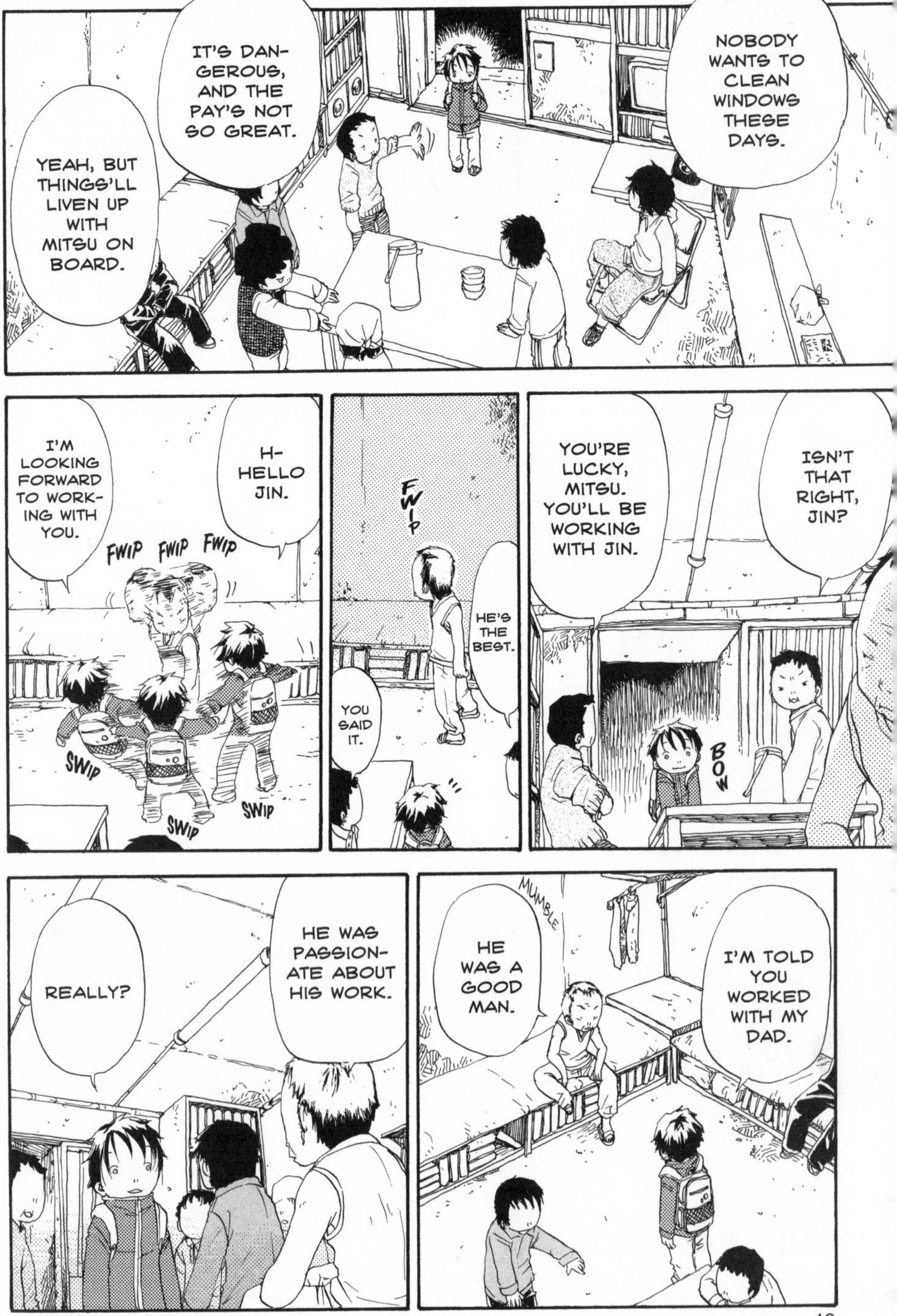

NOBODY WANTS TO CLEAN WINDOWS THESE DAYS.
IT'S DAN-GEROUS, AND THE PAY'S NOT SO GREAT.
YEAH, BUT THINGS'LL LIVEN UP WITH MITSU ON BOARD.
ISN'T THAT RIGHT, JIN?
YOU'RE LUCKY, MITSU. YOU'LL BE WORKING WITH JIN.
BOW
FWIP
HE'S THE BEST.
YOU SAID IT.
H-HELLO JIN.
I'M LOOKING FORWARD TO WORK-ING WITH YOU.
FWIP FWIP FWIP
SWIP SWIP SWIP
I'M TOLD YOU WORKED WITH MY DAD.
MUMBLE
HE WAS A GOOD MAN.
HE WAS PASSION-ATE ABOUT HIS WORK.
REALLY?

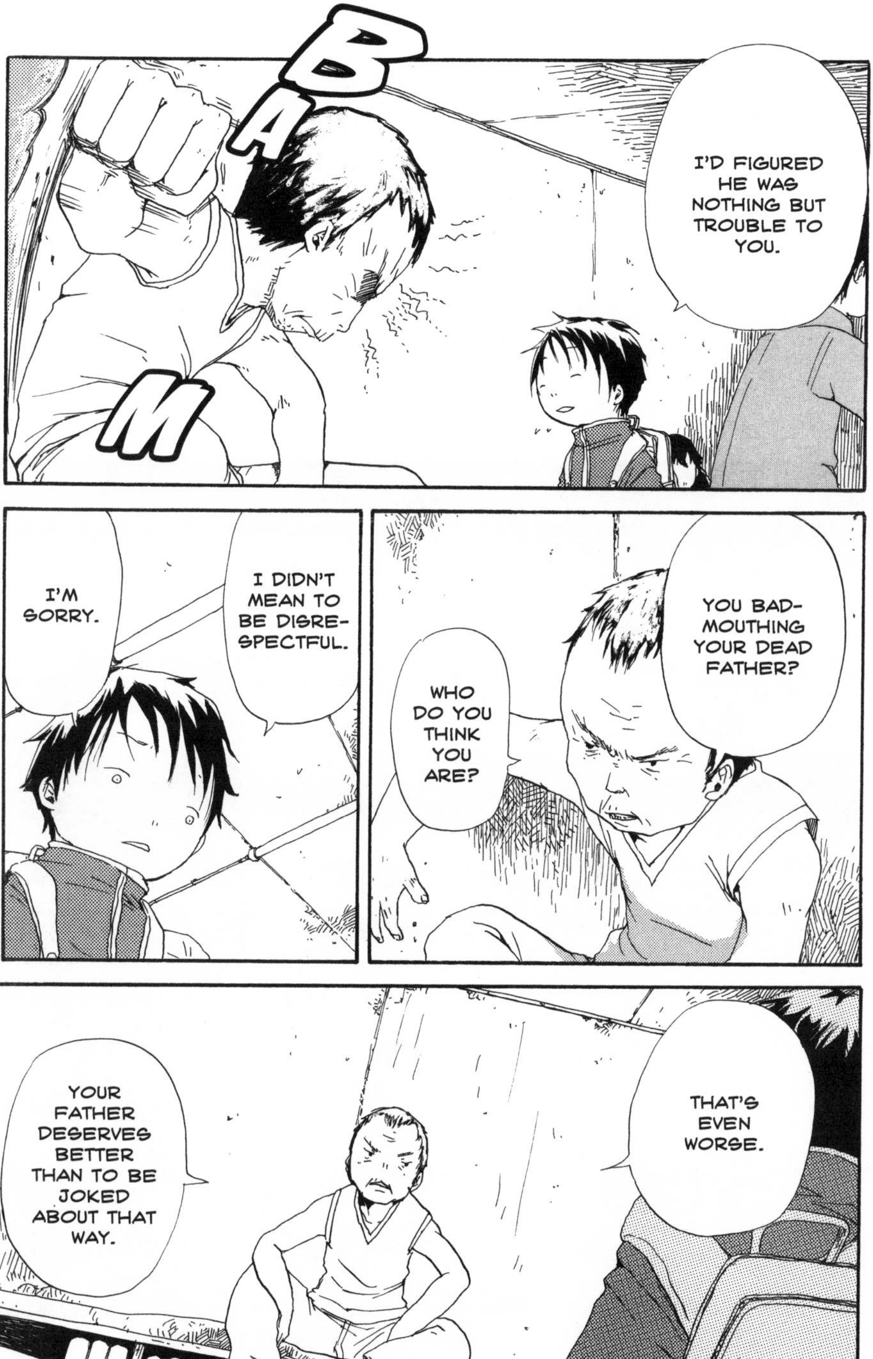
I'D FIGURED HE WAS NOTHING BUT TROUBLE TO YOU.
BAM
YOU BAD-MOUTHING YOUR DEAD FATHER?
WHO DO YOU THINK YOU ARE?
I DIDN'T MEAN TO BE DISRESPECTFUL.
I'M SORRY.
THAT'S EVEN WORSE.
YOUR FATHER DESERVES BETTER THAN TO BE JOKED ABOUT THAT WAY.

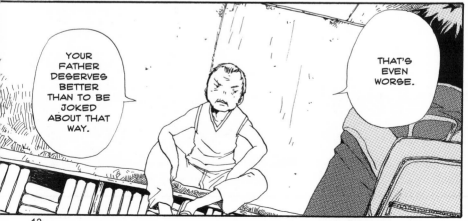

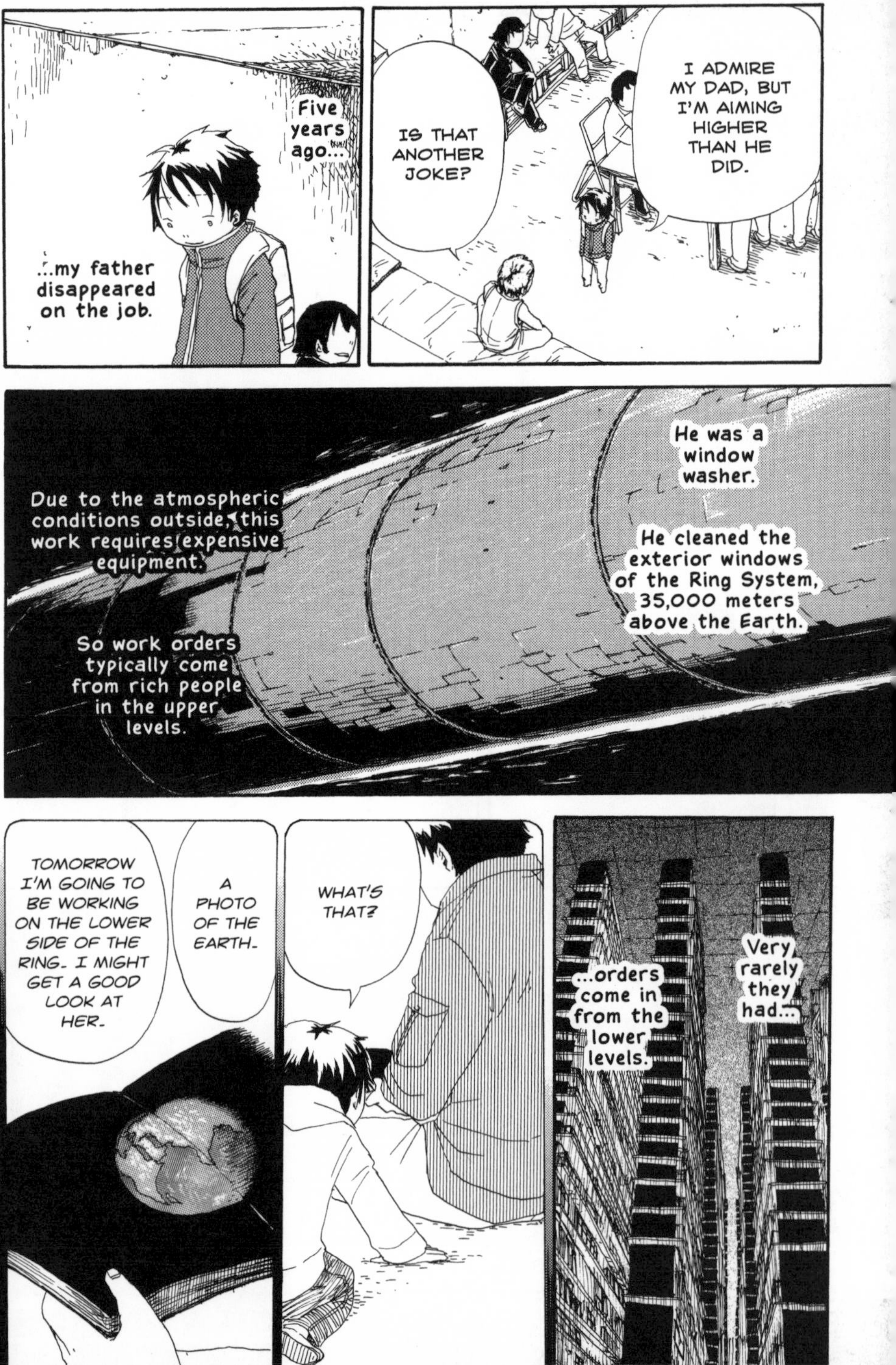
I ADMIRE MY DAD, BUT I'M AIMING HIGHER THAN HE DID.
IS THAT ANOTHER JOKE?
Five years ago...
...my father disappeared on the job.
He was a window washer.
He cleaned the exterior windows of the Ring System, 35,000 meters above the Earth.
Due to the atmospheric conditions outside, this work requires expensive equipment.
So work orders typically come from rich people in the upper levels.
Very rarely they had...
...orders come in from the lower levels.
WHAT'S THAT?
A PHOTO OF THE EARTH.
TOMORROW I'M GOING TO BE WORKING ON THE LOWER SIDE OF THE RING. I MIGHT GET A GOOD LOOK AT HER.

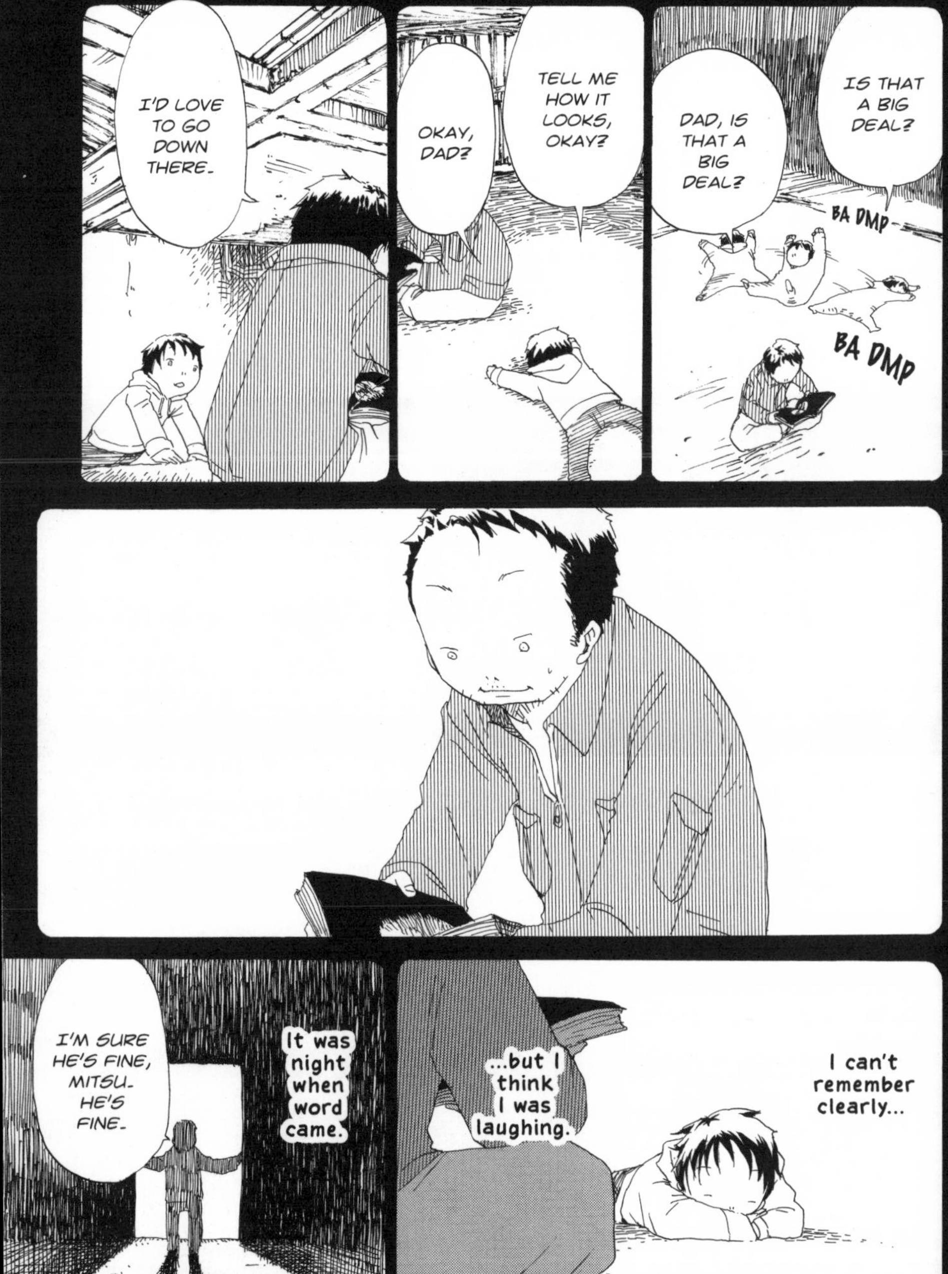
IS THAT A BIG DEAL?
DAD, IS THAT A BIG DEAL?
BA DMP
BA DMP
TELL ME HOW IT LOOKS, OKAY?
OKAY, DAD?
I'D LOVE TO GO DOWN THERE.
I can't remember clearly...
...but I think I was laughing.
It was night when word came.
I'M SURE HE'S FINE, MITSU. HE'S FINE.

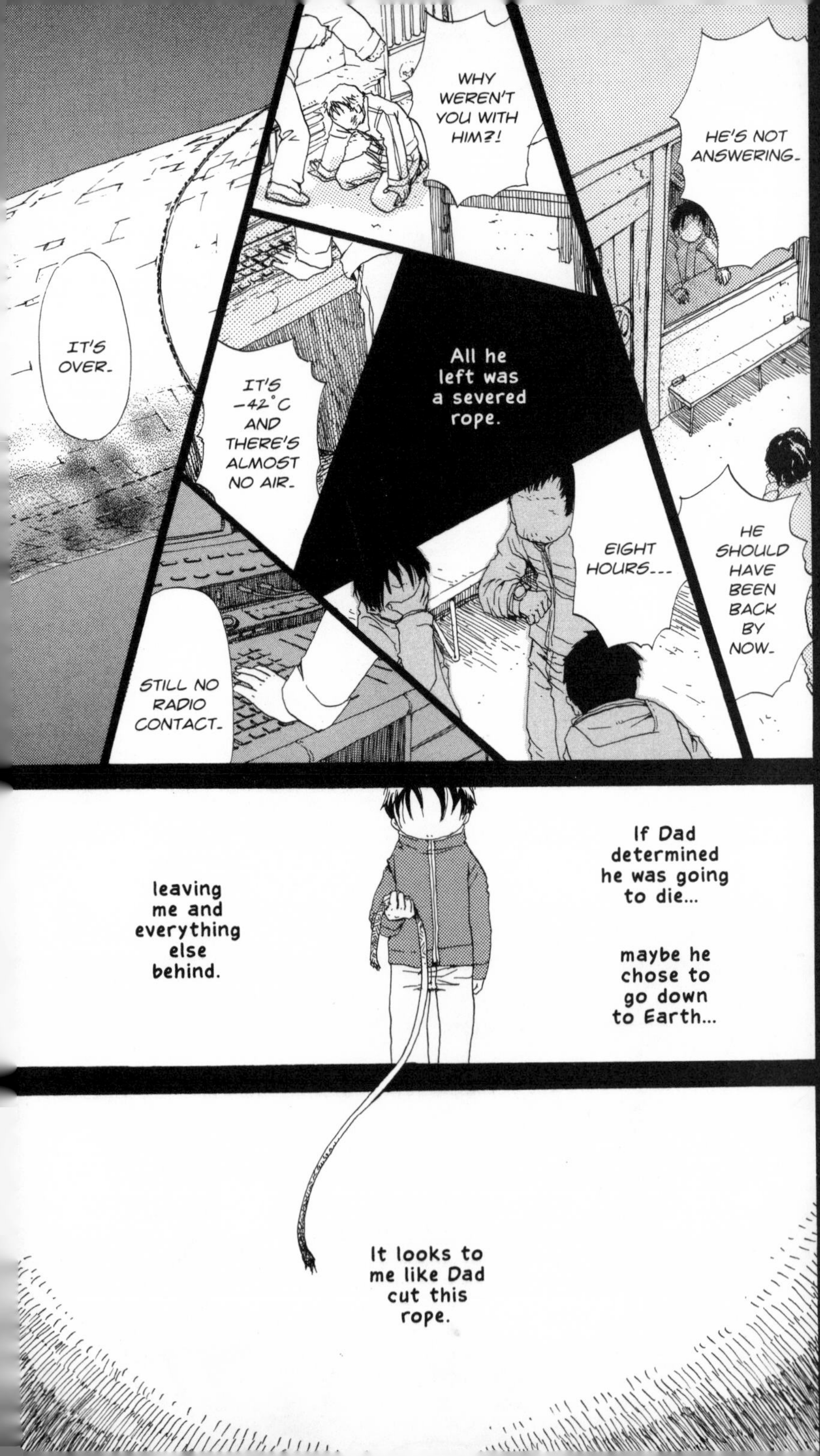
HE'S NOT ANSWERING.
WHY WEREN'T YOU WITH HIM?!
HE SHOULD HAVE BEEN BACK BY NOW.
EIGHT HOURS...
All he left was a severed rope.
IT'S –42°C AND THERE'S ALMOST NO AIR.
STILL NO RADIO CONTACT.
IT'S OVER.
If Dad determined he was going to die...
maybe he chose to go down to Earth...
leaving me and everything else behind.
It looks to me like Dad cut this rope.

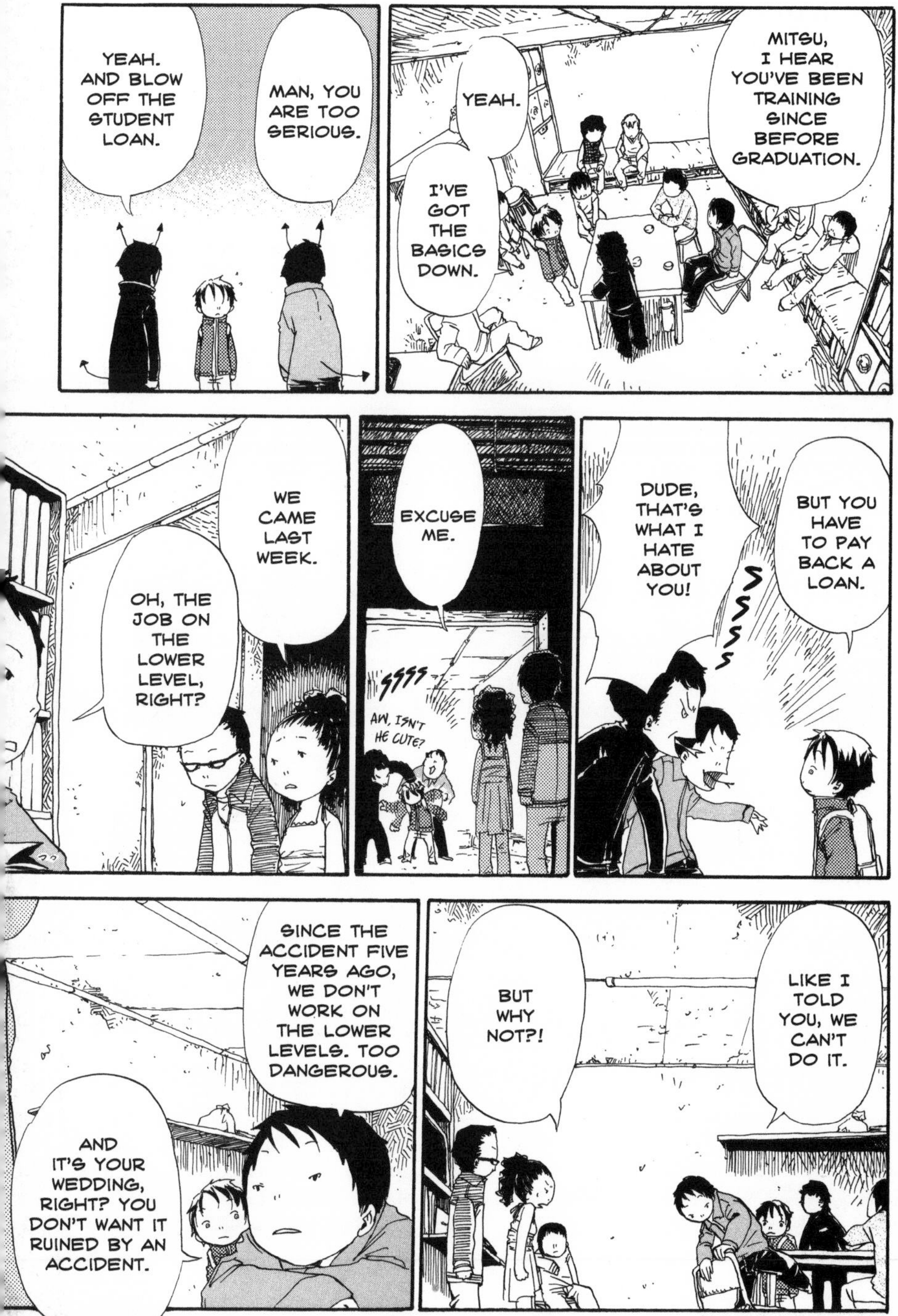
MITSU, I HEAR YOU'VE BEEN TRAINING SINCE BEFORE GRADUATION.
YEAH.
I'VE GOT THE BASICS DOWN.
MAN, YOU ARE TOO SERIOUS.
YEAH. AND BLOW OFF THE STUDENT LOAN.
BUT YOU HAVE TO PAY BACK A LOAN.
SSSS
DUDE, THAT'S WHAT I HATE ABOUT YOU!
EXCUSE ME.
SSSS
AW, ISN'T HE CUTE?
WE CAME LAST WEEK.
OH, THE JOB ON THE LOWER LEVEL, RIGHT?
LIKE I TOLD YOU, WE CAN'T DO IT.
BUT WHY NOT?!
SINCE THE ACCIDENT FIVE YEARS AGO, WE DON'T WORK ON THE LOWER LEVELS. TOO DANGEROUS.
AND IT'S YOUR WEDDING, RIGHT? YOU DON'T WANT IT RUINED BY AN ACCIDENT.

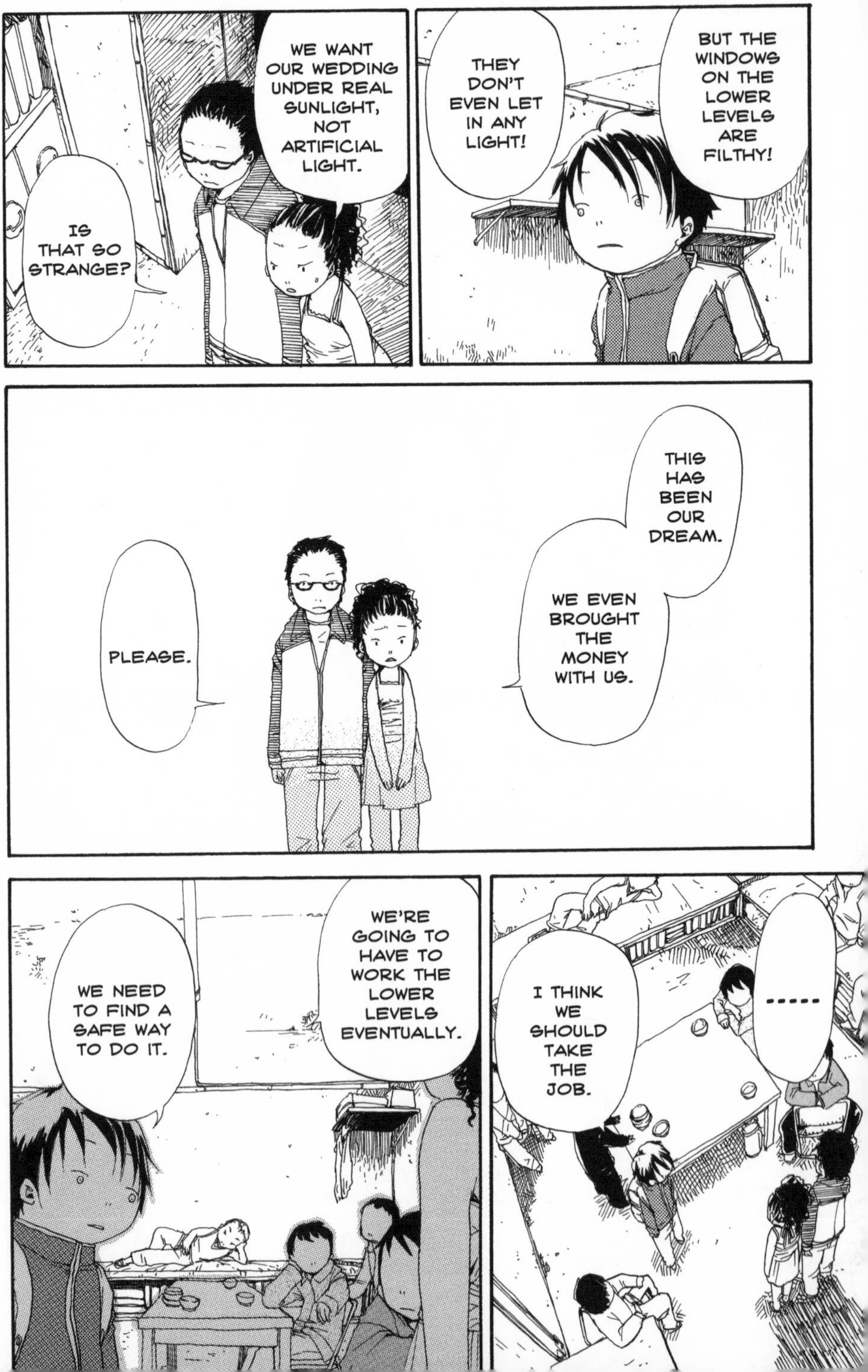
BUT THE WINDOWS ON THE LOWER LEVELS ARE FILTHY!
THEY DON'T EVEN LET IN ANY LIGHT!
WE WANT OUR WEDDING UNDER REAL SUNLIGHT, NOT ARTIFICIAL LIGHT.
IS THAT SO STRANGE?
THIS HAS BEEN OUR DREAM.
WE EVEN BROUGHT THE MONEY WITH US.
PLEASE.
.....
I THINK WE SHOULD TAKE THE JOB.
WE'RE GOING TO HAVE TO WORK THE LOWER LEVELS EVENTUALLY.
WE NEED TO FIND A SAFE WAY TO DO IT.

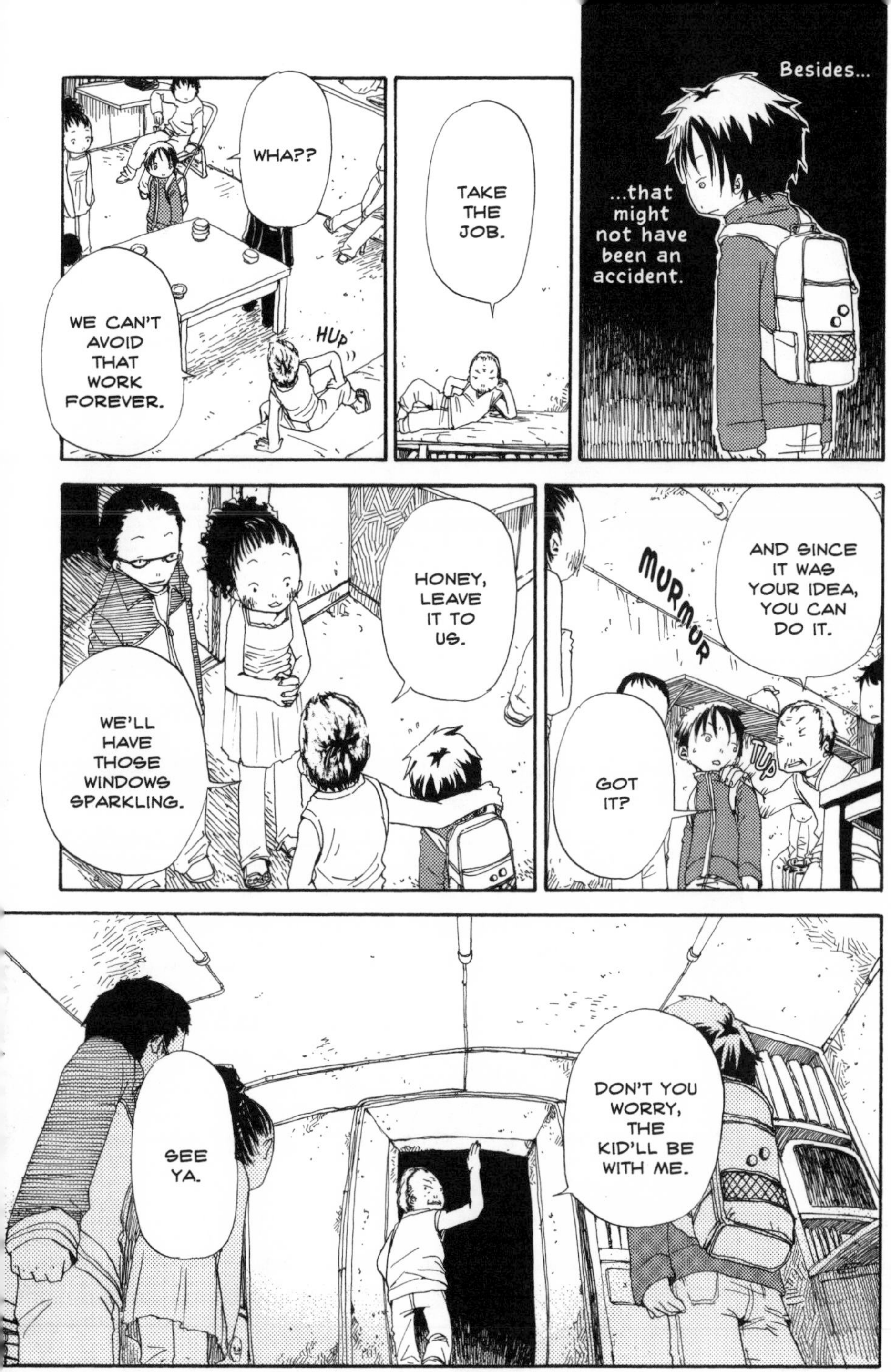
Besides...
...that might not have been an accident.
TAKE THE JOB.
WHA??
HUP
WE CAN'T AVOID THAT WORK FOREVER.
AND SINCE IT WAS YOUR IDEA, YOU CAN DO IT.
MURMUR
TUP
GOT IT?
HONEY, LEAVE IT TO US.
WE'LL HAVE THOSE WINDOWS SPARKLING.
DON'T YOU WORRY, THE KID'LL BE WITH ME.
SEE YA.

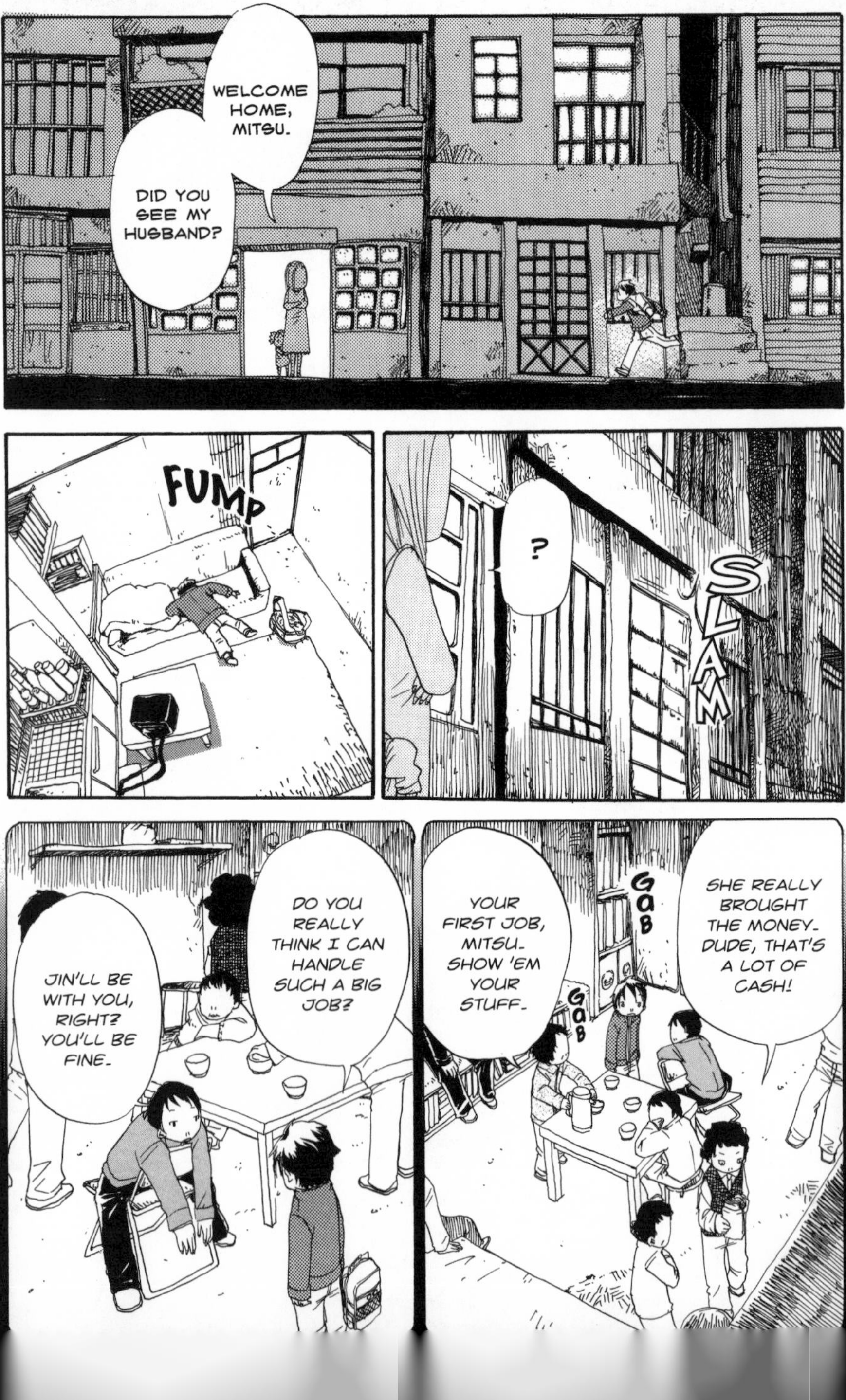
WELCOME HOME, MITSU.
DID YOU SEE MY HUSBAND?
?
SLAM
FUMP
SHE REALLY BROUGHT THE MONEY. DUDE, THAT'S A LOT OF CASH!
GAB
GAB
YOUR FIRST JOB, MITSU. SHOW 'EM YOUR STUFF.
DO YOU REALLY THINK I CAN HANDLE SUCH A BIG JOB?
JIN'LL BE WITH YOU, RIGHT? YOU'LL BE FINE.

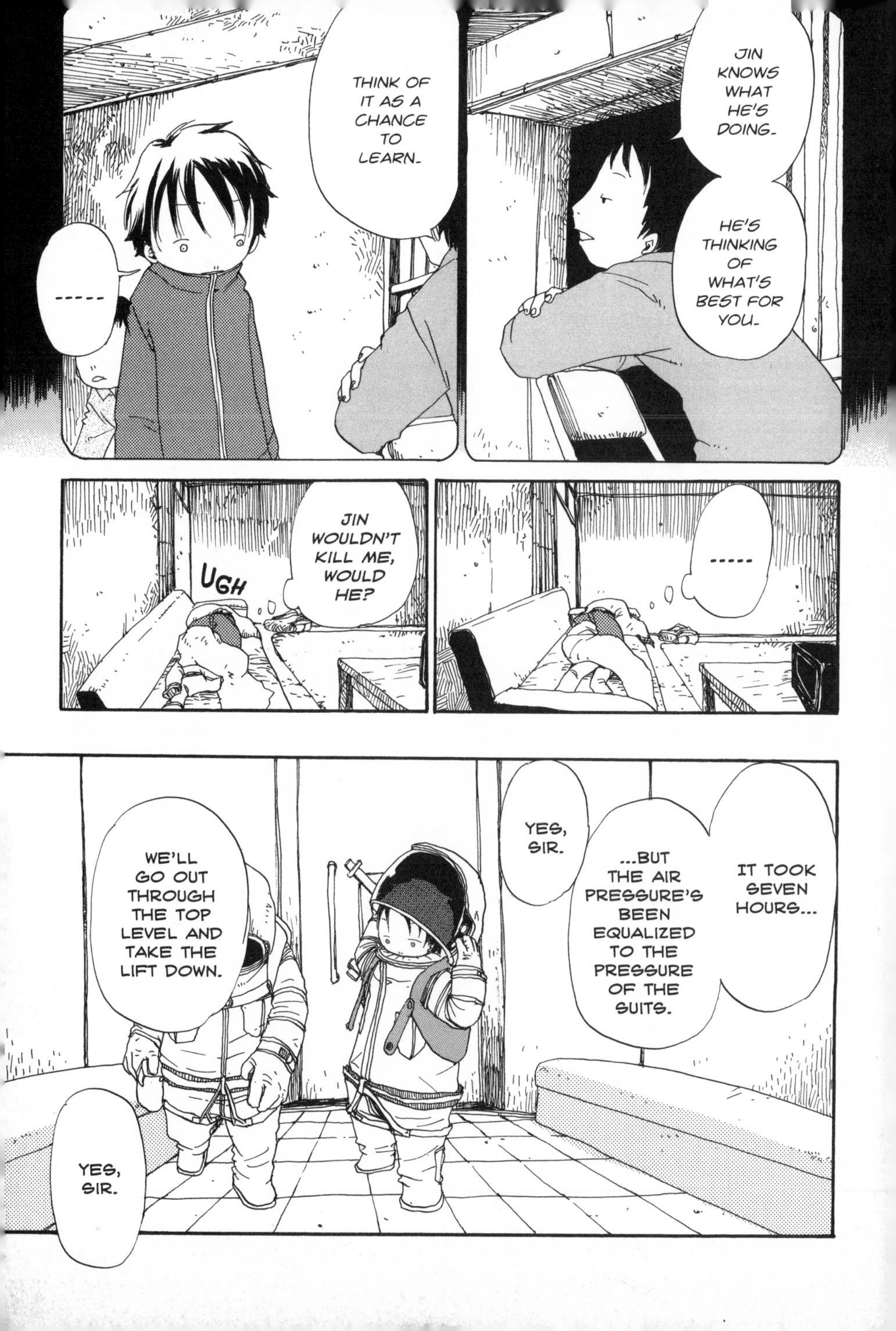
JIN KNOWS WHAT HE'S DOING.
HE'S THINKING OF WHAT'S BEST FOR YOU.
THINK OF IT AS A CHANCE TO LEARN.

JIN WOULDN'T KILL ME, WOULD HE?
UGH
IT TOOK SEVEN HOURS...
...BUT THE AIR PRESSURE'S BEEN EQUALIZED TO THE PRESSURE OF THE SUITS.
YES, SIR.
WE'LL GO OUT THROUGH THE TOP LEVEL AND TAKE THE LIFT DOWN.
YES, SIR.

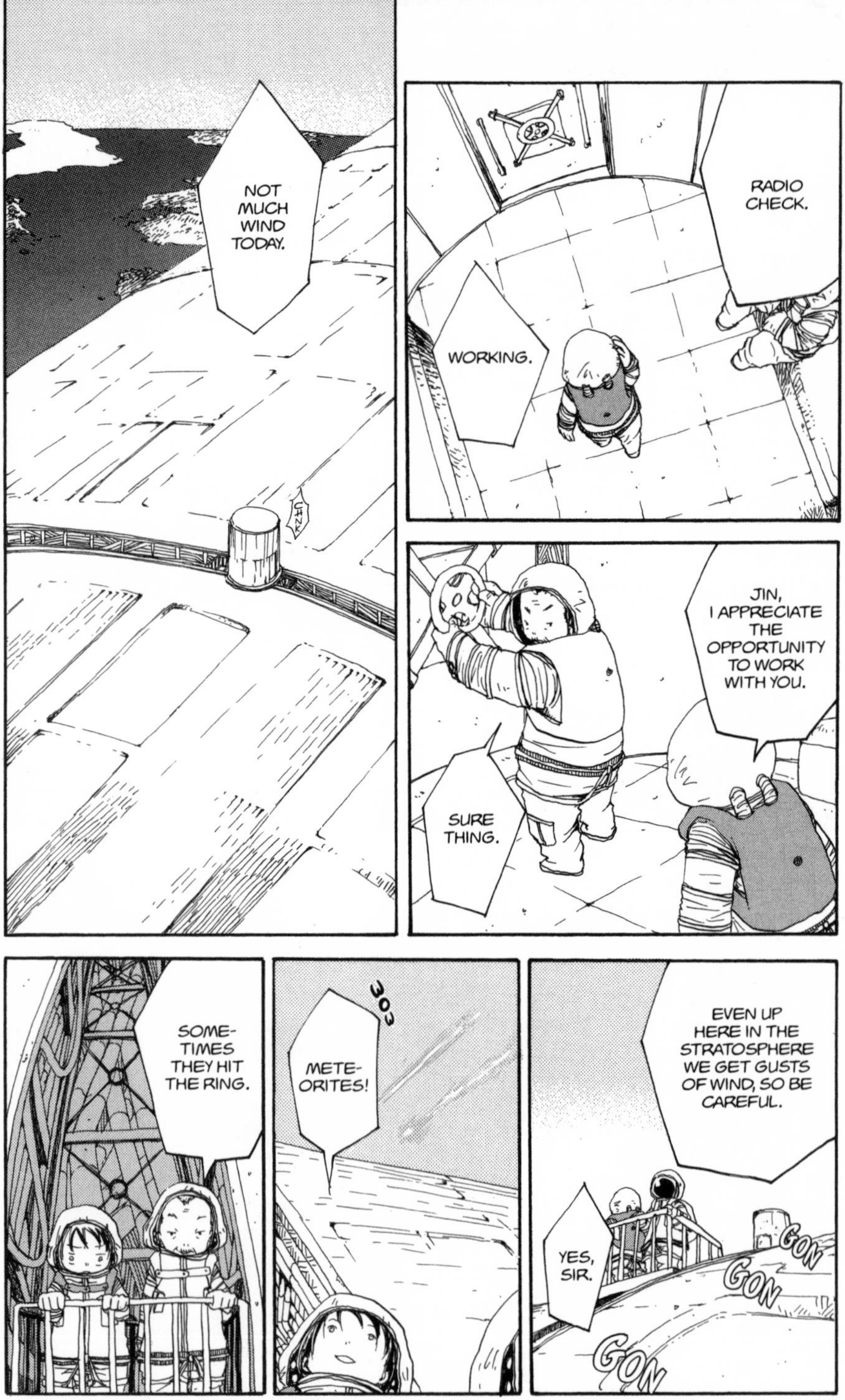
RADIO CHECK.
WORKING.
JIN, I APPRECIATE THE OPPORTUNITY TO WORK WITH YOU.
SURE THING.
NOT MUCH WIND TODAY.
CHNK
EVEN UP HERE IN THE STRATOSPHERE WE GET GUSTS OF WIND, SO BE CAREFUL.
YES, SIR.
GON
GON
GON
METE-ORITES!
SOME-TIMES THEY HIT THE RING.

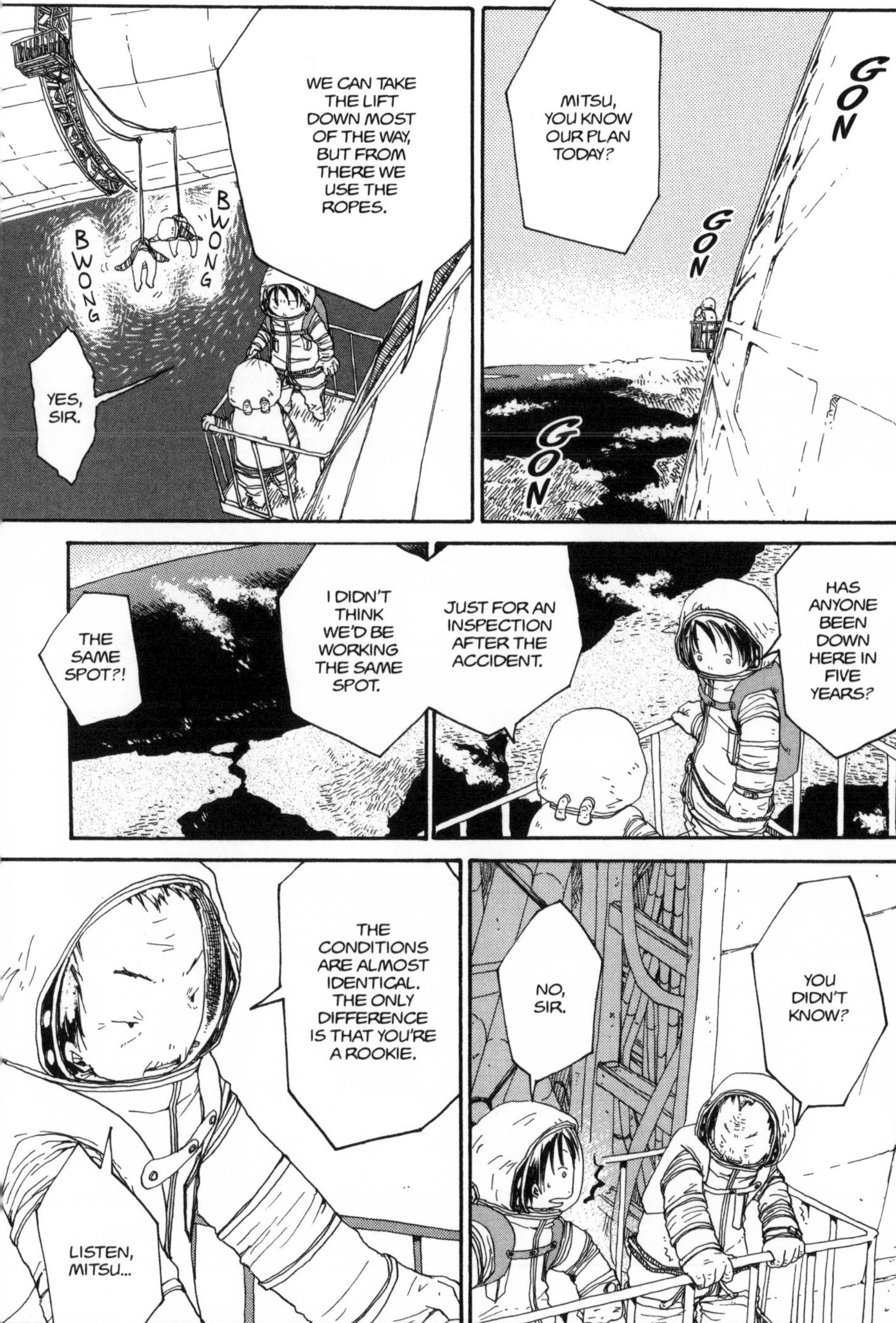
MITSU, YOU KNOW OUR PLAN TODAY?
GON
GON
GON
WE CAN TAKE THE LIFT DOWN MOST OF THE WAY, BUT FROM THERE WE USE THE ROPES.
BWONG
BWONG
YES, SIR.
HAS ANYONE BEEN DOWN HERE IN FIVE YEARS?
JUST FOR AN INSPECTION AFTER THE ACCIDENT.
I DIDN'T THINK WE'D BE WORKING THE SAME SPOT.
THE SAME SPOT?!
YOU DIDN'T KNOW?
NO, SIR.
THE CONDITIONS ARE ALMOST IDENTICAL. THE ONLY DIFFERENCE IS THAT YOU'RE A ROOKIE.
LISTEN, MITSU...

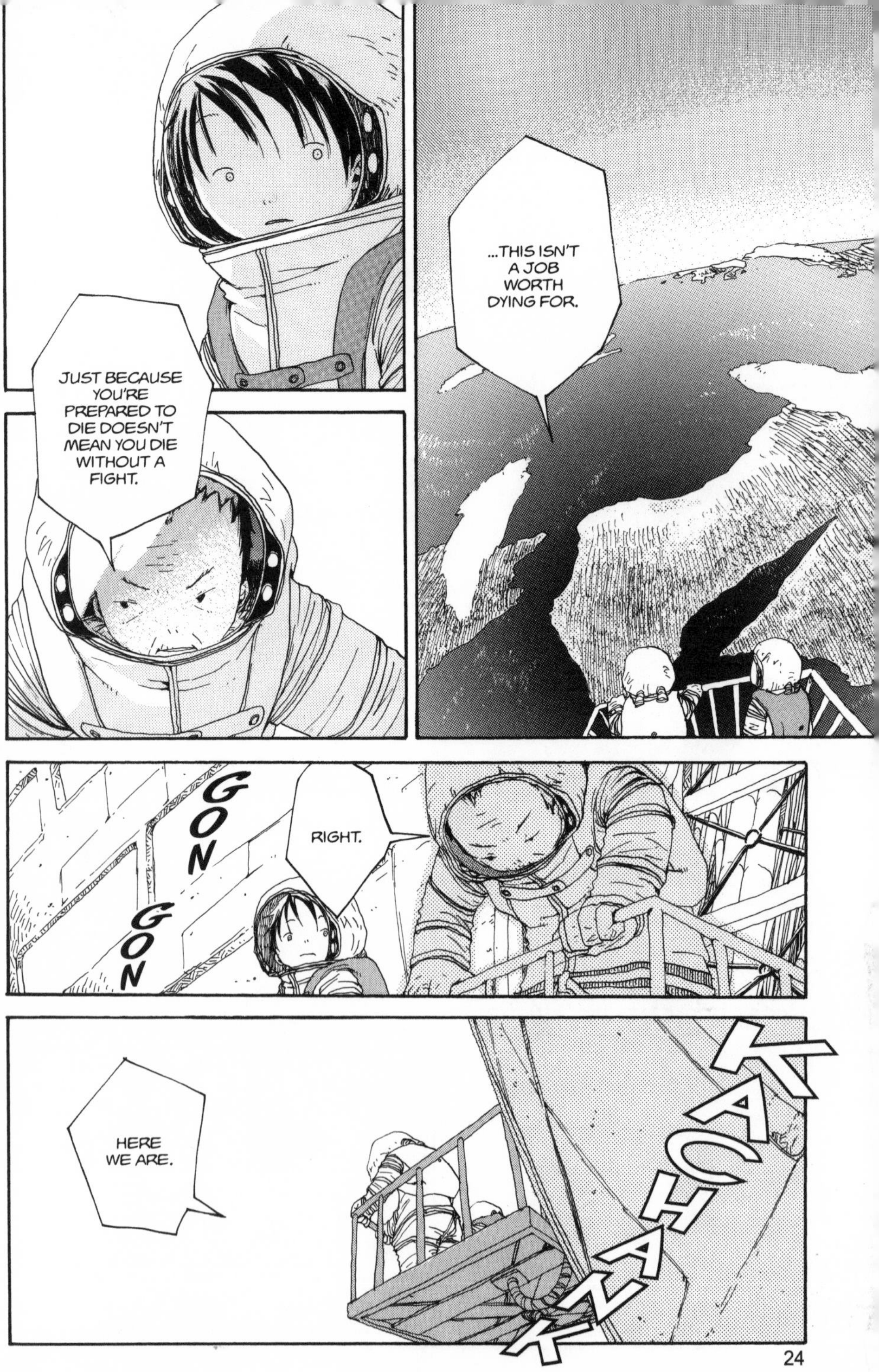
...THIS ISN'T A JOB WORTH DYING FOR.
JUST BECAUSE YOU'RE PREPARED TO DIE DOESN'T MEAN YOU DIE WITHOUT A FIGHT.
RIGHT.
GON GON
KACHANK
HERE WE ARE.

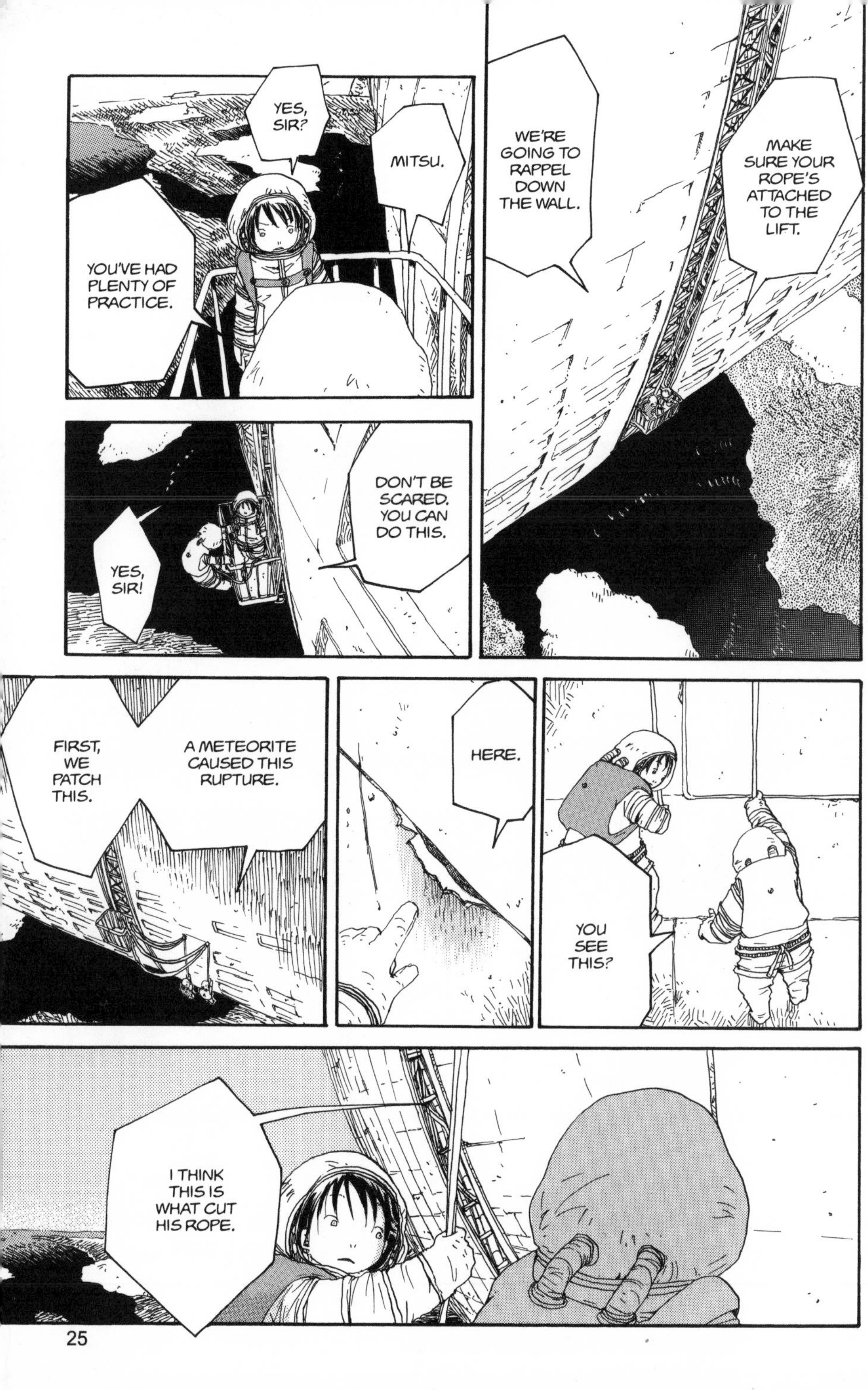
MAKE SURE YOUR ROPE'S ATTACHED TO THE LIFT.
WE'RE GOING TO RAPPEL DOWN THE WALL.
MITSU.
YES, SIR?
YOU'VE HAD PLENTY OF PRACTICE.
DON'T BE SCARED. YOU CAN DO THIS.
YES, SIR!
YOU SEE THIS?
HERE.
A METEORITE CAUSED THIS RUPTURE.
FIRST, WE PATCH THIS.
I THINK THIS IS WHAT CUT HIS ROPE.

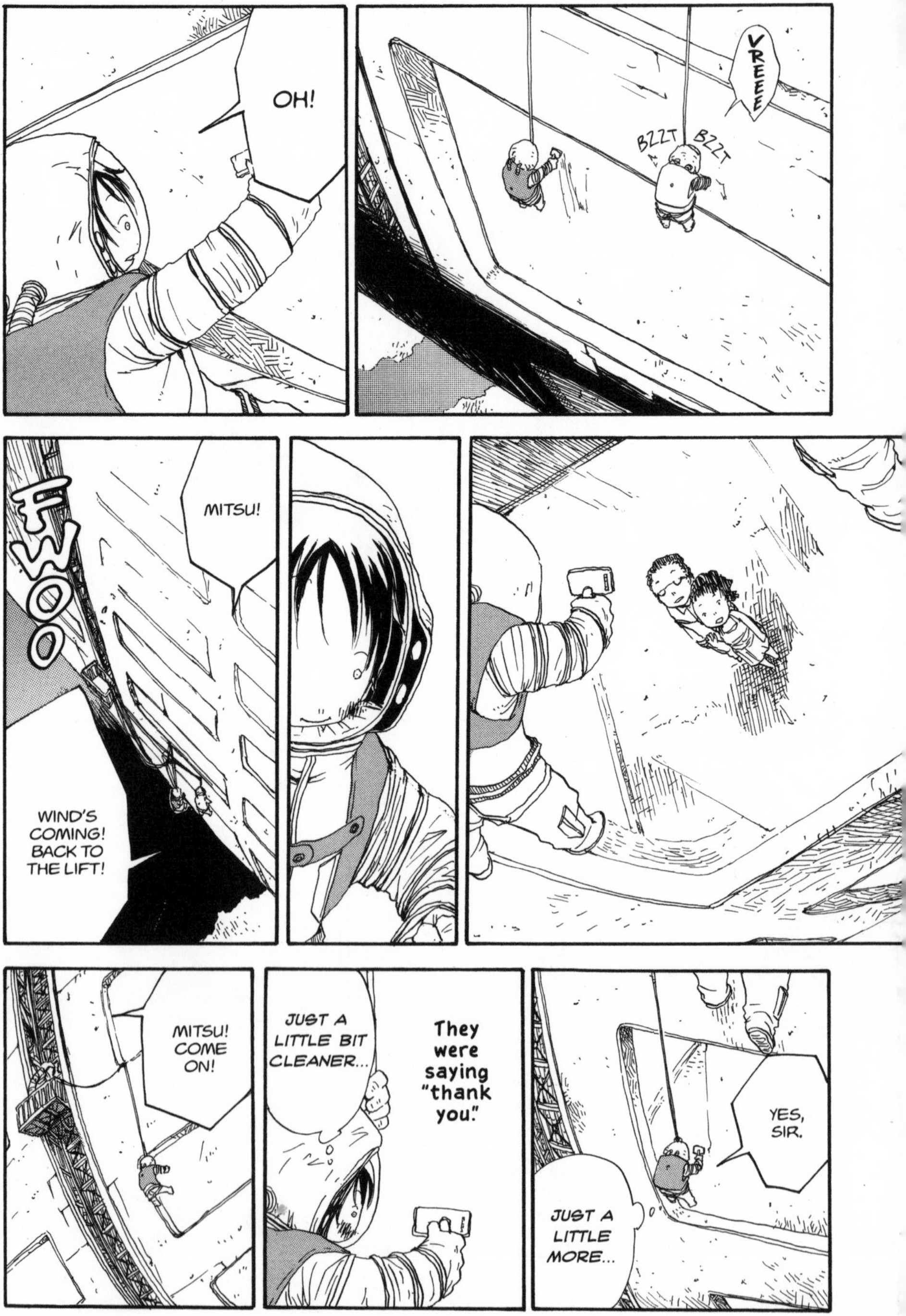
VREEEE
BZZT BZZT
OH!
MITSU!
FWOO
WIND'S COMING! BACK TO THE LIFT!
YES, SIR.
JUST A LITTLE MORE...
They were saying "thank you."
JUST A LITTLE BIT CLEANER...
MITSU! COME ON!

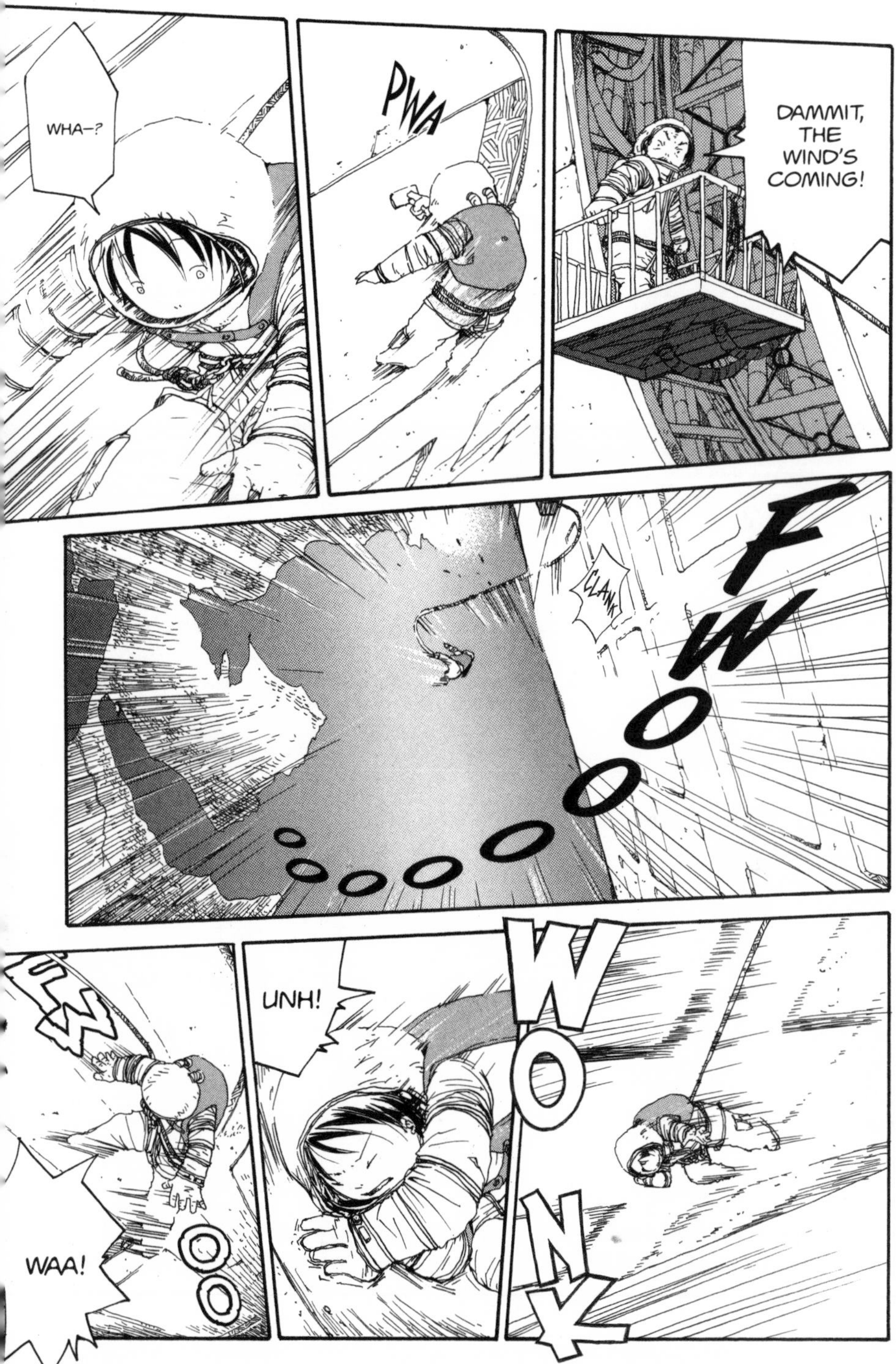
DAMMIT, THE WIND'S COMING!
PWA
WHA-?
CLANK
FWOOOOOOOOO
WONK
UNH!
WAA!

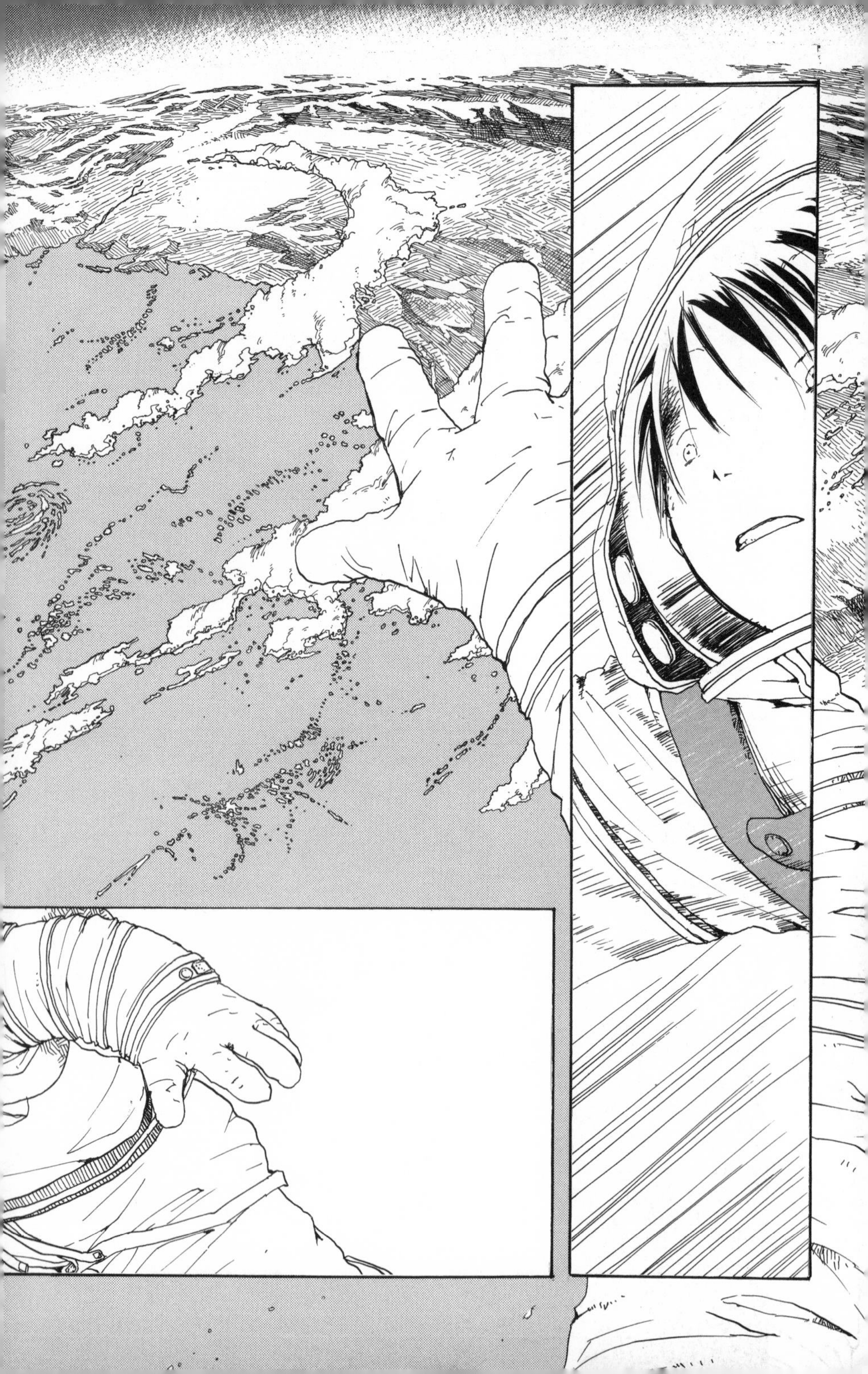

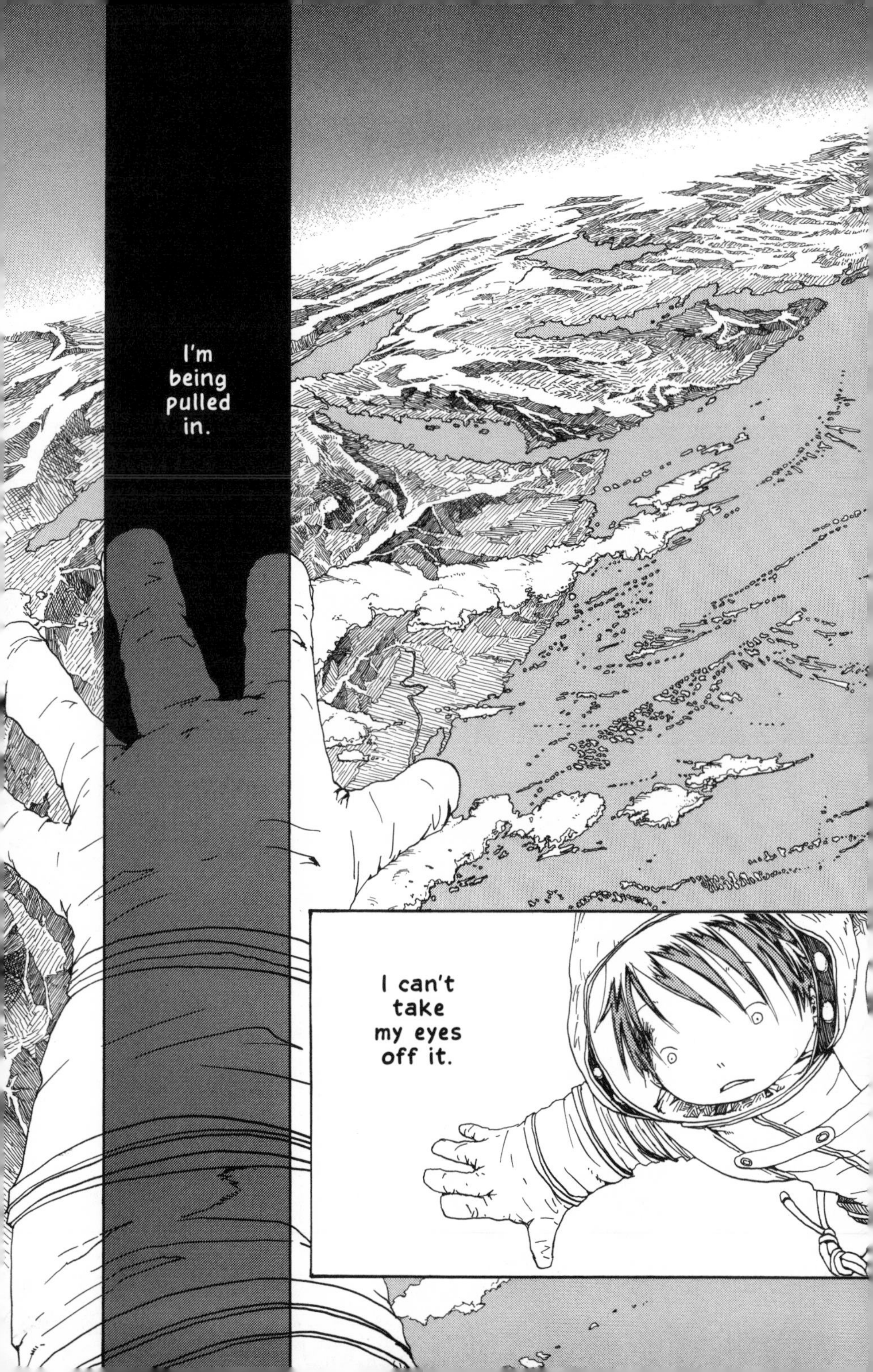
I'm being pulled in.
I can't take my eyes off it.

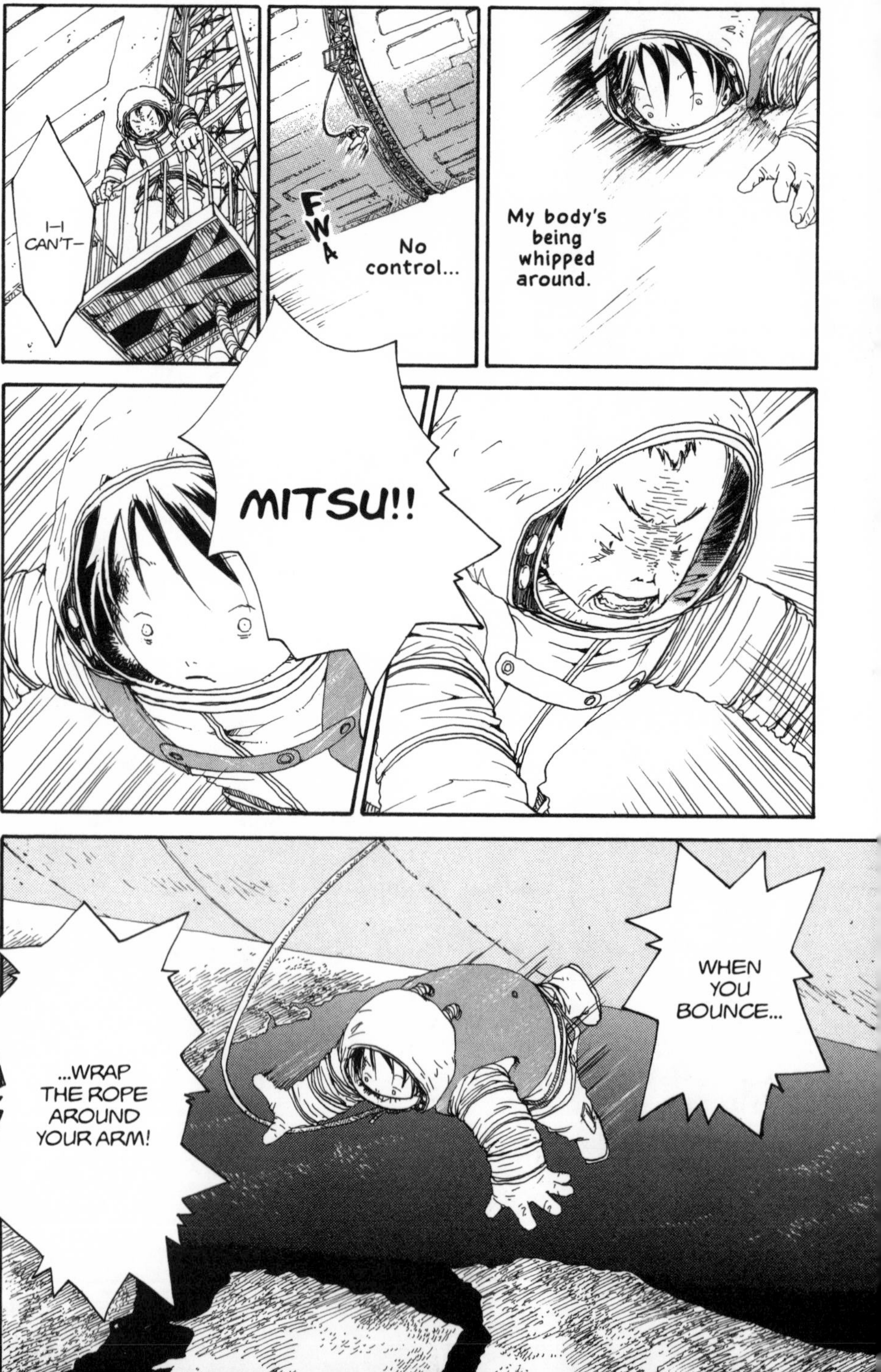
My body's being whipped around.
FWA
No control...
I-I CAN'T—
MITSU!!
WHEN YOU BOUNCE...
...WRAP THE ROPE AROUND YOUR ARM!

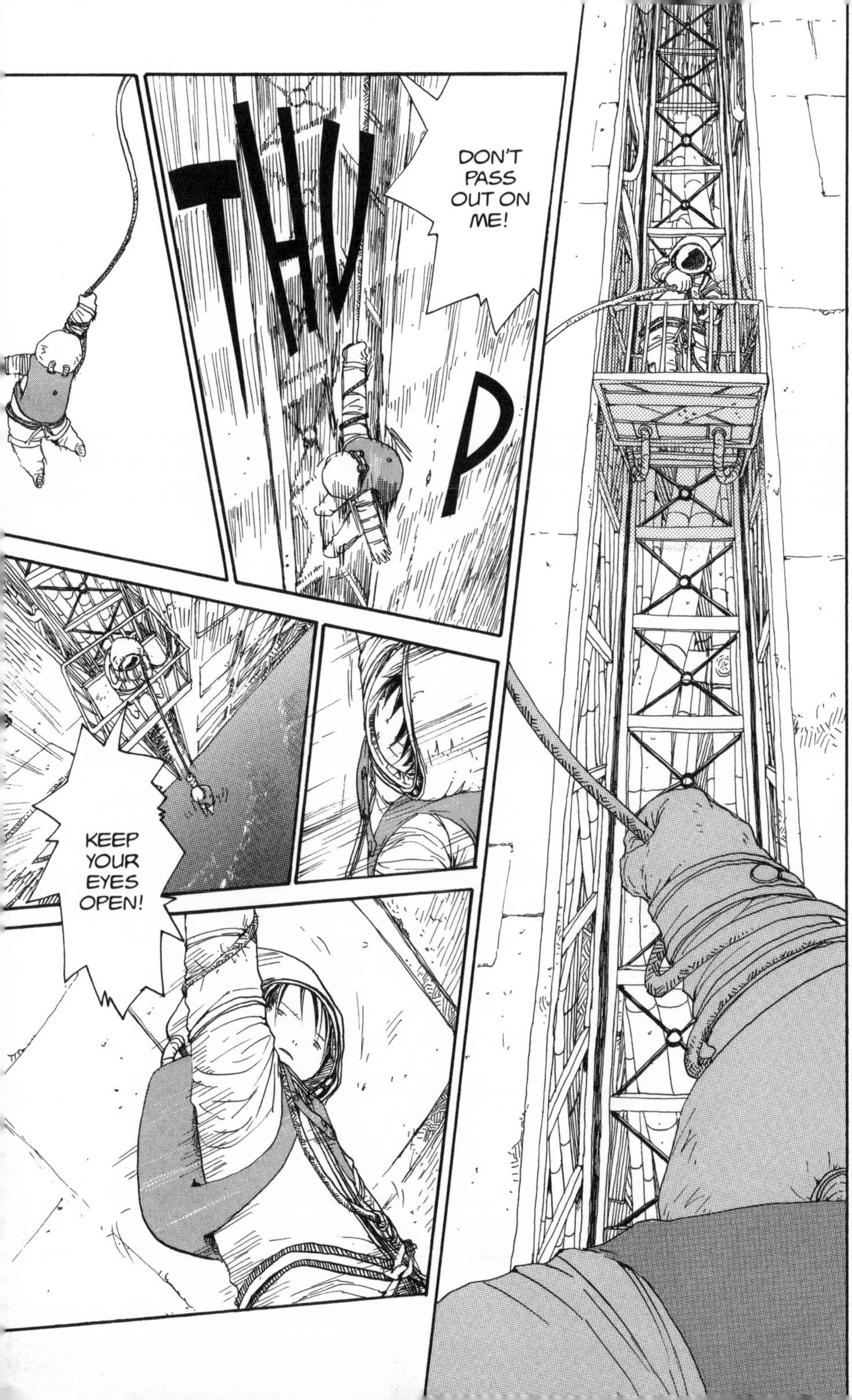
THUD
DON'T PASS OUT ON ME!
KEEP YOUR EYES OPEN!

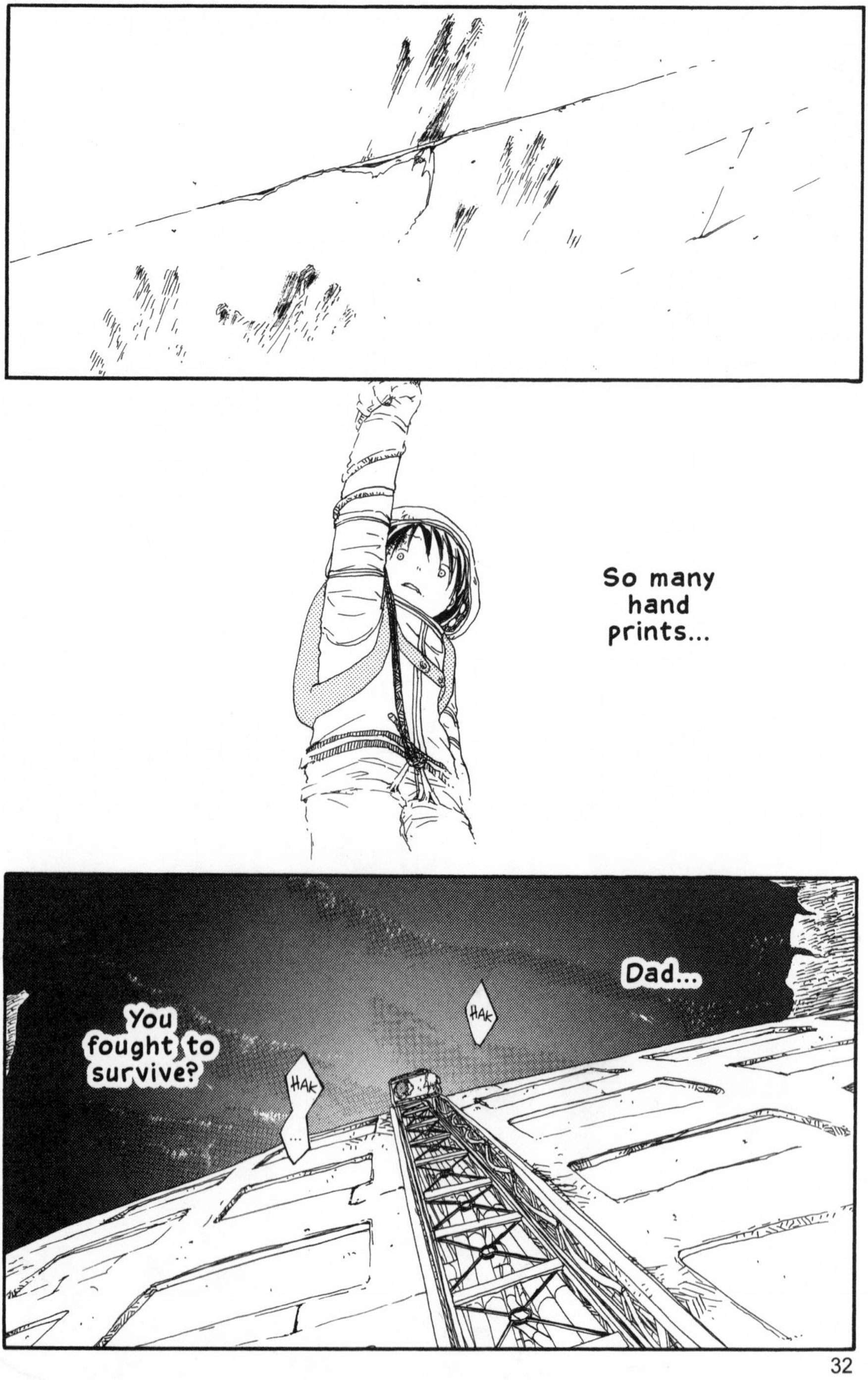
So many hand prints...
Dad...
HAK
You fought to survive?
HAK
...

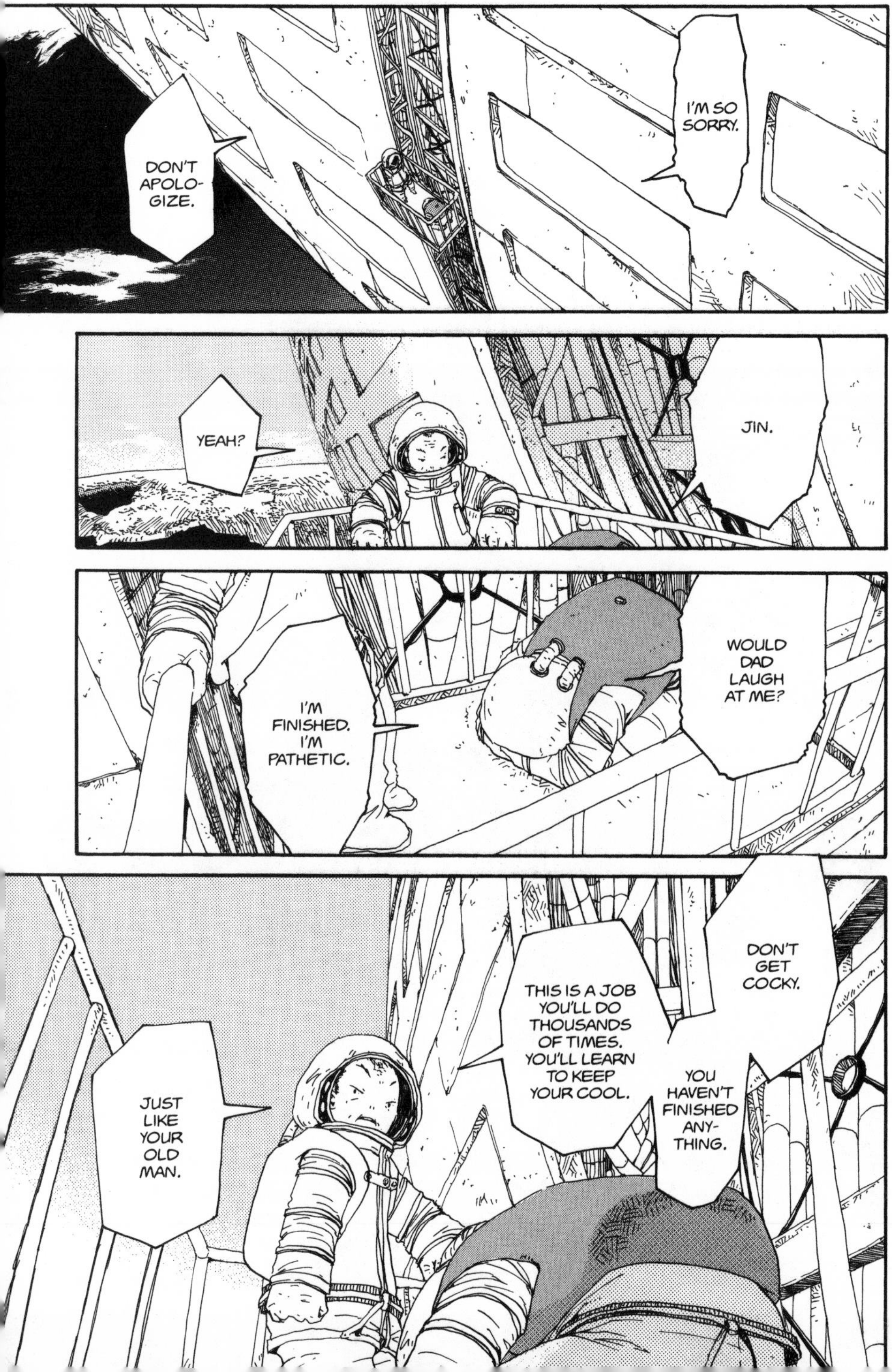
I'M SO SORRY.
DON'T APOLOGIZE.
JIN.
YEAH?
WOULD DAD LAUGH AT ME?
I'M FINISHED. I'M PATHETIC.
DON'T GET COCKY.
YOU HAVEN'T FINISHED ANYTHING.
THIS IS A JOB YOU'LL DO THOUSANDS OF TIMES. YOU'LL LEARN TO KEEP YOUR COOL.
JUST LIKE YOUR OLD MAN.

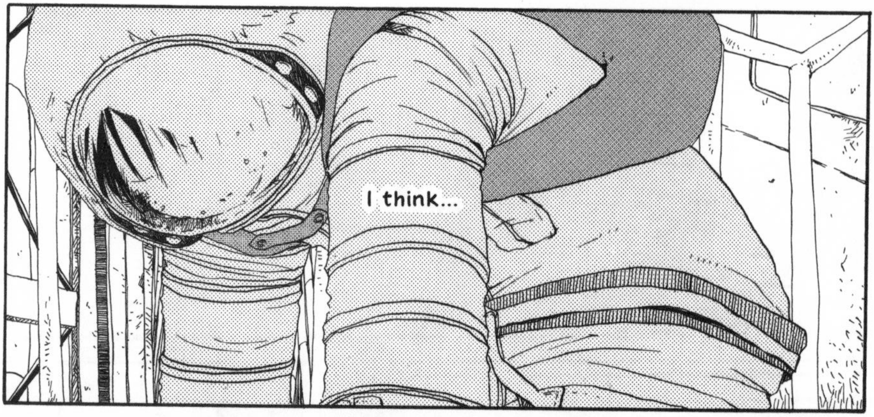
I think...
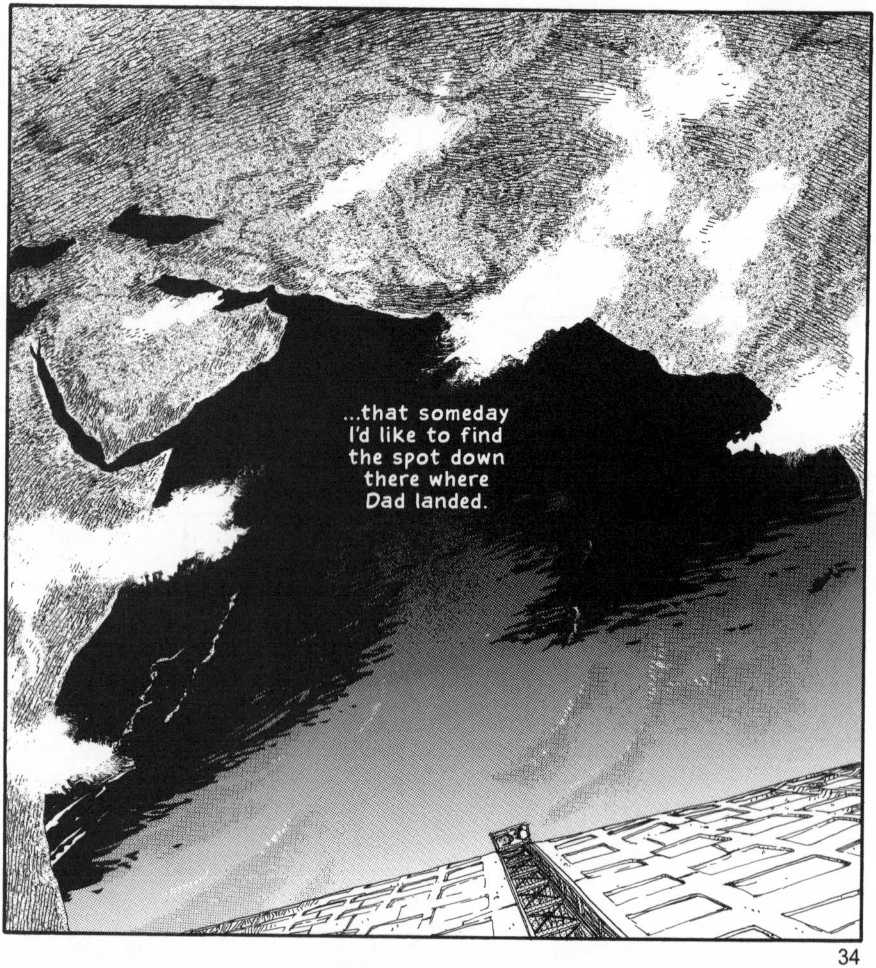
...that someday I'd like to find the spot down there where Dad landed.

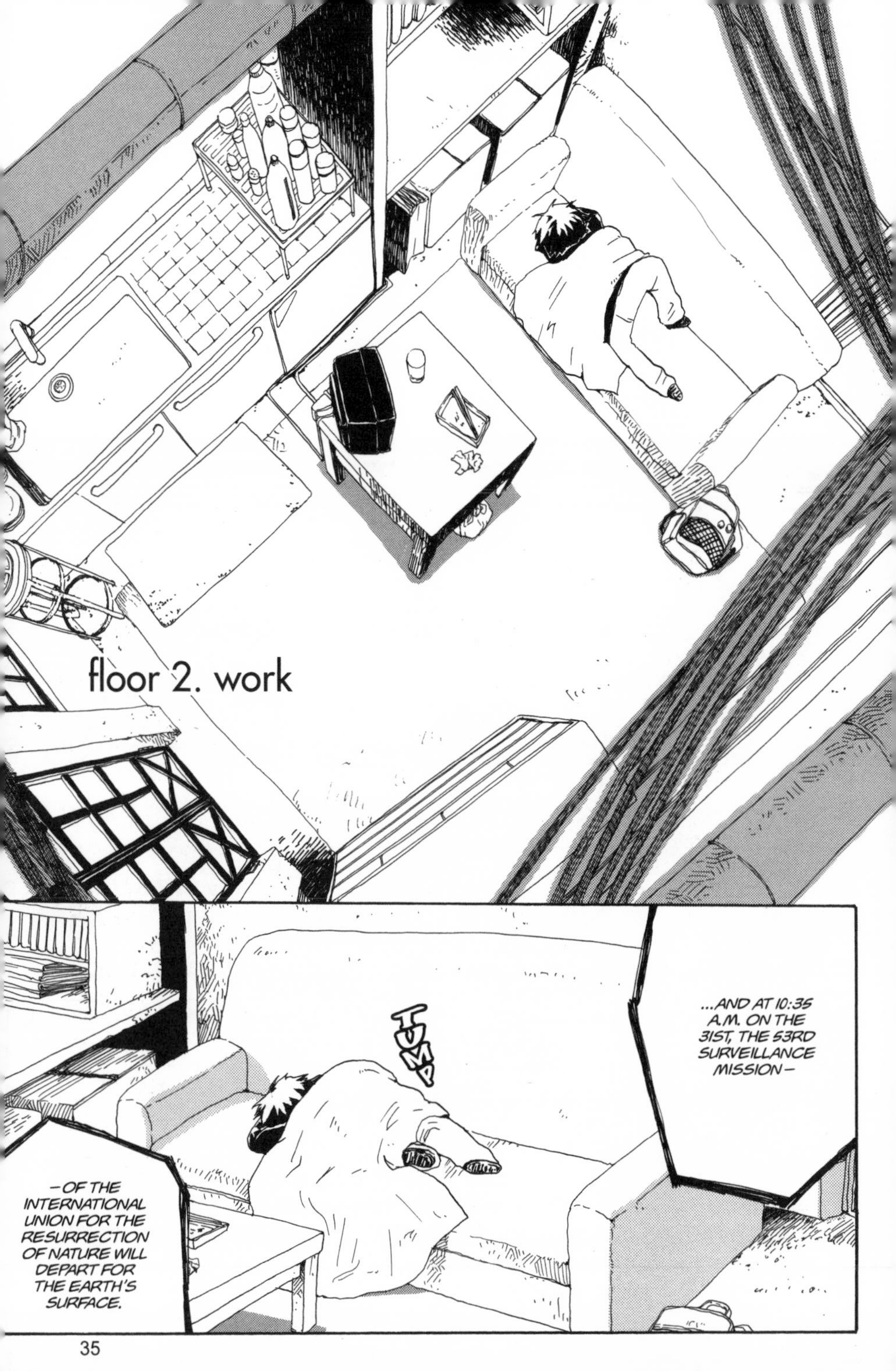
floor 2. work
...AND AT 10:35 A.M. ON THE 31ST, THE 53RD SURVEILLANCE MISSION—
TUMP
—OF THE INTERNATIONAL UNION FOR THE RESURRECTION OF NATURE WILL DEPART FOR THE EARTH'S SURFACE.

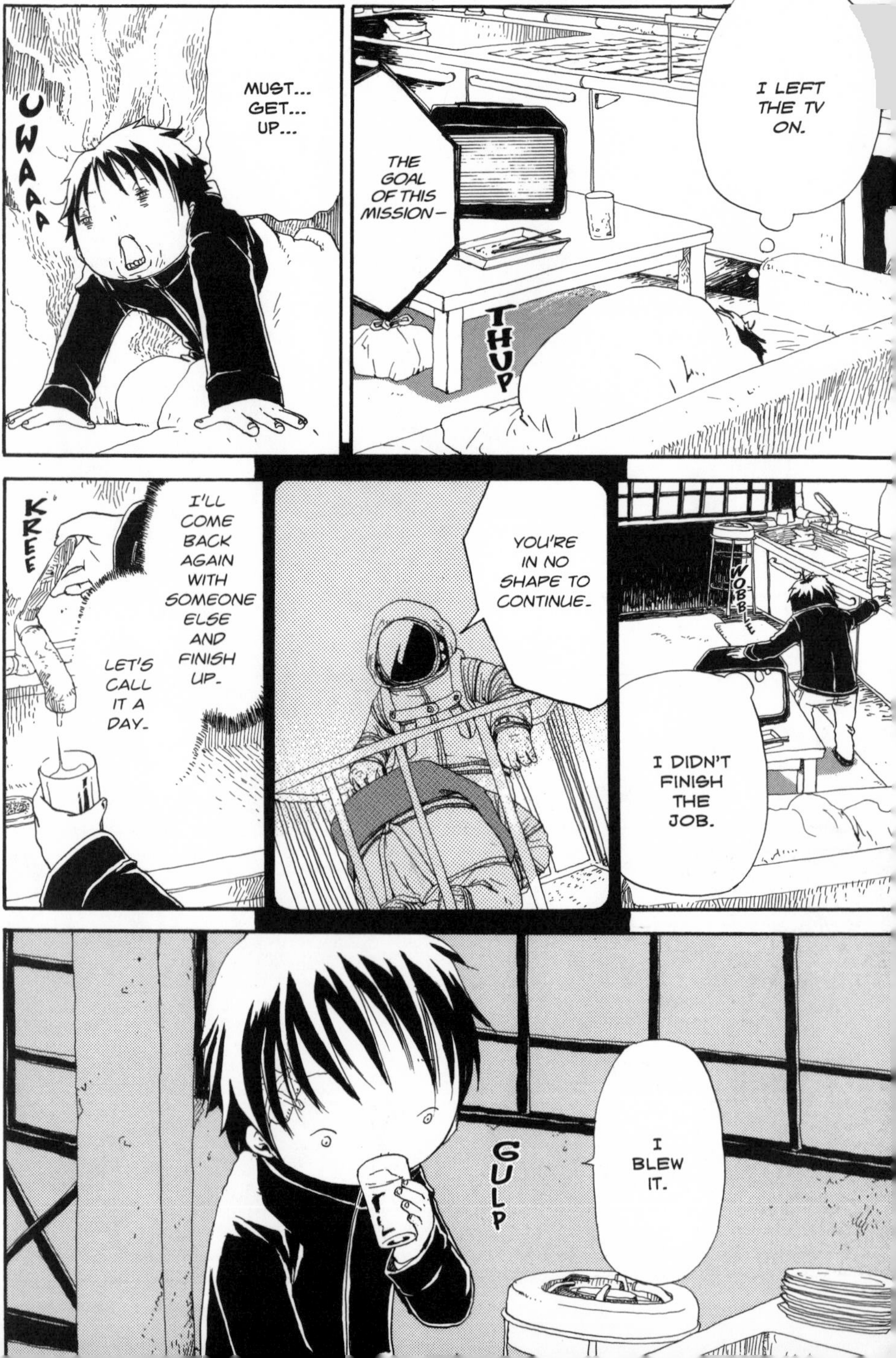
I LEFT THE TV ON.
THE GOAL OF THIS MISSION—
THUP
MUST... GET... UP...
UWAAP
WOBBLE
I DIDN'T FINISH THE JOB.
YOU'RE IN NO SHAPE TO CONTINUE.
I'LL COME BACK AGAIN WITH SOMEONE ELSE AND FINISH UP.
LET'S CALL IT A DAY.
KREE
I BLEW IT.
GULP

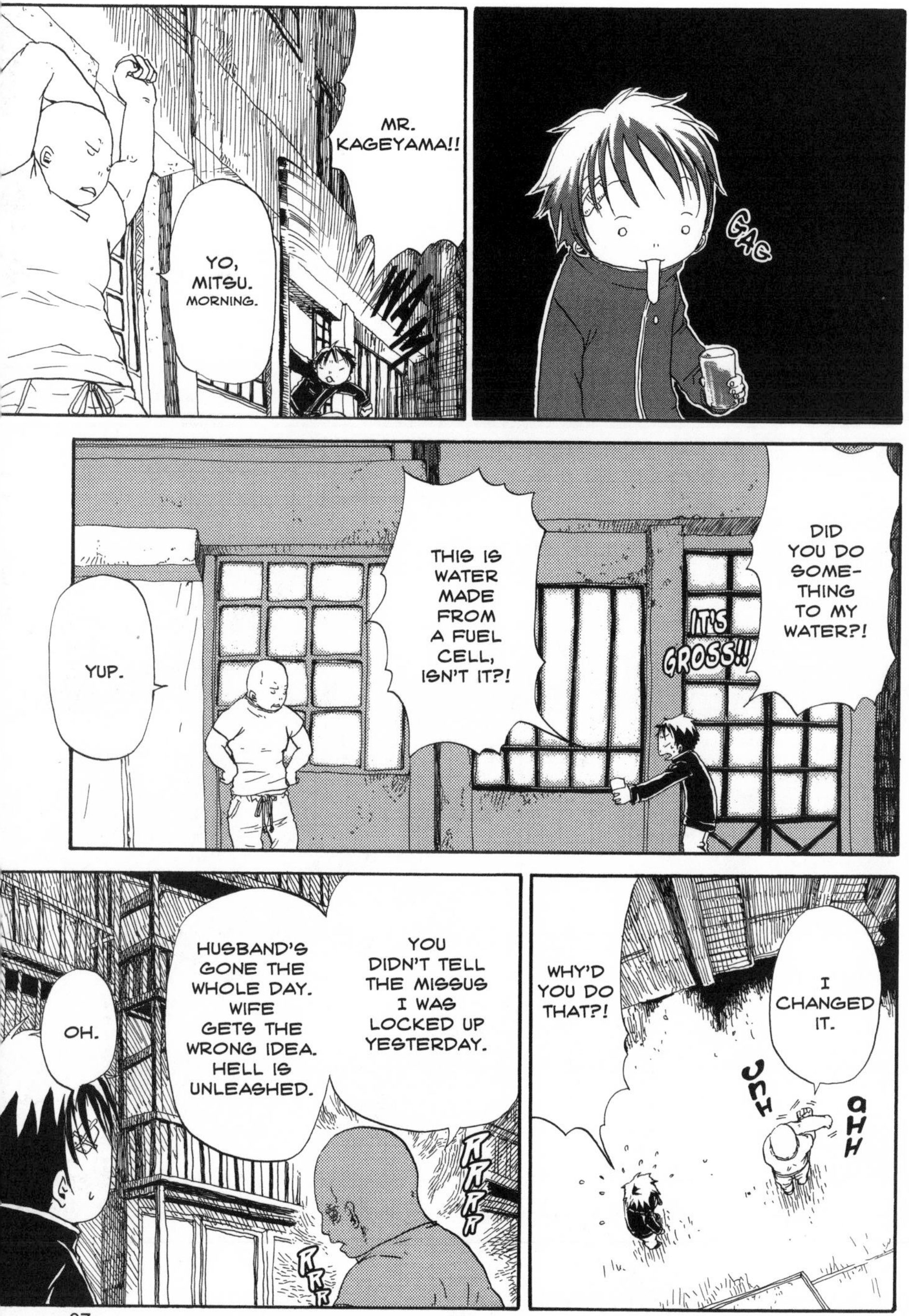
GAG
MR. KAGEYAMA!!
WAM
YO, MITSU. MORNING.
DID YOU DO SOME-THING TO MY WATER?!
IT'S GROSS!!
THIS IS WATER MADE FROM A FUEL CELL, ISN'T IT?!
YUP.
I CHANGED IT.
AHH
UNH
WHY'D YOU DO THAT?!
YOU DIDN'T TELL THE MISSUS I WAS LOCKED UP YESTERDAY.
HUSBAND'S GONE THE WHOLE DAY. WIFE GETS THE WRONG IDEA. HELL IS UNLEASHED.
RRRR
OH.
RRR

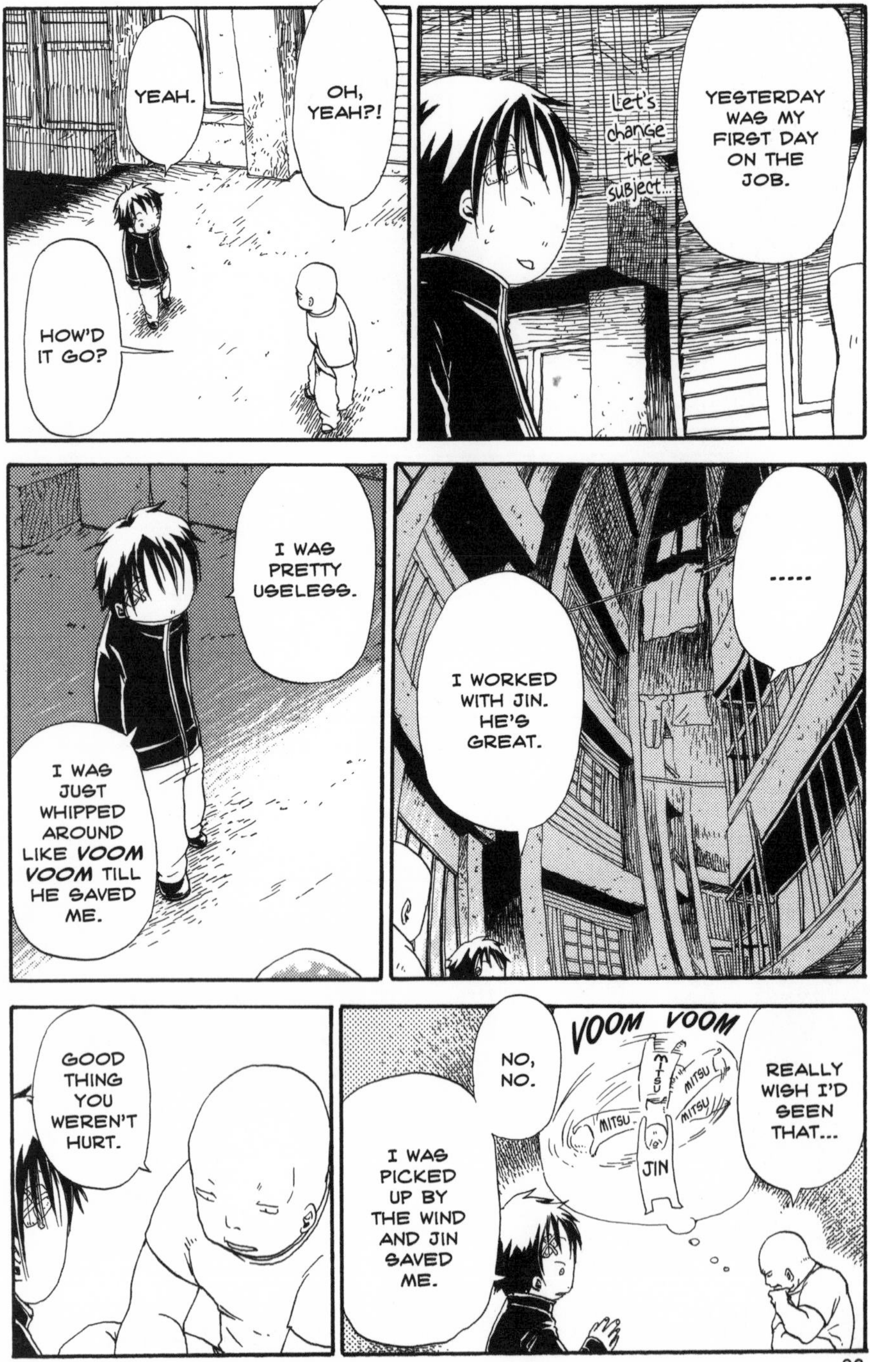
YESTERDAY WAS MY FIRST DAY ON THE JOB.
Let's change the subject...
OH, YEAH?!
YEAH.
HOW'D IT GO?

I WORKED WITH JIN. HE'S GREAT.
I WAS PRETTY USELESS.
I WAS JUST WHIPPED AROUND LIKE *VOOM VOOM* TILL HE SAVED ME.
REALLY WISH I'D SEEN THAT...
VOOM VOOM
MITSU
MITSU
MITSU
MITSU
MITSU
JIN
NO, NO.
I WAS PICKED UP BY THE WIND AND JIN SAVED ME.
GOOD THING YOU WEREN'T HURT.

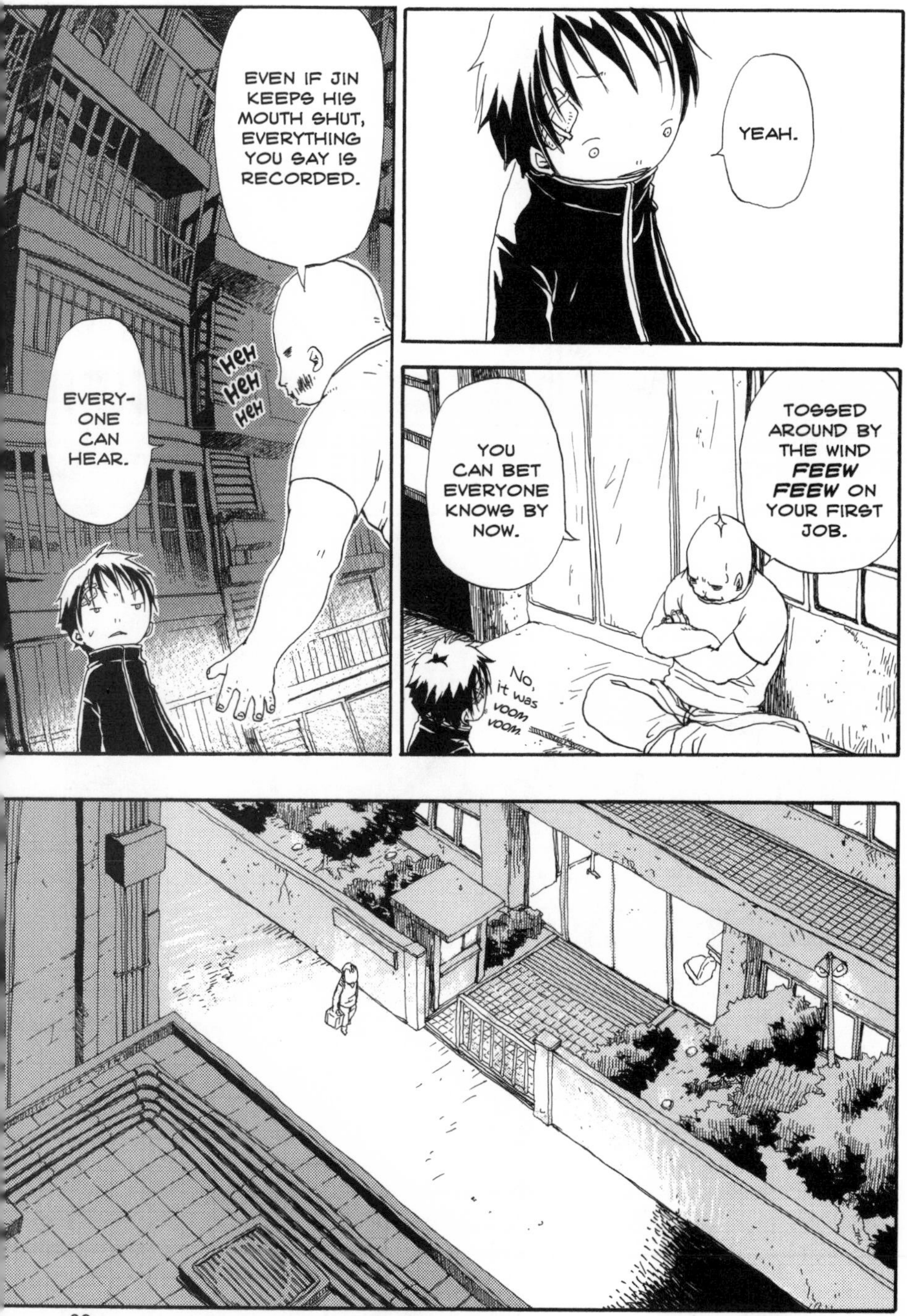
YEAH.
TOSSED AROUND BY THE WIND FEEW FEEW ON YOUR FIRST JOB.
YOU CAN BET EVERYONE KNOWS BY NOW.
No, it was voom voom.
EVEN IF JIN KEEPS HIS MOUTH SHUT, EVERYTHING YOU SAY IS RECORDED.
HEH HEH HEH
EVERY-ONE CAN HEAR.

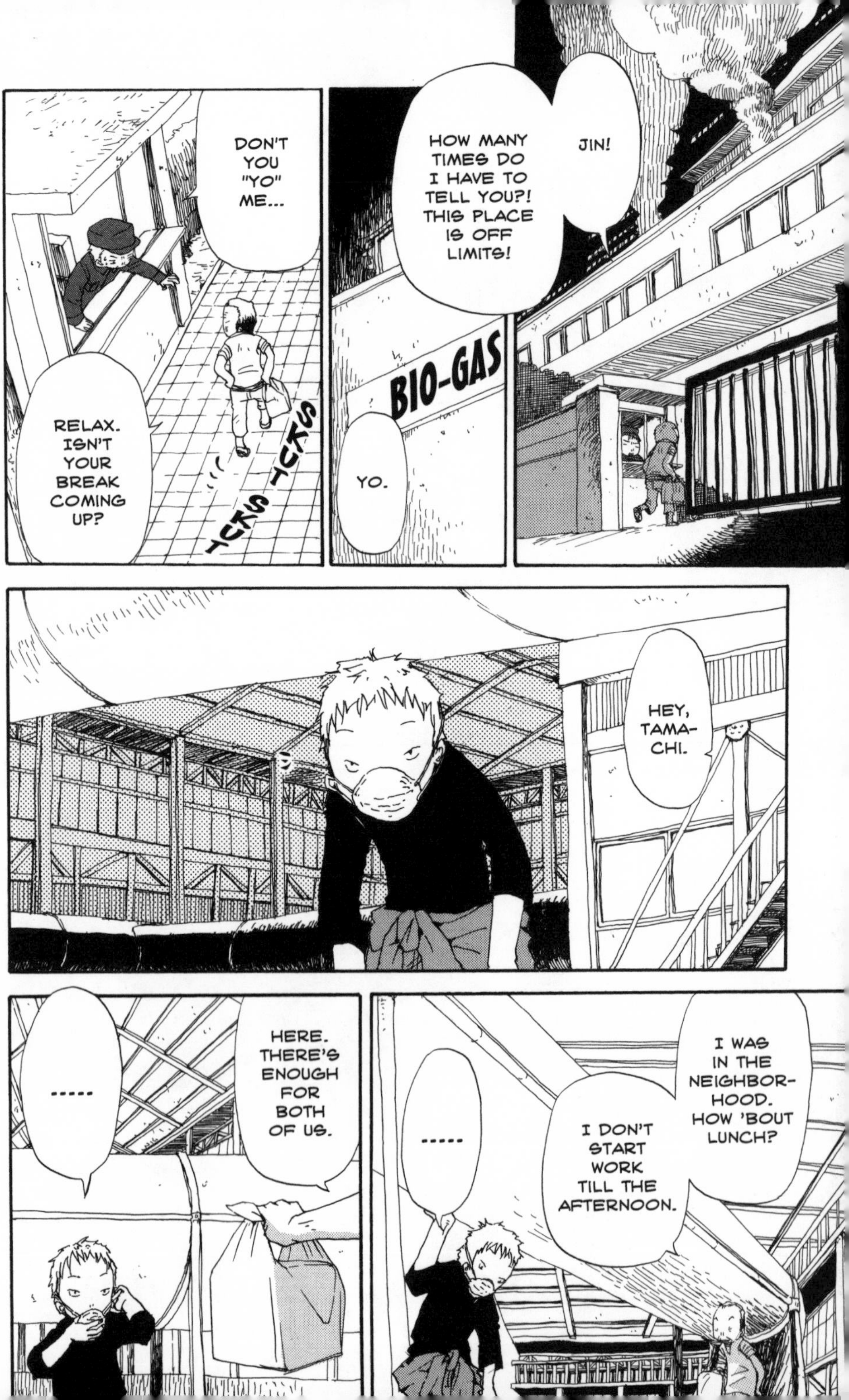
JIN!
HOW MANY TIMES DO I HAVE TO TELL YOU?! THIS PLACE IS OFF LIMITS!
BIO-GAS
YO.
DON'T YOU "YO" ME...
RELAX. ISN'T YOUR BREAK COMING UP?
HEY, TAMA-CHI.
I WAS IN THE NEIGHBOR-HOOD. HOW 'BOUT LUNCH?
I DON'T START WORK TILL THE AFTERNOON.

HERE. THERE'S ENOUGH FOR BOTH OF US.

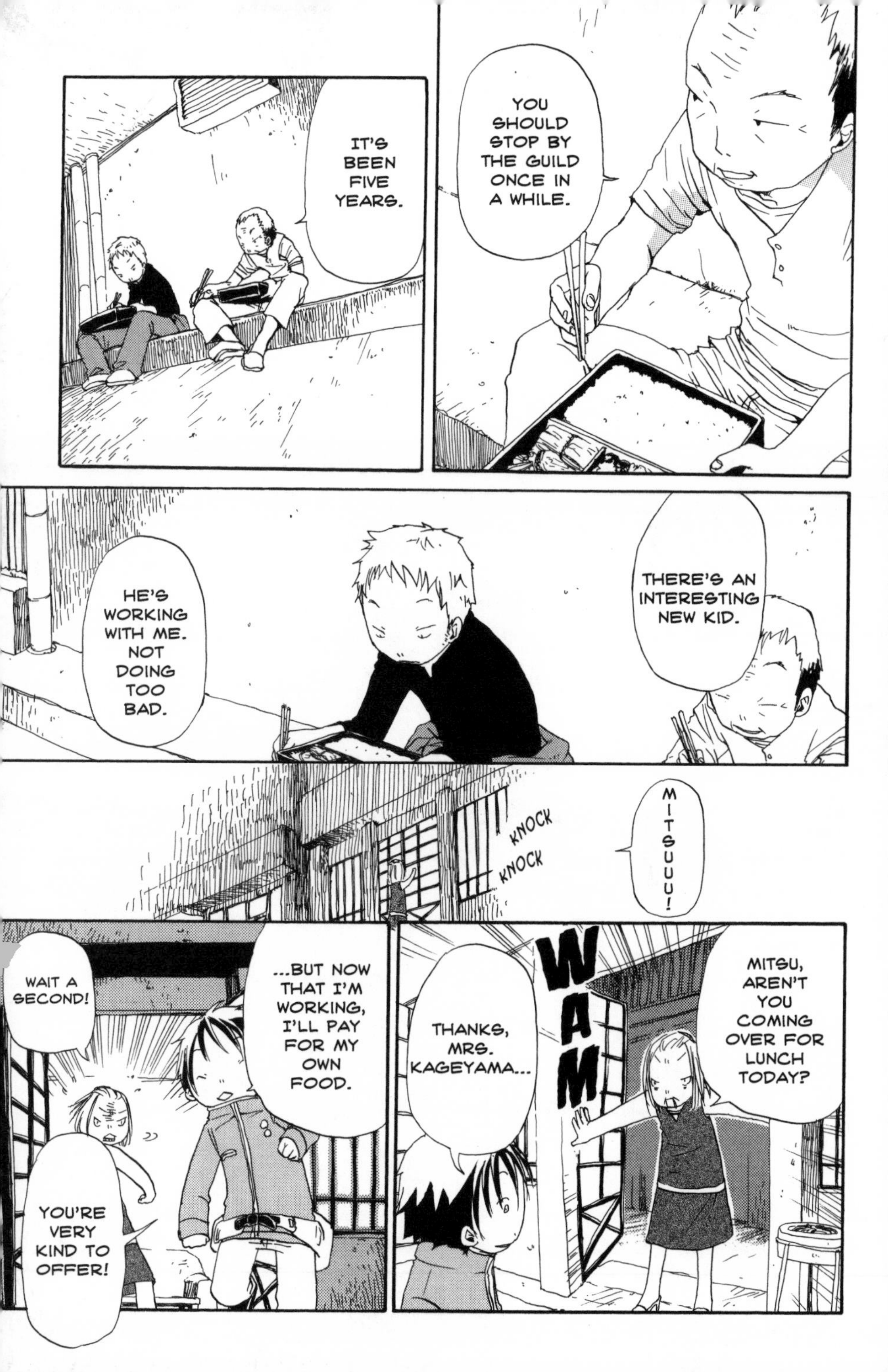
YOU SHOULD STOP BY THE GUILD ONCE IN A WHILE.
IT'S BEEN FIVE YEARS.
THERE'S AN INTERESTING NEW KID.
HE'S WORKING WITH ME. NOT DOING TOO BAD.
MITSUUU!
KNOCK KNOCK
MITSU, AREN'T YOU COMING OVER FOR LUNCH TODAY?
WAM
THANKS, MRS. KAGEYAMA...
...BUT NOW THAT I'M WORKING, I'LL PAY FOR MY OWN FOOD.
WAIT A SECOND!
YOU'RE VERY KIND TO OFFER!

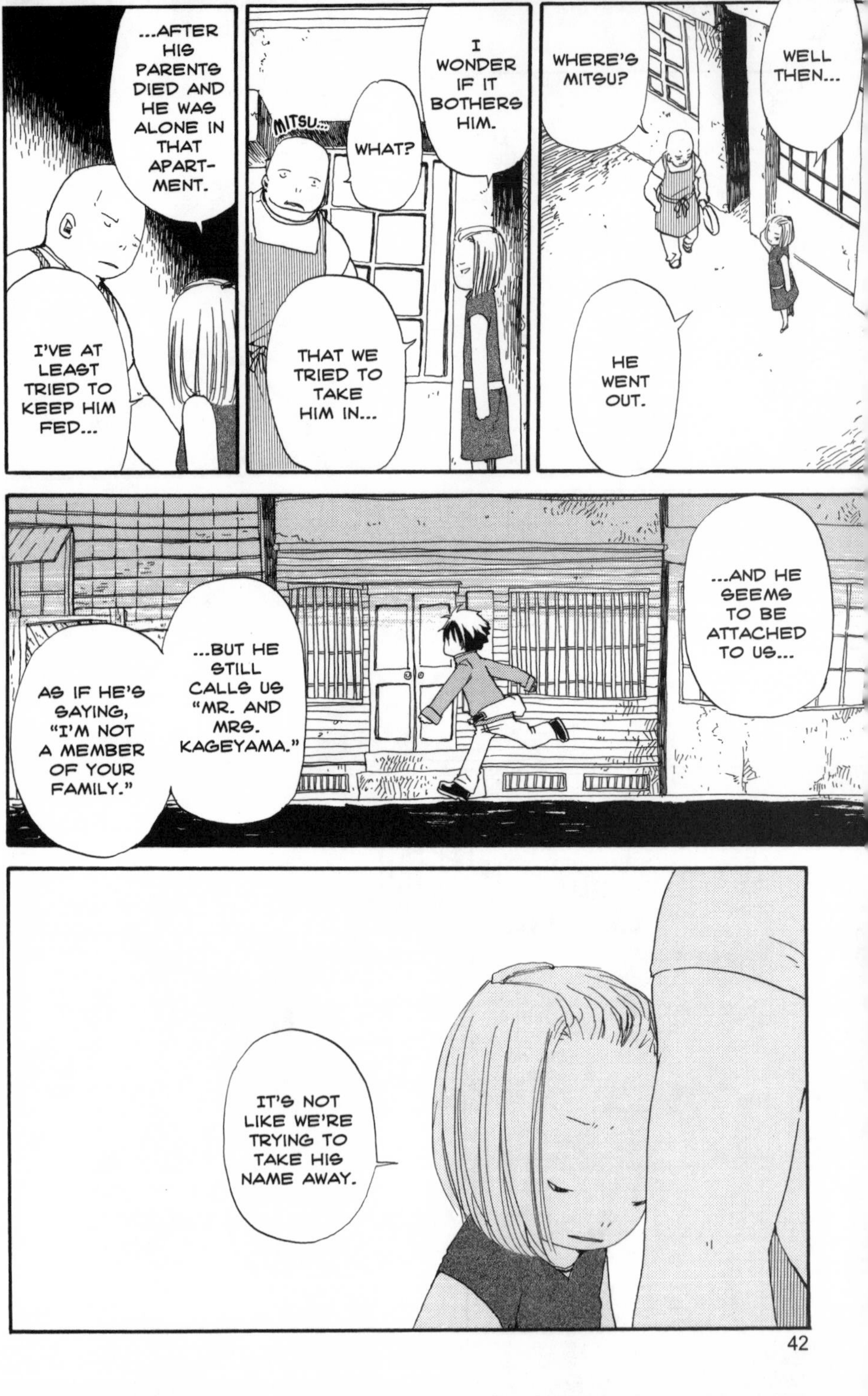
WELL THEN...
WHERE'S MITSU?
HE WENT OUT.
I WONDER IF IT BOTHERS HIM.
MITSU...
WHAT?
THAT WE TRIED TO TAKE HIM IN...
...AFTER HIS PARENTS DIED AND HE WAS ALONE IN THAT APARTMENT.
I'VE AT LEAST TRIED TO KEEP HIM FED...
...AND HE SEEMS TO BE ATTACHED TO US...
...BUT HE STILL CALLS US "MR. AND MRS. KAGEYAMA."
AS IF HE'S SAYING, "I'M NOT A MEMBER OF YOUR FAMILY."
IT'S NOT LIKE WE'RE TRYING TO TAKE HIS NAME AWAY.

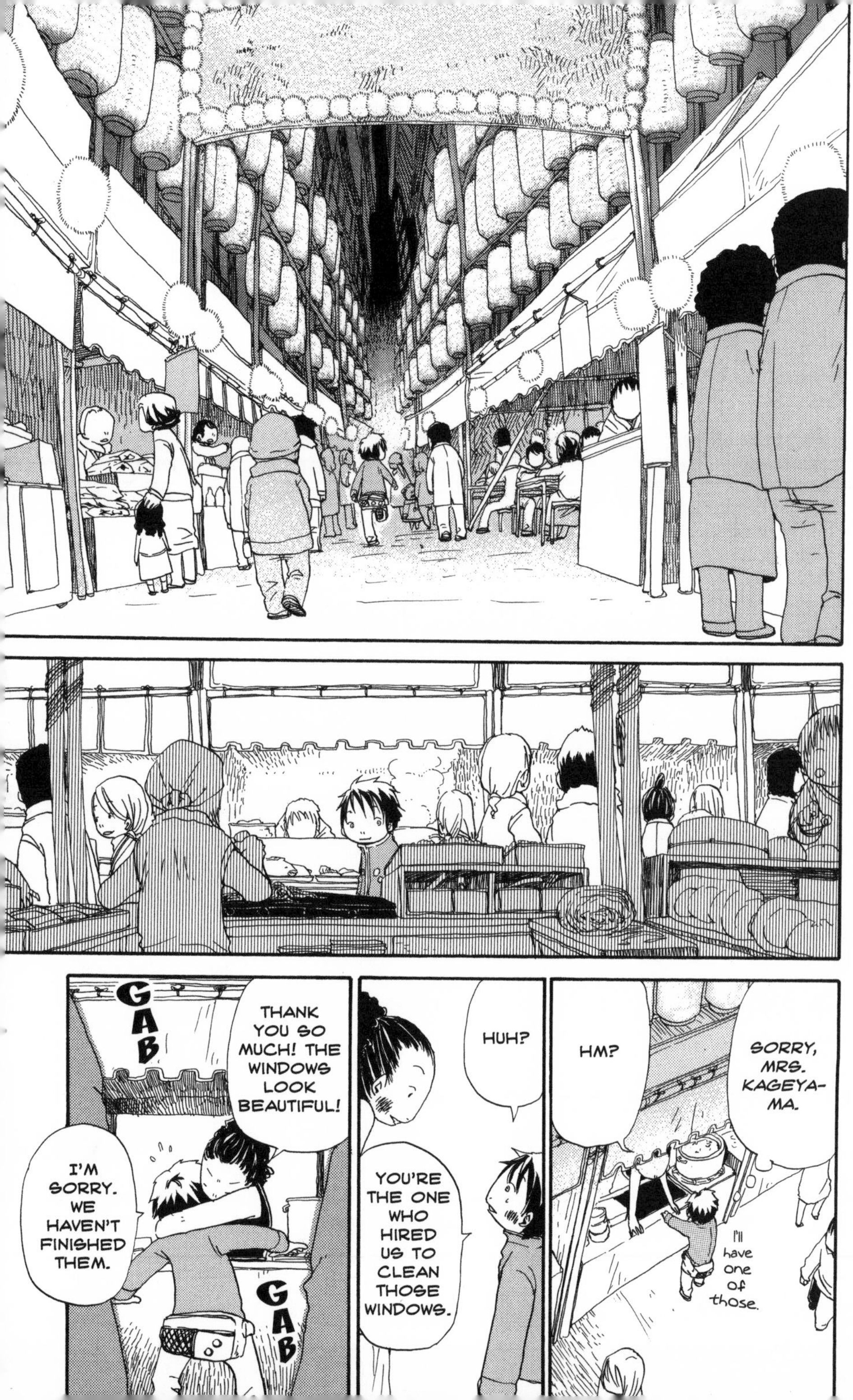
SORRY, MRS. KAGEYAMA.
HM?
I'll have one of those.
HUH?
YOU'RE THE ONE WHO HIRED US TO CLEAN THOSE WINDOWS.
THANK YOU SO MUCH! THE WINDOWS LOOK BEAUTIFUL!
GAB
I'M SORRY. WE HAVEN'T FINISHED THEM.
GAB

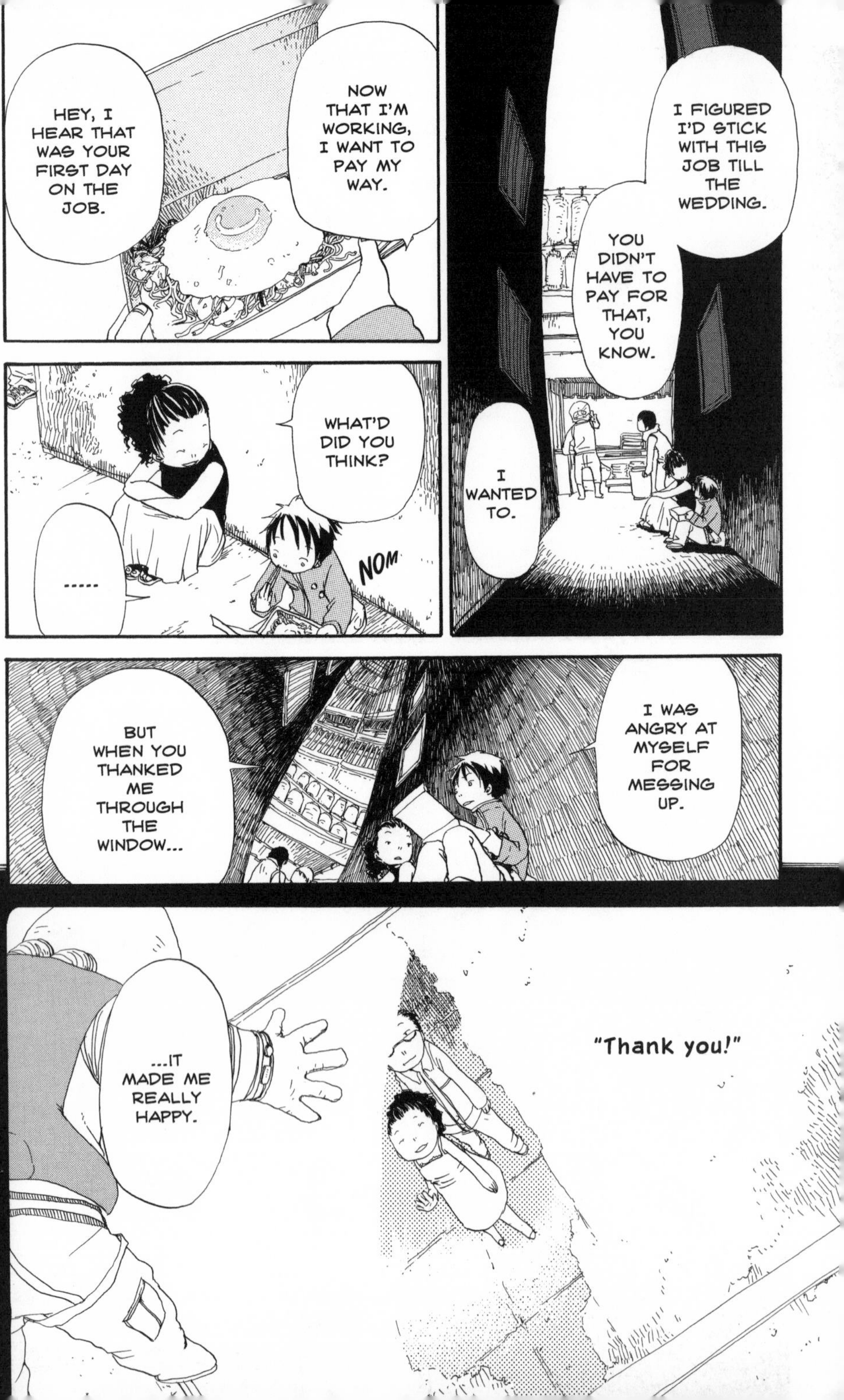
I FIGURED I'D STICK WITH THIS JOB TILL THE WEDDING.
YOU DIDN'T HAVE TO PAY FOR THAT, YOU KNOW.
I WANTED TO.
NOW THAT I'M WORKING, I WANT TO PAY MY WAY.
HEY, I HEAR THAT WAS YOUR FIRST DAY ON THE JOB.
WHAT'D DID YOU THINK?
NOM

I WAS ANGRY AT MYSELF FOR MESSING UP.
BUT WHEN YOU THANKED ME THROUGH THE WINDOW...
"Thank you!"
...IT MADE ME REALLY HAPPY.

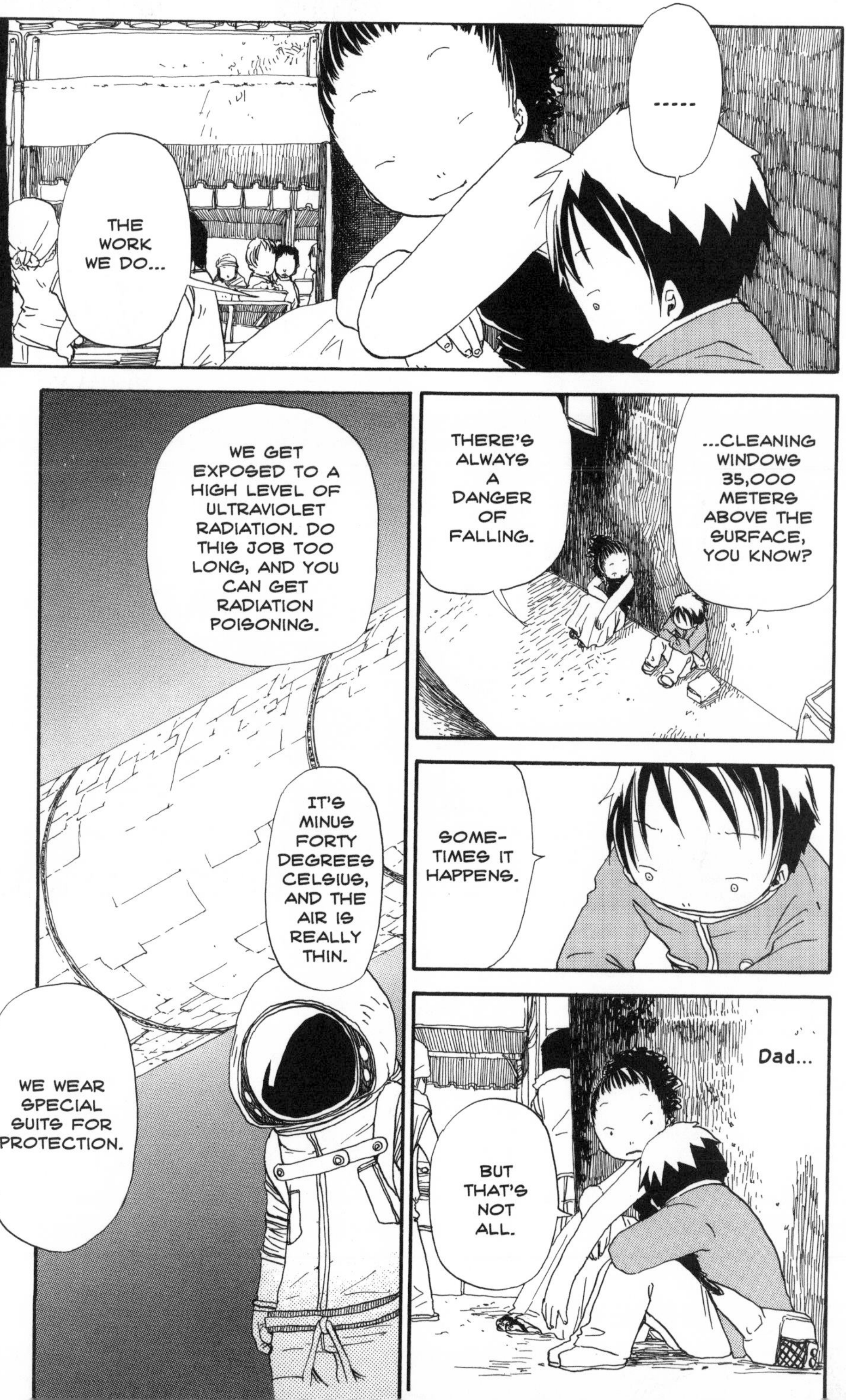

THE WORK WE DO...
...CLEANING WINDOWS 35,000 METERS ABOVE THE SURFACE, YOU KNOW?
THERE'S ALWAYS A DANGER OF FALLING.
SOME-TIMES IT HAPPENS.
Dad...
BUT THAT'S NOT ALL.
WE GET EXPOSED TO A HIGH LEVEL OF ULTRAVIOLET RADIATION. DO THIS JOB TOO LONG, AND YOU CAN GET RADIATION POISONING.
IT'S MINUS FORTY DEGREES CELSIUS, AND THE AIR IS REALLY THIN.
WE WEAR SPECIAL SUITS FOR PROTECTION.

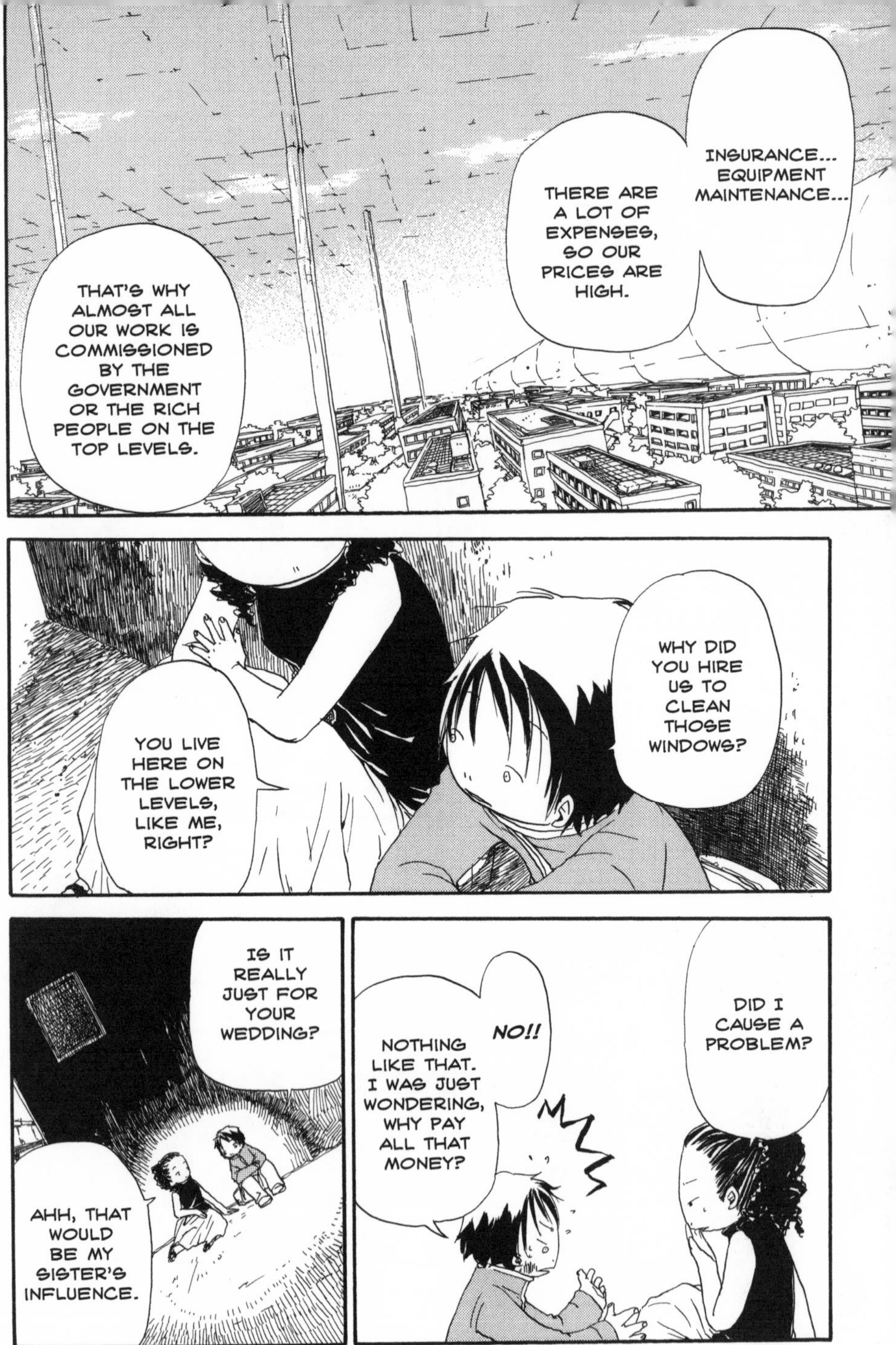
INSURANCE... EQUIPMENT MAINTENANCE...
THERE ARE A LOT OF EXPENSES, SO OUR PRICES ARE HIGH.
THAT'S WHY ALMOST ALL OUR WORK IS COMMISSIONED BY THE GOVERNMENT OR THE RICH PEOPLE ON THE TOP LEVELS.
WHY DID YOU HIRE US TO CLEAN THOSE WINDOWS?
YOU LIVE HERE ON THE LOWER LEVELS, LIKE ME, RIGHT?
DID I CAUSE A PROBLEM?
NO!!
NOTHING LIKE THAT. I WAS JUST WONDERING, WHY PAY ALL THAT MONEY?
IS IT REALLY JUST FOR YOUR WEDDING?
AHH, THAT WOULD BE MY SISTER'S INFLUENCE.

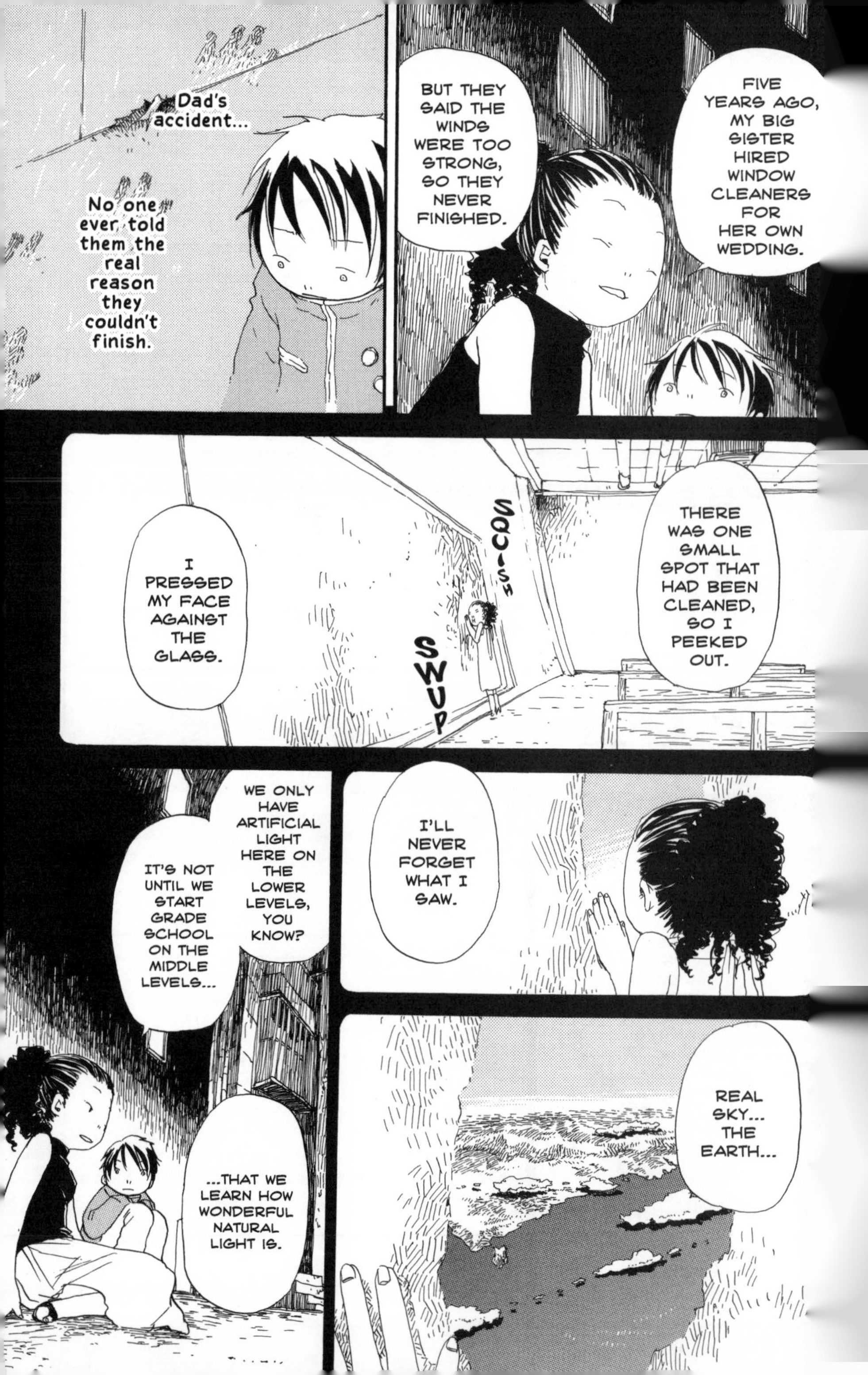
FIVE YEARS AGO, MY BIG SISTER HIRED WINDOW CLEANERS FOR HER OWN WEDDING.
BUT THEY SAID THE WINDS WERE TOO STRONG, SO THEY NEVER FINISHED.
Dad's accident...
No one ever told them the real reason they couldn't finish.
THERE WAS ONE SMALL SPOT THAT HAD BEEN CLEANED, SO I PEEKED OUT.
SQUISH
SWUP
I PRESSED MY FACE AGAINST THE GLASS.
I'LL NEVER FORGET WHAT I SAW.
REAL SKY... THE EARTH...
WE ONLY HAVE ARTIFICIAL LIGHT HERE ON THE LOWER LEVELS, YOU KNOW?
IT'S NOT UNTIL WE START GRADE SCHOOL ON THE MIDDLE LEVELS...
...THAT WE LEARN HOW WONDERFUL NATURAL LIGHT IS.

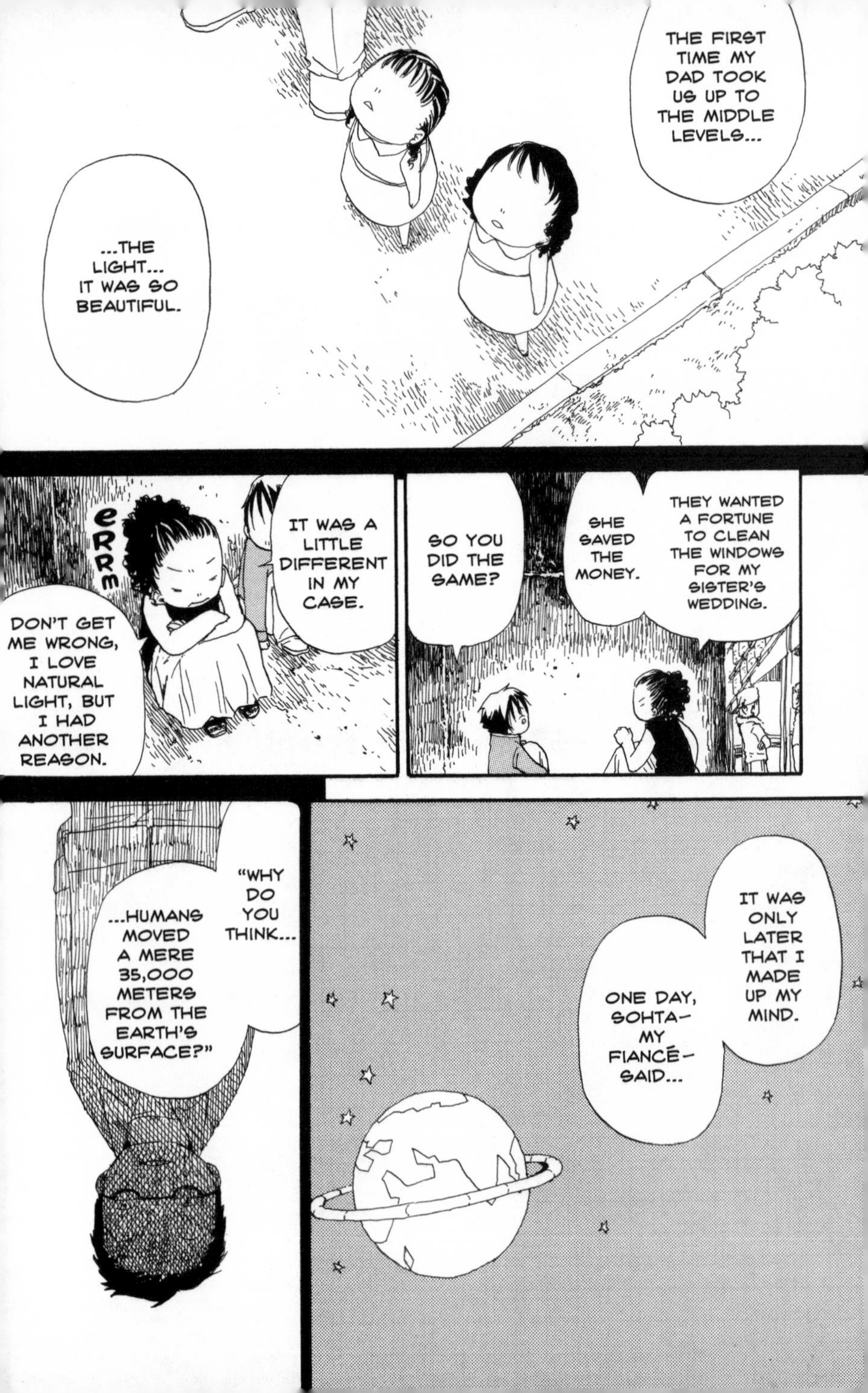
THE FIRST TIME MY DAD TOOK US UP TO THE MIDDLE LEVELS...
...THE LIGHT... IT WAS SO BEAUTIFUL.
THEY WANTED A FORTUNE TO CLEAN THE WINDOWS FOR MY SISTER'S WEDDING.
SHE SAVED THE MONEY.
SO YOU DID THE SAME?
IT WAS A LITTLE DIFFERENT IN MY CASE.
ERRM
DON'T GET ME WRONG, I LOVE NATURAL LIGHT, BUT I HAD ANOTHER REASON.
IT WAS ONLY LATER THAT I MADE UP MY MIND.
ONE DAY, SOHTA—MY FIANCÉ—SAID...
"WHY DO YOU THINK...
...HUMANS MOVED A MERE 35,000 METERS FROM THE EARTH'S SURFACE?"

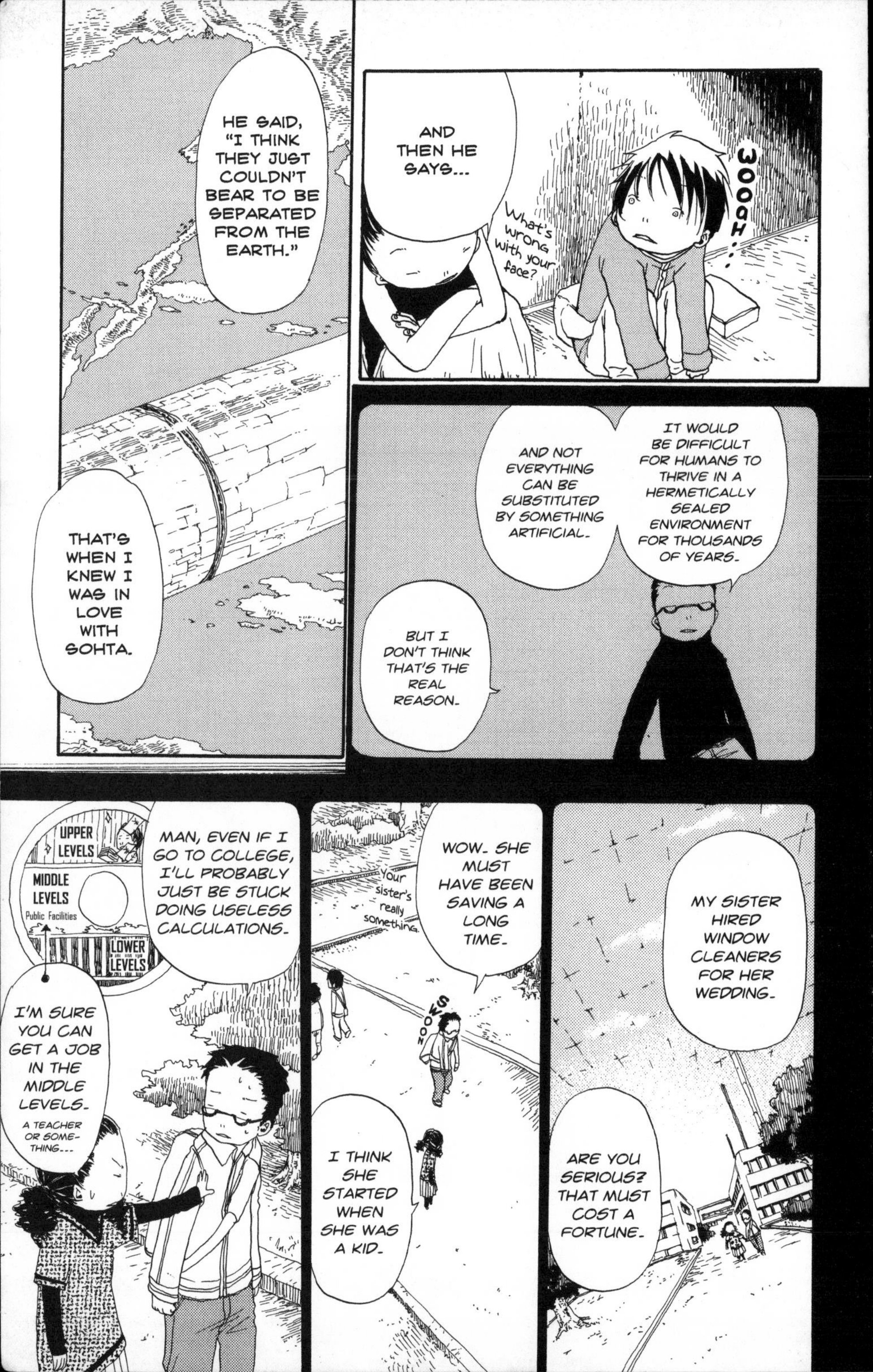
AND THEN HE SAYS...
What's wrong with your face?
WOOOAH...
IT WOULD BE DIFFICULT FOR HUMANS TO THRIVE IN A HERMETICALLY SEALED ENVIRONMENT FOR THOUSANDS OF YEARS.
AND NOT EVERYTHING CAN BE SUBSTITUTED BY SOMETHING ARTIFICIAL.
BUT I DON'T THINK THAT'S THE REAL REASON.
HE SAID, "I THINK THEY JUST COULDN'T BEAR TO BE SEPARATED FROM THE EARTH."
THAT'S WHEN I KNEW I WAS IN LOVE WITH SOHTA.
MY SISTER HIRED WINDOW CLEANERS FOR HER WEDDING.
ARE YOU SERIOUS? THAT MUST COST A FORTUNE.
WOW. SHE MUST HAVE BEEN SAVING A LONG TIME.
Your sister's really something.
I THINK SHE STARTED WHEN SHE WAS A KID.
MAN, EVEN IF I GO TO COLLEGE, I'LL PROBABLY JUST BE STUCK DOING USELESS CALCULATIONS.
UPPER LEVELS
MIDDLE LEVELS
Public Facilities
LOWER LEVELS
I'M SURE YOU CAN GET A JOB IN THE MIDDLE LEVELS.
A TEACHER OR SOMETHING...

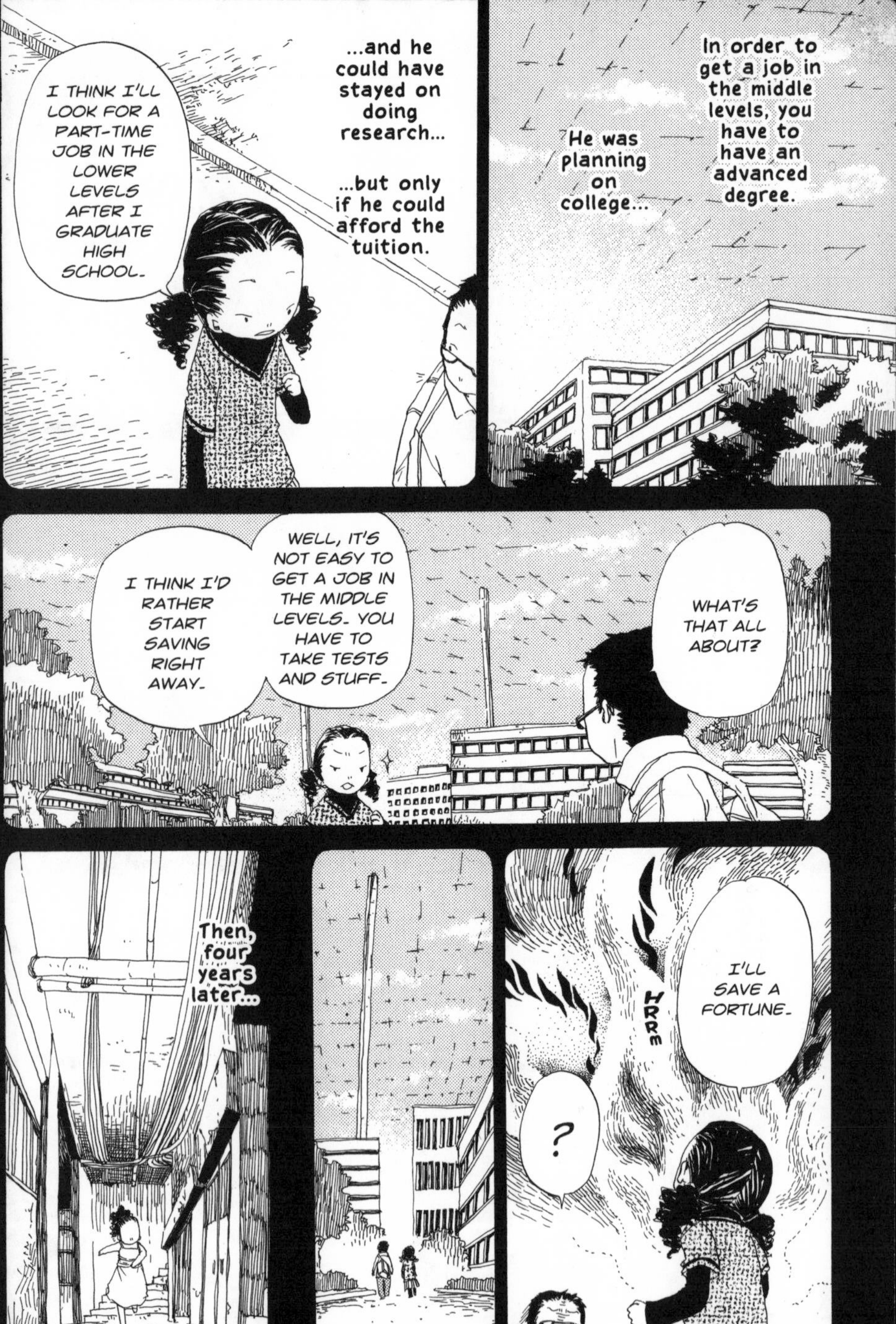

In order to get a job in the middle levels, you have to have an advanced degree.
He was planning on college...
...and he could have stayed on doing research...
...but only if he could afford the tuition.
I THINK I'LL LOOK FOR A PART-TIME JOB IN THE LOWER LEVELS AFTER I GRADUATE HIGH SCHOOL.
WHAT'S THAT ALL ABOUT?
WELL, IT'S NOT EASY TO GET A JOB IN THE MIDDLE LEVELS. YOU HAVE TO TAKE TESTS AND STUFF.
I THINK I'D RATHER START SAVING RIGHT AWAY.
I'LL SAVE A FORTUNE.
HRRM
?
Then, four years later...

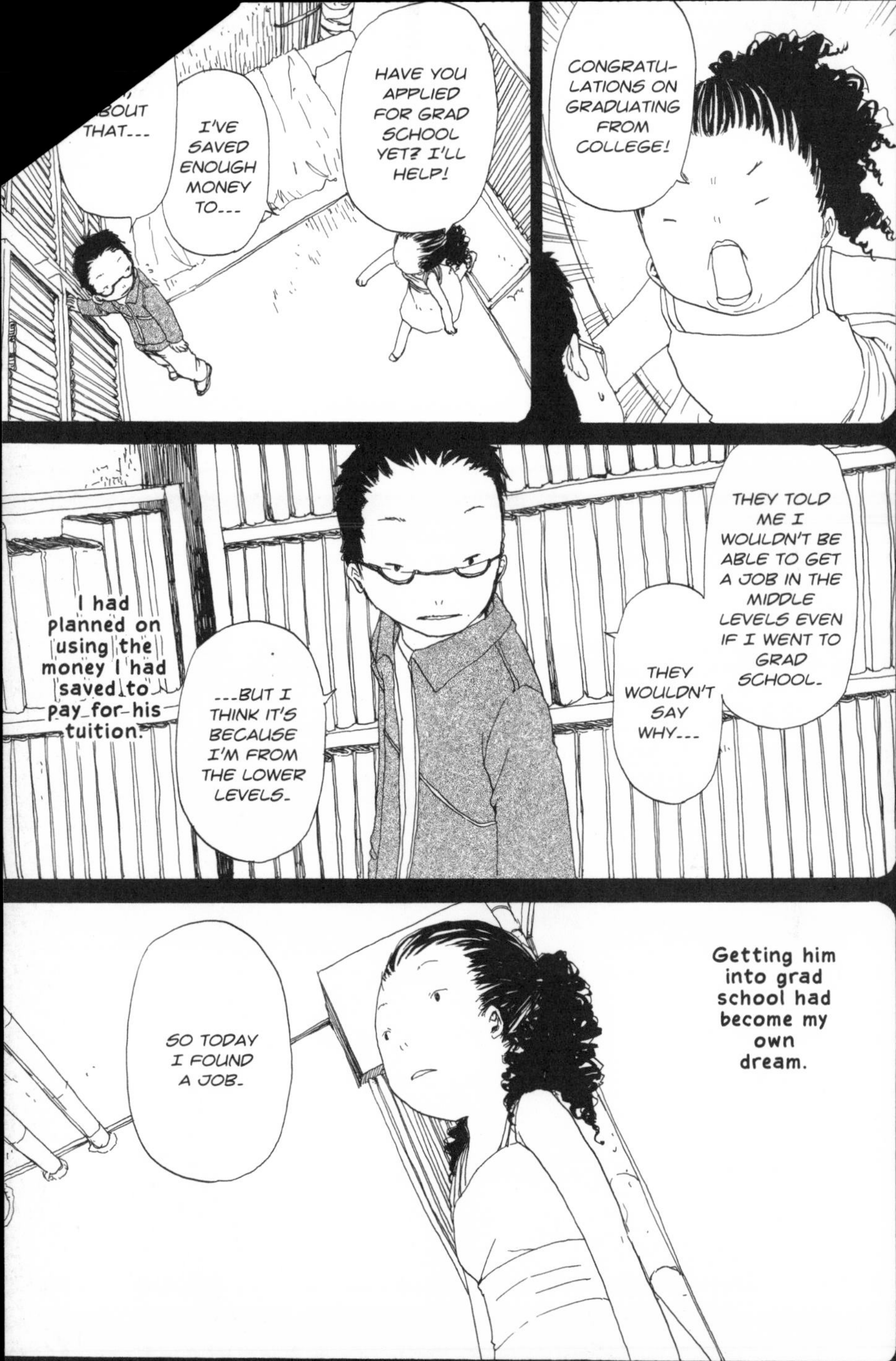
CONGRATULATIONS ON GRADUATING FROM COLLEGE!
HAVE YOU APPLIED FOR GRAD SCHOOL YET? I'LL HELP!
I'VE SAVED ENOUGH MONEY TO...
ABOUT THAT...
THEY TOLD ME I WOULDN'T BE ABLE TO GET A JOB IN THE MIDDLE LEVELS EVEN IF I WENT TO GRAD SCHOOL.
THEY WOULDN'T SAY WHY...
...BUT I THINK IT'S BECAUSE I'M FROM THE LOWER LEVELS.
I had planned on using the money I had saved to pay for his tuition.
Getting him into grad school had become my own dream.
SO TODAY I FOUND A JOB.

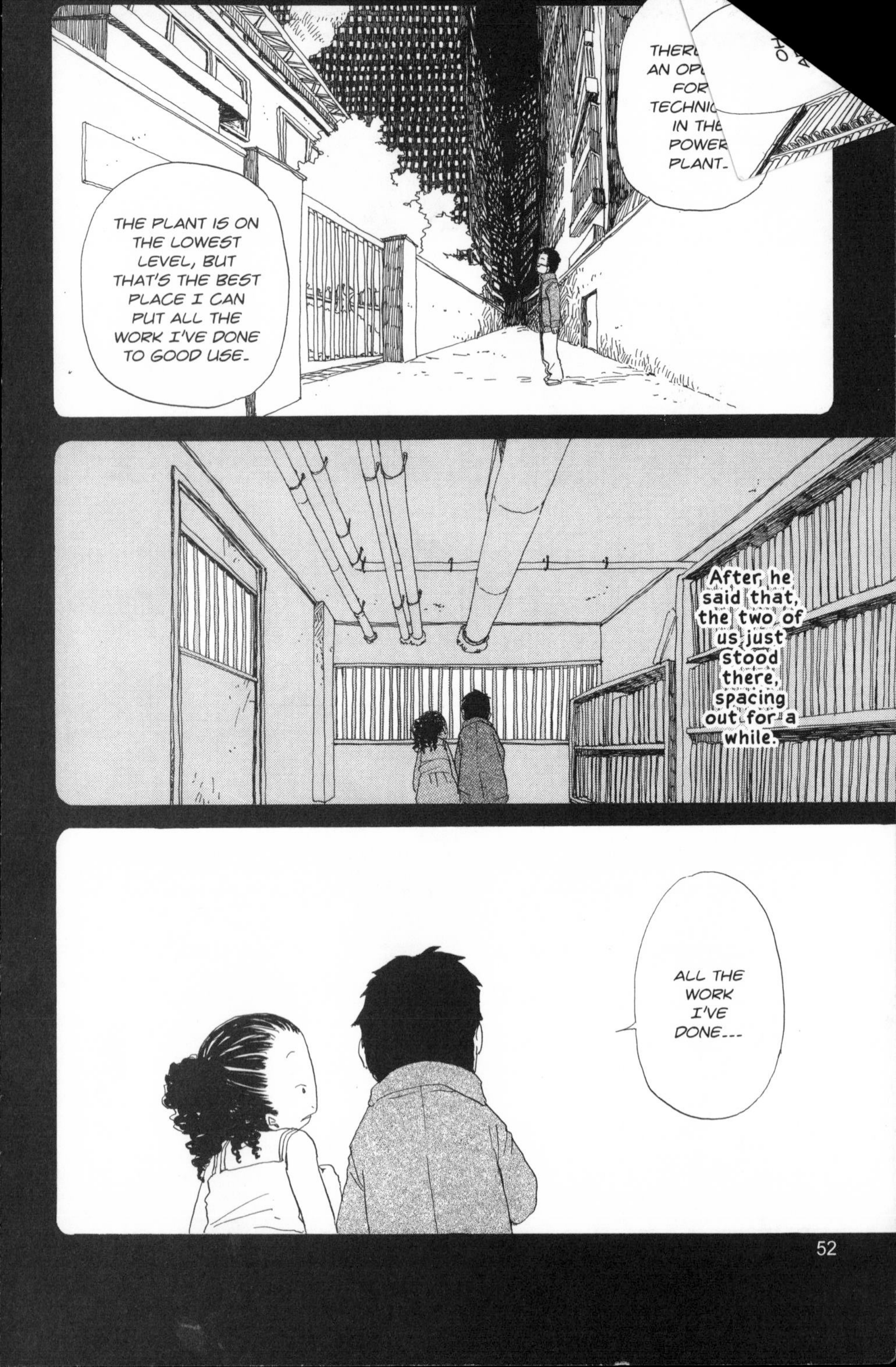
THERE AN OP FOR TECHNIC IN THE POWER PLANT.
THE PLANT IS ON THE LOWEST LEVEL, BUT THAT'S THE BEST PLACE I CAN PUT ALL THE WORK I'VE DONE TO GOOD USE.
After he said that, the two of us just stood there, spacing out for a while.
ALL THE WORK I'VE DONE...

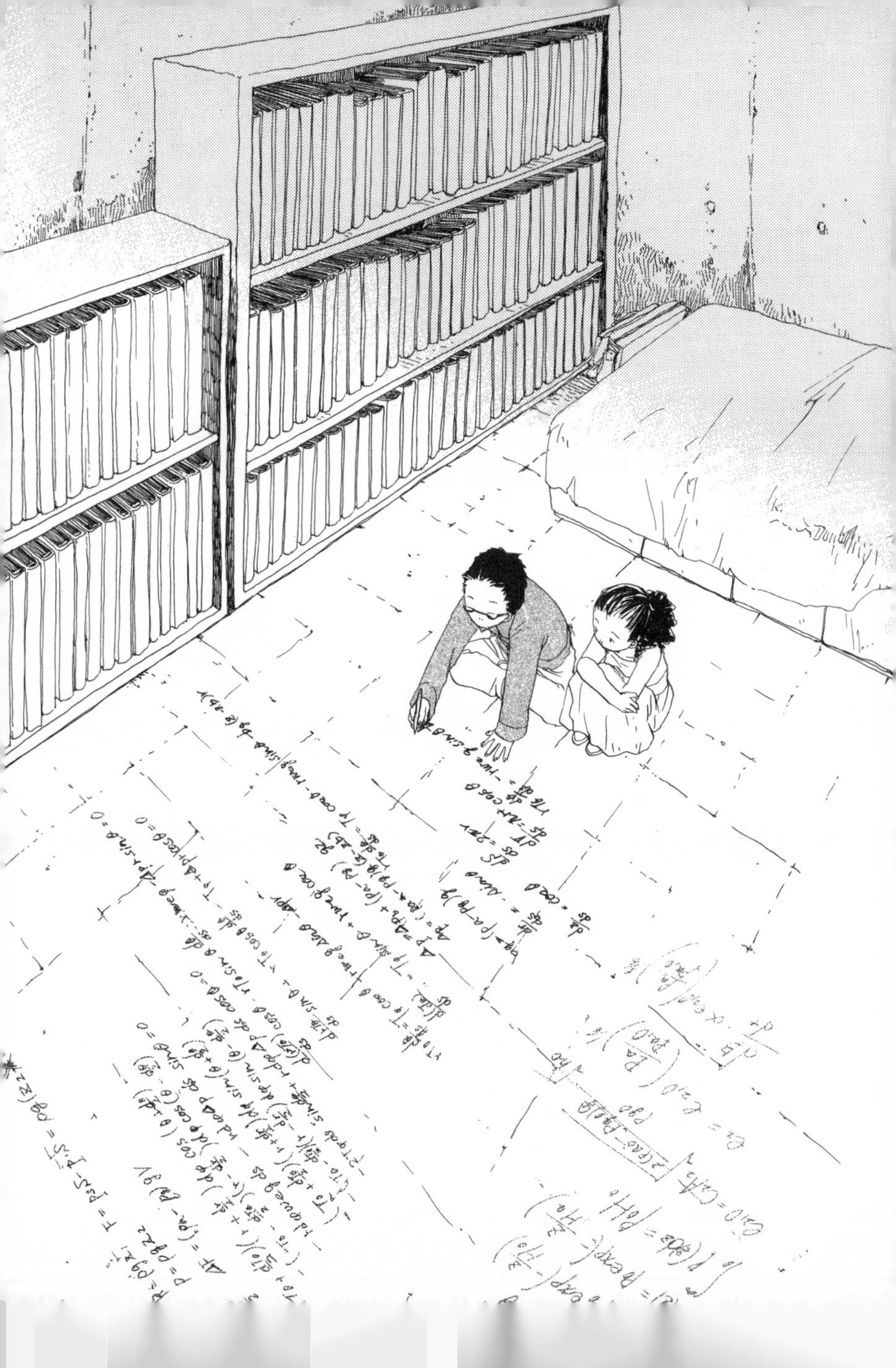

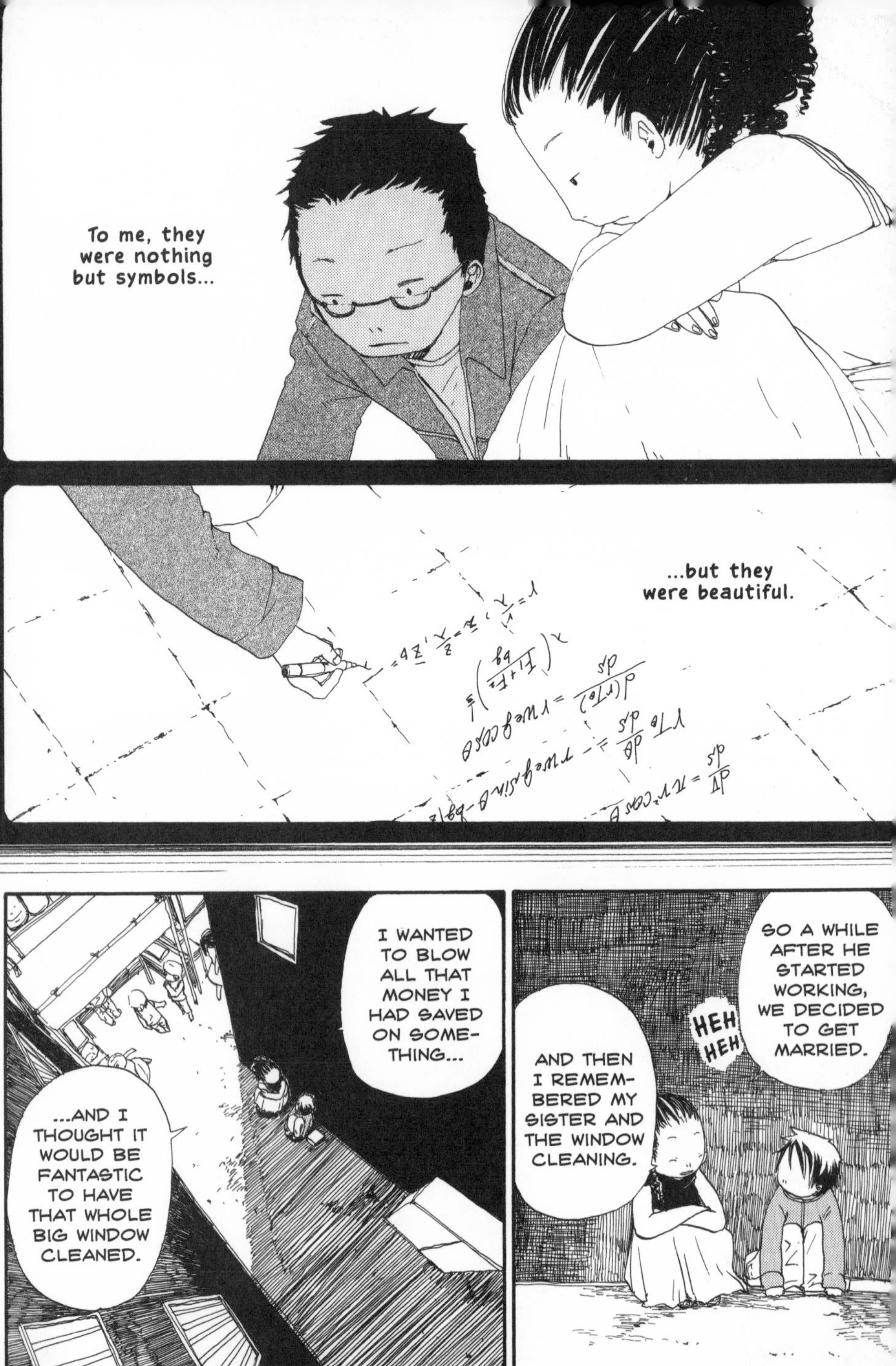
To me, they were nothing but symbols...
...but they were beautiful.
SO A WHILE AFTER HE STARTED WORKING, WE DECIDED TO GET MARRIED.
HEH HEH
AND THEN I REMEM-BERED MY SISTER AND THE WINDOW CLEANING.
I WANTED TO BLOW ALL THAT MONEY I HAD SAVED ON SOME-THING...
...AND I THOUGHT IT WOULD BE FANTASTIC TO HAVE THAT WHOLE BIG WINDOW CLEANED.

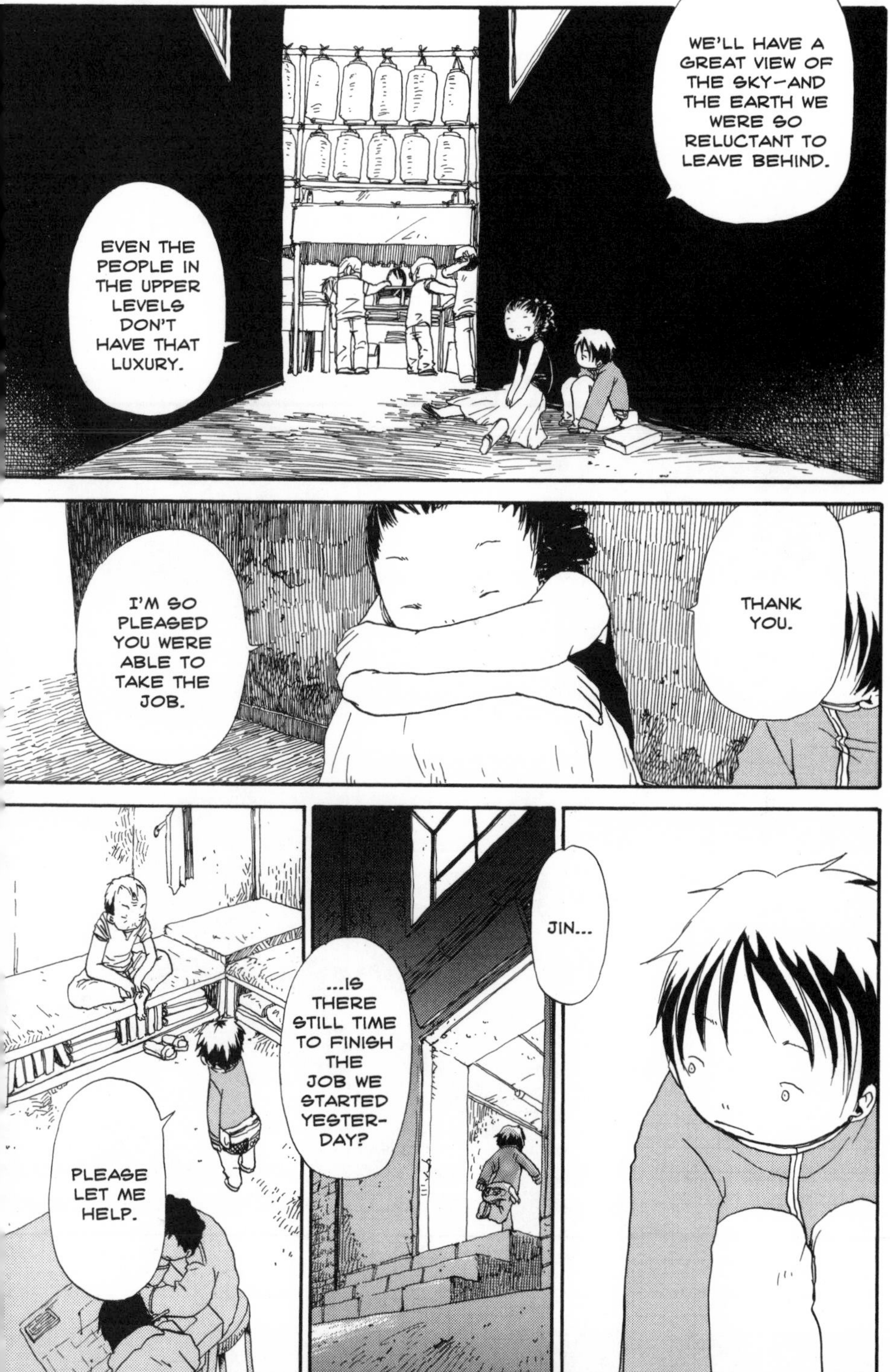
WE'LL HAVE A GREAT VIEW OF THE SKY—AND THE EARTH WE WERE SO RELUCTANT TO LEAVE BEHIND.
EVEN THE PEOPLE IN THE UPPER LEVELS DON'T HAVE THAT LUXURY.
THANK YOU.
I'M SO PLEASED YOU WERE ABLE TO TAKE THE JOB.
JIN...
...IS THERE STILL TIME TO FINISH THE JOB WE STARTED YESTER-DAY?
PLEASE LET ME HELP.

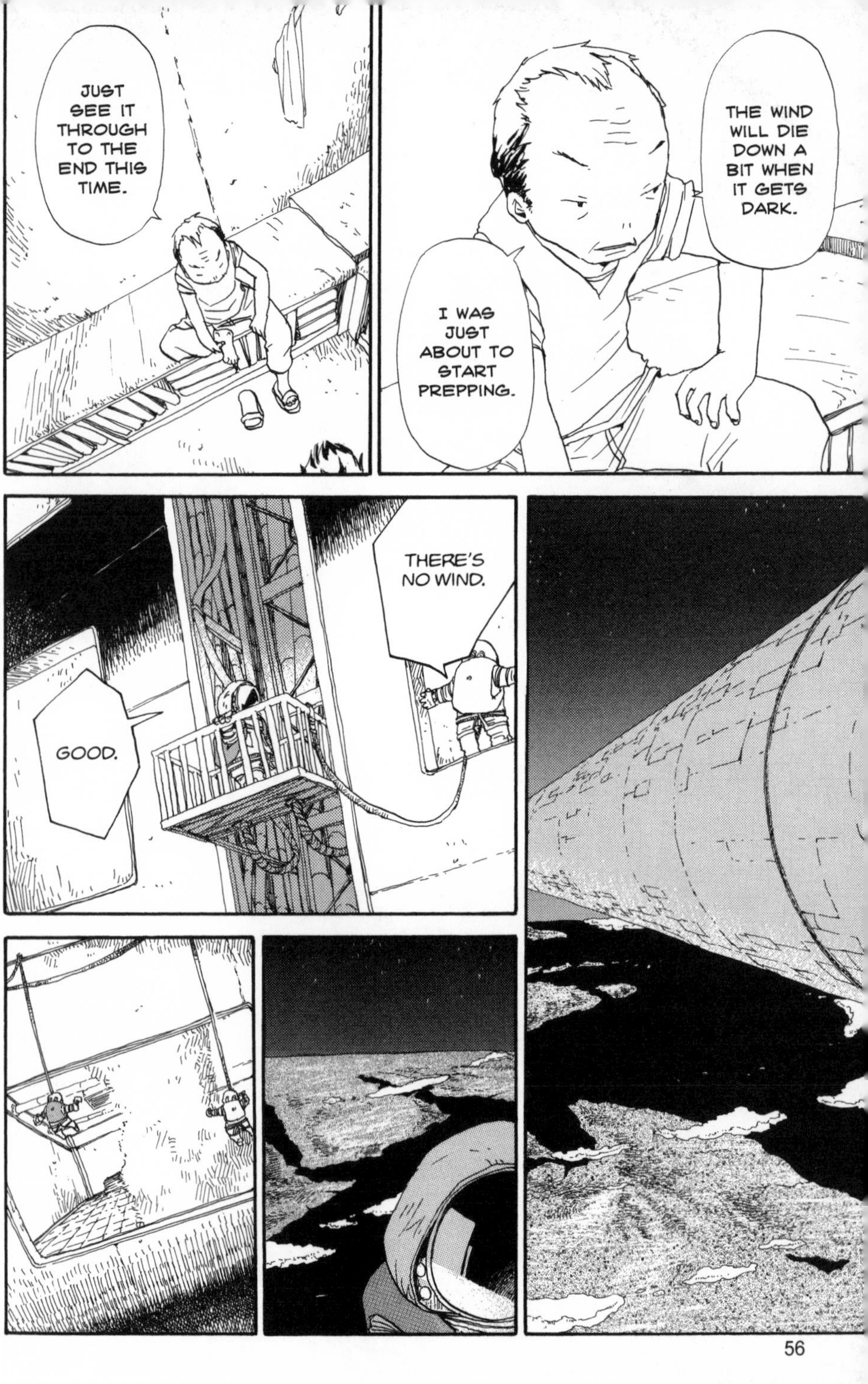
THE WIND WILL DIE DOWN A BIT WHEN IT GETS DARK.
I WAS JUST ABOUT TO START PREPPING.
JUST SEE IT THROUGH TO THE END THIS TIME.
THERE'S NO WIND.
GOOD.

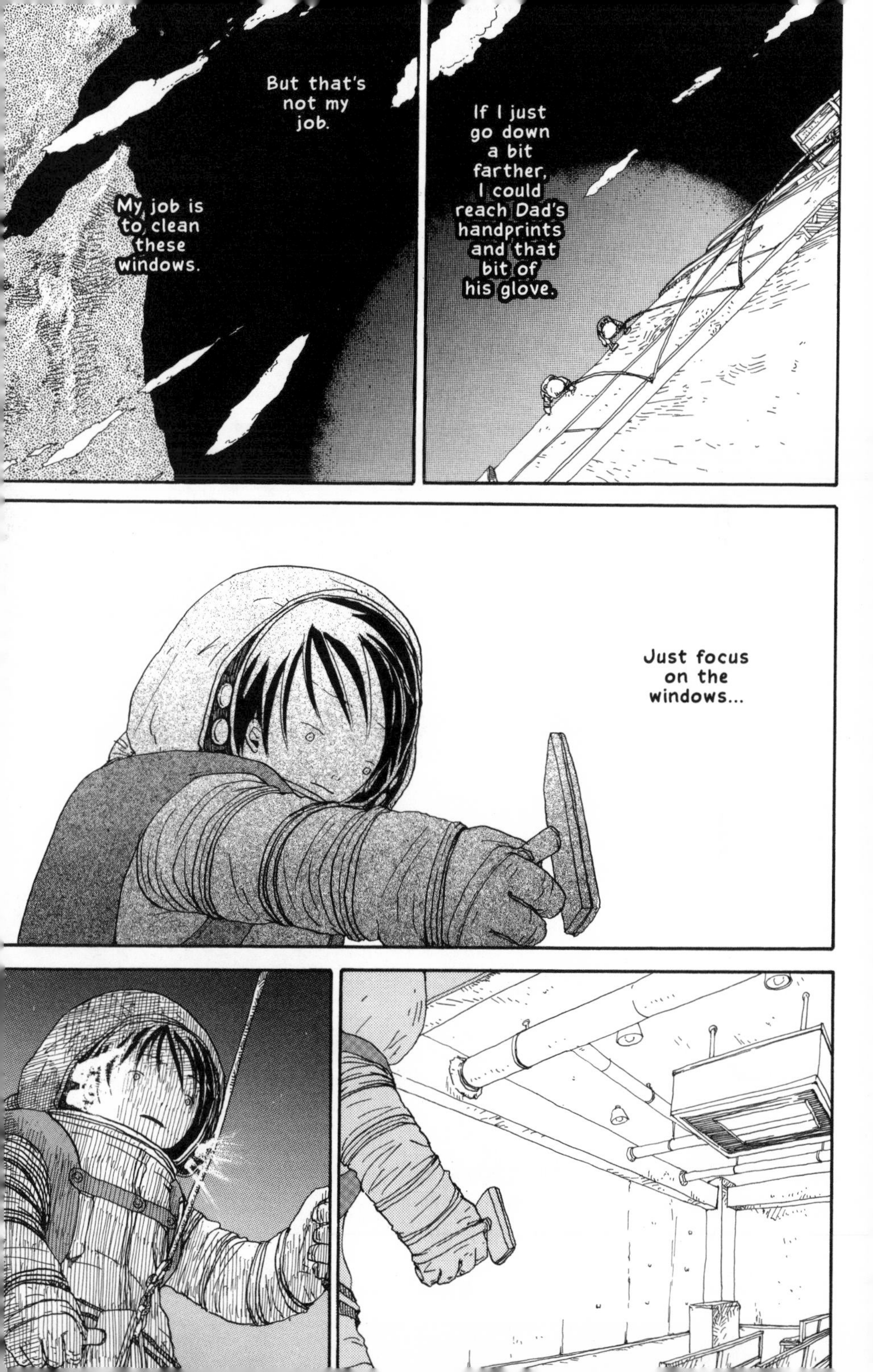

If I just go down a bit farther, I could reach Dad's handprints and that bit of his glove.
But that's not my job.
My job is to clean these windows.
Just focus on the windows...

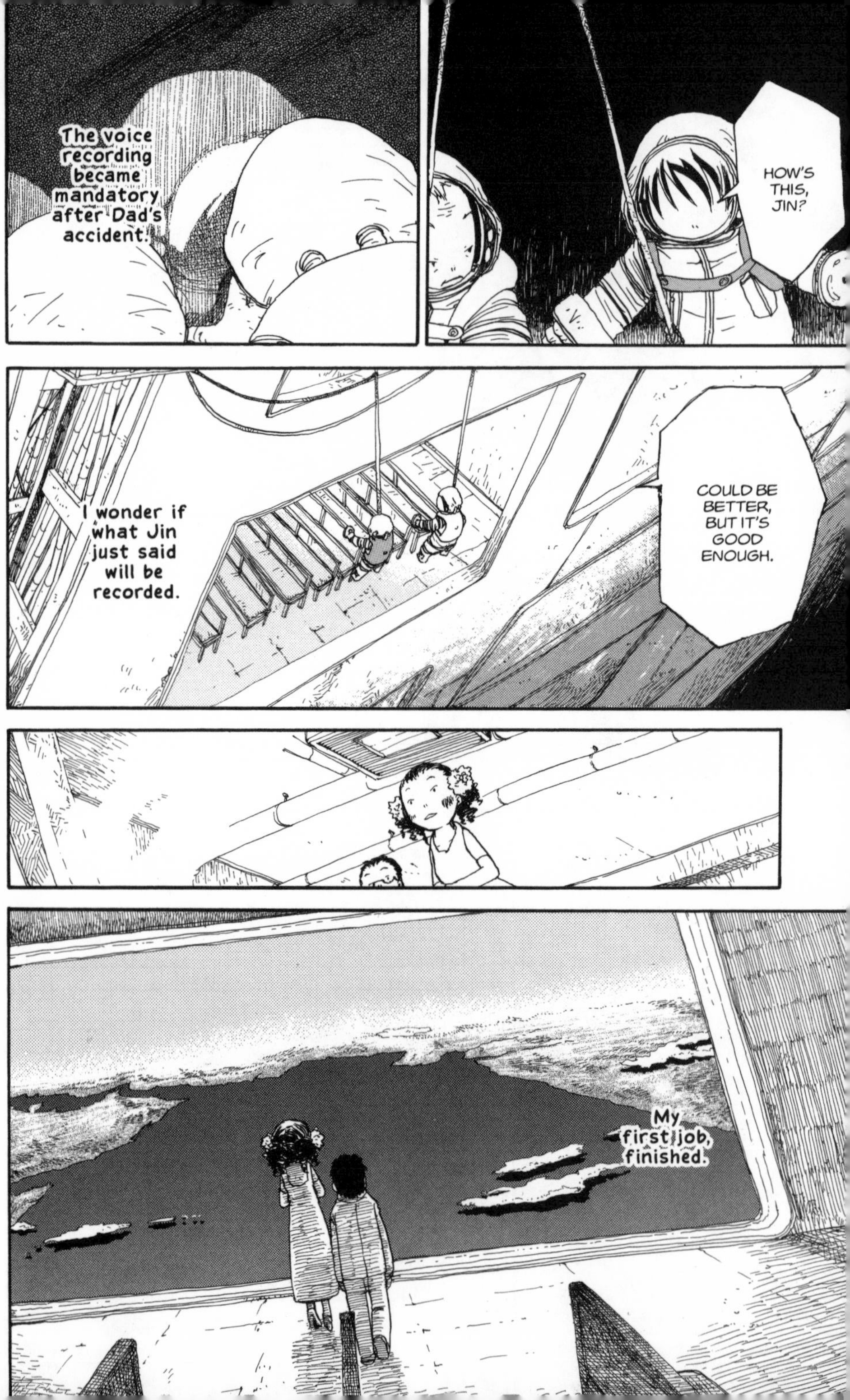
HOW'S THIS, JIN?
The voice recording became mandatory after Dad's accident.
COULD BE BETTER, BUT IT'S GOOD ENOUGH.
I wonder if what Jin just said will be recorded.
My first job, finished.

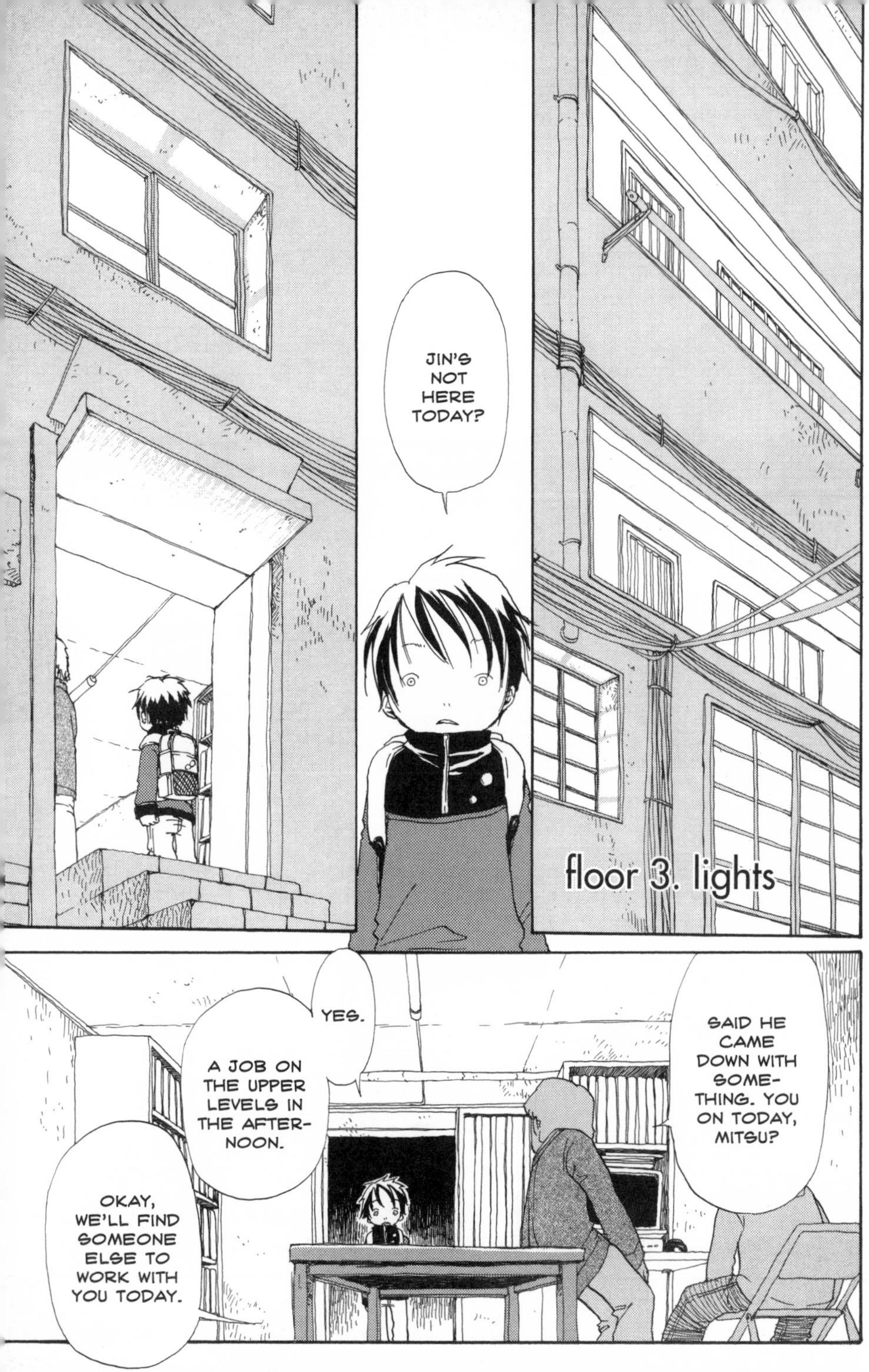
floor 3. lights
JIN'S NOT HERE TODAY?
SAID HE CAME DOWN WITH SOME-THING. YOU ON TODAY, MITSU?
YES.
A JOB ON THE UPPER LEVELS IN THE AFTER-NOON.
OKAY, WE'LL FIND SOMEONE ELSE TO WORK WITH YOU TODAY.

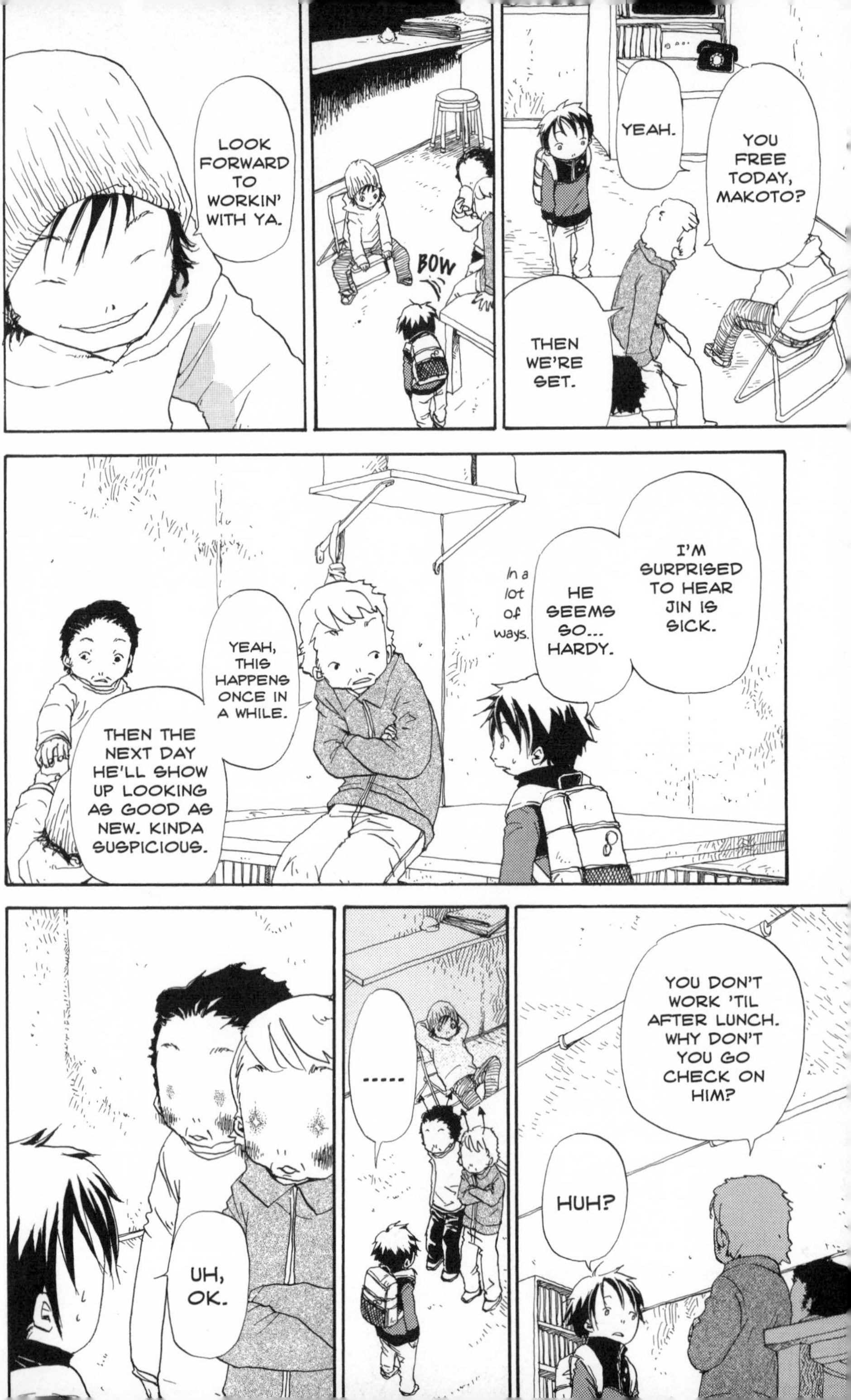
YOU FREE TODAY, MAKOTO?
YEAH.
THEN WE'RE SET.
BOW
LOOK FORWARD TO WORKIN' WITH YA.
I'M SURPRISED TO HEAR JIN IS SICK.
HE SEEMS SO... HARDY.
In a lot of ways.
YEAH, THIS HAPPENS ONCE IN A WHILE.
THEN THE NEXT DAY HE'LL SHOW UP LOOKING AS GOOD AS NEW. KINDA SUSPICIOUS.
YOU DON'T WORK 'TIL AFTER LUNCH. WHY DON'T YOU GO CHECK ON HIM?
HUH?

UH, OK.

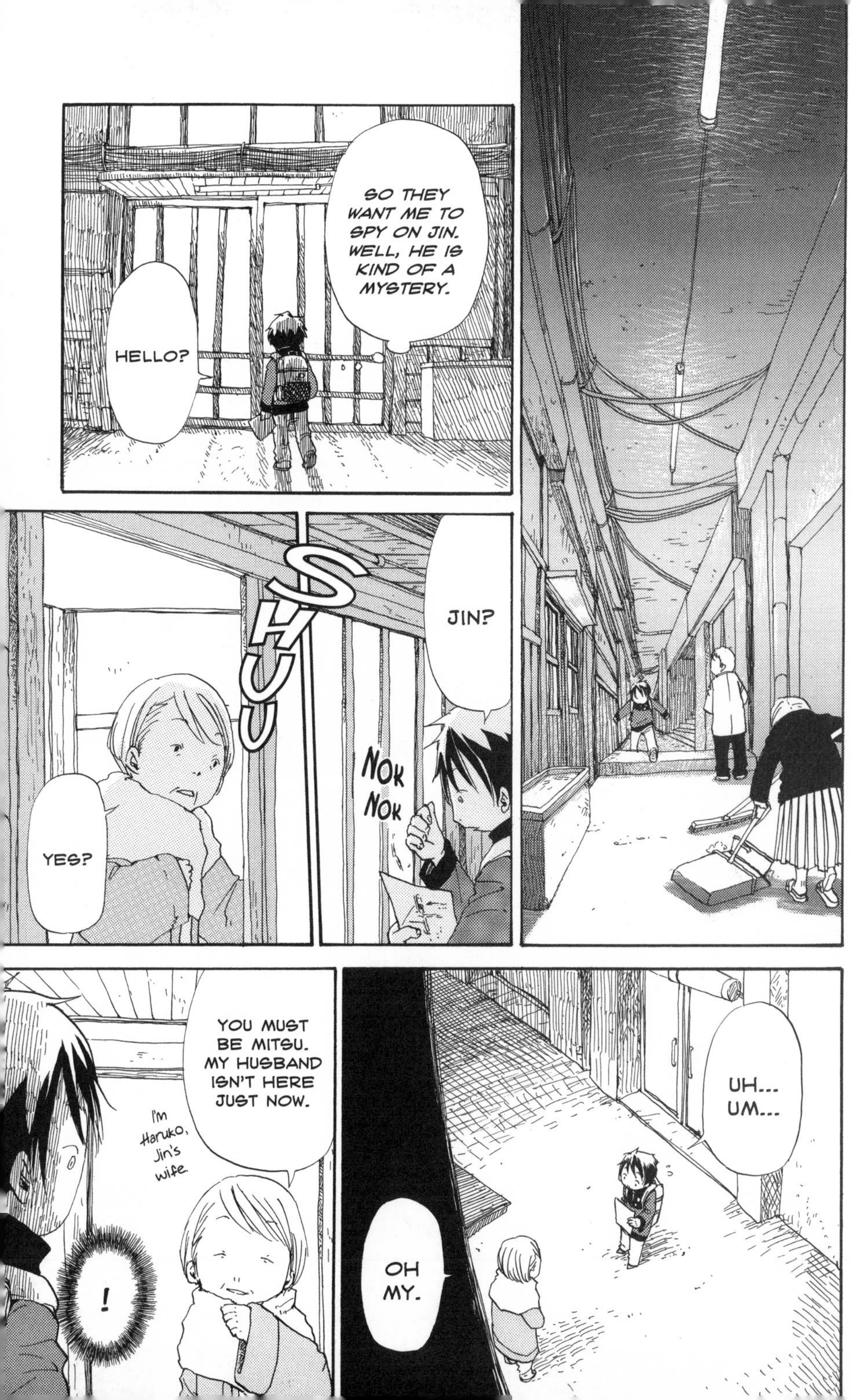
SO THEY WANT ME TO SPY ON JIN. WELL, HE IS KIND OF A MYSTERY.
HELLO?
JIN?
NOK NOK
SHUU
YES?
UH... UM...
OH MY.
YOU MUST BE MITSU. MY HUSBAND ISN'T HERE JUST NOW.
I'm Haruko, Jin's wife.
!

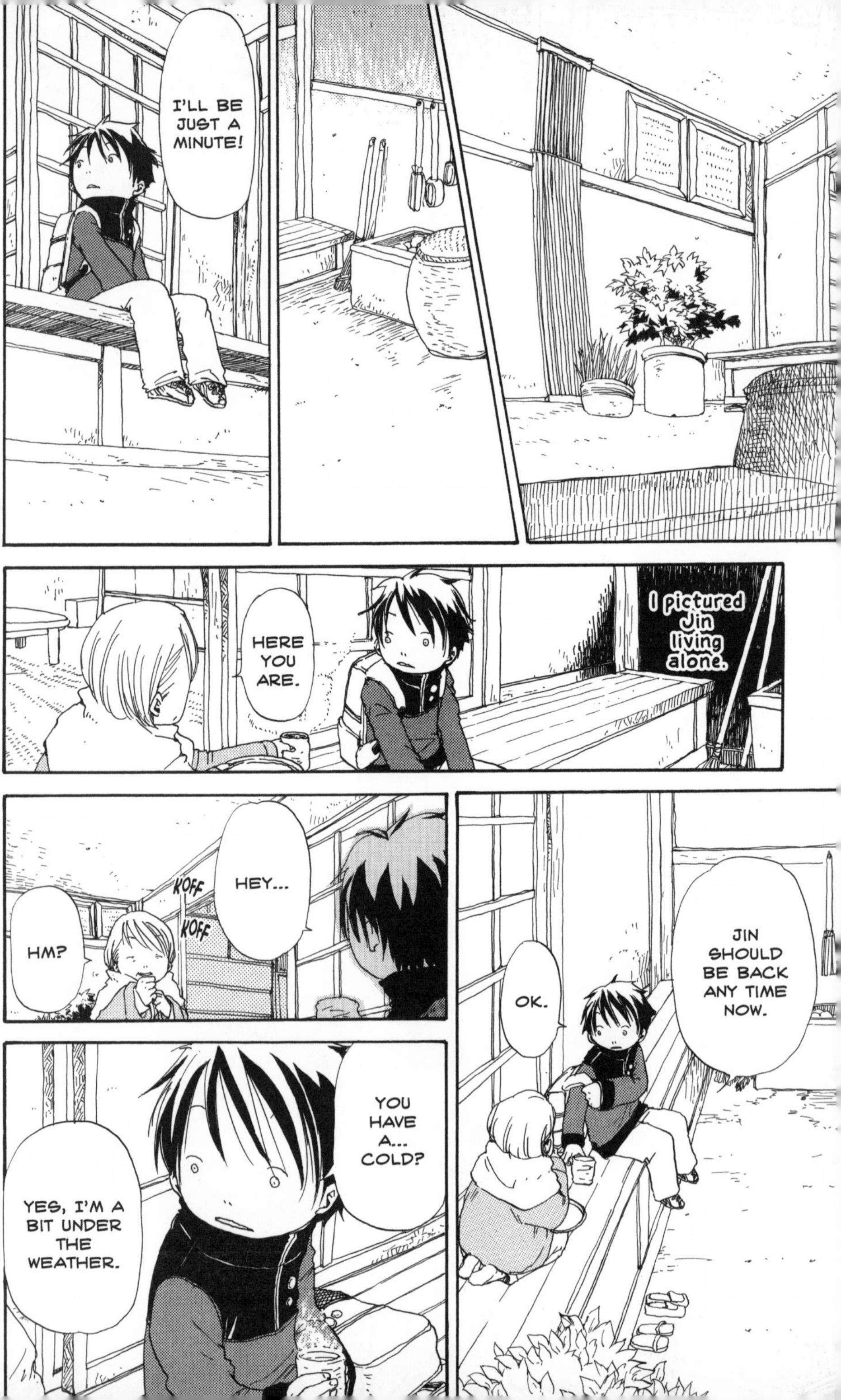
I'LL BE JUST A MINUTE!
I pictured Jin living alone.
HERE YOU ARE.
JIN SHOULD BE BACK ANY TIME NOW.
OK.
HEY...
KOFF
KOFF
HM?
YOU HAVE A... COLD?
YES, I'M A BIT UNDER THE WEATHER.

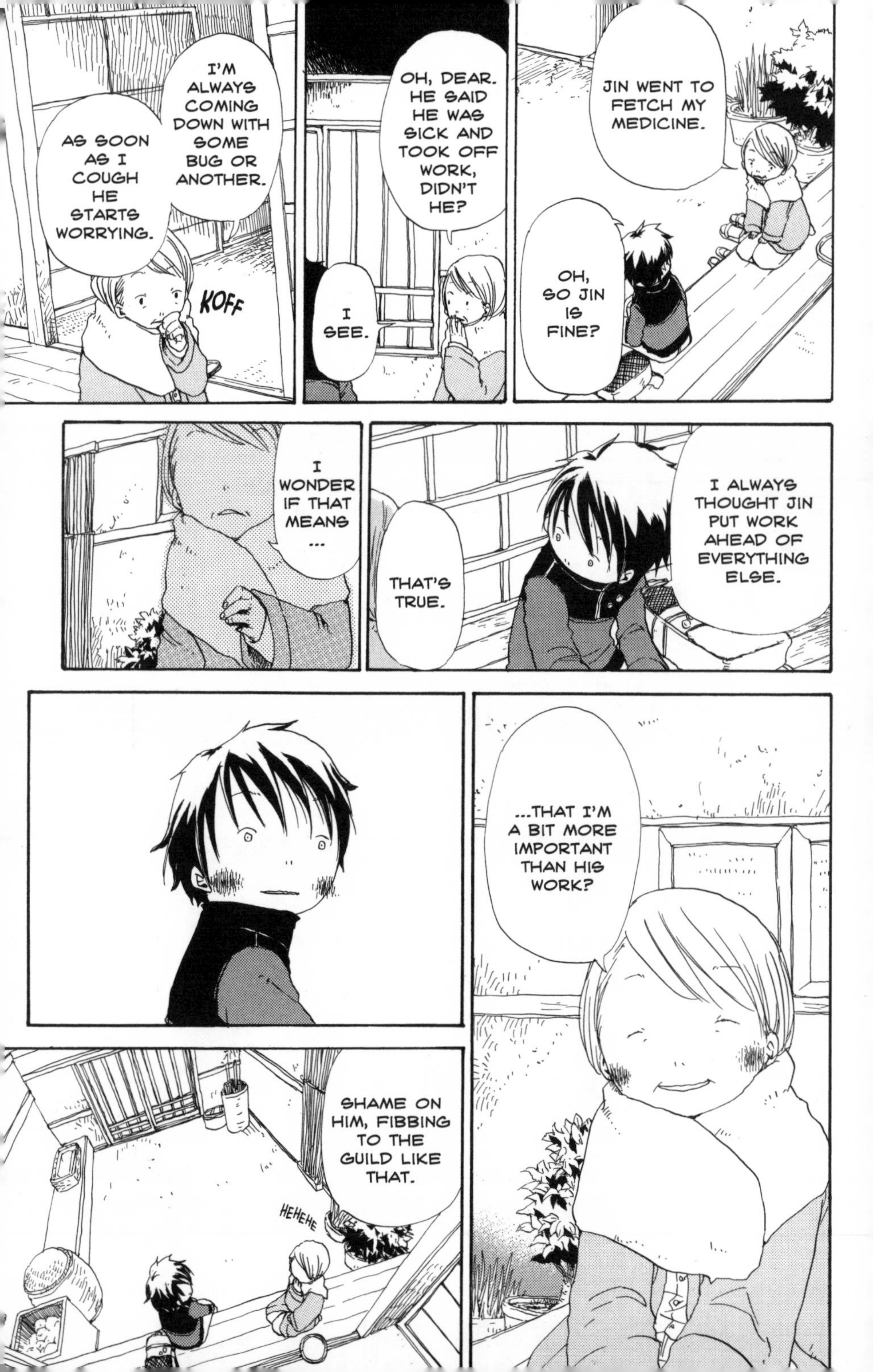
JIN WENT TO FETCH MY MEDICINE.
OH, SO JIN IS FINE?
OH, DEAR. HE SAID HE WAS SICK AND TOOK OFF WORK, DIDN'T HE?
I SEE.
I'M ALWAYS COMING DOWN WITH SOME BUG OR ANOTHER.
AS SOON AS I COUGH HE STARTS WORRYING.
KOFF
I ALWAYS THOUGHT JIN PUT WORK AHEAD OF EVERYTHING ELSE.
THAT'S TRUE.
I WONDER IF THAT MEANS ...
...THAT I'M A BIT MORE IMPORTANT THAN HIS WORK?
SHAME ON HIM, FIBBING TO THE GUILD LIKE THAT.
HEHEHE

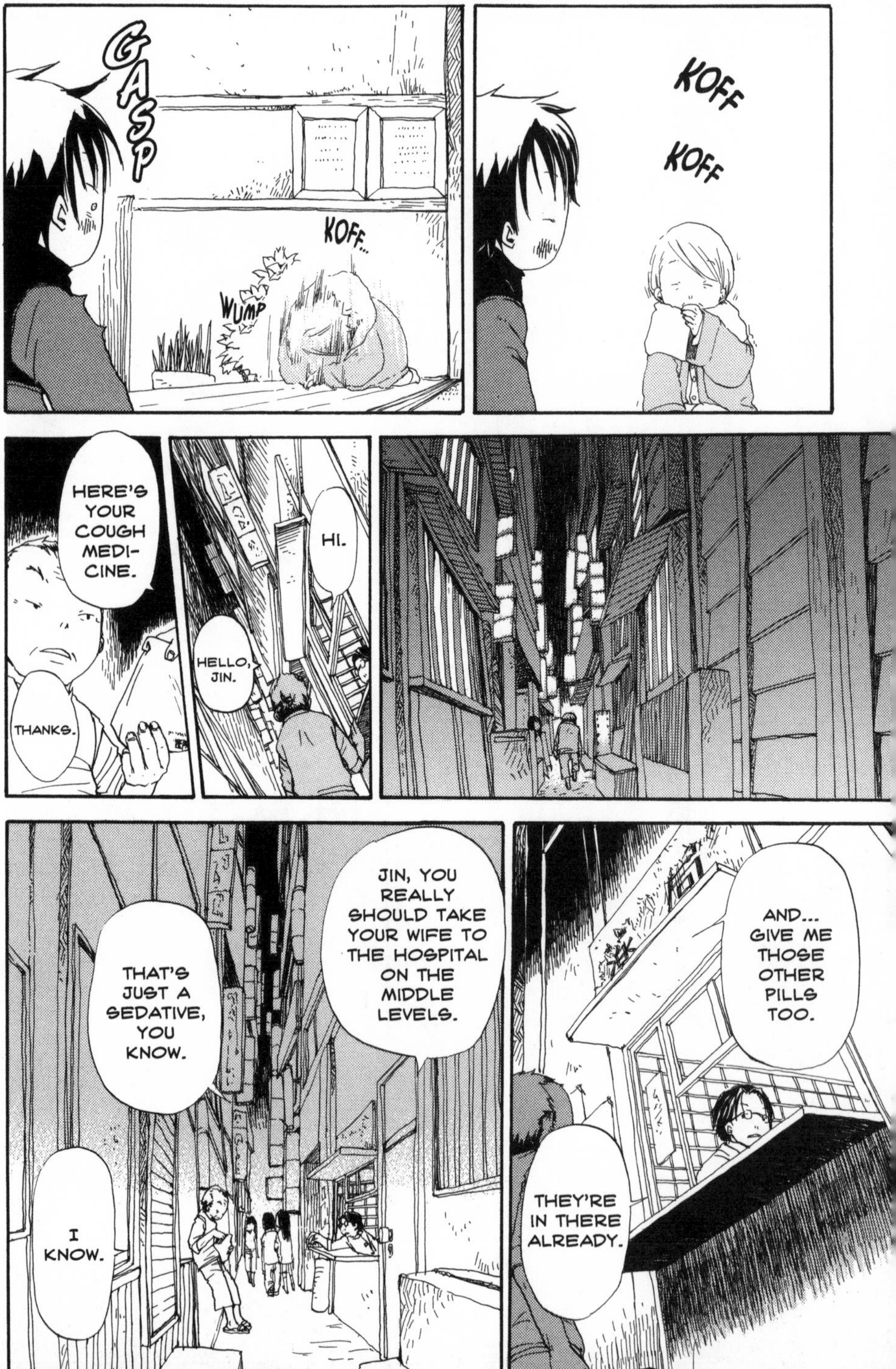
KOFF
KOFF
GASP
KOFF...
WUMP
HI.
HELLO, JIN.
HERE'S YOUR COUGH MEDI-CINE.
THANKS.
AND... GIVE ME THOSE OTHER PILLS TOO.
THEY'RE IN THERE ALREADY.
JIN, YOU REALLY SHOULD TAKE YOUR WIFE TO THE HOSPITAL ON THE MIDDLE LEVELS.
THAT'S JUST A SEDATIVE, YOU KNOW.
I KNOW.

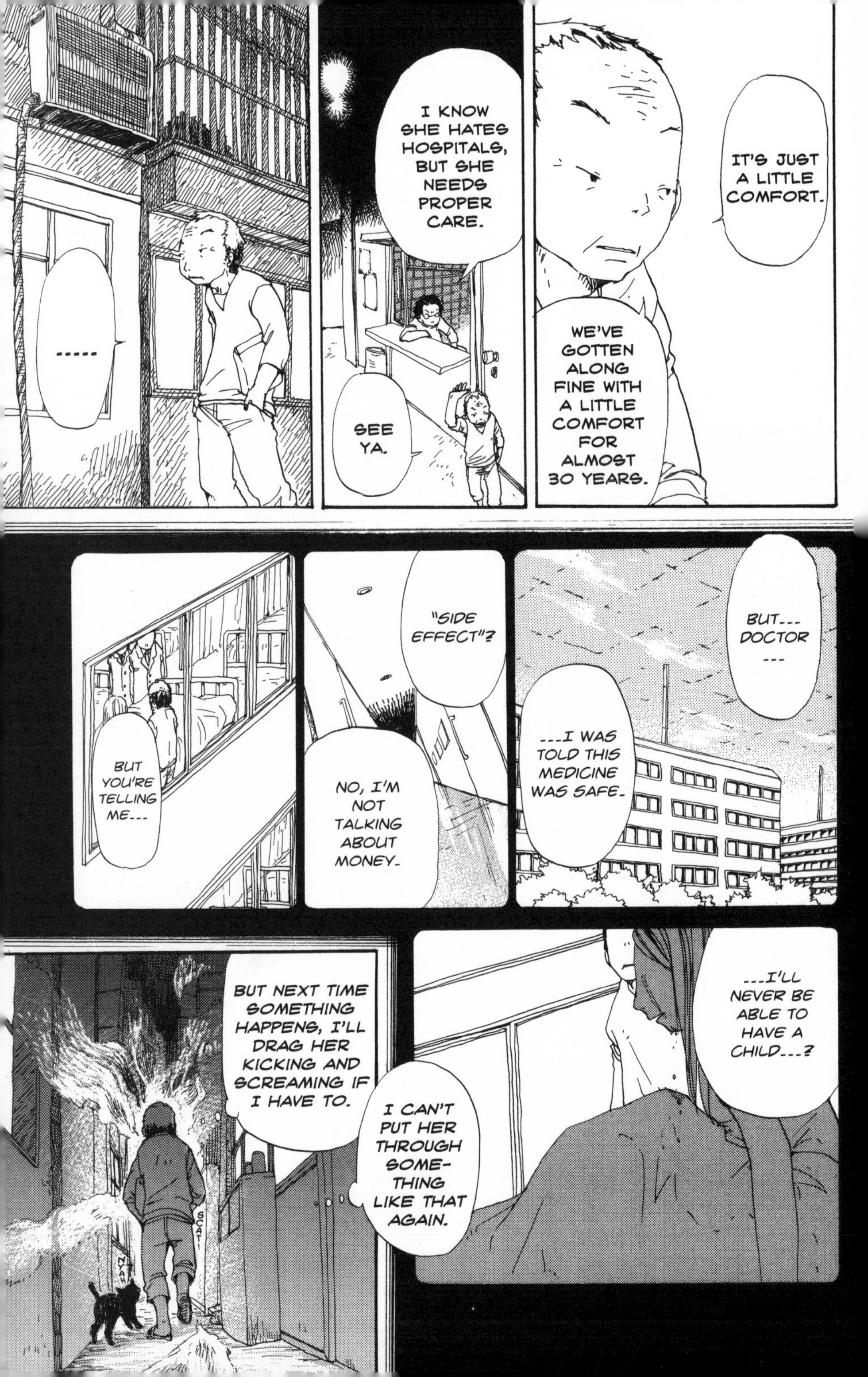
IT'S JUST A LITTLE COMFORT.
WE'VE GOTTEN ALONG FINE WITH A LITTLE COMFORT FOR ALMOST 30 YEARS.
I KNOW SHE HATES HOSPITALS, BUT SHE NEEDS PROPER CARE.
SEE YA.
.....
BUT... DOCTOR ...
...I WAS TOLD THIS MEDICINE WAS SAFE.
"SIDE EFFECT"?
NO, I'M NOT TALKING ABOUT MONEY.
BUT YOU'RE TELLING ME...
...I'LL NEVER BE ABLE TO HAVE A CHILD...?
BUT NEXT TIME SOMETHING HAPPENS, I'LL DRAG HER KICKING AND SCREAMING IF I HAVE TO.
I CAN'T PUT HER THROUGH SOME-THING LIKE THAT AGAIN.
SCAT!
NYA!

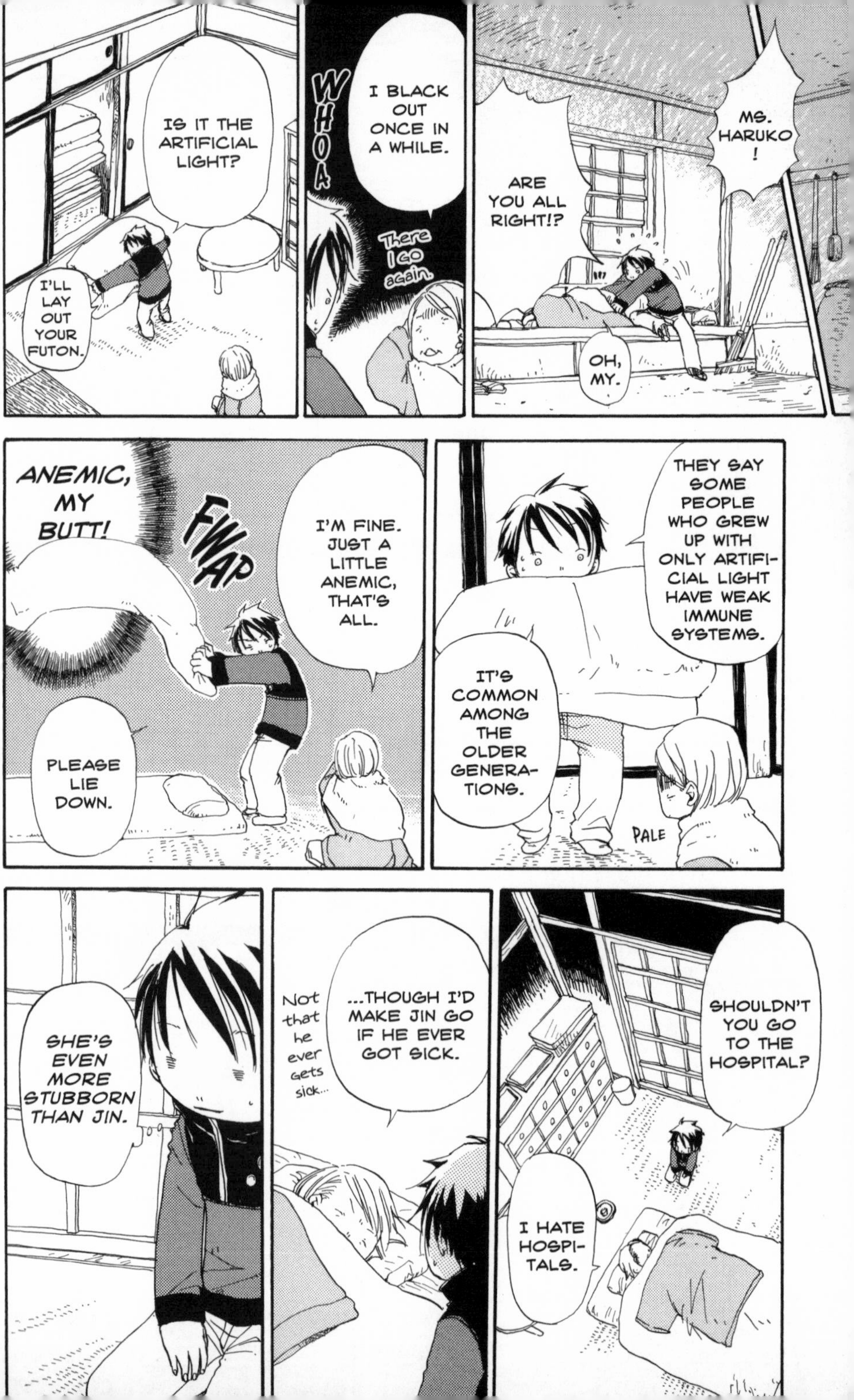
MS. HARUKO!
ARE YOU ALL RIGHT!?
OH, MY.
I BLACK OUT ONCE IN A WHILE.
WHOA
There I go again.
IS IT THE ARTIFICIAL LIGHT?
I'LL LAY OUT YOUR FUTON.
THEY SAY SOME PEOPLE WHO GREW UP WITH ONLY ARTIFI-CIAL LIGHT HAVE WEAK IMMUNE SYSTEMS.
IT'S COMMON AMONG THE OLDER GENERA-TIONS.
PALE
I'M FINE. JUST A LITTLE ANEMIC, THAT'S ALL.
FWAP
ANEMIC, MY BUTT!
PLEASE LIE DOWN.
SHOULDN'T YOU GO TO THE HOSPITAL?
I HATE HOSPI-TALS.
...THOUGH I'D MAKE JIN GO IF HE EVER GOT SICK.
Not that he ever gets sick...
SHE'S EVEN MORE STUBBORN THAN JIN.

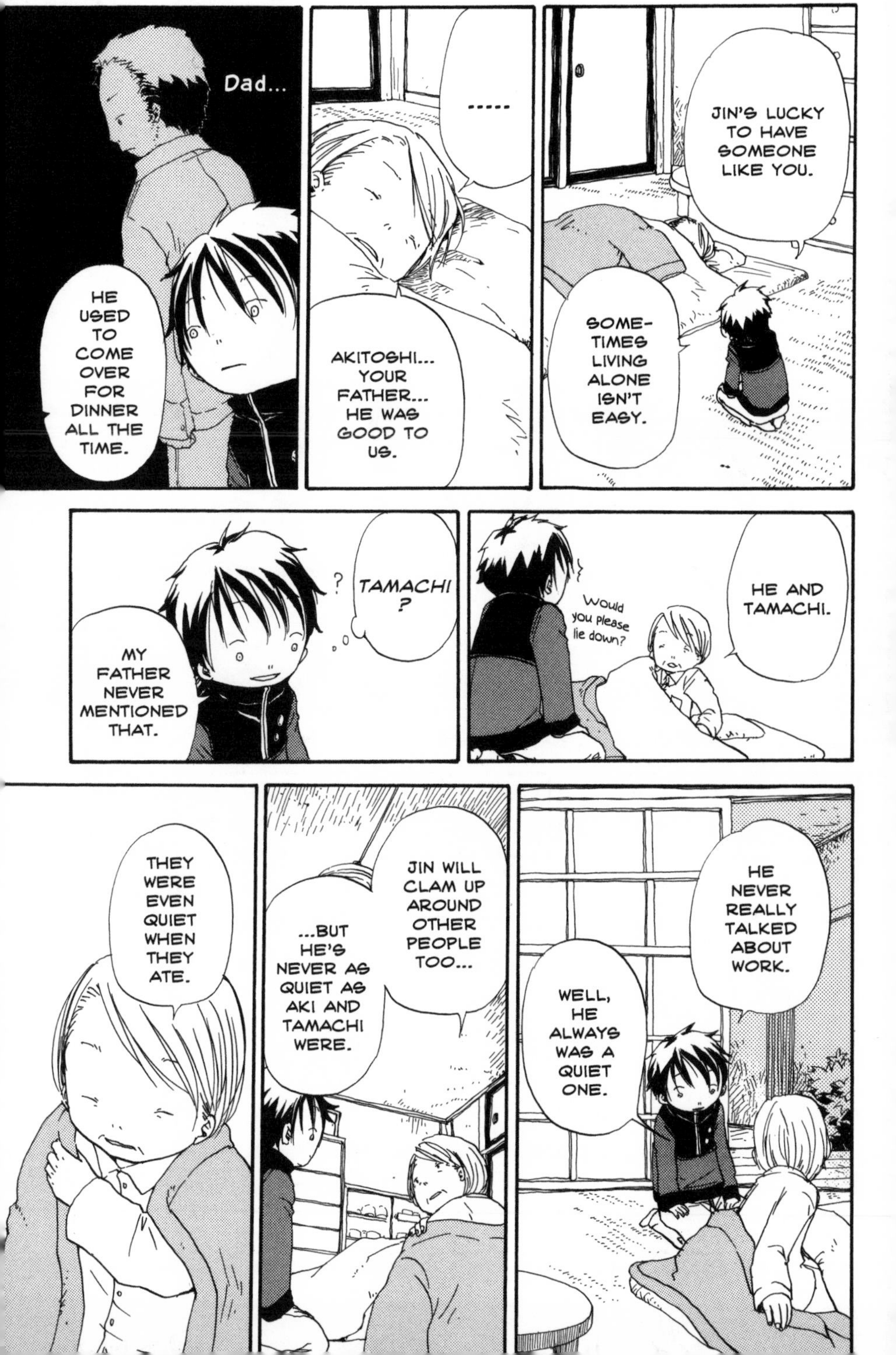
JIN'S LUCKY TO HAVE SOMEONE LIKE YOU.
SOME-TIMES LIVING ALONE ISN'T EASY.
.....
AKITOSHI... YOUR FATHER... HE WAS GOOD TO US.
Dad...
HE USED TO COME OVER FOR DINNER ALL THE TIME.
HE AND TAMACHI.
Would you please lie down?
TAMACHI?
MY FATHER NEVER MENTIONED THAT.
HE NEVER REALLY TALKED ABOUT WORK.
WELL, HE ALWAYS WAS A QUIET ONE.
JIN WILL CLAM UP AROUND OTHER PEOPLE TOO...
...BUT HE'S NEVER AS QUIET AS AKI AND TAMACHI WERE.
THEY WERE EVEN QUIET WHEN THEY ATE.

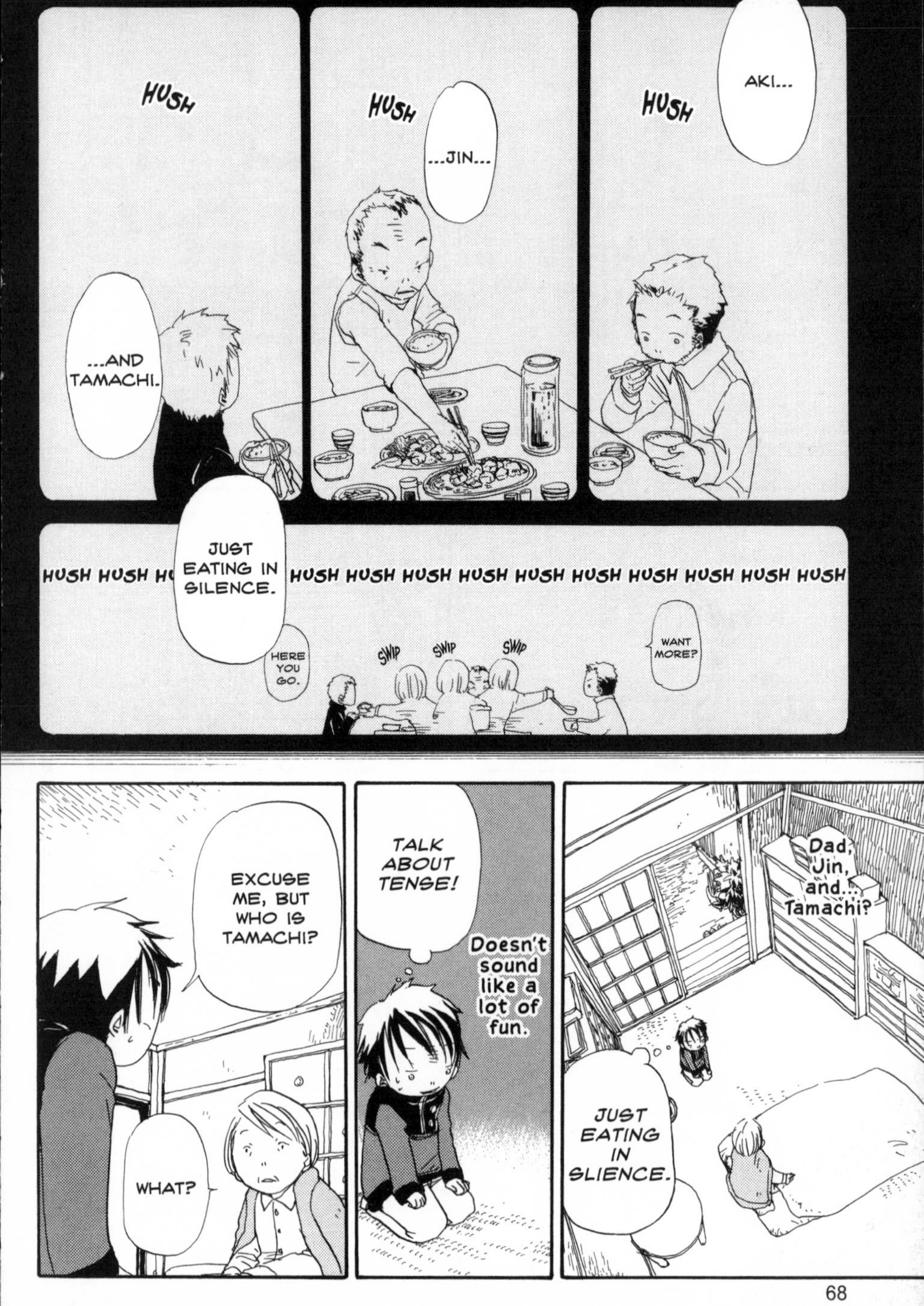

AKI...
HUSH
...JIN...
HUSH
HUSH
...AND TAMACHI.
JUST EATING IN SILENCE.
HUSH HUSH HUSH HUSH HUSH HUSH HUSH HUSH HUSH HUSH HUSH HUSH HU
WANT MORE?
SWIP
SWIP
SWIP
HERE YOU GO.
Dad, Jin, and... Tamachi?
JUST EATING IN SLIENCE.
TALK ABOUT TENSE!
Doesn't sound like a lot of fun.
EXCUSE ME, BUT WHO IS TAMACHI?
WHAT?

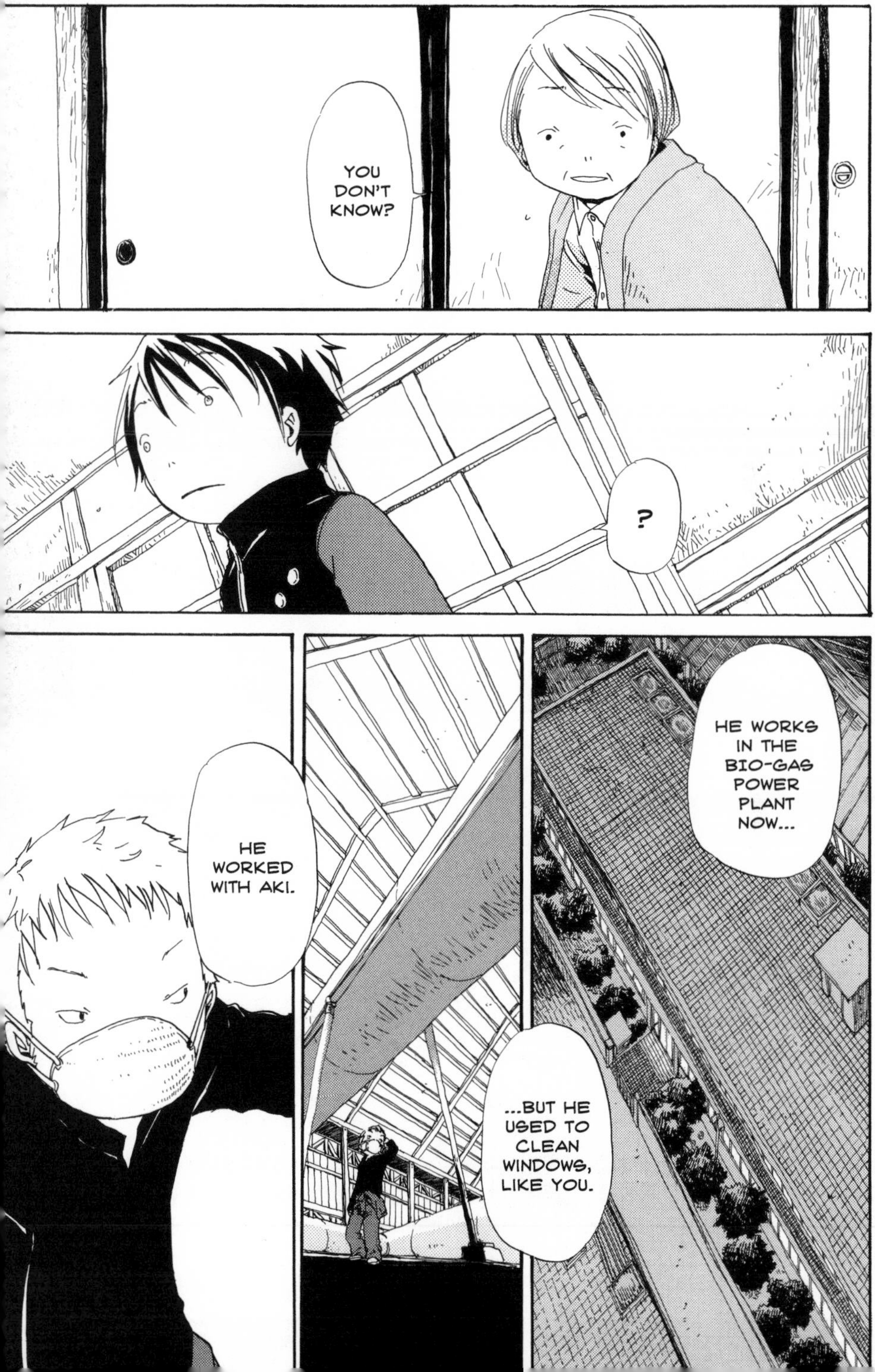
YOU DON'T KNOW?
?
HE WORKS IN THE BIO-GAS POWER PLANT NOW...
...BUT HE USED TO CLEAN WINDOWS, LIKE YOU.
HE WORKED WITH AKI.

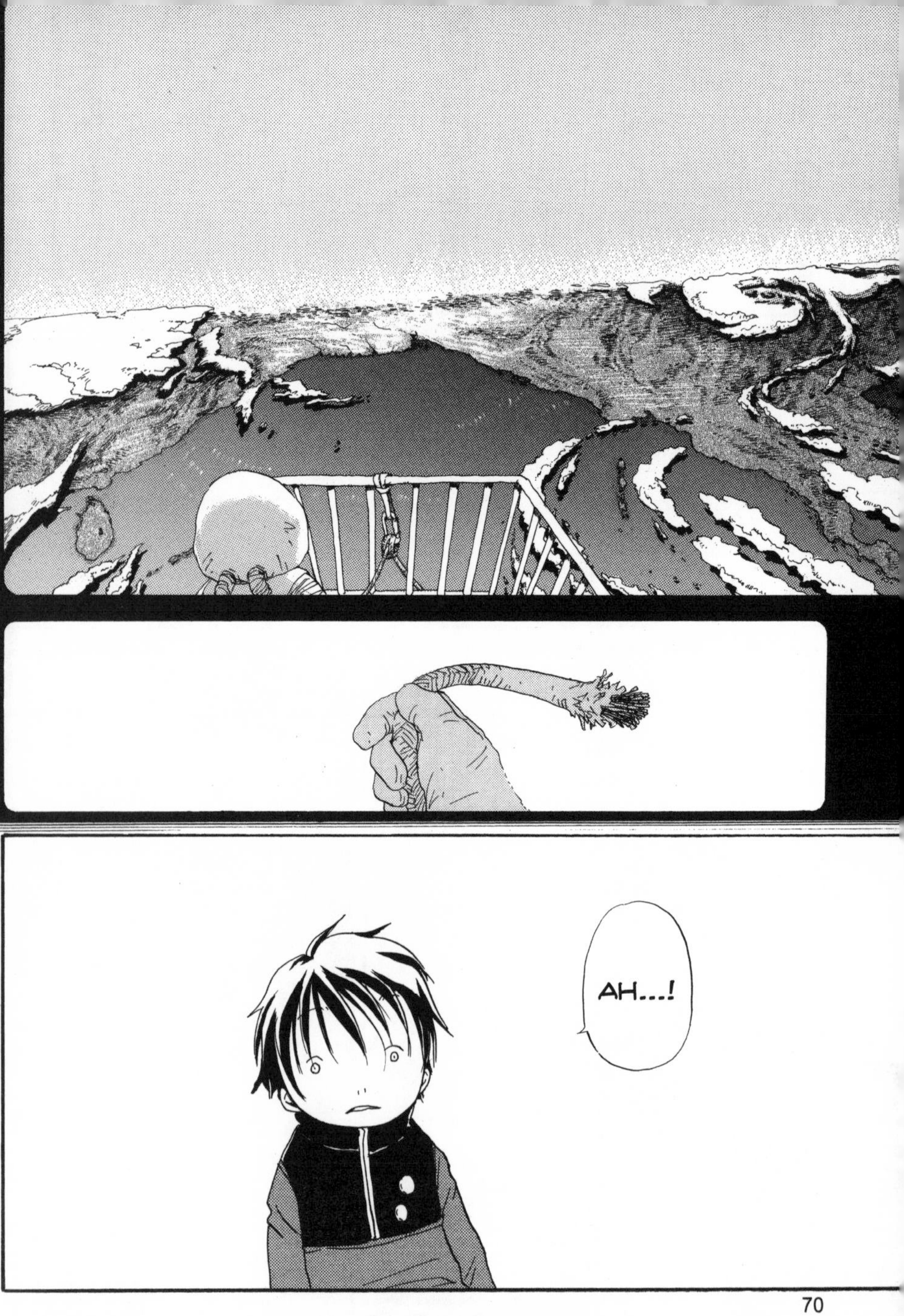
AH...!

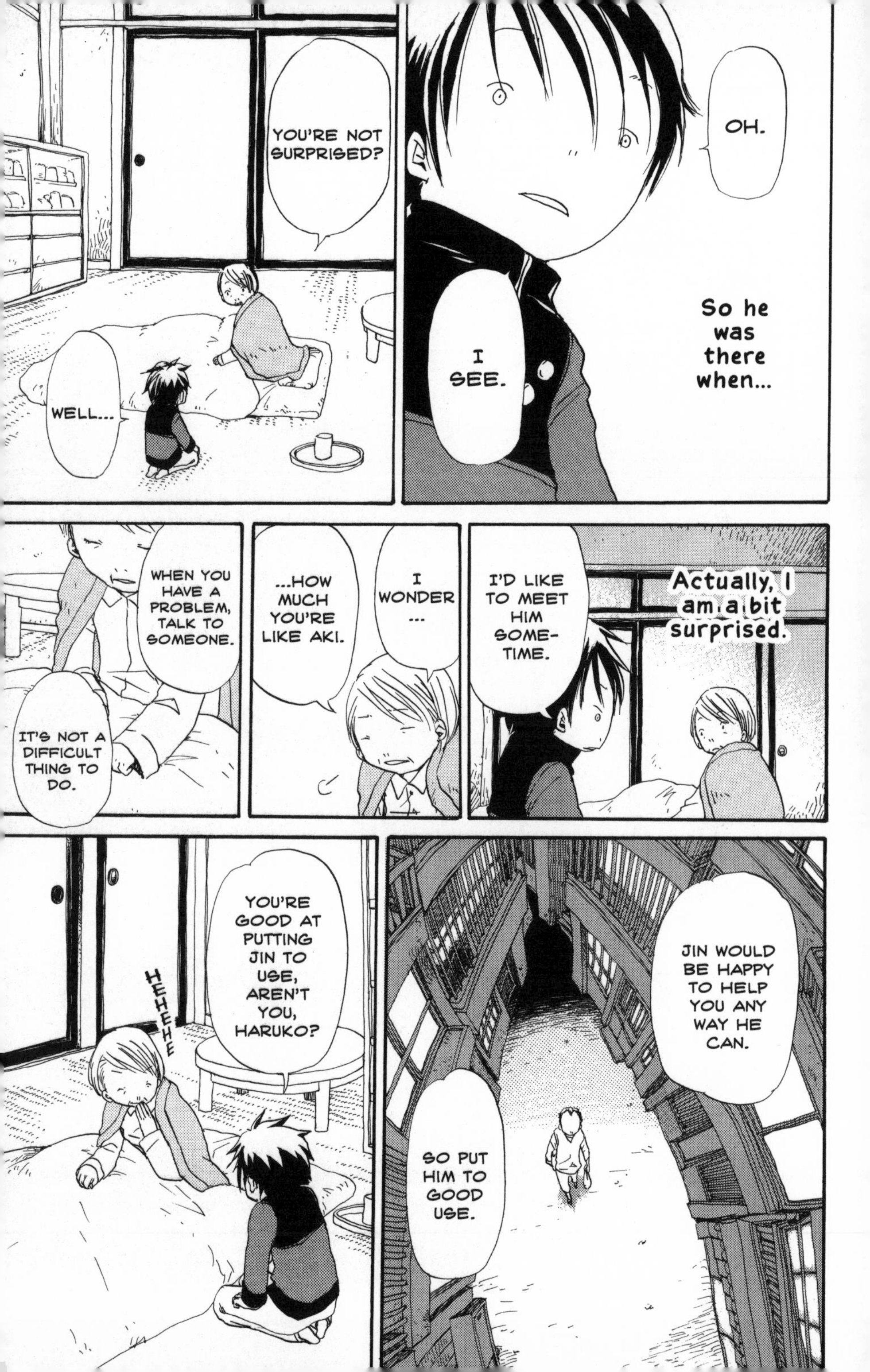
OH.
I SEE.
So he was there when...
YOU'RE NOT SURPRISED?
WELL...
Actually, I am a bit surprised.
I'D LIKE TO MEET HIM SOMETIME.
I WONDER...
...HOW MUCH YOU'RE LIKE AKI.
WHEN YOU HAVE A PROBLEM, TALK TO SOMEONE.
IT'S NOT A DIFFICULT THING TO DO.
JIN WOULD BE HAPPY TO HELP YOU ANY WAY HE CAN.
SO PUT HIM TO GOOD USE.
YOU'RE GOOD AT PUTTING JIN TO USE, AREN'T YOU, HARUKO?
HEHEHE

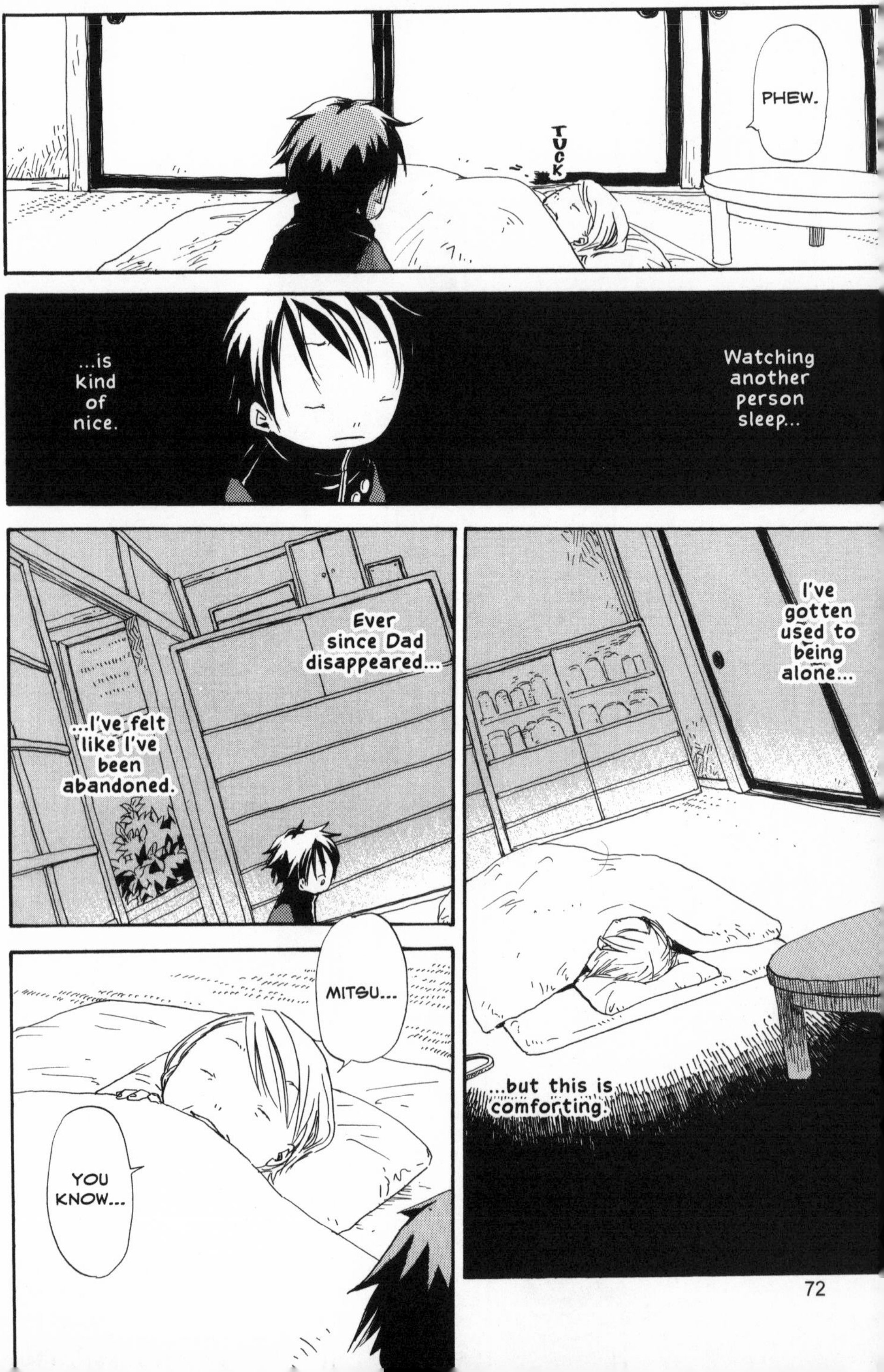
PHEW.
TUCK
Watching another person sleep...
...is kind of nice.
I've gotten used to being alone...
...but this is comforting.
Ever since Dad disappeared...
...I've felt like I've been abandoned.
MITSU...
YOU KNOW...

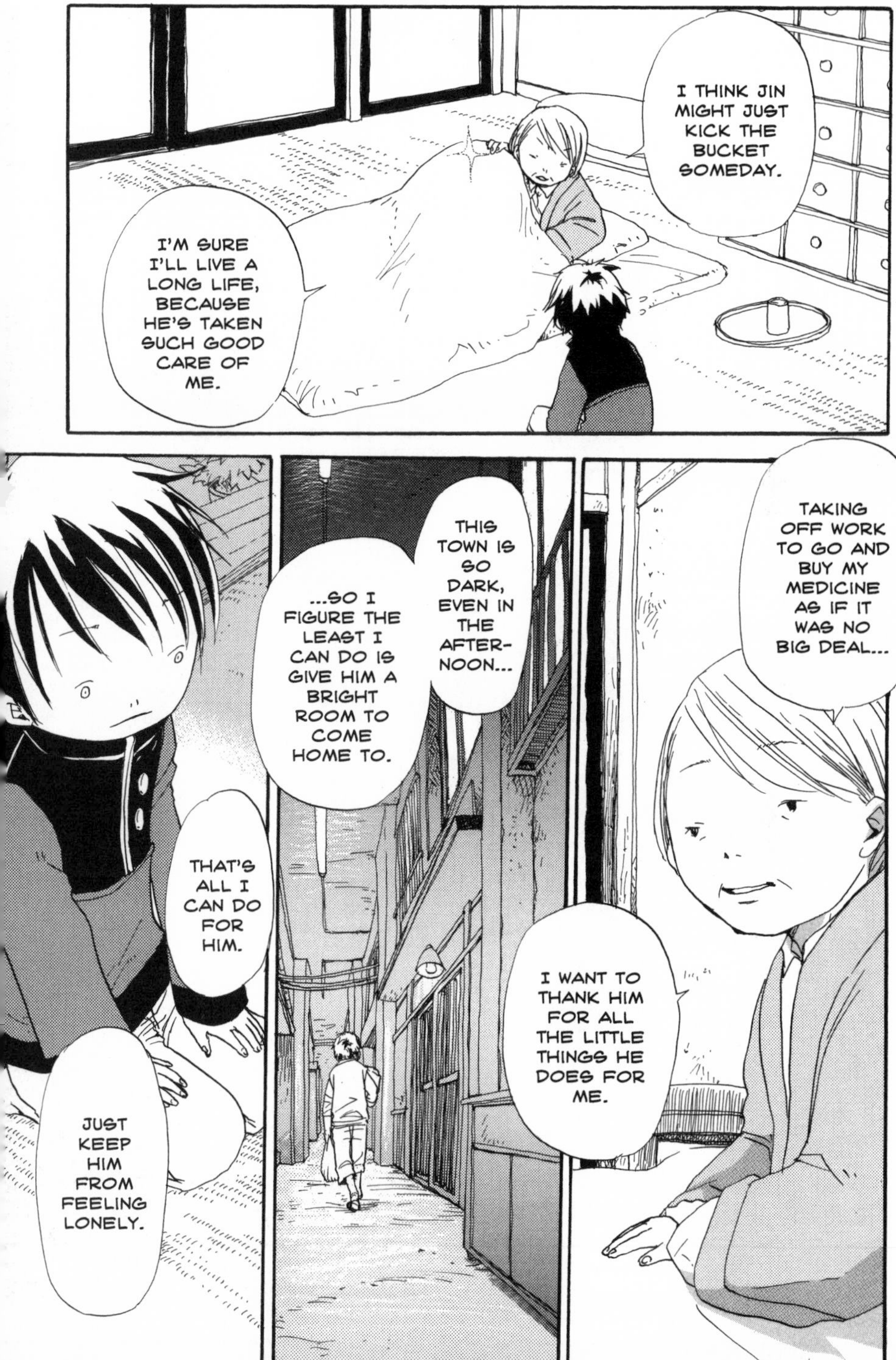
I THINK JIN MIGHT JUST KICK THE BUCKET SOMEDAY.
I'M SURE I'LL LIVE A LONG LIFE, BECAUSE HE'S TAKEN SUCH GOOD CARE OF ME.
TAKING OFF WORK TO GO AND BUY MY MEDICINE AS IF IT WAS NO BIG DEAL...
I WANT TO THANK HIM FOR ALL THE LITTLE THINGS HE DOES FOR ME.
THIS TOWN IS SO DARK, EVEN IN THE AFTER-NOON...
...SO I FIGURE THE LEAST I CAN DO IS GIVE HIM A BRIGHT ROOM TO COME HOME TO.
THAT'S ALL I CAN DO FOR HIM.
JUST KEEP HIM FROM FEELING LONELY.

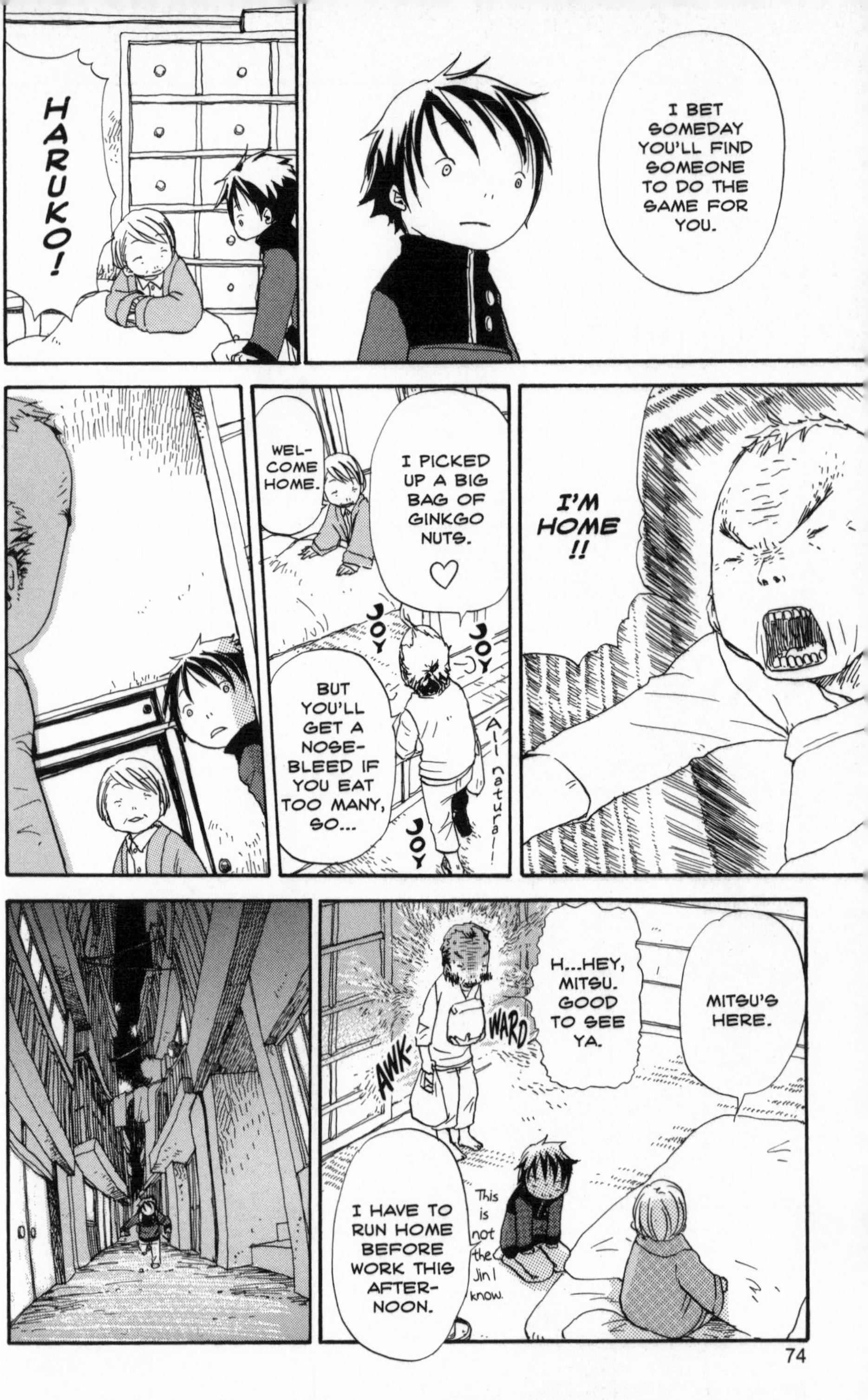
I BET SOMEDAY YOU'LL FIND SOMEONE TO DO THE SAME FOR YOU.
HARUKO!
I'M HOME !!
I PICKED UP A BIG BAG OF GINKGO NUTS. ♡
WEL-COME HOME.
JOY JOY
BUT YOU'LL GET A NOSE-BLEED IF YOU EAT TOO MANY, SO...
All natural!
JOY
MITSU'S HERE.
H...HEY, MITSU. GOOD TO SEE YA.
AWK-WARD
This is not the Jin I know.
I HAVE TO RUN HOME BEFORE WORK THIS AFTER-NOON.

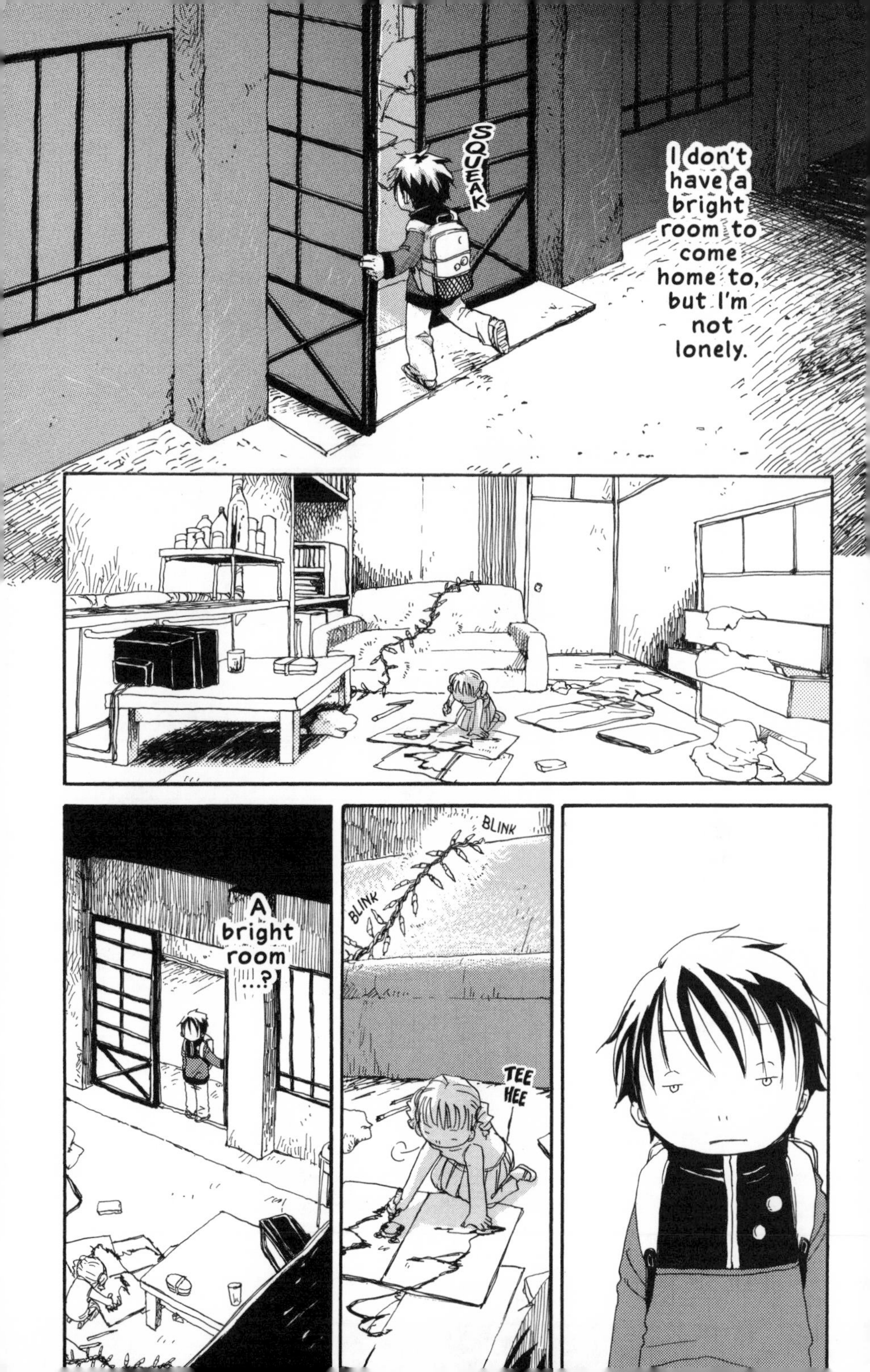
I don't have a bright room to come home to, but I'm not lonely.
SQUEAK
BLINK
BLINK
TEE HEE
A bright room ...?

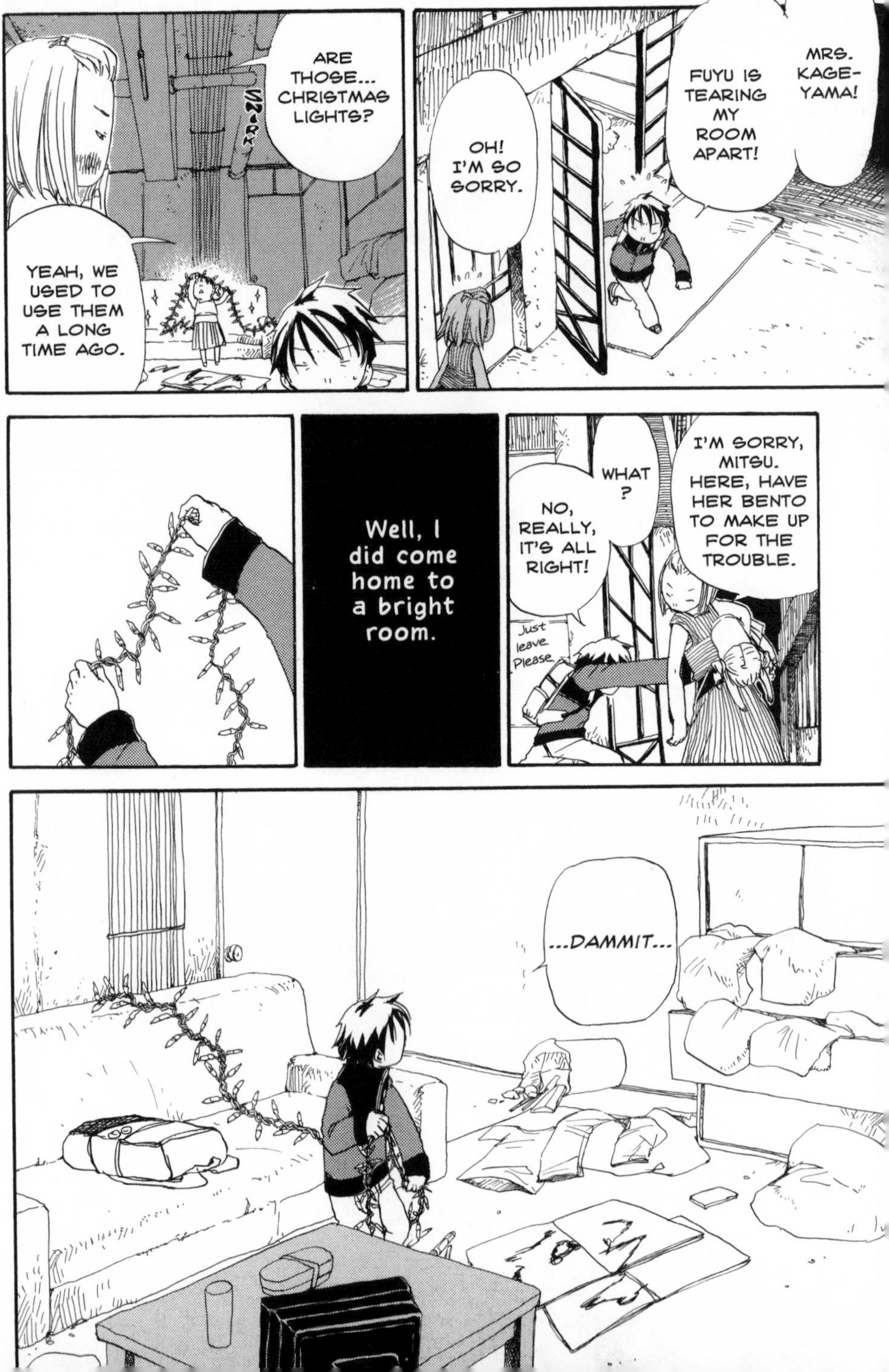
MRS. KAGE-YAMA!
FUYU IS TEARING MY ROOM APART!
OH! I'M SO SORRY.
ARE THOSE... CHRISTMAS LIGHTS?
SNIRK
YEAH, WE USED TO USE THEM A LONG TIME AGO.
I'M SORRY, MITSU. HERE, HAVE HER BENTO TO MAKE UP FOR THE TROUBLE.
WHAT ?
NO, REALLY, IT'S ALL RIGHT!
Just leave. Please.
Well, I did come home to a bright room.
...DAMMIT...

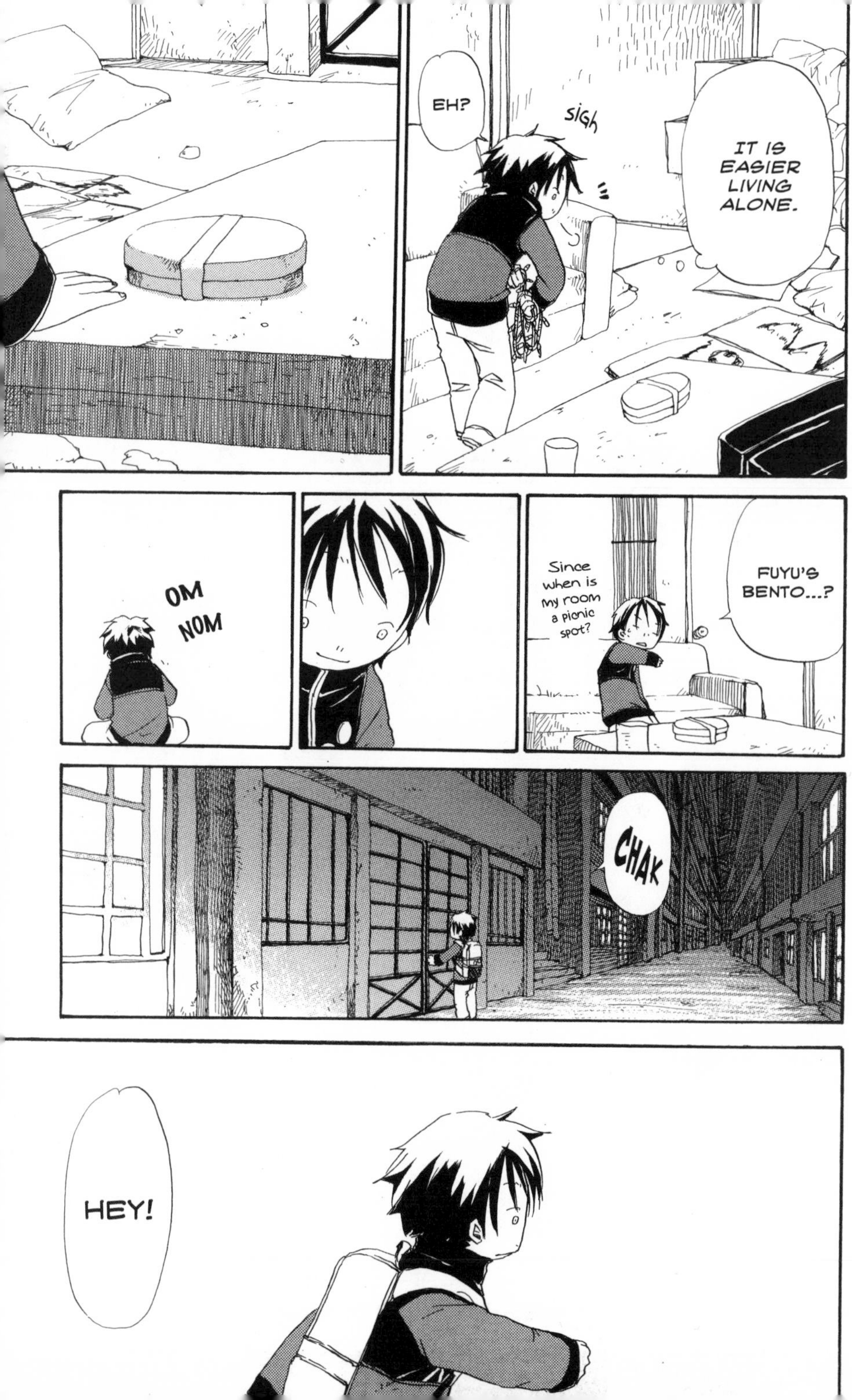
IT IS EASIER LIVING ALONE.
SIGH
EH?
FUYU'S BENTO...?
Since when is my room a picnic spot?
OM NOM
CHAK
HEY!

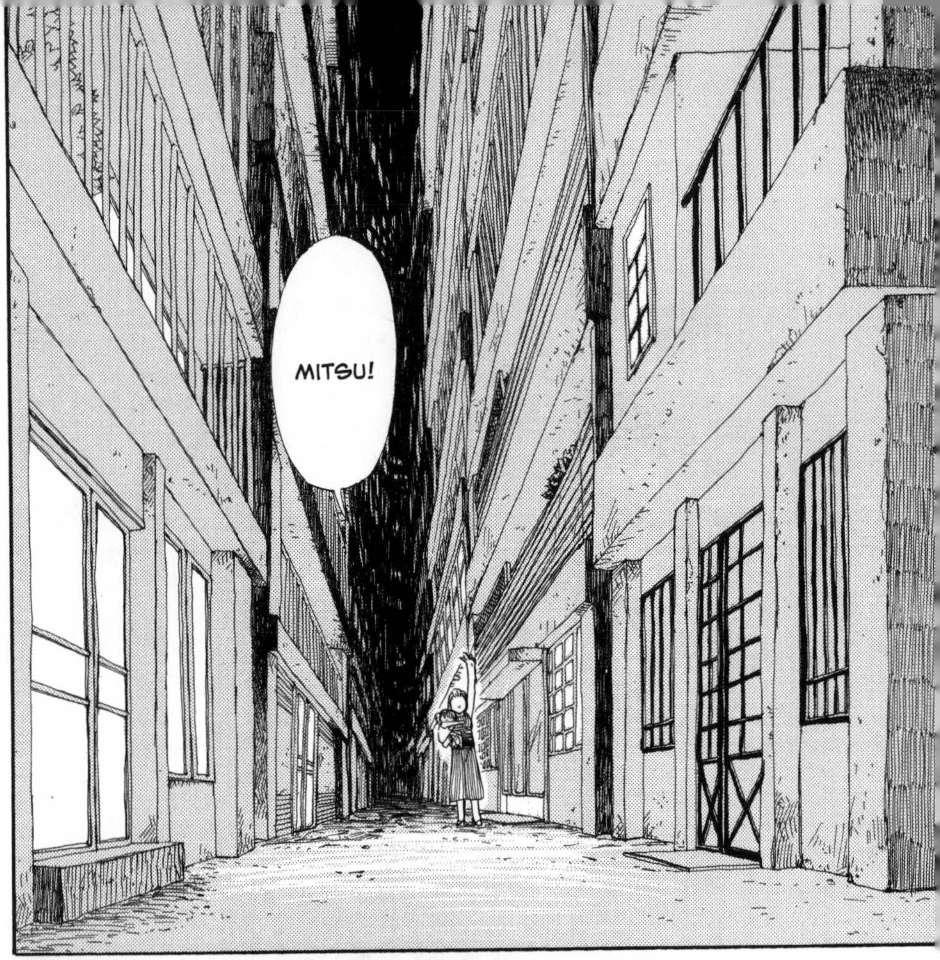
MITSU!
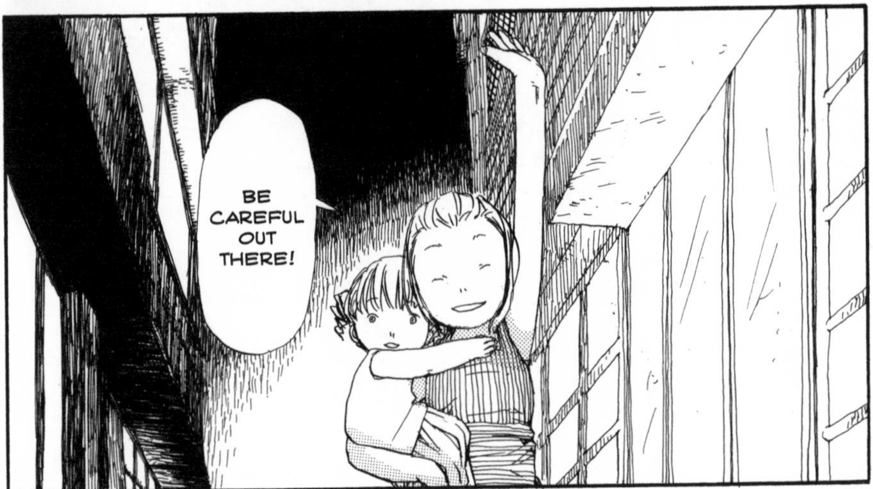
BE CAREFUL OUT THERE!

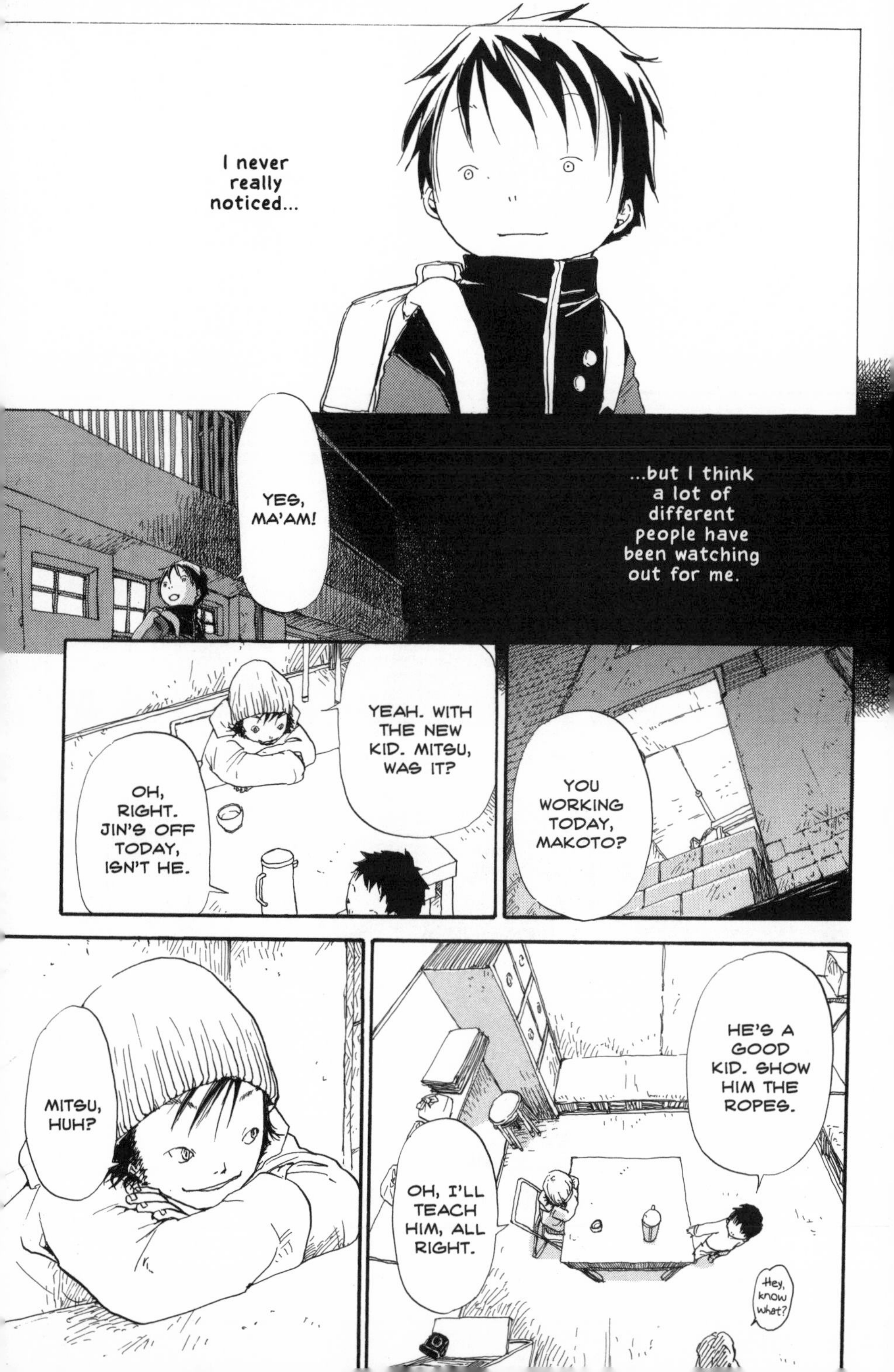
I never really noticed...
...but I think a lot of different people have been watching out for me.
YES, MA'AM!
YOU WORKING TODAY, MAKOTO?
YEAH. WITH THE NEW KID. MITSU, WAS IT?
OH, RIGHT. JIN'S OFF TODAY, ISN'T HE.
HE'S A GOOD KID. SHOW HIM THE ROPES.
OH, I'LL TEACH HIM, ALL RIGHT.
Hey, know what?
MITSU, HUH?

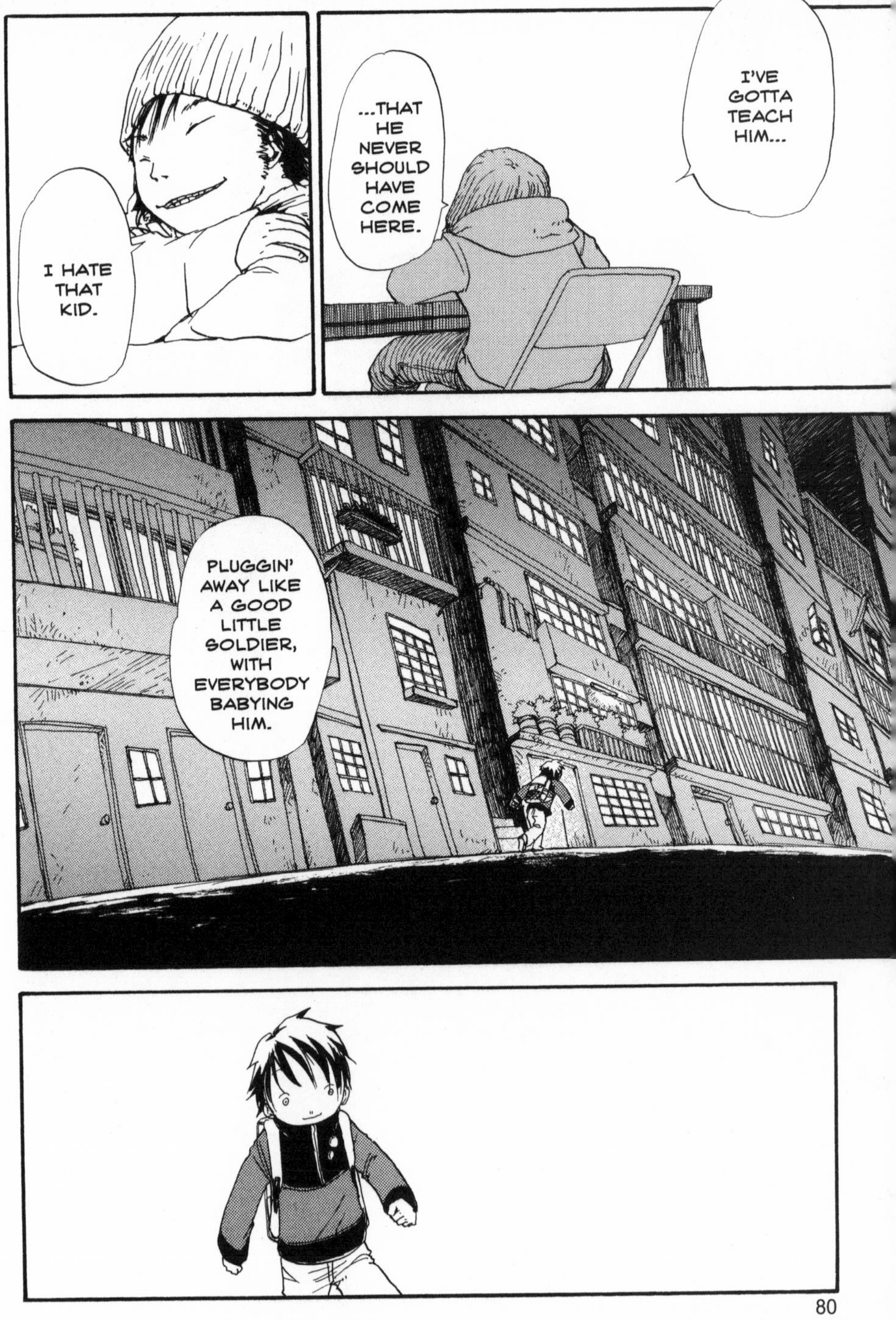
I'VE GOTTA TEACH HIM...
...THAT HE NEVER SHOULD HAVE COME HERE.
I HATE THAT KID.
PLUGGIN' AWAY LIKE A GOOD LITTLE SOLDIER, WITH EVERYBODY BABYING HIM.

floor 4: a place far away

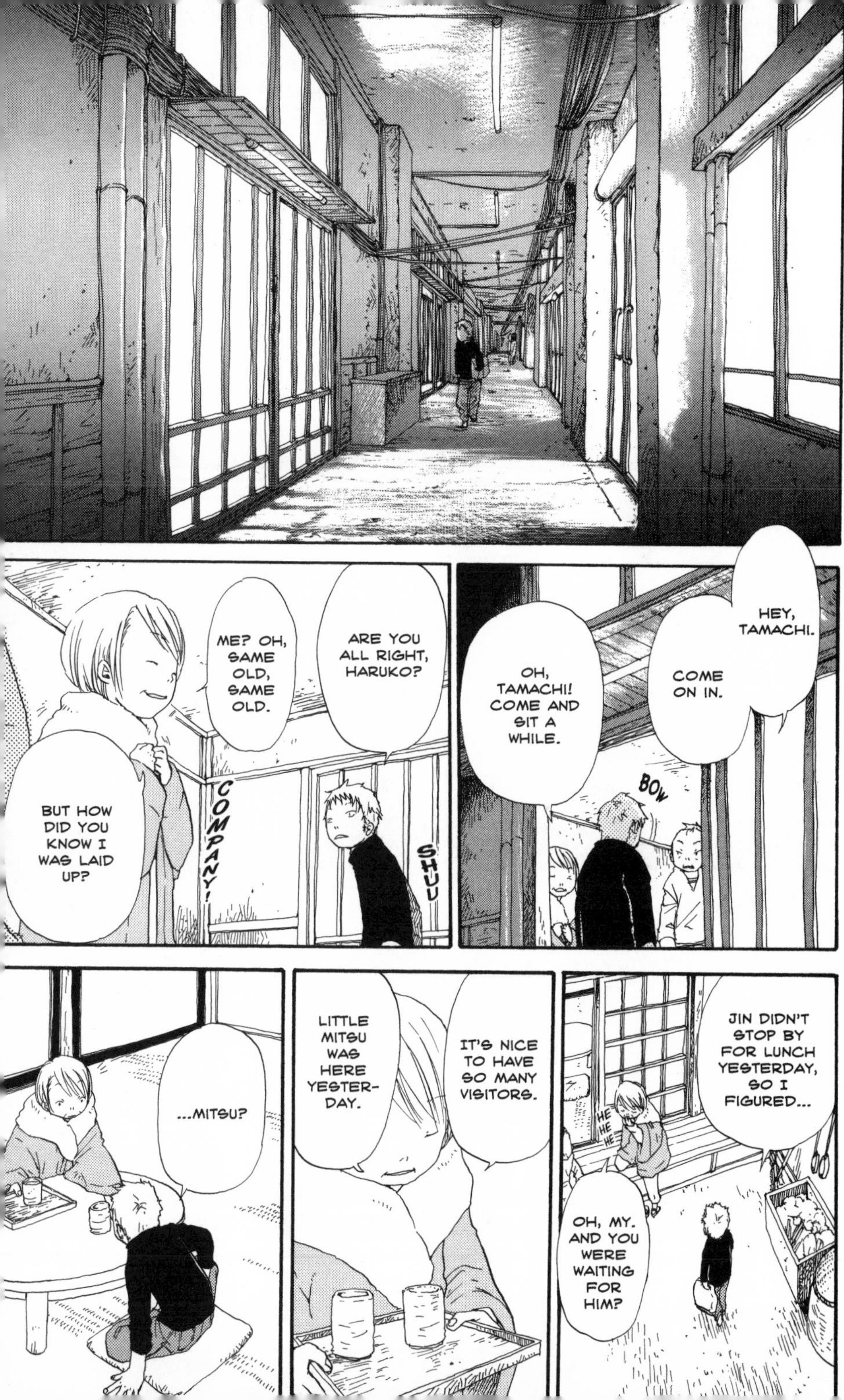
HEY, TAMACHI.
COME ON IN.
OH, TAMACHI! COME AND SIT A WHILE.
BOW
ARE YOU ALL RIGHT, HARUKO?
ME? OH, SAME OLD, SAME OLD.
SHUU
COMPANY!
BUT HOW DID YOU KNOW I WAS LAID UP?
JIN DIDN'T STOP BY FOR LUNCH YESTERDAY, SO I FIGURED...
HE HE HE
OH, MY. AND YOU WERE WAITING FOR HIM?
IT'S NICE TO HAVE SO MANY VISITORS.
LITTLE MITSU WAS HERE YESTER-DAY.
...MITSU?

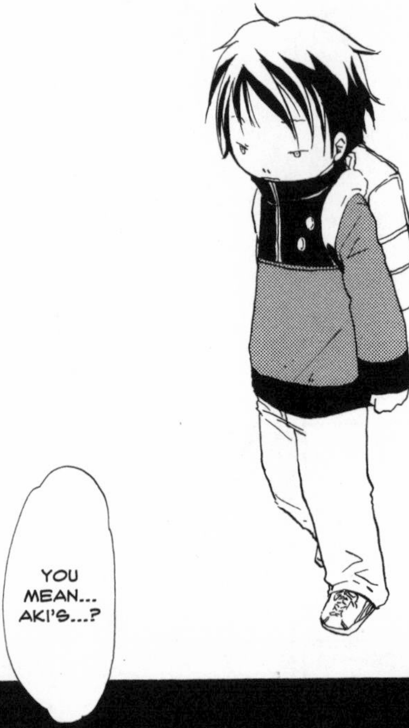
YOU MEAN... AKI'S...?

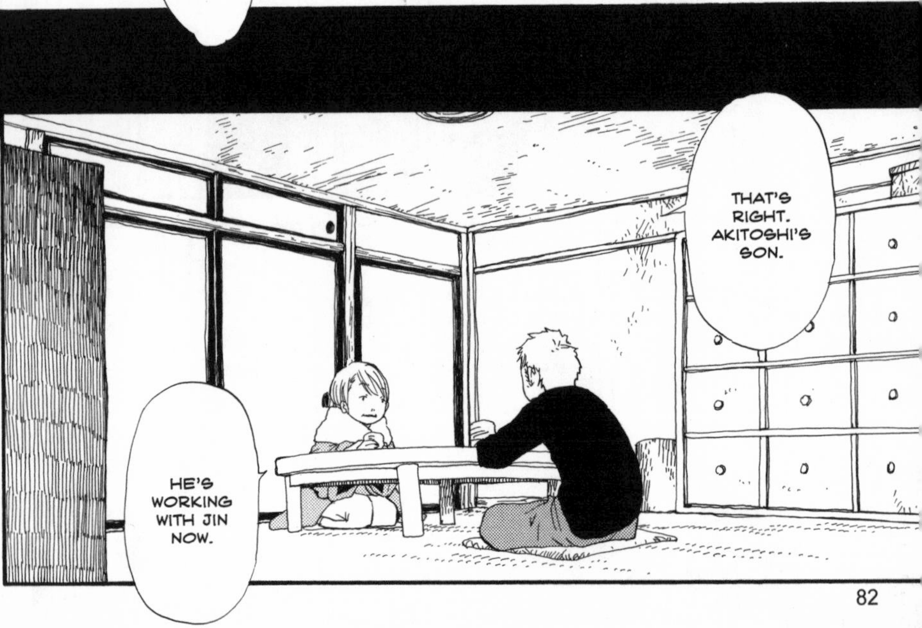
THAT'S RIGHT. AKITOSHI'S SON.
HE'S WORKING WITH JIN NOW.

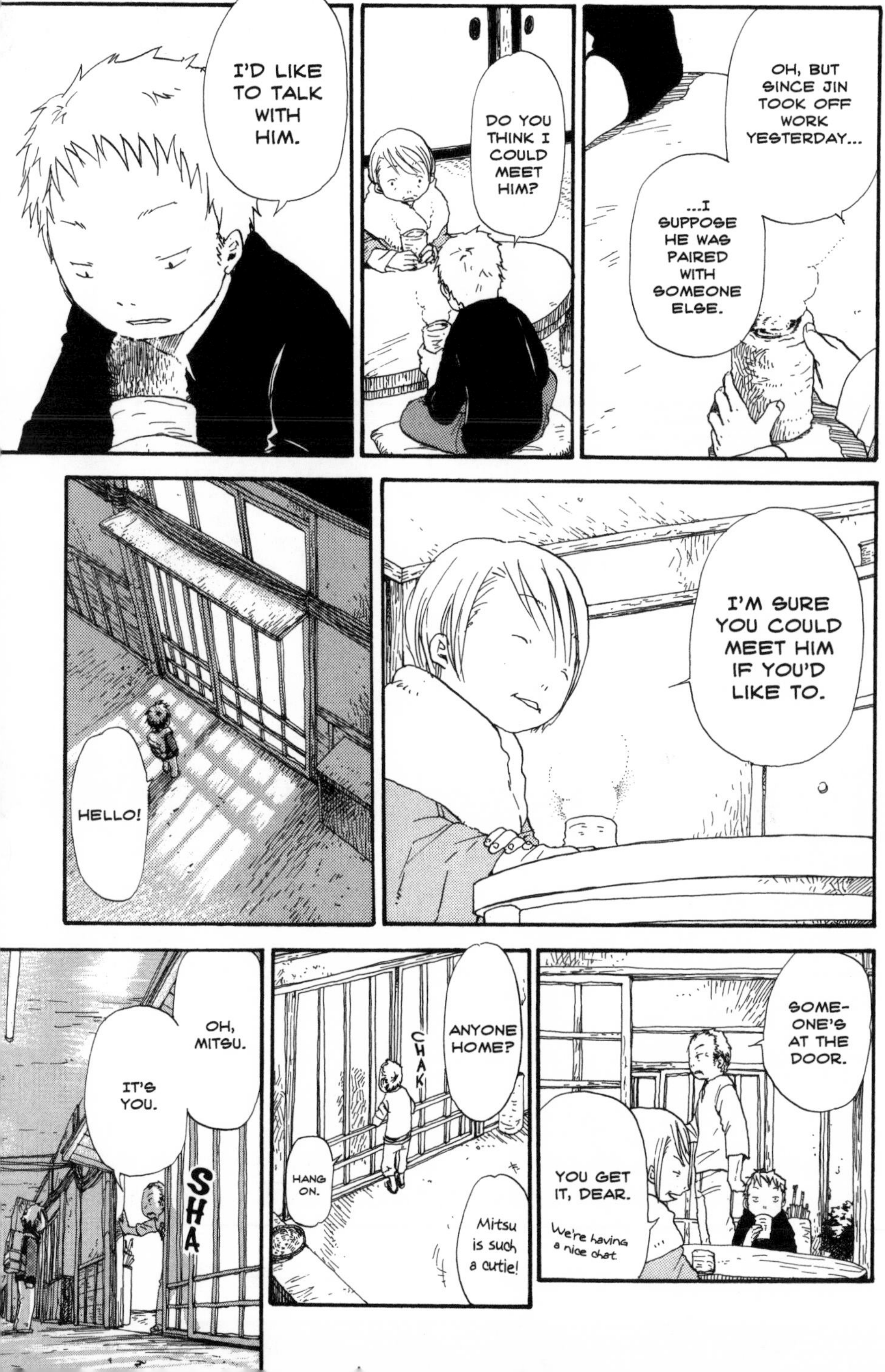
OH, BUT SINCE JIN TOOK OFF WORK YESTERDAY...
...I SUPPOSE HE WAS PAIRED WITH SOMEONE ELSE.
DO YOU THINK I COULD MEET HIM?
I'D LIKE TO TALK WITH HIM.
I'M SURE YOU COULD MEET HIM IF YOU'D LIKE TO.
HELLO!
SOME-ONE'S AT THE DOOR.
YOU GET IT, DEAR.
We're having a nice chat.
ANYONE HOME?
CHAK
Mitsu is such a cutie!
HANG ON.
OH, MITSU.
IT'S YOU.
SHA

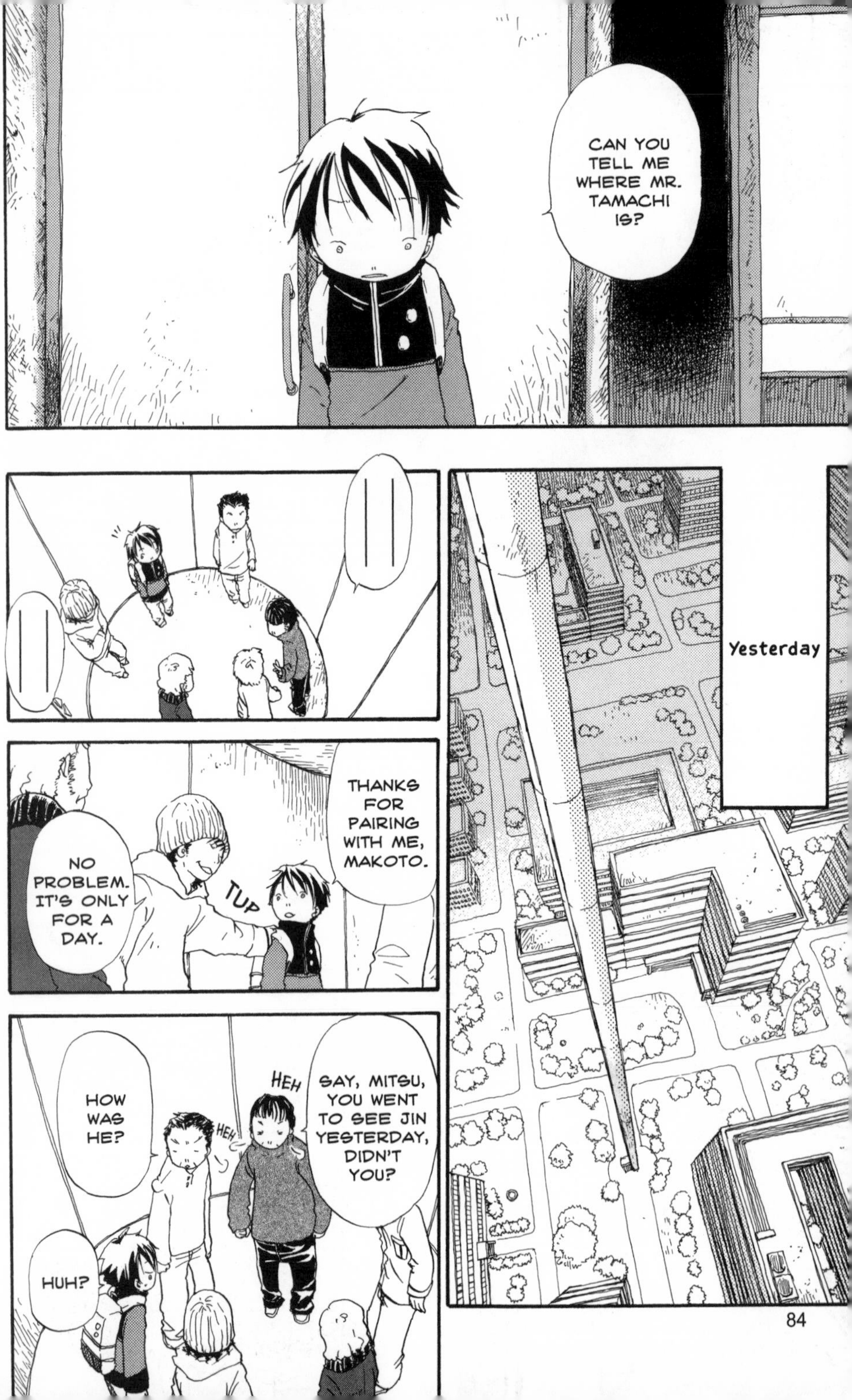
CAN YOU TELL ME WHERE MR. TAMACHI IS?
Yesterday
THANKS FOR PAIRING WITH ME, MAKOTO.
NO PROBLEM. IT'S ONLY FOR A DAY.
TUP
HEH
SAY, MITSU, YOU WENT TO SEE JIN YESTERDAY, DIDN'T YOU?
HEH
HOW WAS HE?
HUH?

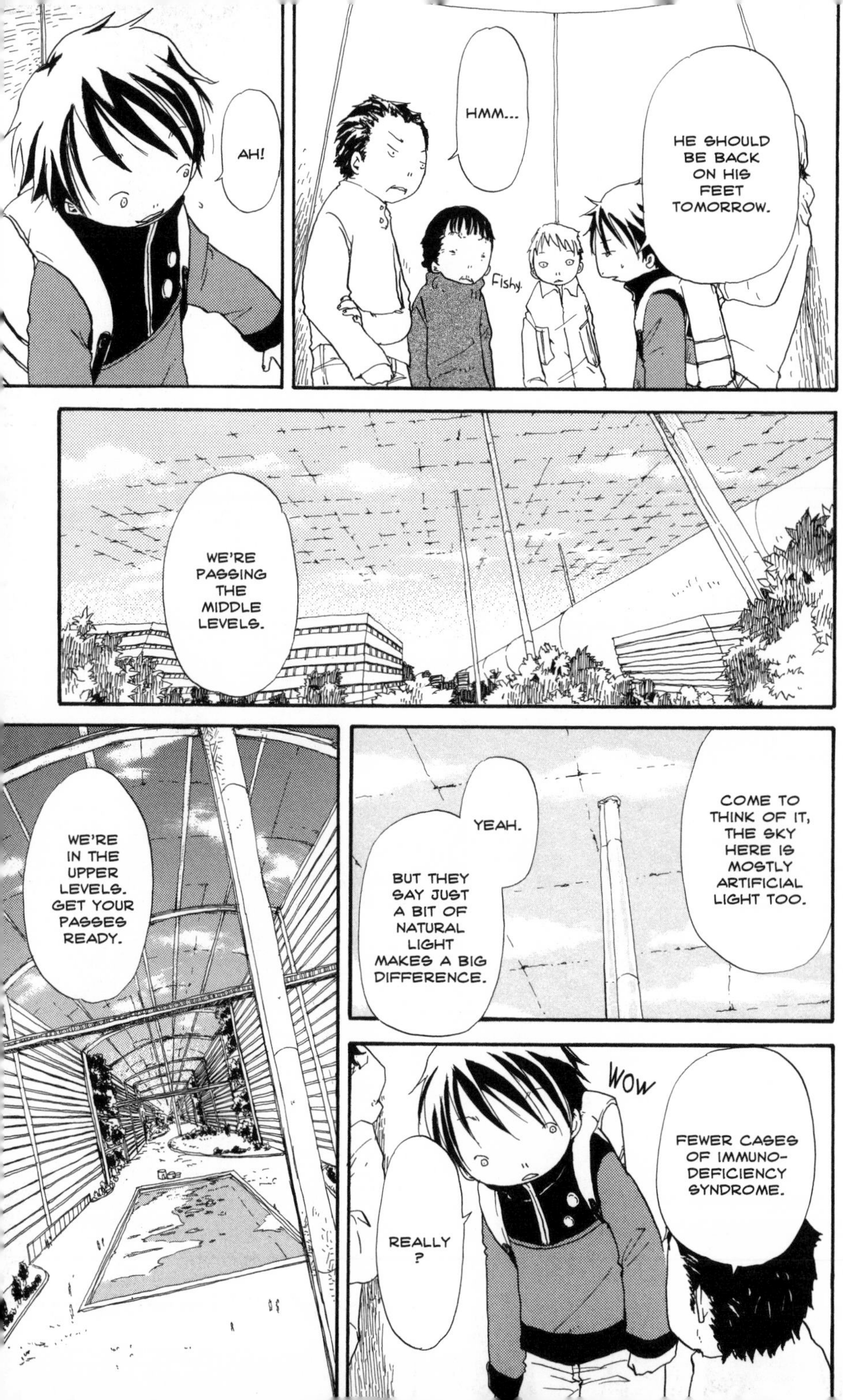
HE SHOULD BE BACK ON HIS FEET TOMORROW.
HMM...
Fishy.
AH!
WE'RE PASSING THE MIDDLE LEVELS.
COME TO THINK OF IT, THE SKY HERE IS MOSTLY ARTIFICIAL LIGHT TOO.
YEAH.
BUT THEY SAY JUST A BIT OF NATURAL LIGHT MAKES A BIG DIFFERENCE.
FEWER CASES OF IMMUNO-DEFICIENCY SYNDROME.
WOW
REALLY ?
WE'RE IN THE UPPER LEVELS. GET YOUR PASSES READY.

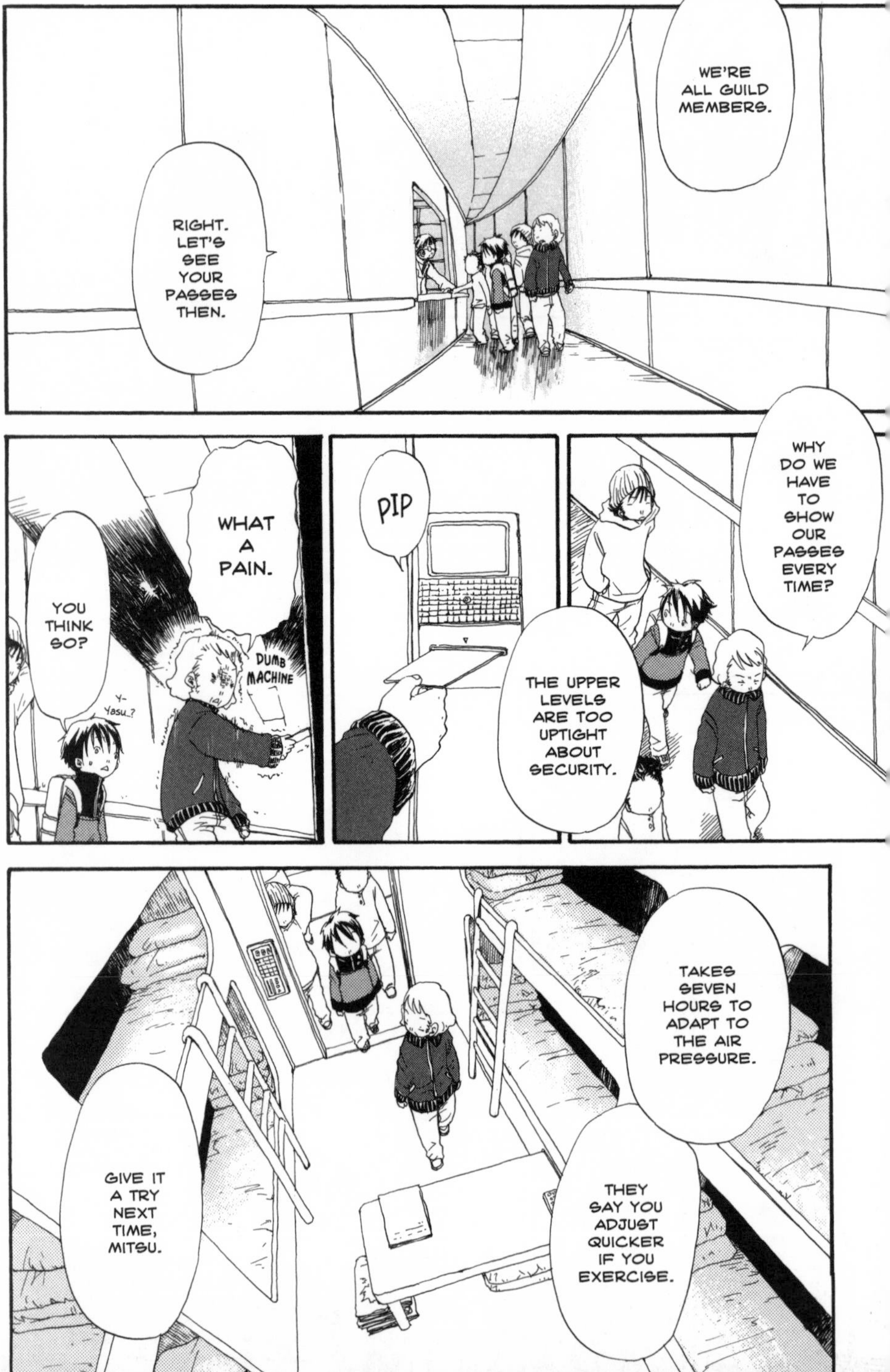
WE'RE ALL GUILD MEMBERS.
RIGHT. LET'S SEE YOUR PASSES THEN.
WHY DO WE HAVE TO SHOW OUR PASSES EVERY TIME?
THE UPPER LEVELS ARE TOO UPTIGHT ABOUT SECURITY.
PIP
WHAT A PAIN.
DUMB MACHINE
YOU THINK SO?
Y-Yasu...?
TAKES SEVEN HOURS TO ADAPT TO THE AIR PRESSURE.
THEY SAY YOU ADJUST QUICKER IF YOU EXERCISE.
GIVE IT A TRY NEXT TIME, MITSU.

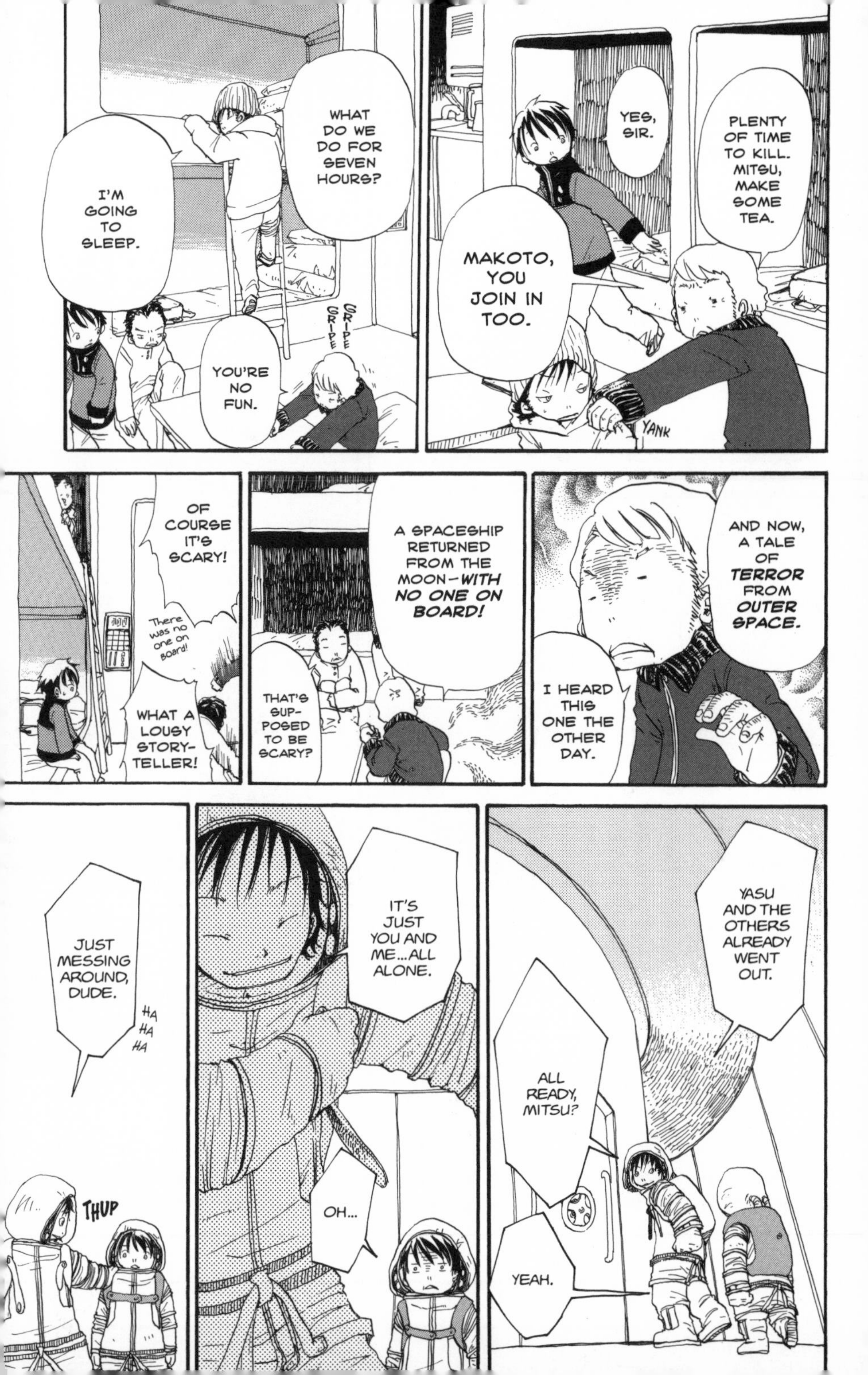
PLENTY OF TIME TO KILL. MITSU, MAKE SOME TEA.
YES, SIR.
MAKOTO, YOU JOIN IN TOO.
YANK
WHAT DO WE DO FOR SEVEN HOURS?
I'M GOING TO SLEEP.
GRIPE GRIPE
YOU'RE NO FUN.
AND NOW, A TALE OF *TERROR* FROM *OUTER SPACE.*
I HEARD THIS ONE THE OTHER DAY.
A SPACESHIP RETURNED FROM THE MOON—*WITH NO ONE ON BOARD!*
THAT'S SUPPOSED TO BE SCARY?
OF COURSE IT'S SCARY!
There was no one on board!
WHAT A LOUSY STORYTELLER!
YASU AND THE OTHERS ALREADY WENT OUT.
ALL READY, MITSU?
YEAH.
IT'S JUST YOU AND ME...ALL ALONE.
OH...
JUST MESSING AROUND, DUDE.
HA HA HA
THUP

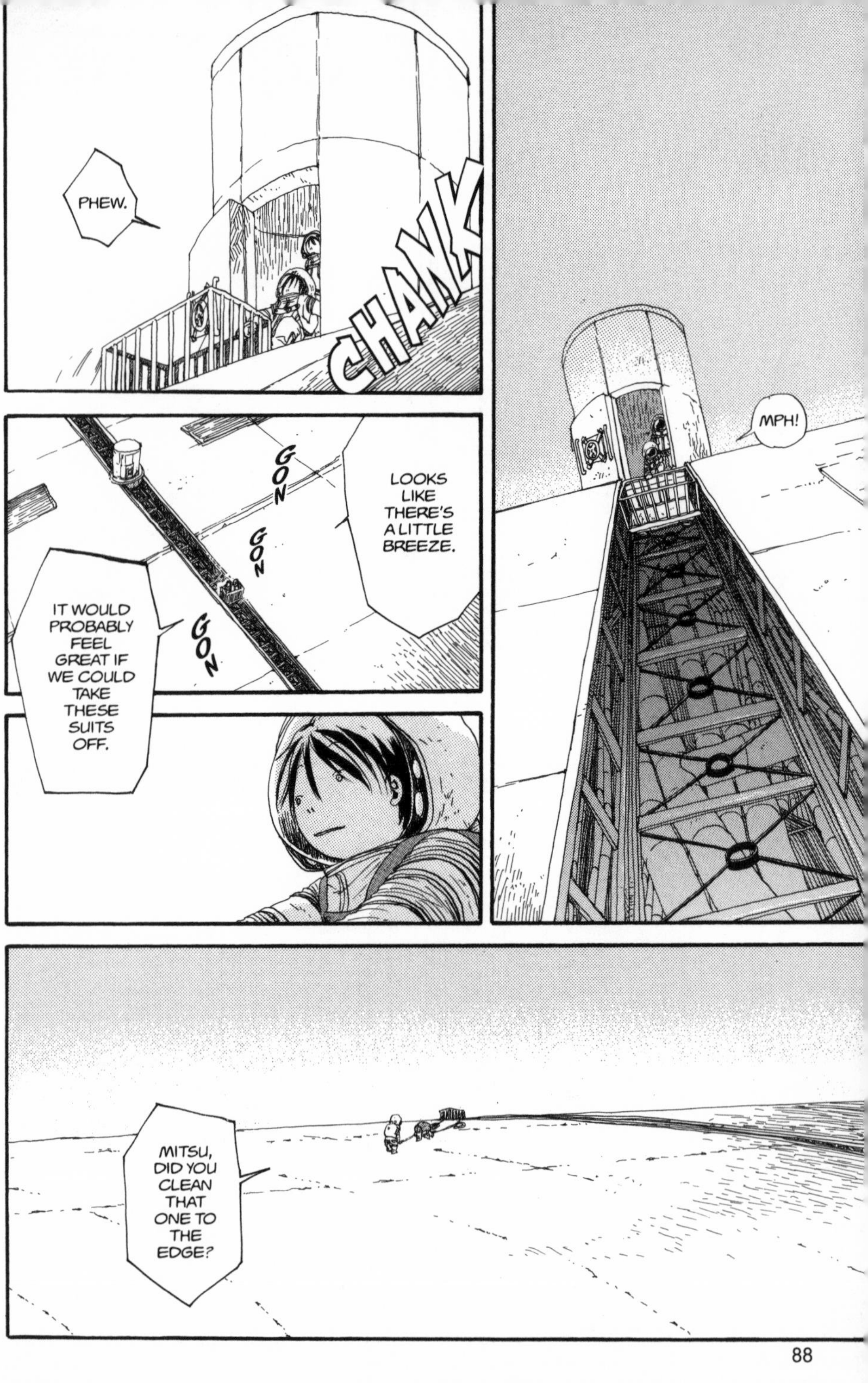
MPH!
PHEW.
CHANK
LOOKS LIKE THERE'S A LITTLE BREEZE.
GON GON GON
IT WOULD PROBABLY FEEL GREAT IF WE COULD TAKE THESE SUITS OFF.
MITSU, DID YOU CLEAN THAT ONE TO THE EDGE?

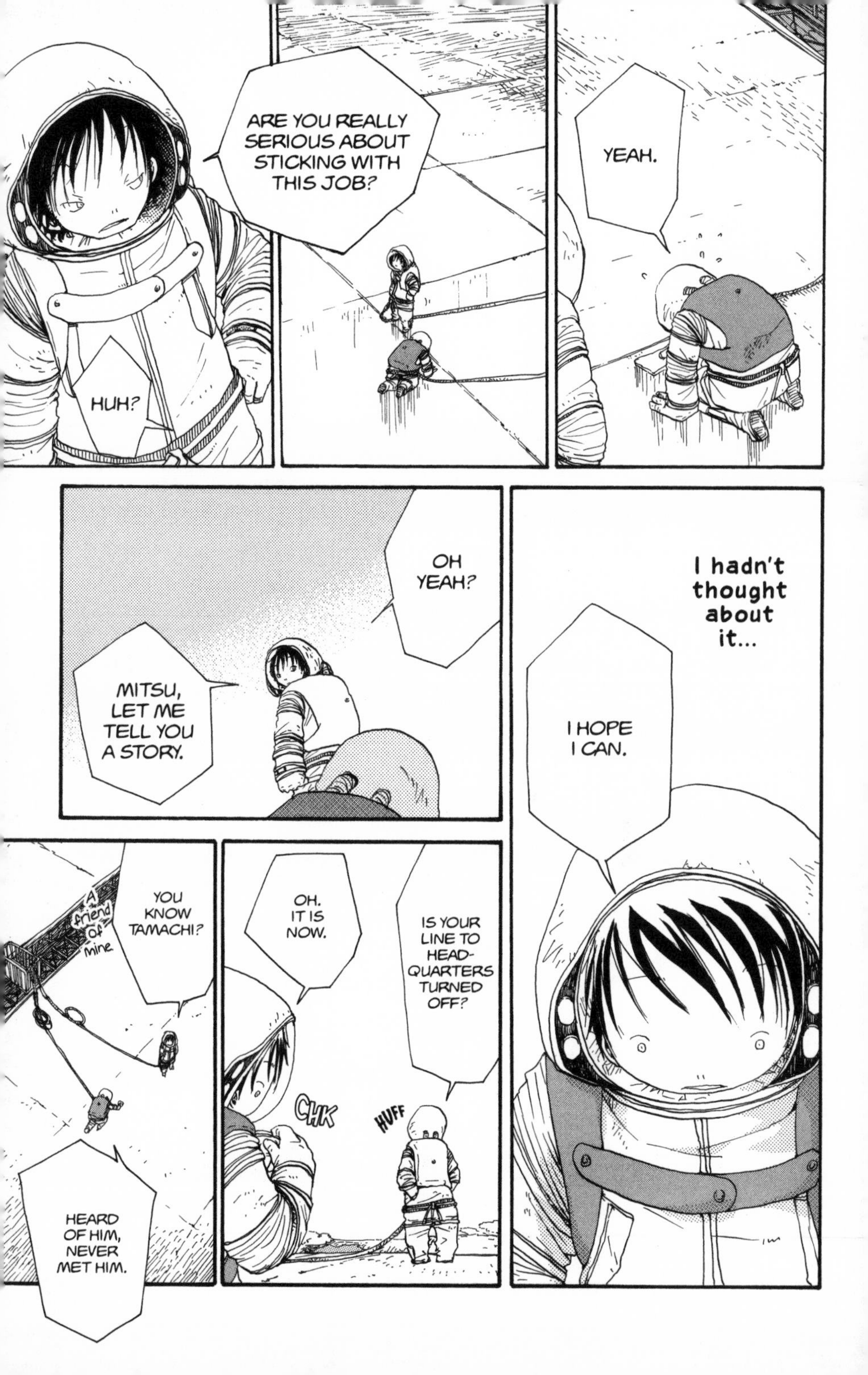

YEAH.
ARE YOU REALLY SERIOUS ABOUT STICKING WITH THIS JOB?
HUH?
I hadn't thought about it...
I HOPE I CAN.
OH YEAH?
MITSU, LET ME TELL YOU A STORY.
IS YOUR LINE TO HEAD-QUARTERS TURNED OFF?
OH. IT IS NOW.
HUFF
CHK
YOU KNOW TAMACHI?
A friend of mine.
HEARD OF HIM, NEVER MET HIM.

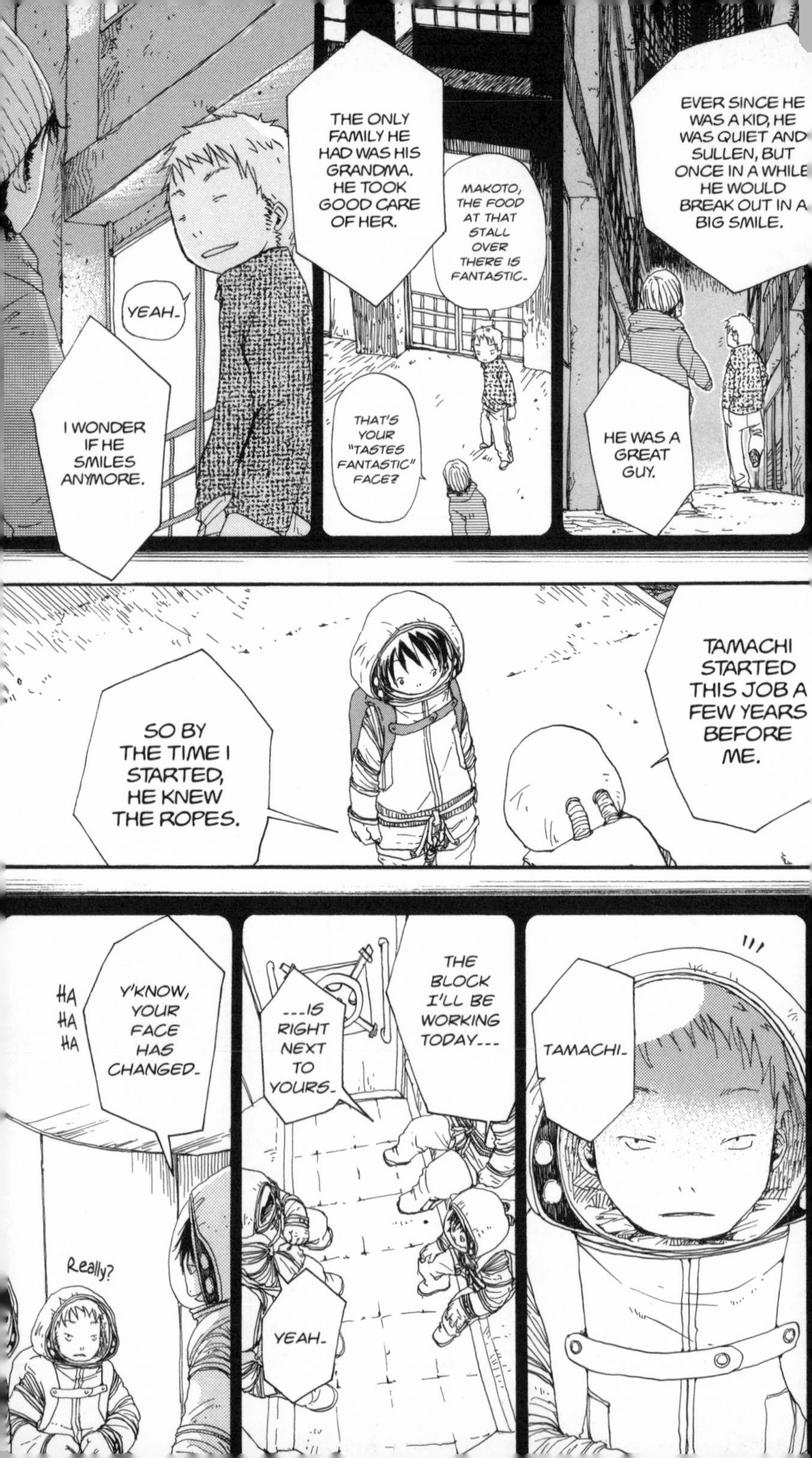
EVER SINCE HE WAS A KID, HE WAS QUIET AND SULLEN, BUT ONCE IN A WHILE HE WOULD BREAK OUT IN A BIG SMILE.
HE WAS A GREAT GUY.
THE ONLY FAMILY HE HAD WAS HIS GRANDMA. HE TOOK GOOD CARE OF HER.
MAKOTO, THE FOOD AT THAT STALL OVER THERE IS FANTASTIC...
THAT'S YOUR "TASTES FANTASTIC" FACE?
YEAH...
I WONDER IF HE SMILES ANYMORE.
TAMACHI STARTED THIS JOB A FEW YEARS BEFORE ME.
SO BY THE TIME I STARTED, HE KNEW THE ROPES.
TAMACHI...
THE BLOCK I'LL BE WORKING TODAY...
...IS RIGHT NEXT TO YOURS...
YEAH...
Y'KNOW, YOUR FACE HAS CHANGED...
HA HA HA
Really?

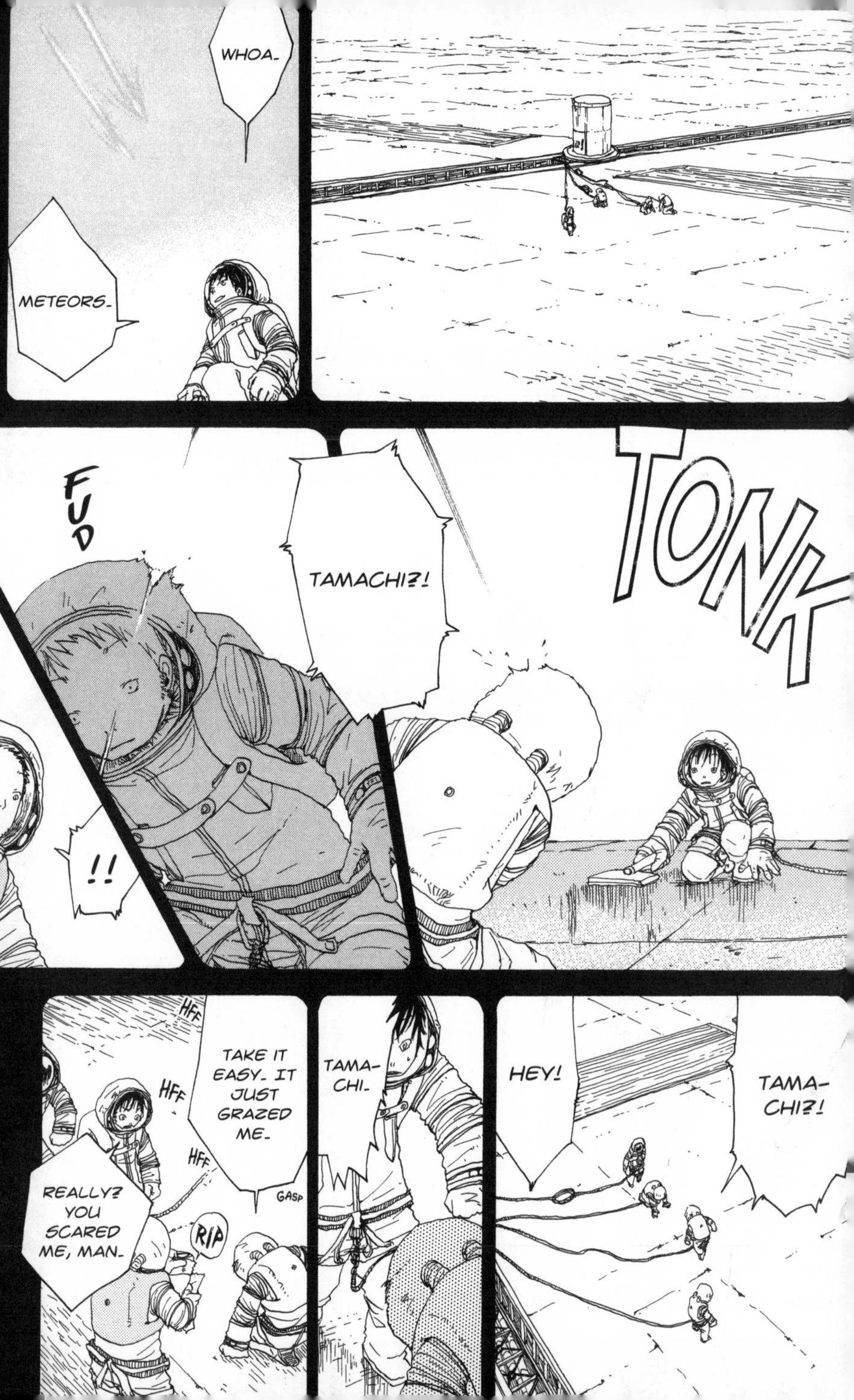
WHOA...
METEORS...
TONK
TAMACHI?!
FUD
!!
TAMA-CHI?!
HEY!
TAMA-CHI...
HFF
TAKE IT EASY... IT JUST GRAZED ME...
GASP
HFF
HFF
RIP
REALLY? YOU SCARED ME, MAN...

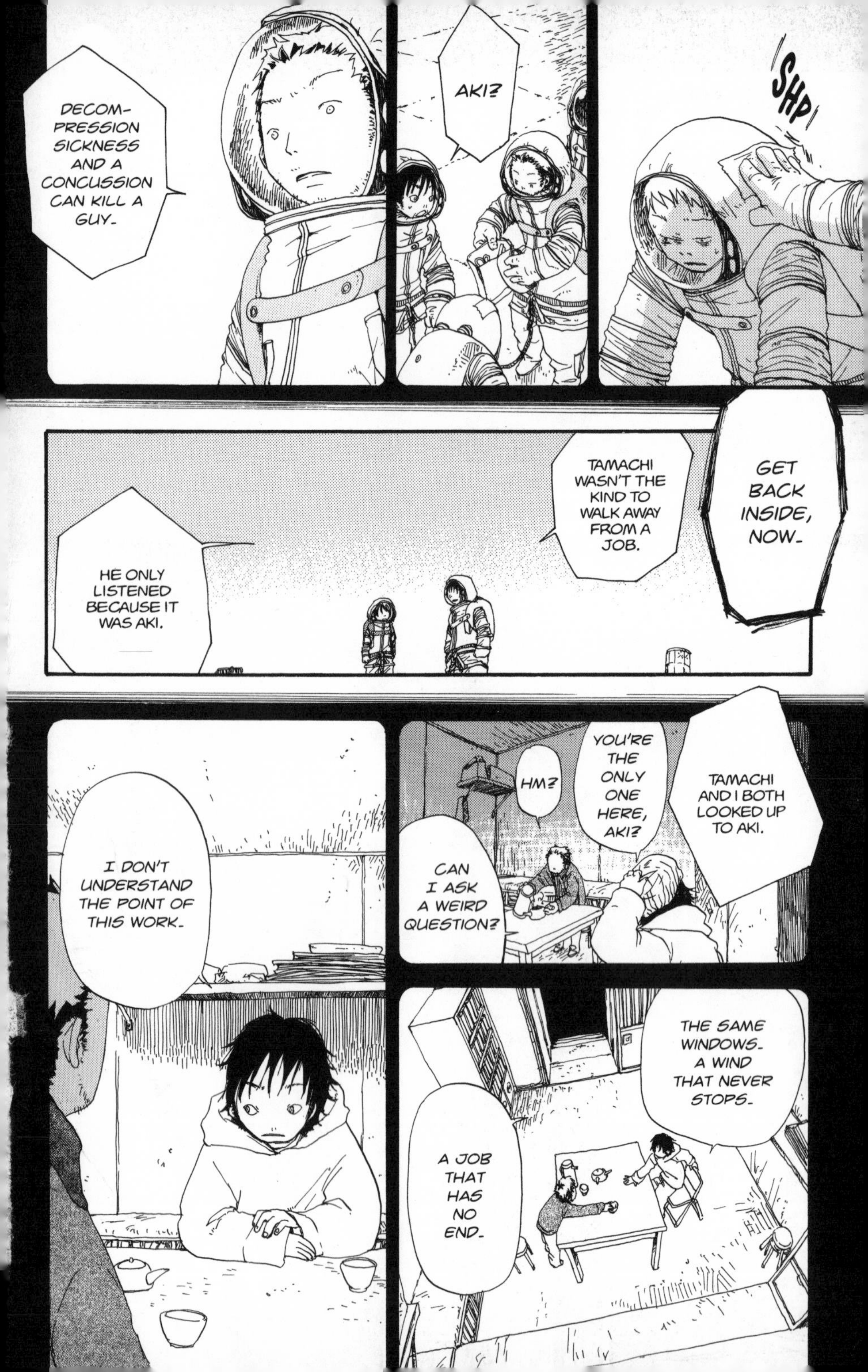
SHP
AKI?
DECOMPRESSION SICKNESS AND A CONCUSSION CAN KILL A GUY.
GET BACK INSIDE, NOW.
TAMACHI WASN'T THE KIND TO WALK AWAY FROM A JOB.
HE ONLY LISTENED BECAUSE IT WAS AKI.
TAMACHI AND I BOTH LOOKED UP TO AKI.
YOU'RE THE ONLY ONE HERE, AKI?
HM?
CAN I ASK A WEIRD QUESTION?
THE SAME WINDOWS. A WIND THAT NEVER STOPS.
A JOB THAT HAS NO END.
I DON'T UNDERSTAND THE POINT OF THIS WORK.

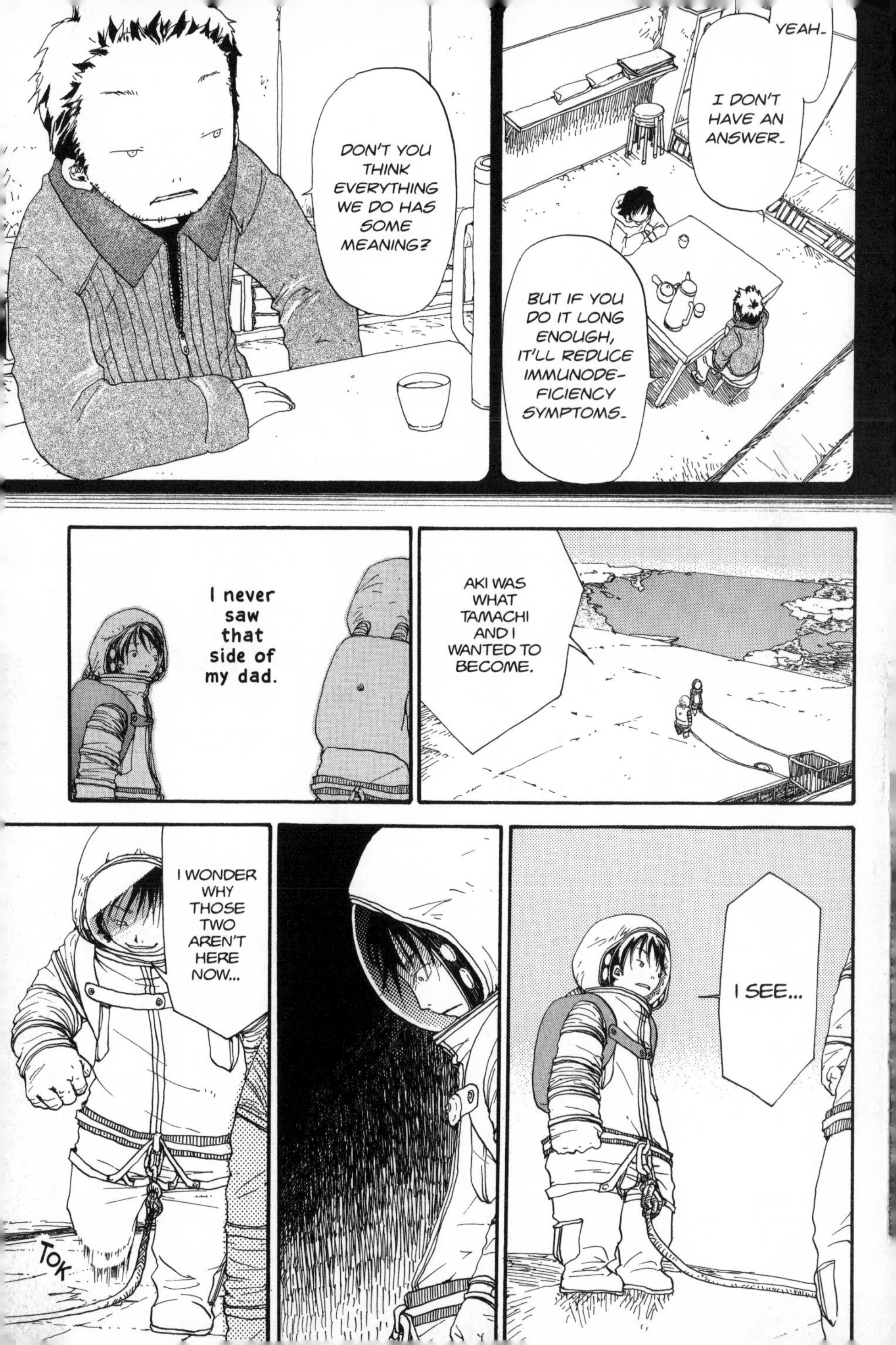
YEAH...
I DON'T HAVE AN ANSWER...
BUT IF YOU DO IT LONG ENOUGH, IT'LL REDUCE IMMUNODE-FICIENCY SYMPTOMS...
DON'T YOU THINK EVERYTHING WE DO HAS SOME MEANING?
AKI WAS WHAT TAMACHI AND I WANTED TO BECOME.
I never saw that side of my dad.
I SEE...
I WONDER WHY THOSE TWO AREN'T HERE NOW...
TOK

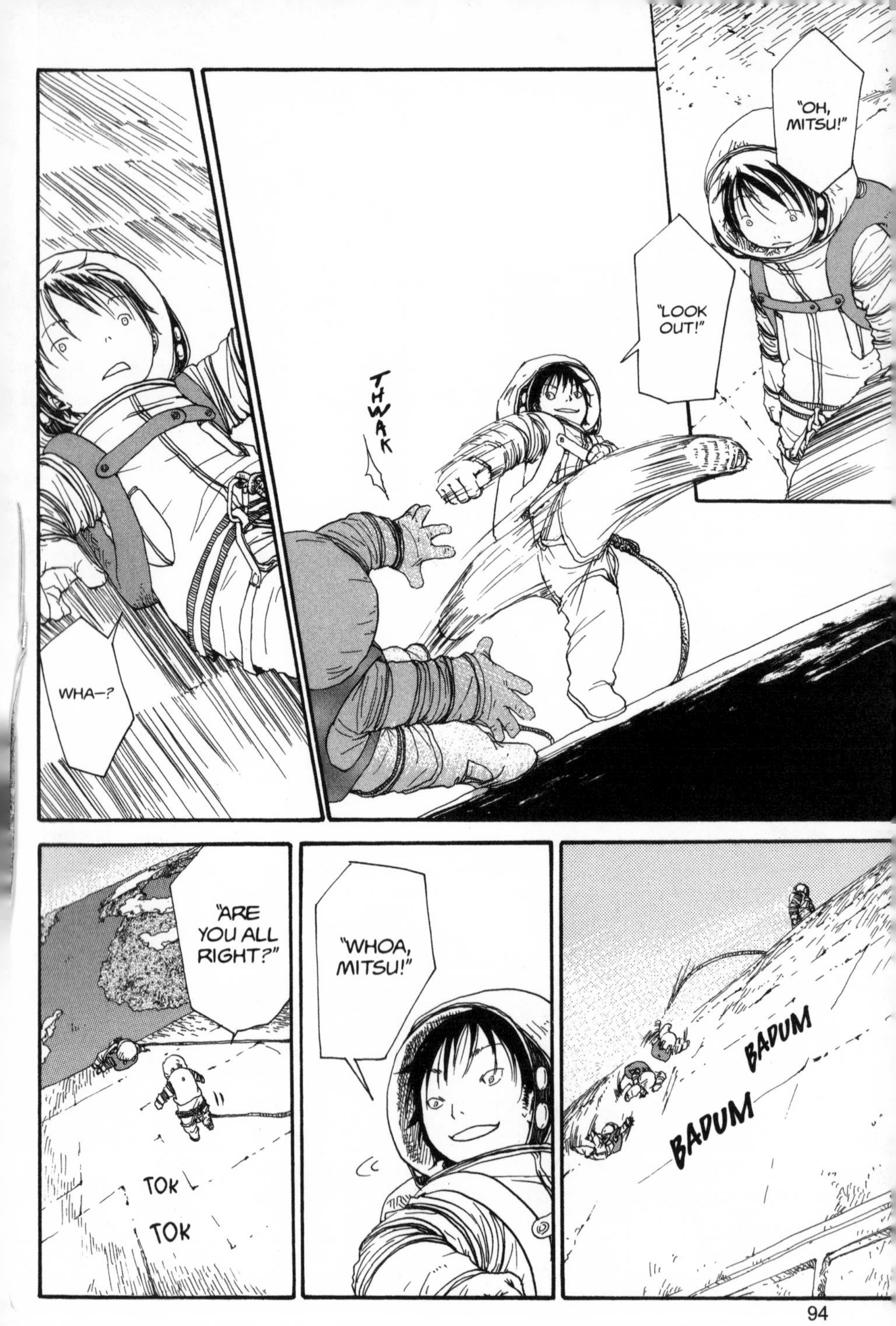
"OH, MITSU!"
"LOOK OUT!"
THWAK
WHA–?
BADUM
BADUM
"WHOA, MITSU!"
"ARE YOU ALL RIGHT?"
TOK
TOK

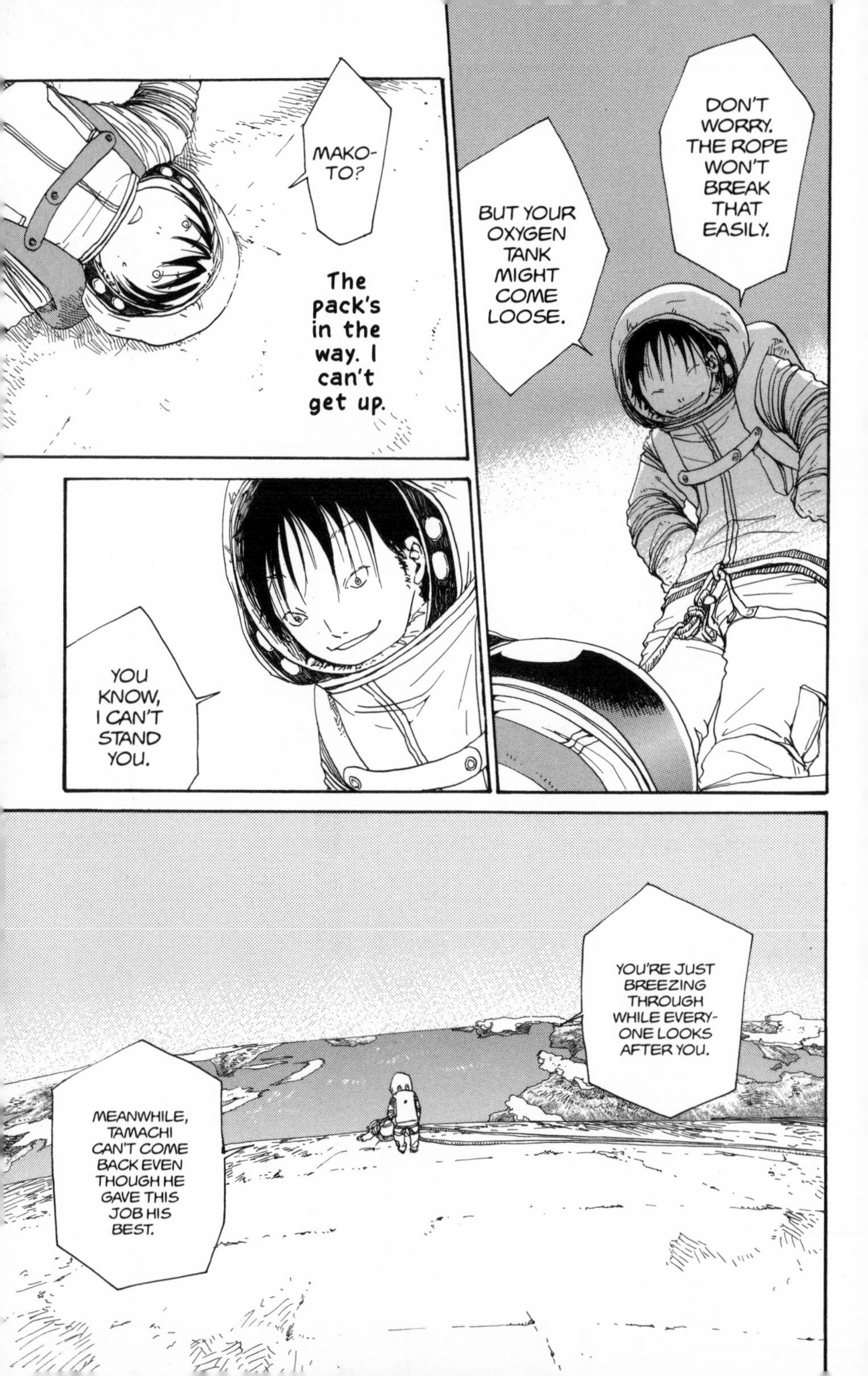
DON'T WORRY. THE ROPE WON'T BREAK THAT EASILY.
BUT YOUR OXYGEN TANK MIGHT COME LOOSE.
MAKO-TO?
The pack's in the way. I can't get up.
YOU KNOW, I CAN'T STAND YOU.
YOU'RE JUST BREEZING THROUGH WHILE EVERY-ONE LOOKS AFTER YOU.
MEANWHILE, TAMACHI CAN'T COME BACK EVEN THOUGH HE GAVE THIS JOB HIS BEST.

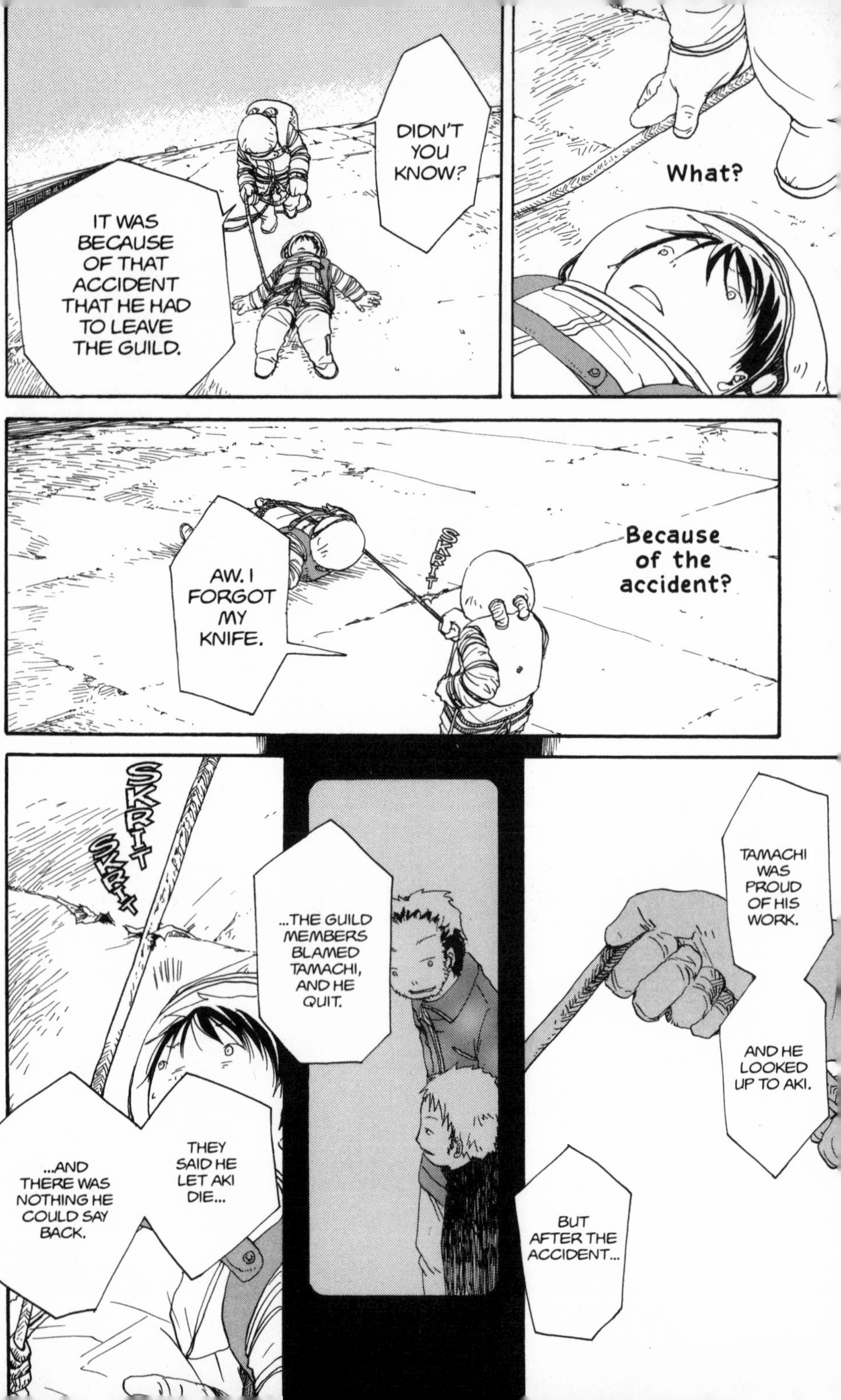
What?
DIDN'T YOU KNOW?
IT WAS BECAUSE OF THAT ACCIDENT THAT HE HAD TO LEAVE THE GUILD.
Because of the accident?
SKRIT
AW. I FORGOT MY KNIFE.
TAMACHI WAS PROUD OF HIS WORK.
AND HE LOOKED UP TO AKI.
BUT AFTER THE ACCIDENT...
...THE GUILD MEMBERS BLAMED TAMACHI, AND HE QUIT.
SKRIT
SKRIT
THEY SAID HE LET AKI DIE...
...AND THERE WAS NOTHING HE COULD SAY BACK.

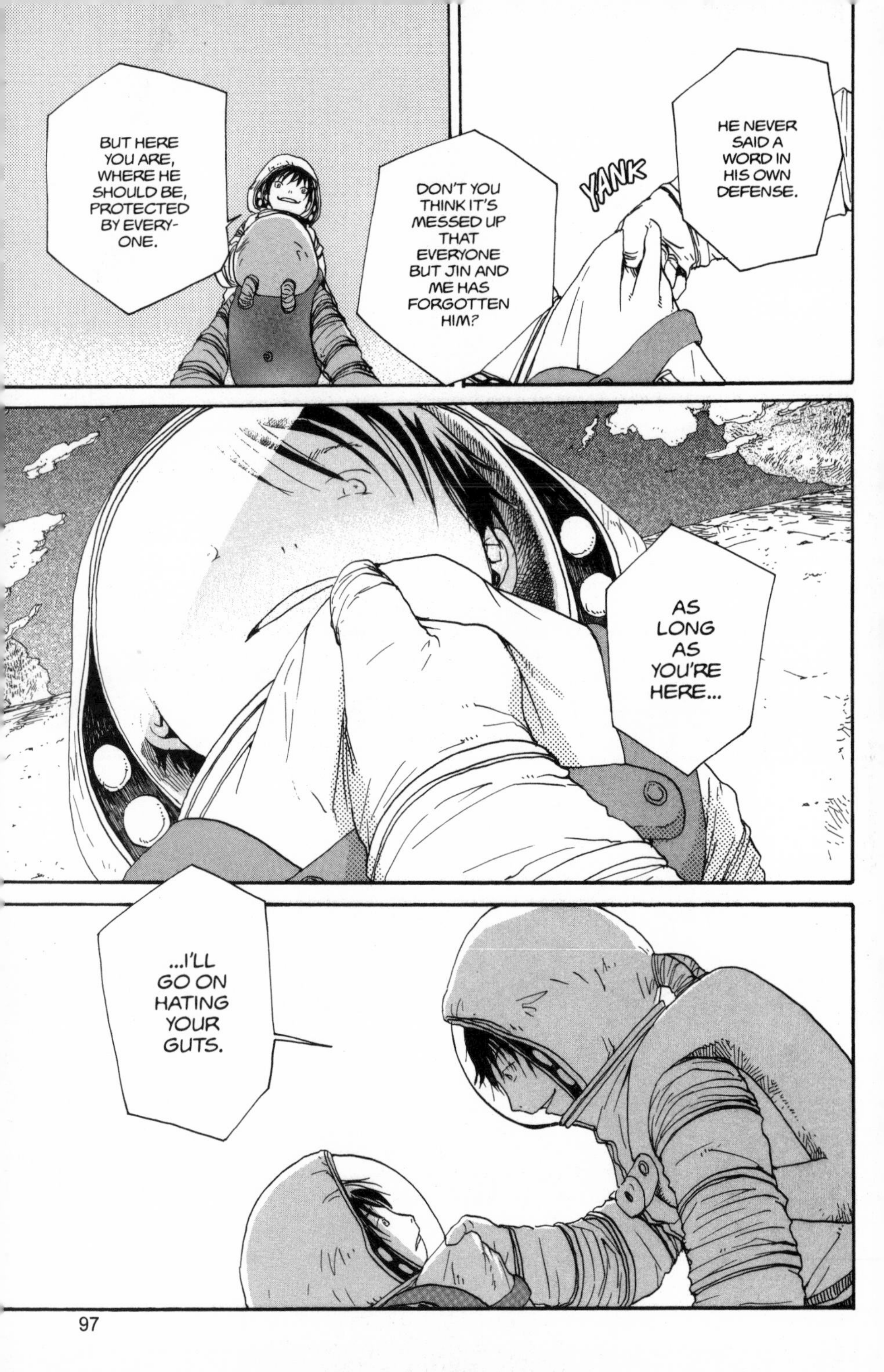
HE NEVER SAID A WORD IN HIS OWN DEFENSE.
YANK
DON'T YOU THINK IT'S MESSED UP THAT EVERYONE BUT JIN AND ME HAS FORGOTTEN HIM?
BUT HERE YOU ARE, WHERE HE SHOULD BE, PROTECTED BY EVERY-ONE.
AS LONG AS YOU'RE HERE...
...I'LL GO ON HATING YOUR GUTS.

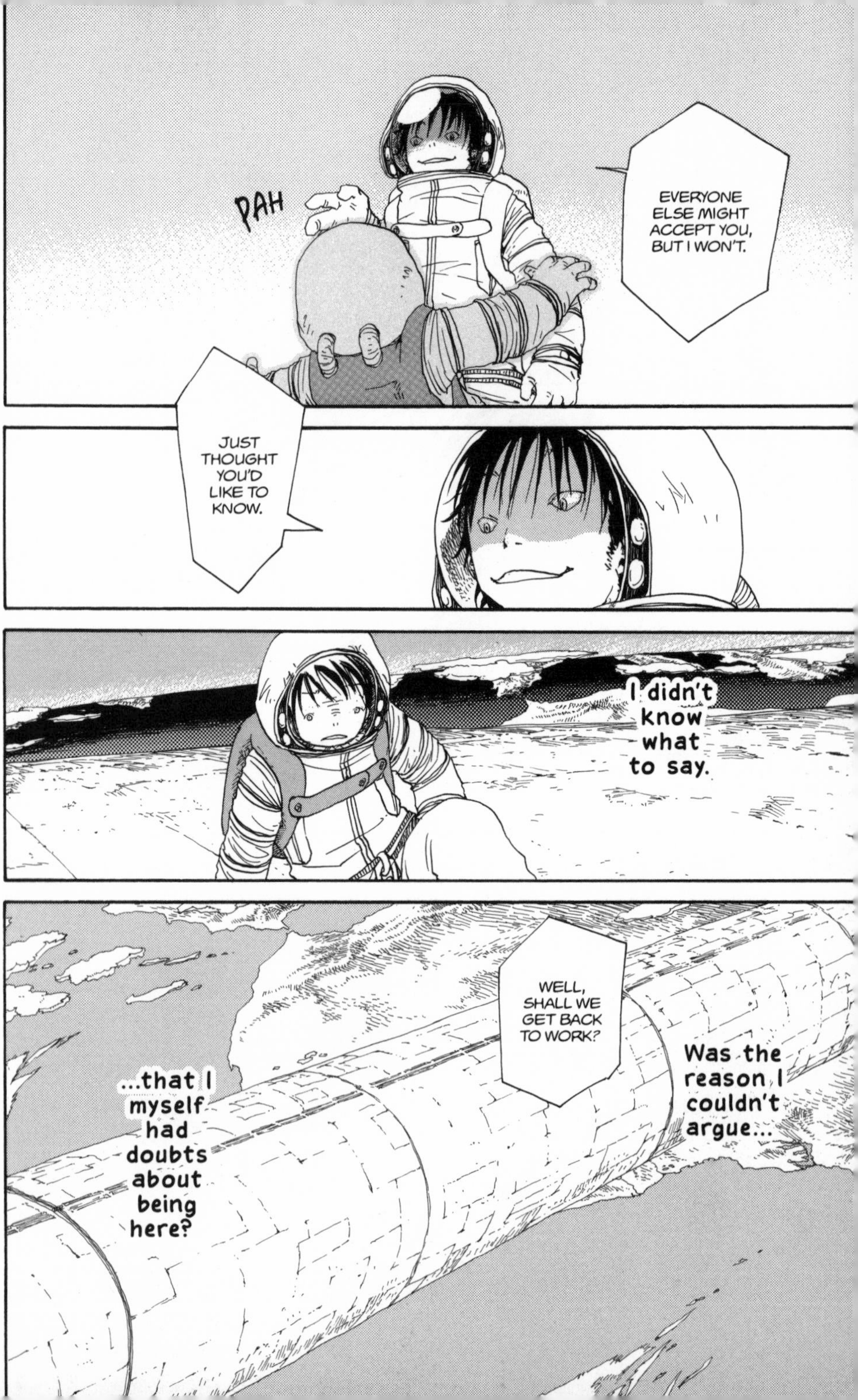
EVERYONE ELSE MIGHT ACCEPT YOU, BUT I WON'T.
PAH
JUST THOUGHT YOU'D LIKE TO KNOW.
I didn't know what to say.
WELL, SHALL WE GET BACK TO WORK?
Was the reason I couldn't argue...
...that I myself had doubts about being here?

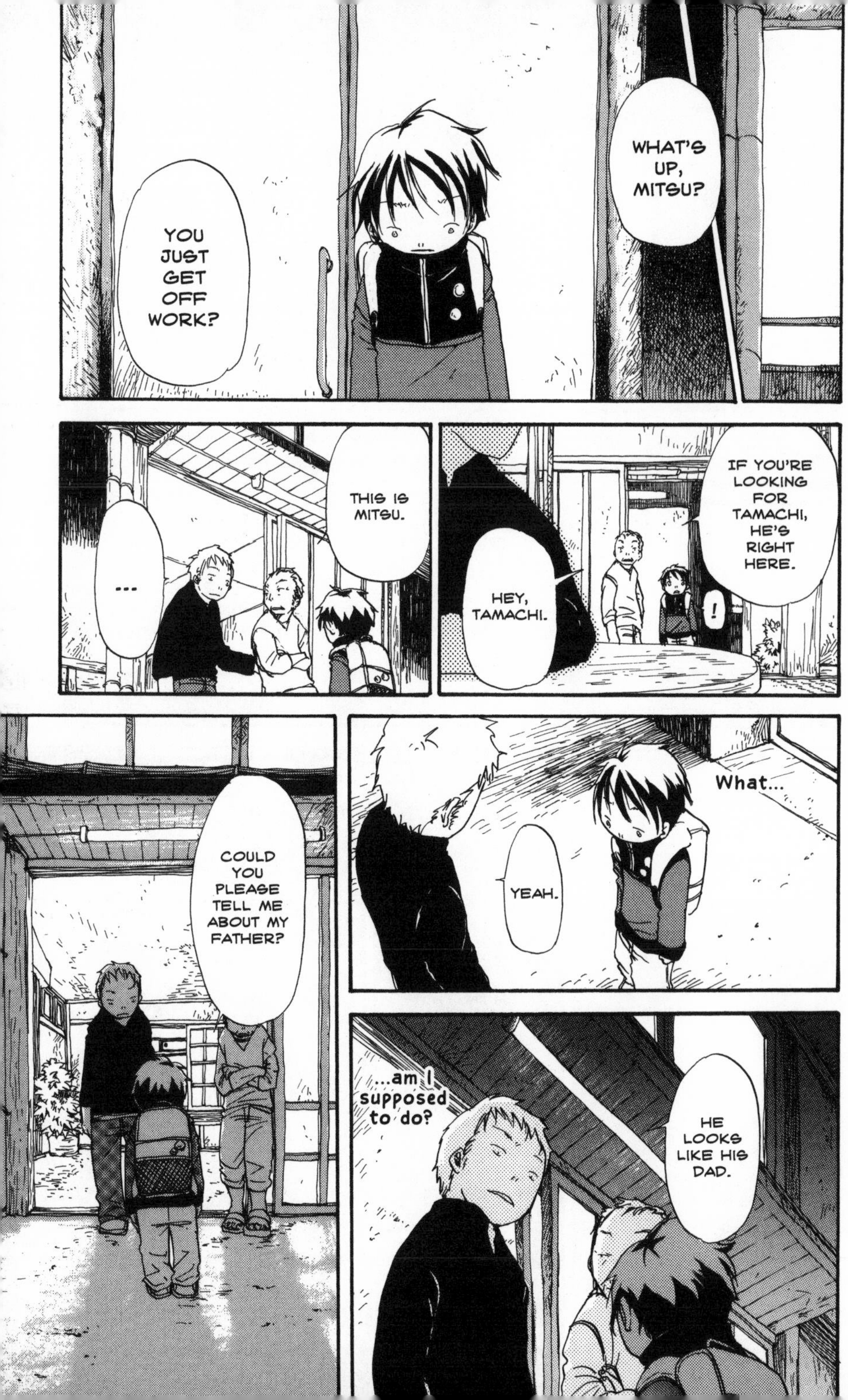
WHAT'S UP, MITSU?
YOU JUST GET OFF WORK?
IF YOU'RE LOOKING FOR TAMACHI, HE'S RIGHT HERE.
!
HEY, TAMACHI.
THIS IS MITSU.
...
What...
YEAH.
...am I supposed to do?
HE LOOKS LIKE HIS DAD.
COULD YOU PLEASE TELL ME ABOUT MY FATHER?

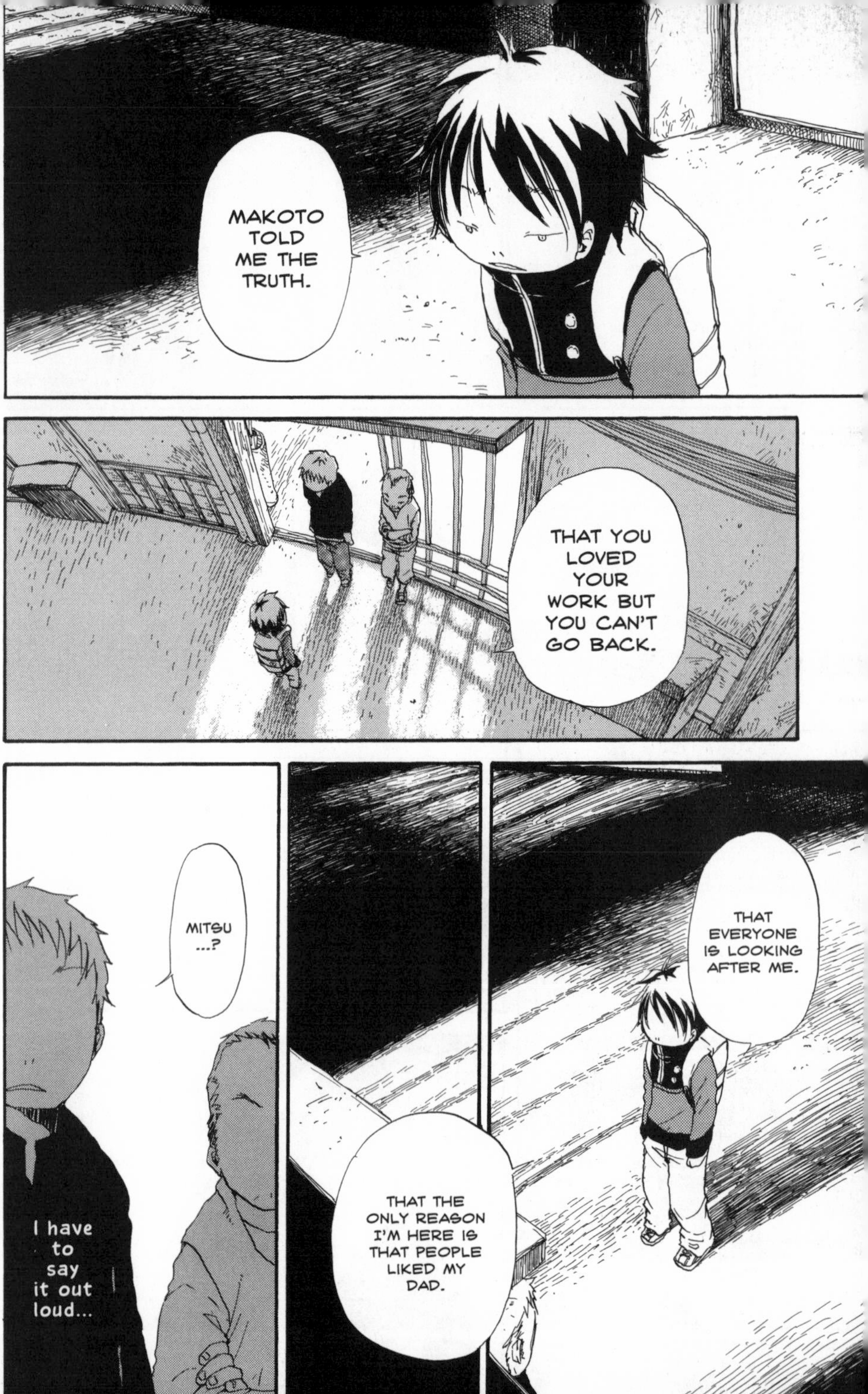
MAKOTO TOLD ME THE TRUTH.
THAT YOU LOVED YOUR WORK BUT YOU CAN'T GO BACK.
THAT EVERYONE IS LOOKING AFTER ME.
THAT THE ONLY REASON I'M HERE IS THAT PEOPLE LIKED MY DAD.
MITSU ...?
I have to say it out loud...

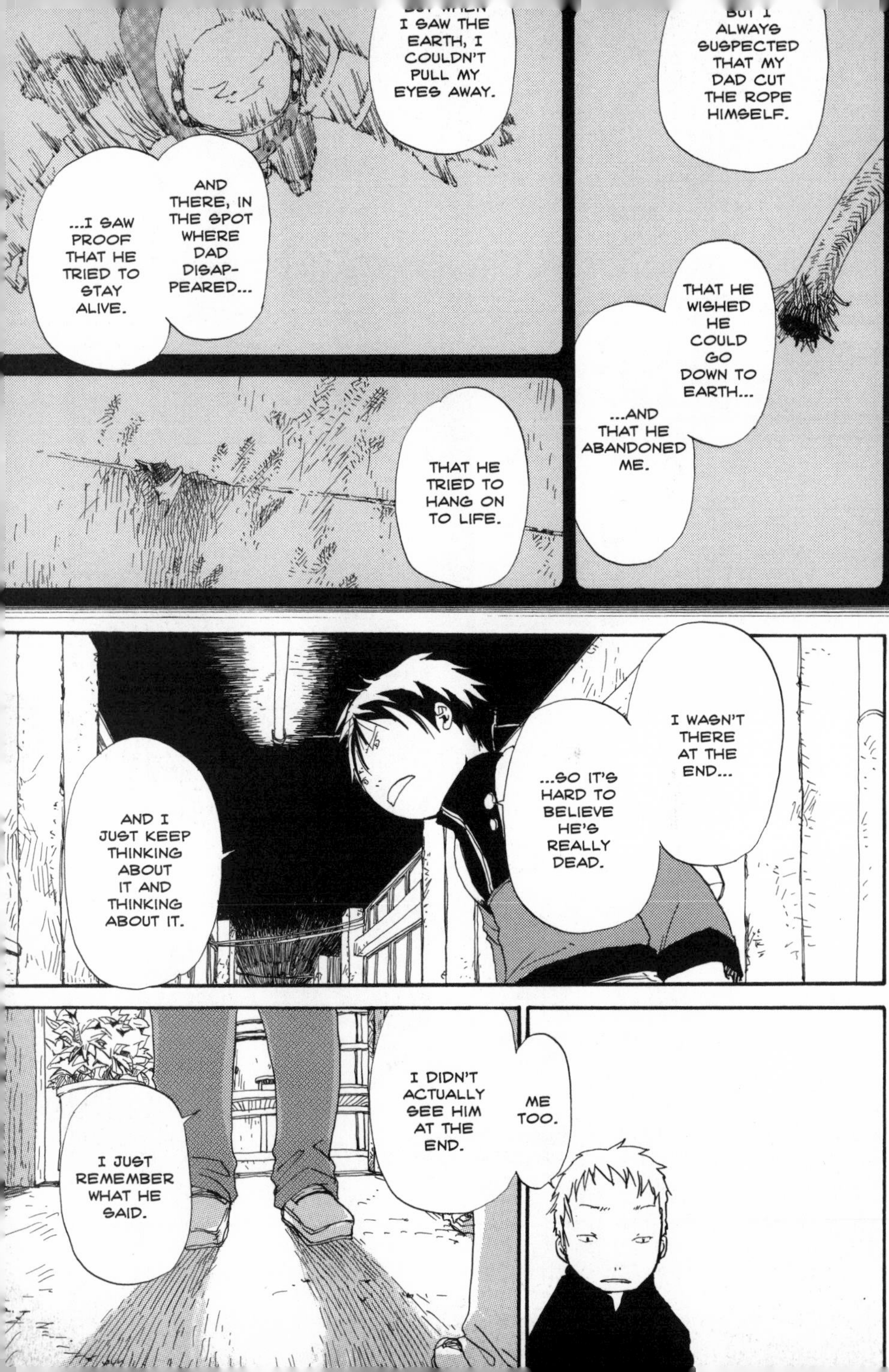
BUT I ALWAYS SUSPECTED THAT MY DAD CUT THE ROPE HIMSELF.
THAT HE WISHED HE COULD GO DOWN TO EARTH...
...AND THAT HE ABANDONED ME.
I SAW THE EARTH, I COULDN'T PULL MY EYES AWAY.
AND THERE, IN THE SPOT WHERE DAD DISAP- PEARED...
...I SAW PROOF THAT HE TRIED TO STAY ALIVE.
THAT HE TRIED TO HANG ON TO LIFE.
I WASN'T THERE AT THE END...
...SO IT'S HARD TO BELIEVE HE'S REALLY DEAD.
AND I JUST KEEP THINKING ABOUT IT AND THINKING ABOUT IT.
ME TOO.
I DIDN'T ACTUALLY SEE HIM AT THE END.
I JUST REMEMBER WHAT HE SAID.

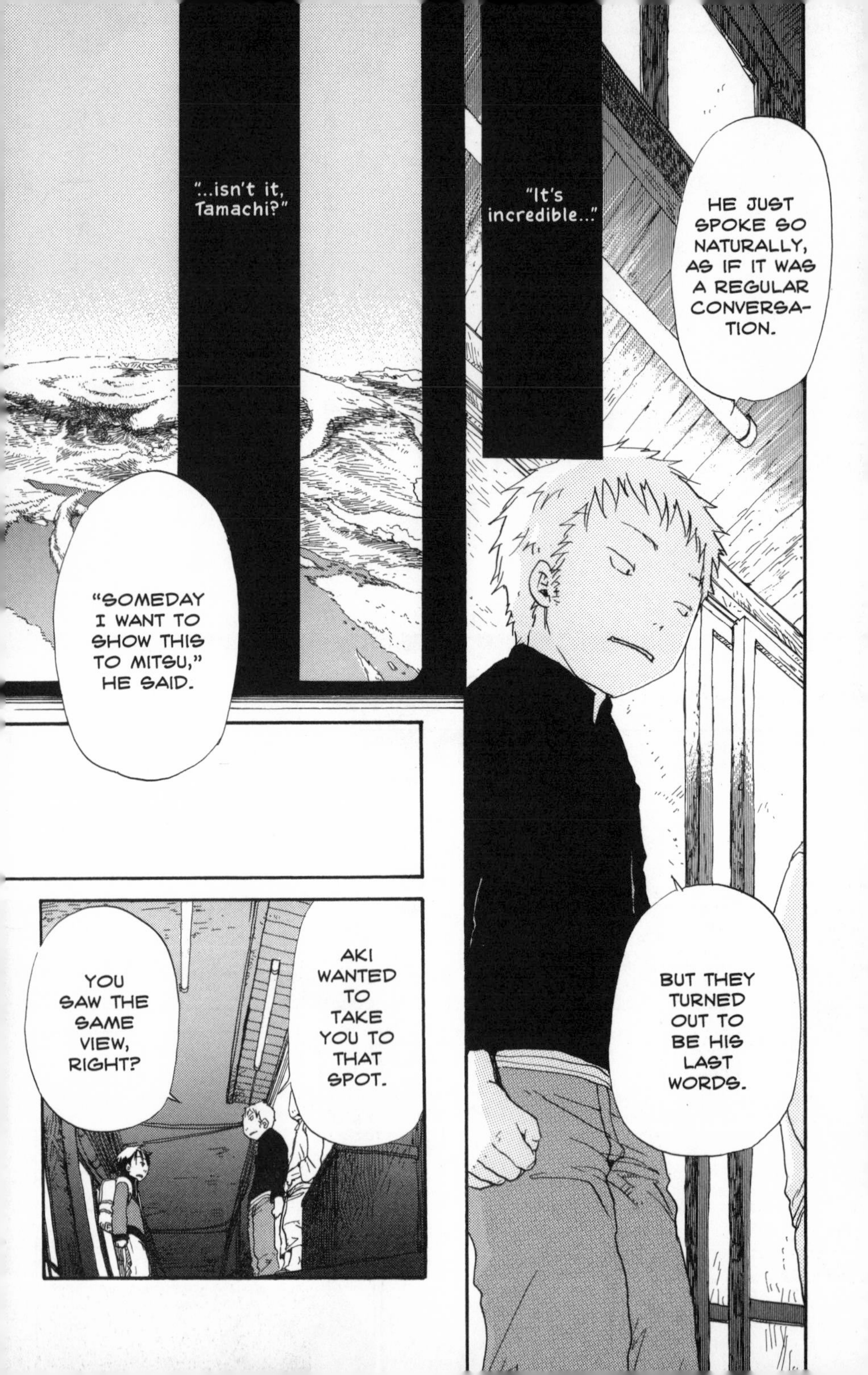
"It's incredible..."
"...isn't it, Tamachi?"
"SOMEDAY I WANT TO SHOW THIS TO MITSU," HE SAID.
HE JUST SPOKE SO NATURALLY, AS IF IT WAS A REGULAR CONVERSA-TION.
BUT THEY TURNED OUT TO BE HIS LAST WORDS.
AKI WANTED TO TAKE YOU TO THAT SPOT.
YOU SAW THE SAME VIEW, RIGHT?

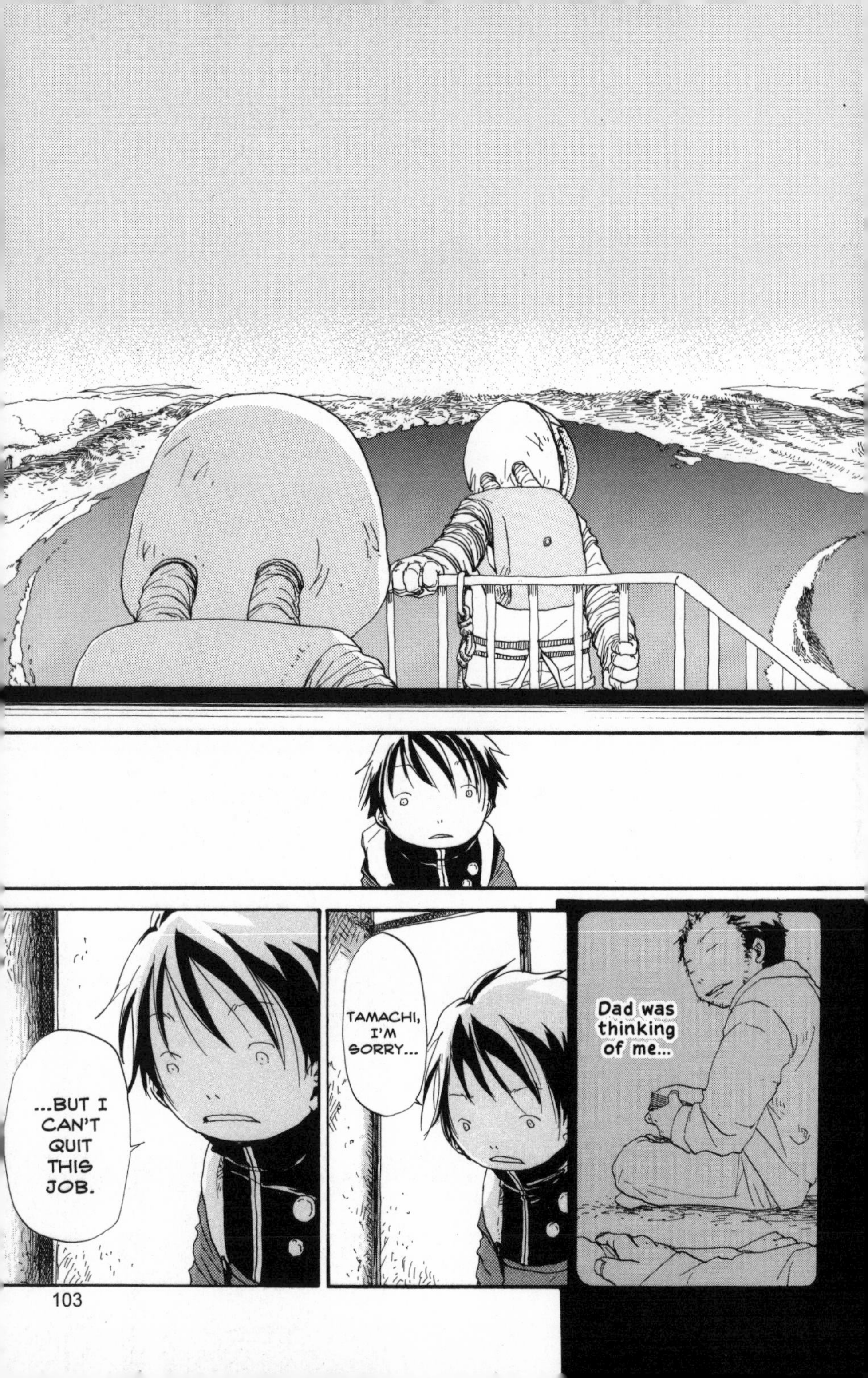
Dad was thinking of me...
TAMACHI, I'M SORRY...
...BUT I CAN'T QUIT THIS JOB.

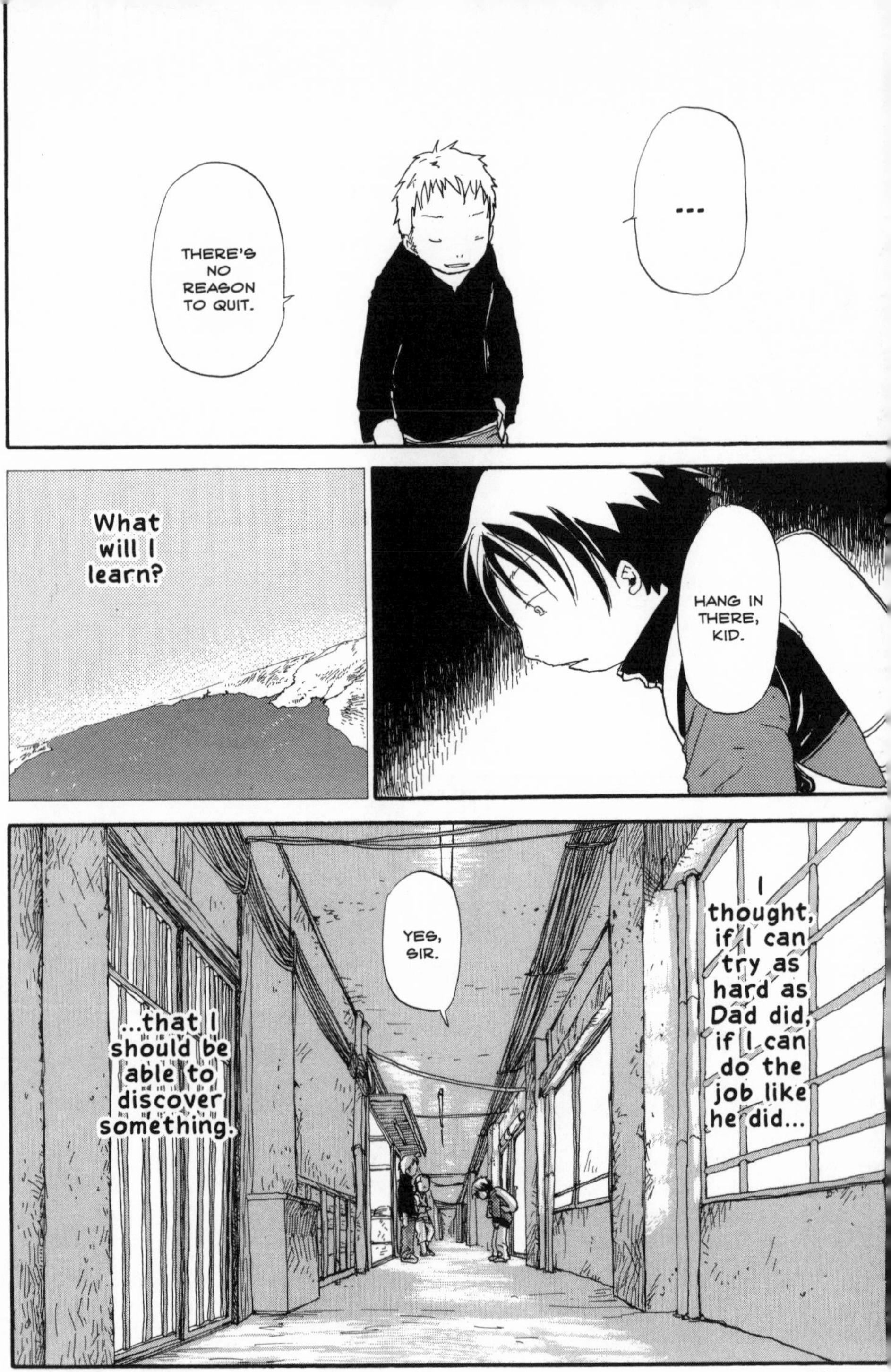
...
THERE'S NO REASON TO QUIT.
HANG IN THERE, KID.
What will I learn?
I thought, if I can try as hard as Dad did, if I can do the job like he did...
YES, SIR.
...that I should be able to discover something.

floor 5: an ocean

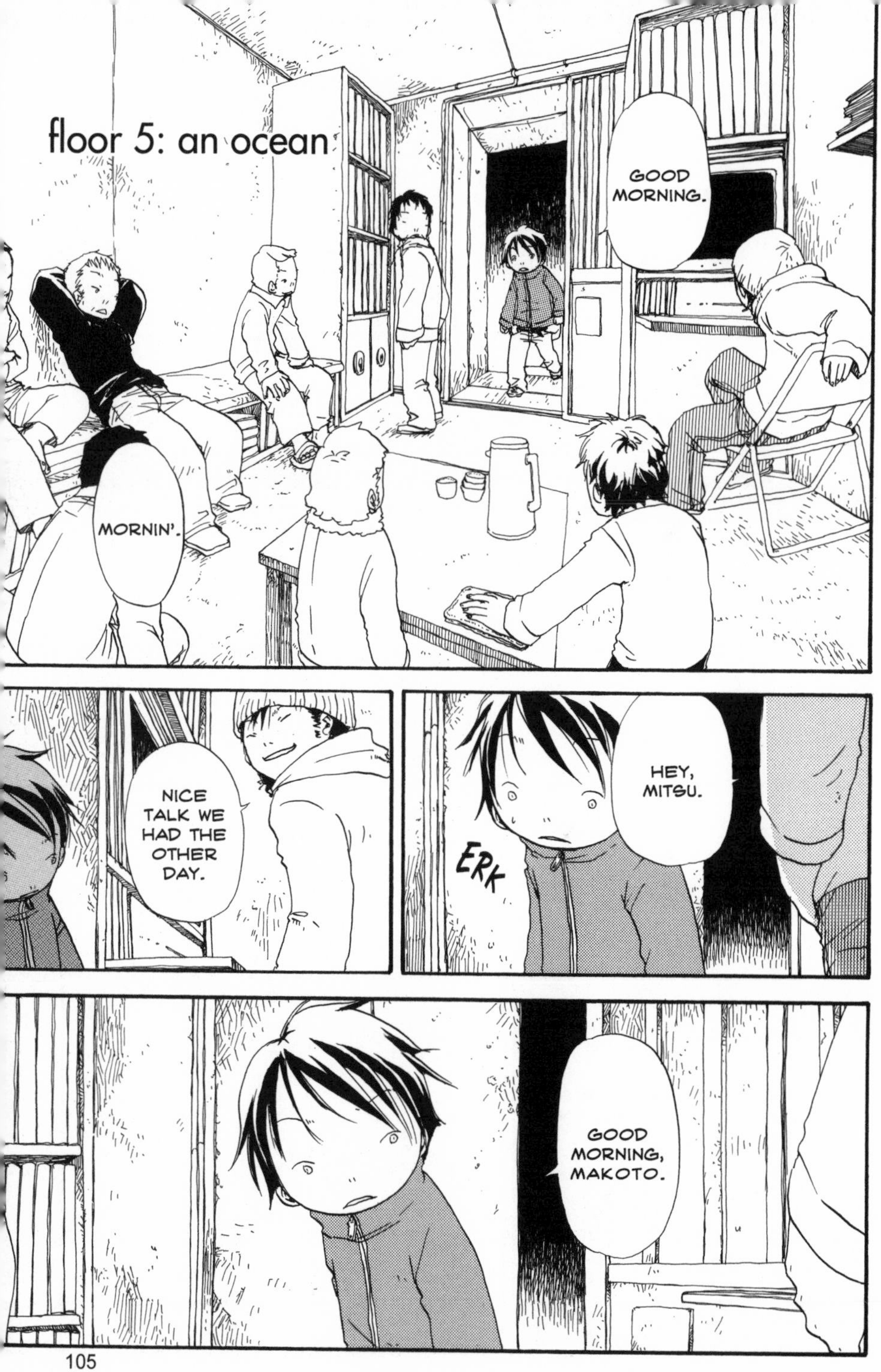
GOOD MORNING.
MORNIN'.
HEY, MITSU.
ERK
NICE TALK WE HAD THE OTHER DAY.
GOOD MORNING, MAKOTO.

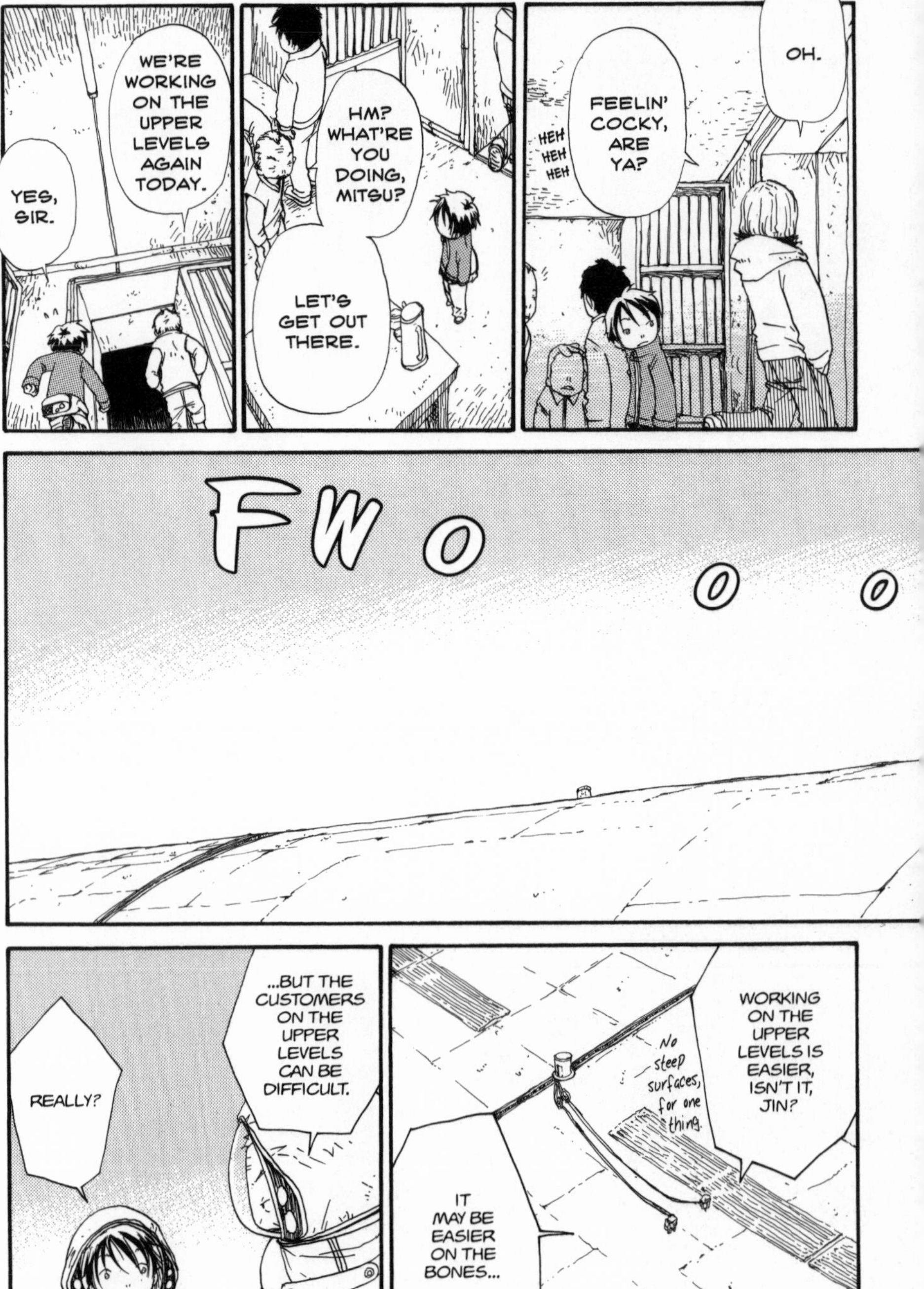
OH.
FEELIN' COCKY, ARE YA?
HEH HEH HEH
HM? WHAT'RE YOU DOING, MITSU?
LET'S GET OUT THERE.
WE'RE WORKING ON THE UPPER LEVELS AGAIN TODAY.
YES, SIR.
FWOOO
WORKING ON THE UPPER LEVELS IS EASIER, ISN'T IT, JIN?
No steep surfaces, for one thing.
IT MAY BE EASIER ON THE BONES...
...BUT THE CUSTOMERS ON THE UPPER LEVELS CAN BE DIFFICULT.
REALLY?

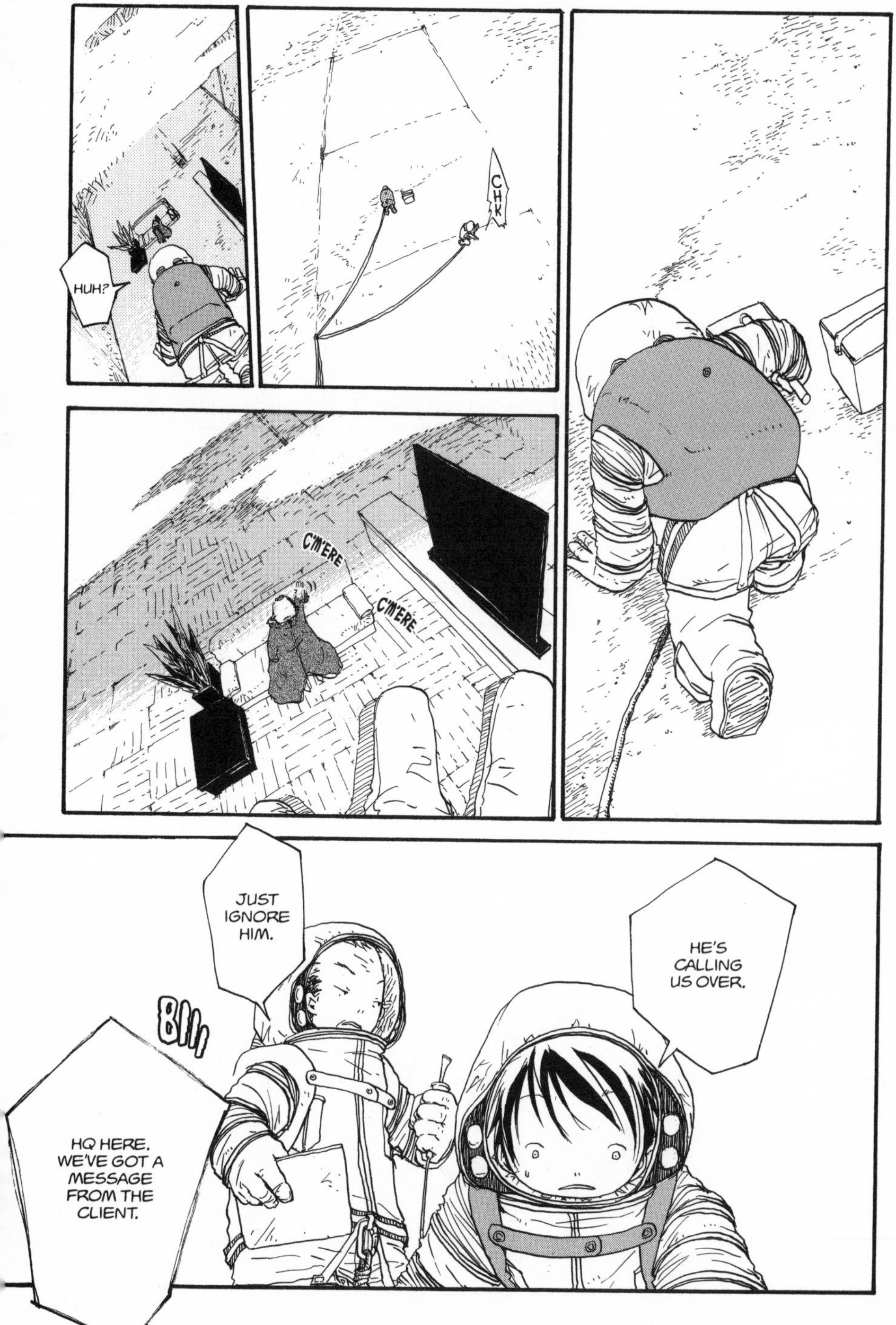
CHK
HUH?
C'M'ERE
C'M'ERE
HE'S CALLING US OVER.
JUST IGNORE HIM.
BIII
HQ HERE. WE'VE GOT A MESSAGE FROM THE CLIENT.

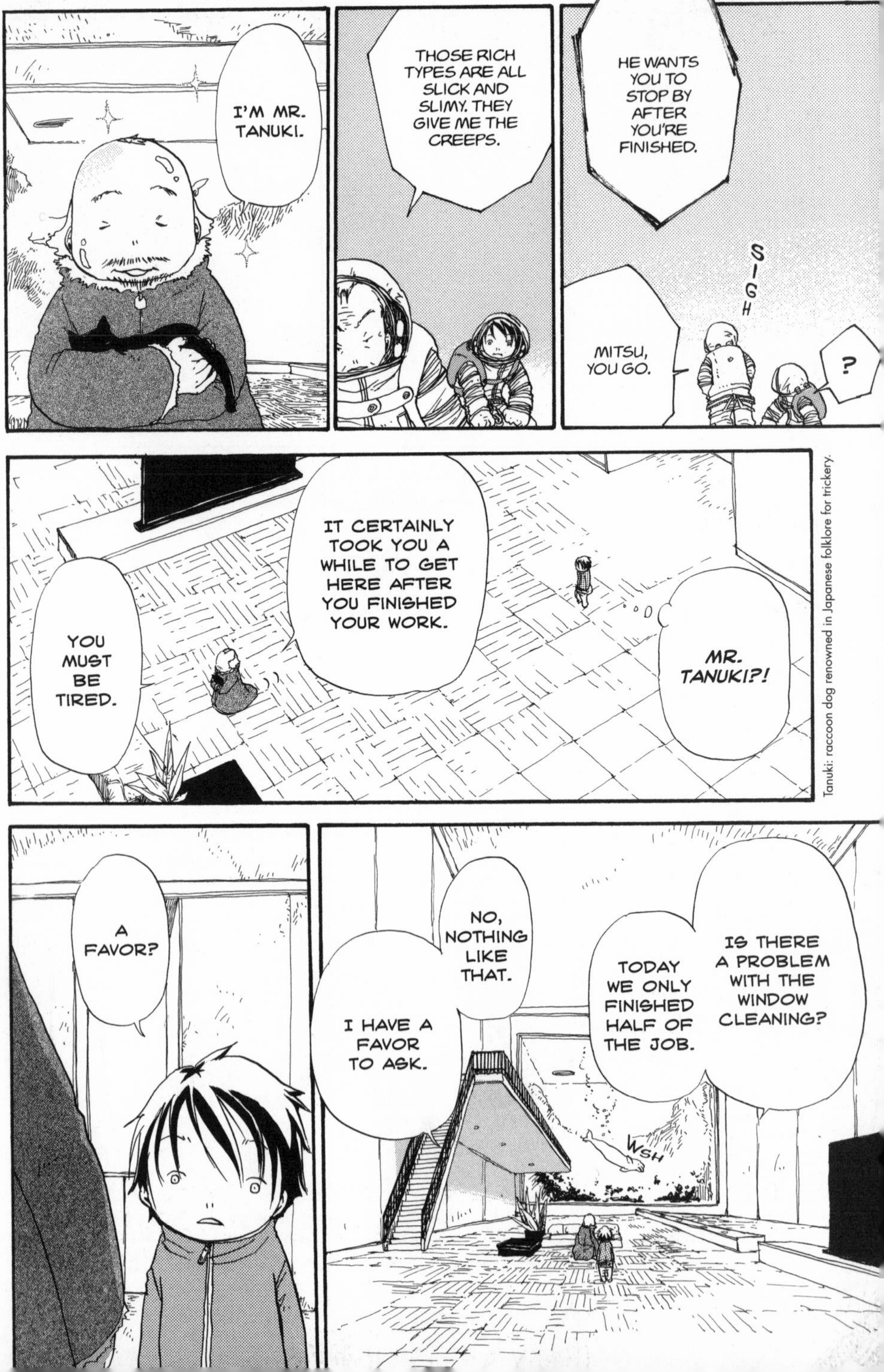
HE WANTS YOU TO STOP BY AFTER YOU'RE FINISHED.
SIGH
?
MITSU, YOU GO.
THOSE RICH TYPES ARE ALL SLICK AND SLIMY. THEY GIVE ME THE CREEPS.
I'M MR. TANUKI.
MR. TANUKI?!
IT CERTAINLY TOOK YOU A WHILE TO GET HERE AFTER YOU FINISHED YOUR WORK.
YOU MUST BE TIRED.
IS THERE A PROBLEM WITH THE WINDOW CLEANING?
TODAY WE ONLY FINISHED HALF OF THE JOB.
NO, NOTHING LIKE THAT.
I HAVE A FAVOR TO ASK.
WSH
A FAVOR?

Tanuki: raccoon dog renowned in Japanese folklore for trickery.

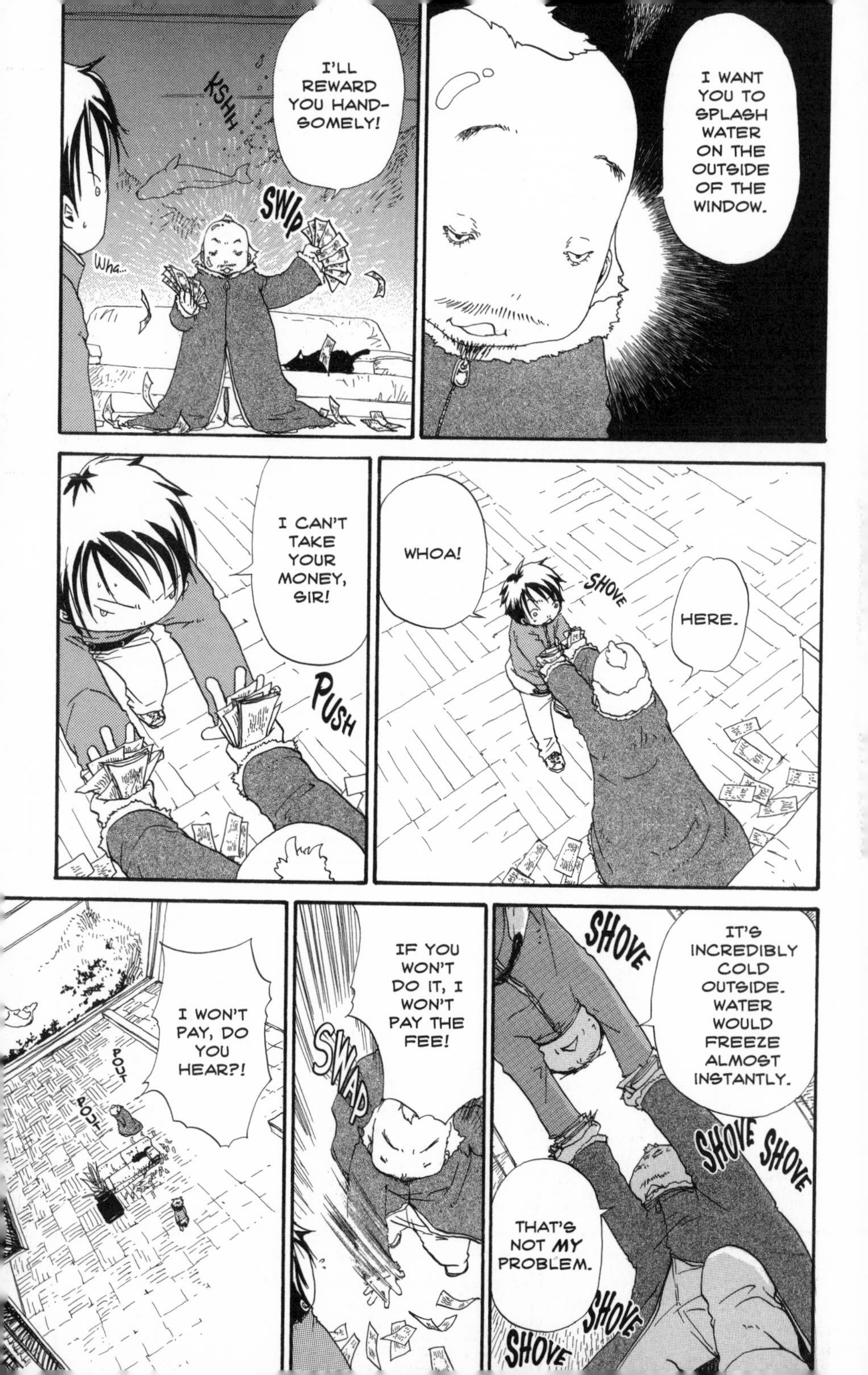
I WANT YOU TO SPLASH WATER ON THE OUTSIDE OF THE WINDOW.
I'LL REWARD YOU HAND-SOMELY!
KSHH
SWIP
Wha...
HERE.
SHOVE
WHOA!
I CAN'T TAKE YOUR MONEY, SIR!
PUSH
IT'S INCREDIBLY COLD OUTSIDE. WATER WOULD FREEZE ALMOST INSTANTLY.
SHOVE
SHOVE SHOVE
THAT'S NOT MY PROBLEM.
SHOVE
SHOVE
IF YOU WON'T DO IT, I WON'T PAY THE FEE!
SWAP
I WON'T PAY, DO YOU HEAR?!
POUT
POUT

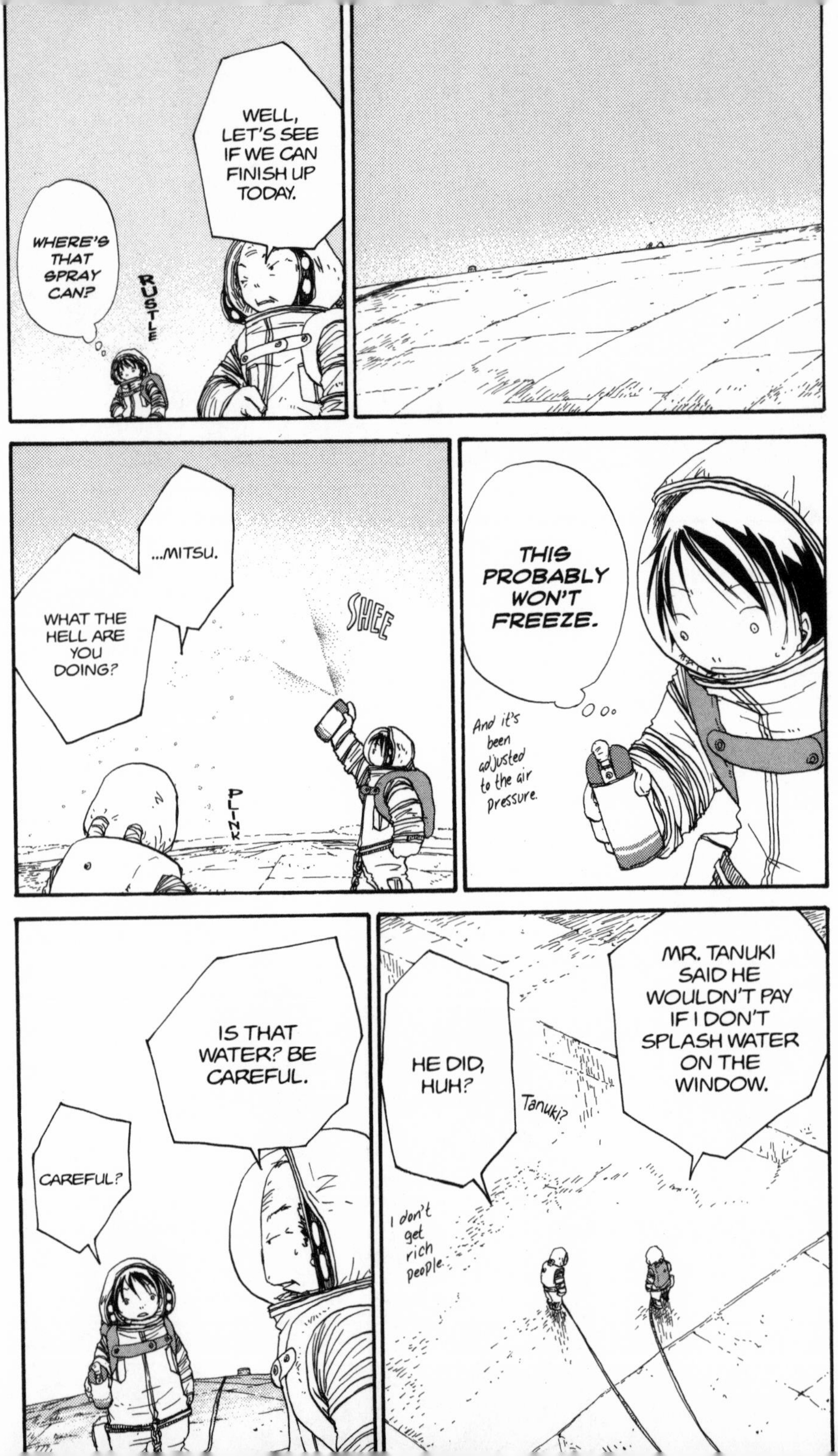
WELL, LET'S SEE IF WE CAN FINISH UP TODAY.
RUSTLE
WHERE'S THAT SPRAY CAN?
THIS PROBABLY WON'T FREEZE.
And it's been adjusted to the air pressure.
SHEE
...MITSU.
WHAT THE HELL ARE YOU DOING?
PLINK
MR. TANUKI SAID HE WOULDN'T PAY IF I DON'T SPLASH WATER ON THE WINDOW.
Tanuki?
HE DID, HUH?
I don't get rich people.
IS THAT WATER? BE CAREFUL.
CAREFUL?

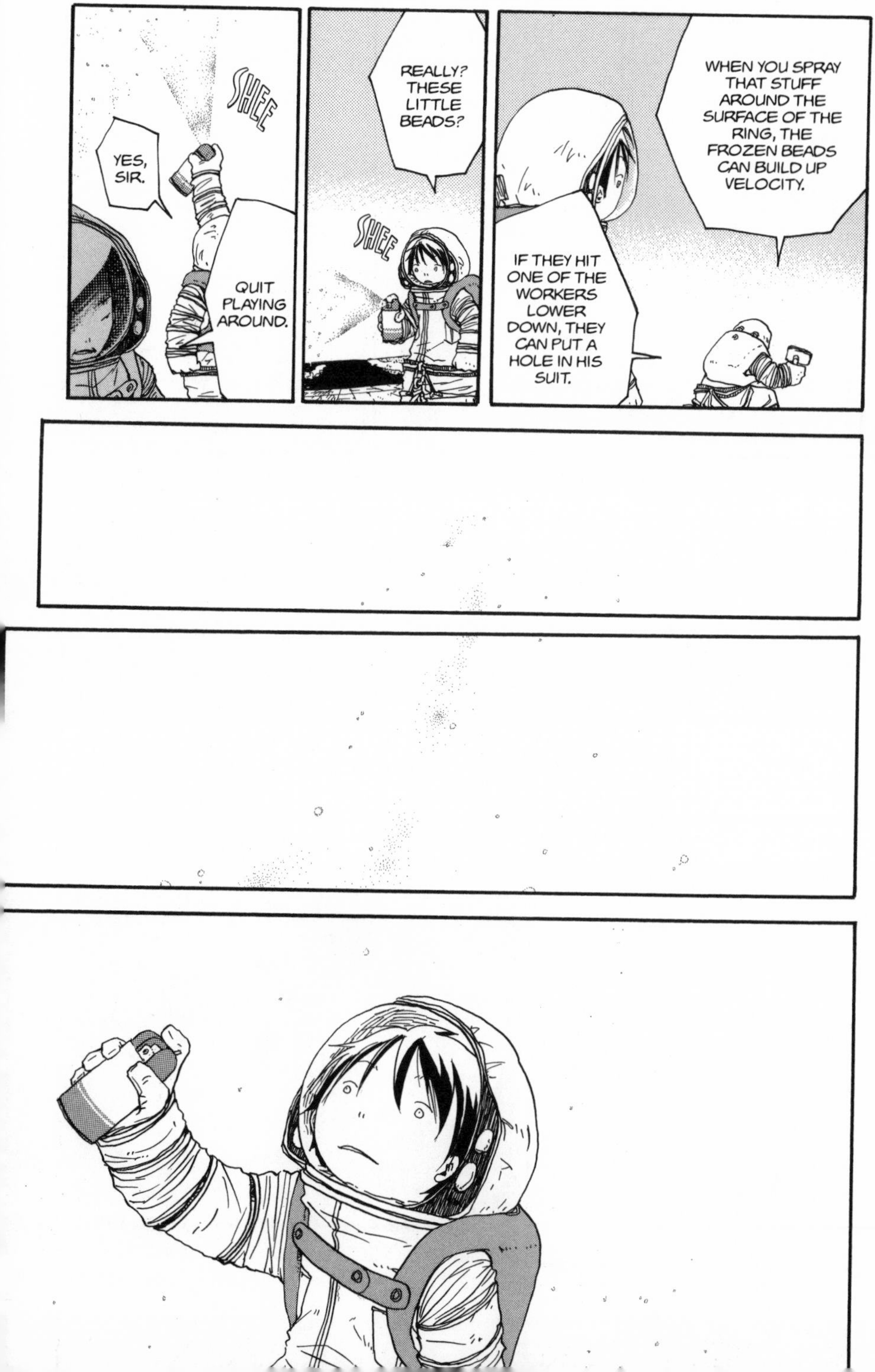
WHEN YOU SPRAY THAT STUFF AROUND THE SURFACE OF THE RING, THE FROZEN BEADS CAN BUILD UP VELOCITY.
IF THEY HIT ONE OF THE WORKERS LOWER DOWN, THEY CAN PUT A HOLE IN HIS SUIT.
REALLY? THESE LITTLE BEADS?
SHEE
SHEE
YES, SIR.
QUIT PLAYING AROUND.

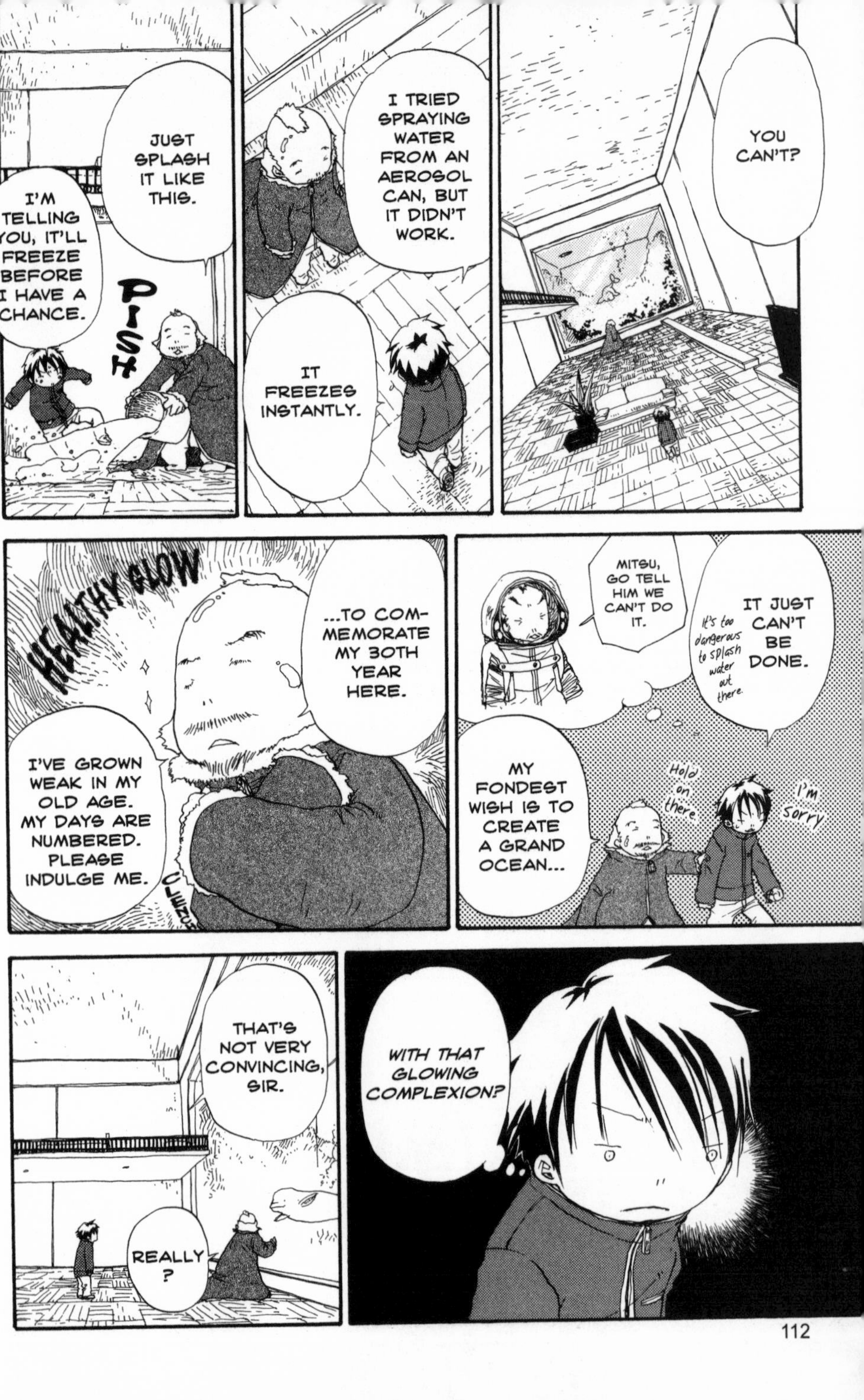
YOU CAN'T?
I TRIED SPRAYING WATER FROM AN AEROSOL CAN, BUT IT DIDN'T WORK.
IT FREEZES INSTANTLY.
JUST SPLASH IT LIKE THIS.
PISH
I'M TELLING YOU, IT'LL FREEZE BEFORE I HAVE A CHANCE.
IT JUST CAN'T BE DONE.
It's too dangerous to splash water out there.
MITSU, GO TELL HIM WE CAN'T DO IT.
I'm Sorry
Hold on there.
MY FONDEST WISH IS TO CREATE A GRAND OCEAN...
HEALTHY GLOW
...TO COMMEMORATE MY 30TH YEAR HERE.
I'VE GROWN WEAK IN MY OLD AGE. MY DAYS ARE NUMBERED. PLEASE INDULGE ME.
CLENCH
WITH THAT GLOWING COMPLEXION?
THAT'S NOT VERY CONVINCING, SIR.
REALLY?

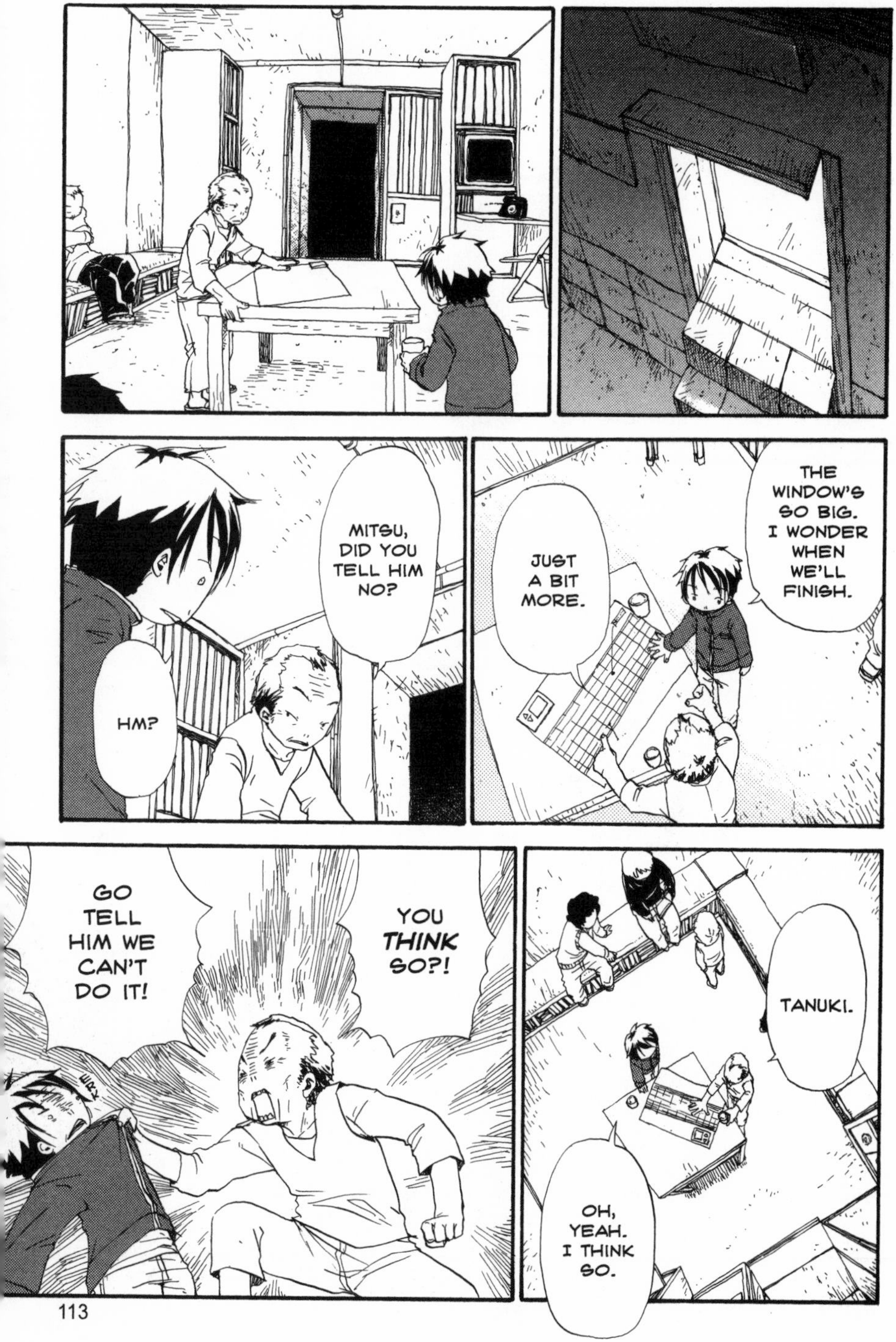
THE WINDOW'S SO BIG. I WONDER WHEN WE'LL FINISH.
JUST A BIT MORE.
MITSU, DID YOU TELL HIM NO?
HM?
TANUKI.
OH, YEAH. I THINK SO.
YOU *THINK* SO?!
GO TELL HIM WE CAN'T DO IT!
ERK

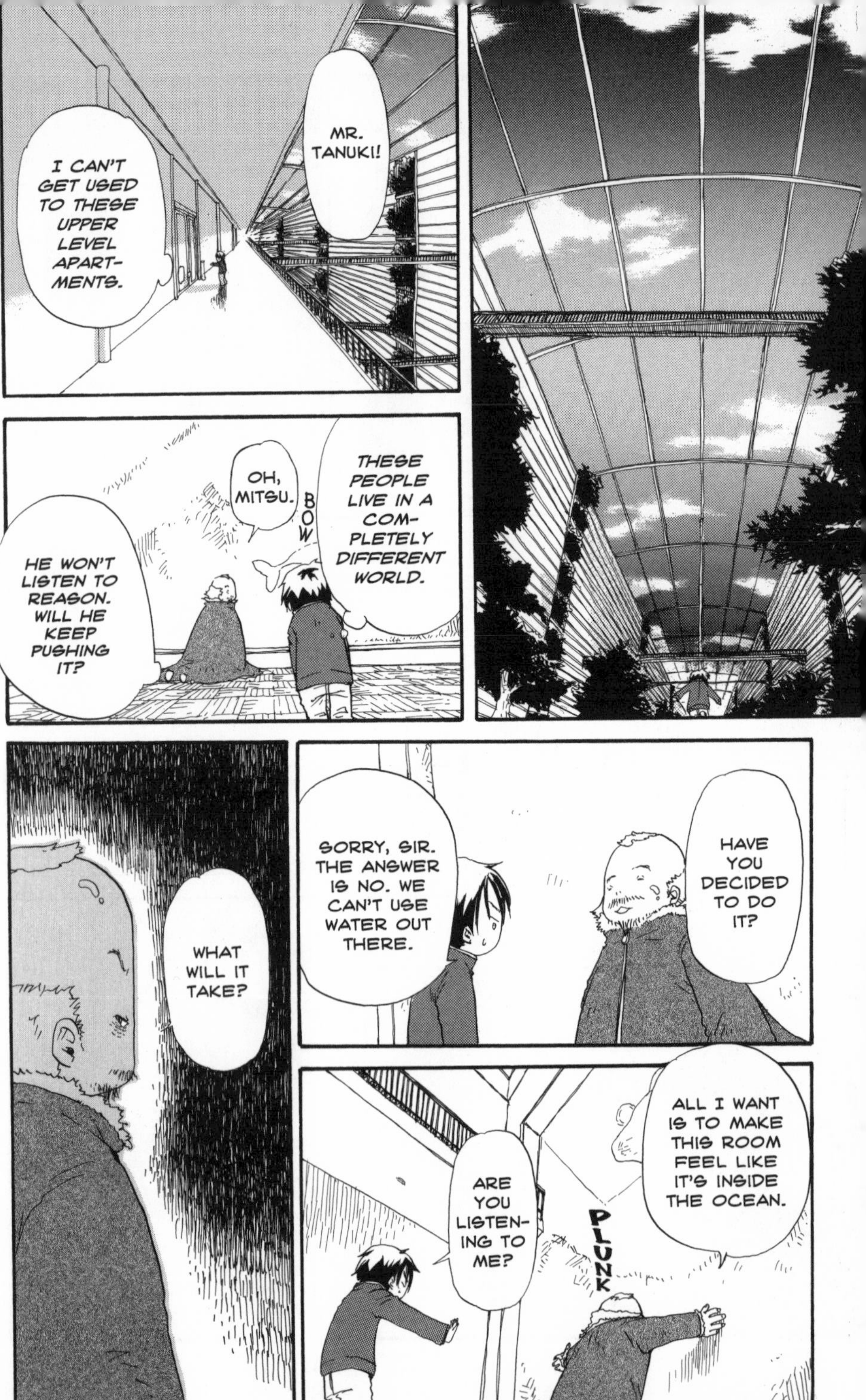
MR. TANUKI!
I CAN'T GET USED TO THESE UPPER LEVEL APART-MENTS.
THESE PEOPLE LIVE IN A COM-PLETELY DIFFERENT WORLD.
BOW
OH, MITSU.
HE WON'T LISTEN TO REASON. WILL HE KEEP PUSHING IT?
HAVE YOU DECIDED TO DO IT?
SORRY, SIR. THE ANSWER IS NO. WE CAN'T USE WATER OUT THERE.
ALL I WANT IS TO MAKE THIS ROOM FEEL LIKE IT'S INSIDE THE OCEAN.
PLUNK
ARE YOU LISTEN-ING TO ME?
WHAT WILL IT TAKE?

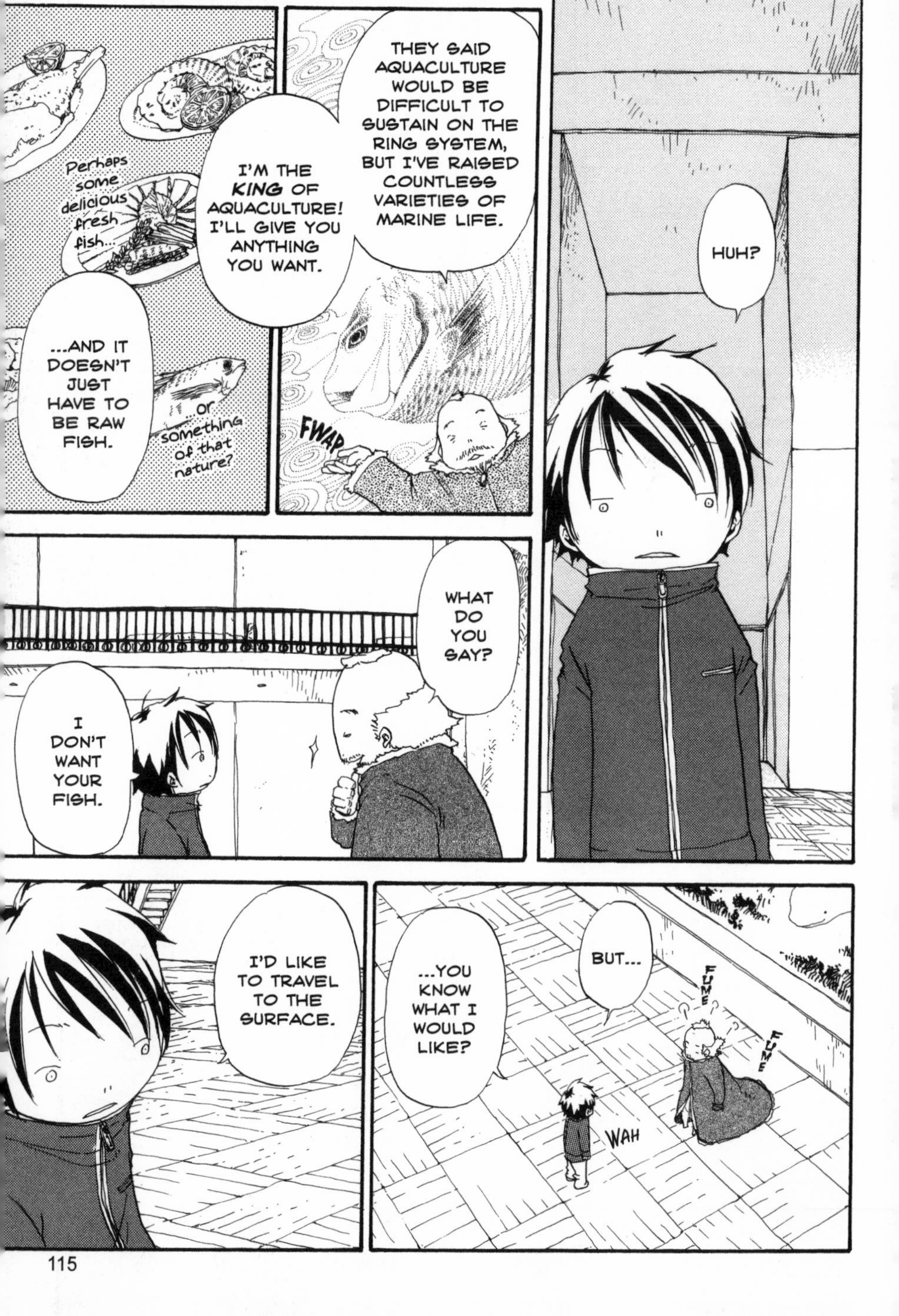
HUH?
THEY SAID AQUACULTURE WOULD BE DIFFICULT TO SUSTAIN ON THE RING SYSTEM, BUT I'VE RAISED COUNTLESS VARIETIES OF MARINE LIFE.
I'M THE KING OF AQUACULTURE! I'LL GIVE YOU ANYTHING YOU WANT.
FWAP
Perhaps some delicious fresh fish...
...or something of that nature?
...AND IT DOESN'T JUST HAVE TO BE RAW FISH.
WHAT DO YOU SAY?
I DON'T WANT YOUR FISH.
BUT...
FUME
FUME
...YOU KNOW WHAT I WOULD LIKE?
WAH
I'D LIKE TO TRAVEL TO THE SURFACE.

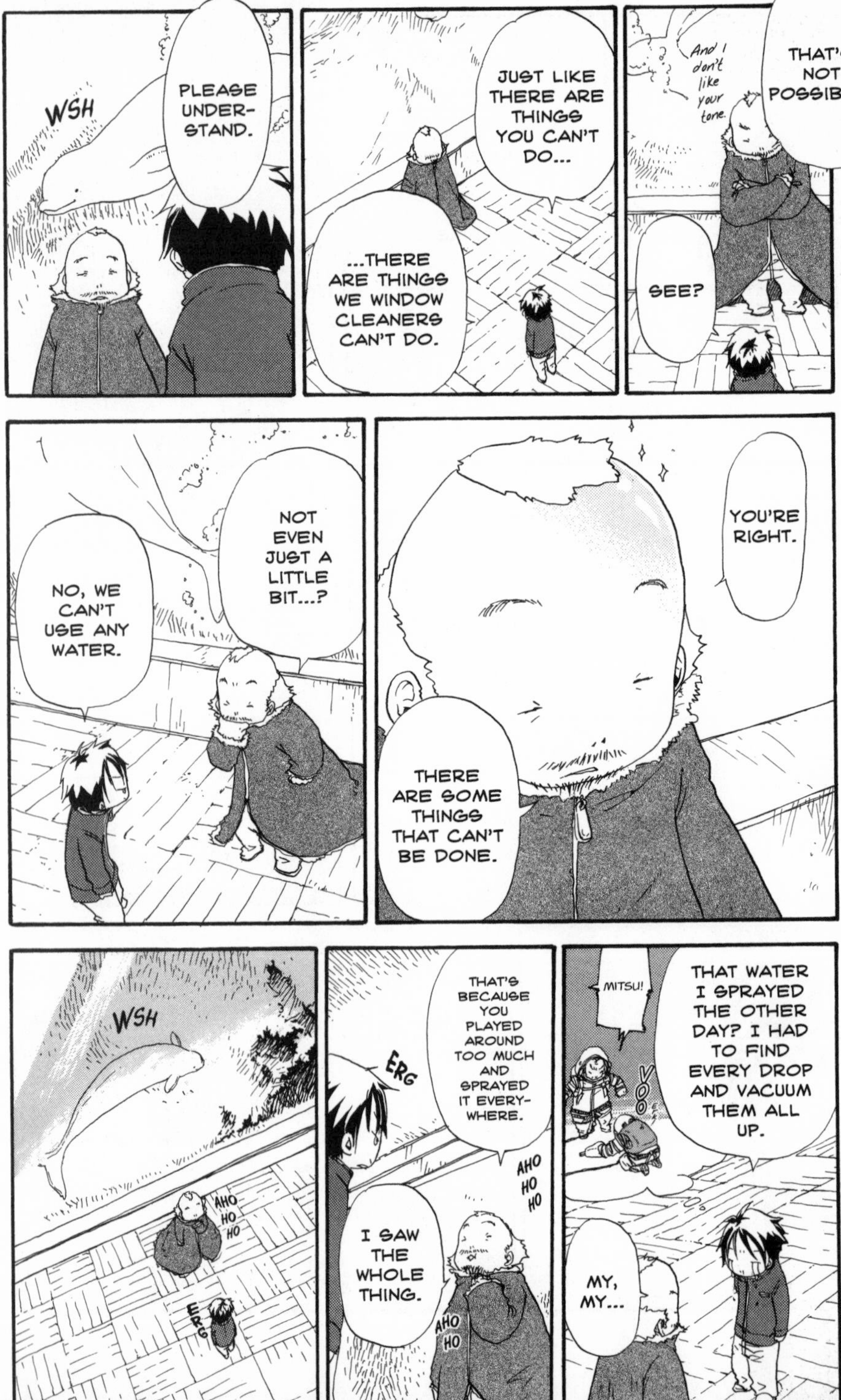
THAT'S NOT POSSIBLE.
And I don't like your tone.
SEE?
JUST LIKE THERE ARE THINGS YOU CAN'T DO...
...THERE ARE THINGS WE WINDOW CLEANERS CAN'T DO.
PLEASE UNDER-STAND.
WSH
YOU'RE RIGHT.
THERE ARE SOME THINGS THAT CAN'T BE DONE.
NOT EVEN JUST A LITTLE BIT...?
NO, WE CAN'T USE ANY WATER.
THAT WATER I SPRAYED THE OTHER DAY? I HAD TO FIND EVERY DROP AND VACUUM THEM ALL UP.
MITSU!
VOO
MY, MY...
THAT'S BECAUSE YOU PLAYED AROUND TOO MUCH AND SPRAYED IT EVERY-WHERE.
ERG
AHO HO HO
I SAW THE WHOLE THING.
AHO HO
WSH
AHO HO HO
ERG

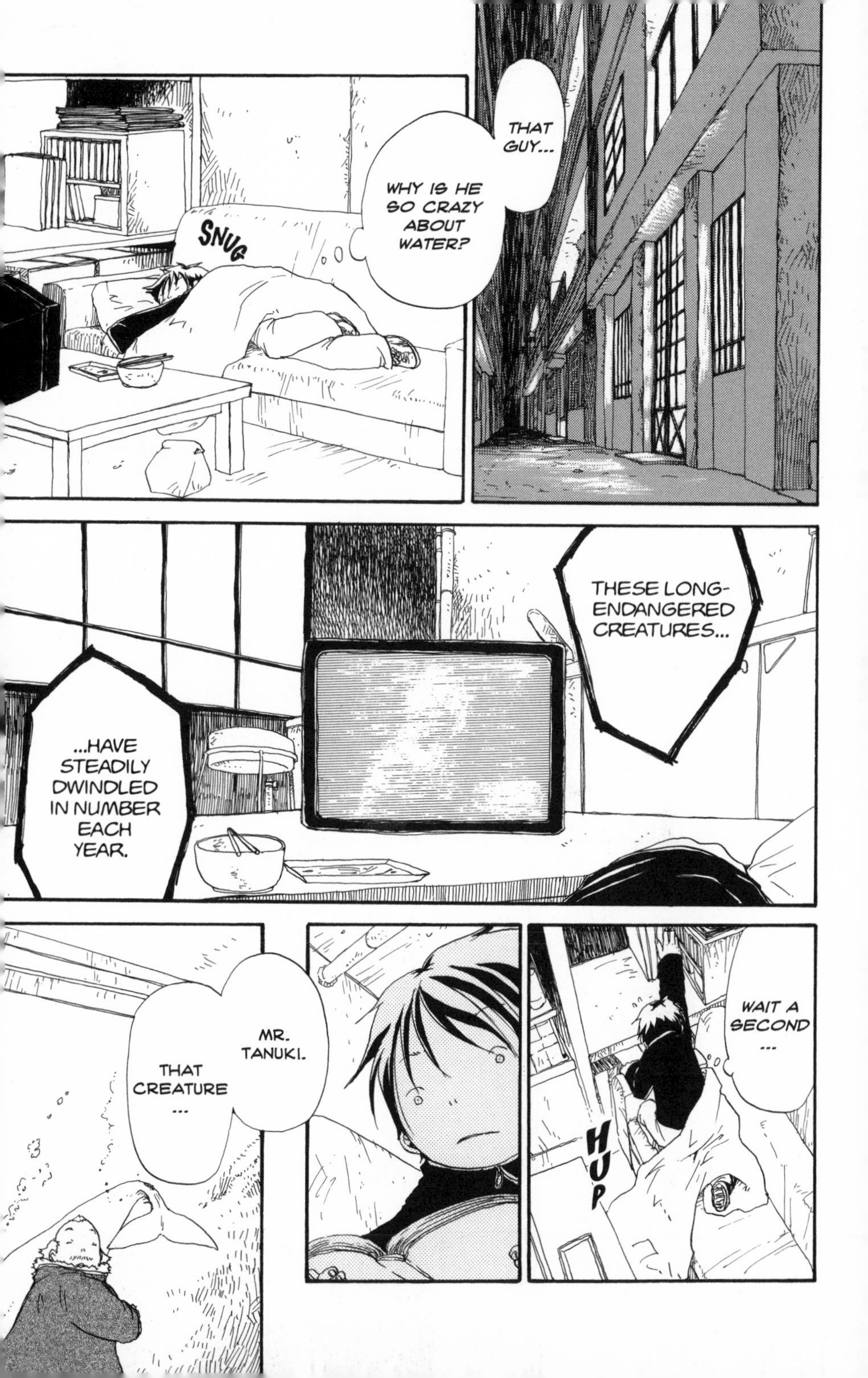
THAT GUY...
WHY IS HE SO CRAZY ABOUT WATER?
SNUG
THESE LONG-ENDANGERED CREATURES...
...HAVE STEADILY DWINDLED IN NUMBER EACH YEAR.
WAIT A SECOND ...
HUP
MR. TANUKI.
THAT CREATURE ...

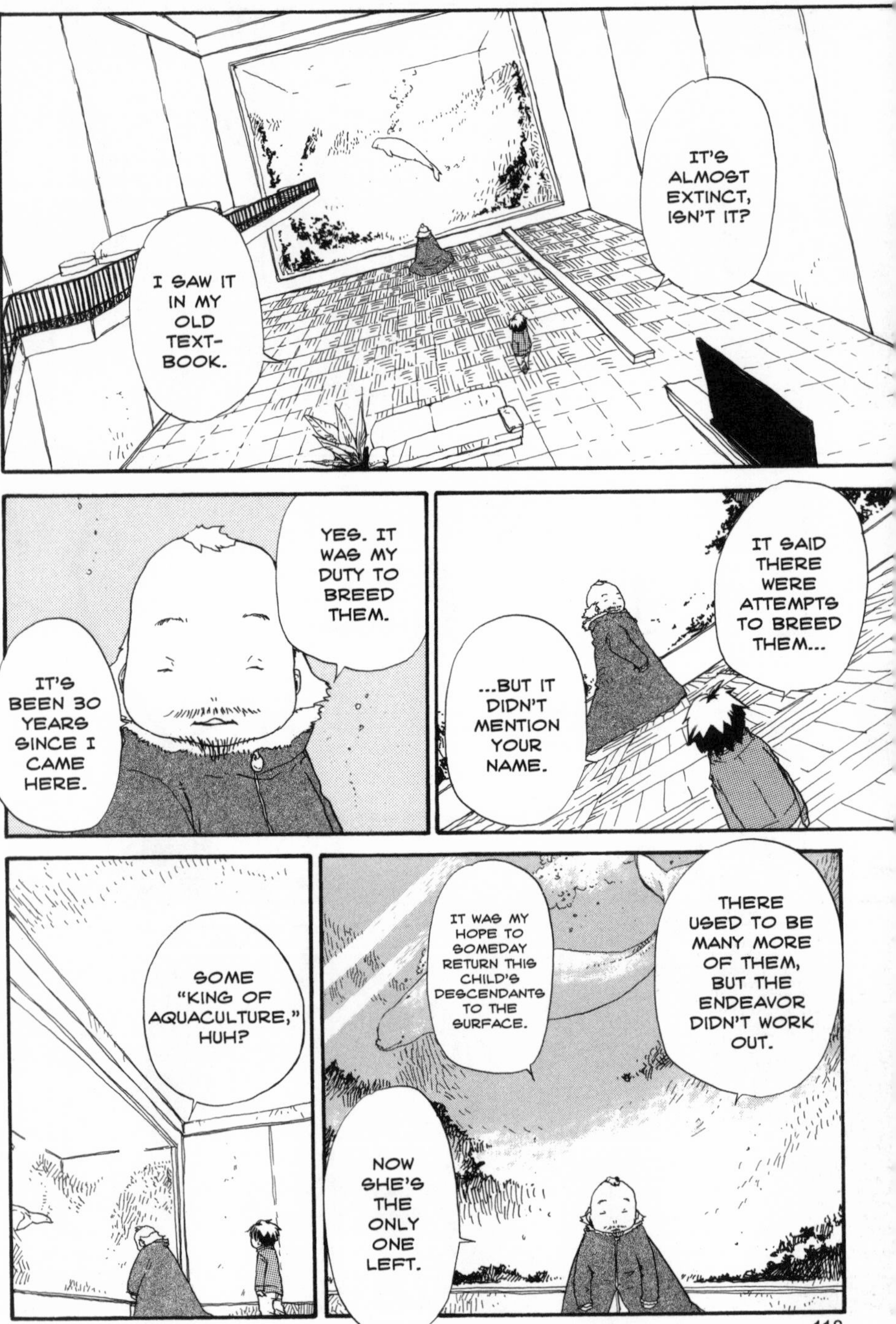
IT'S ALMOST EXTINCT, ISN'T IT?
I SAW IT IN MY OLD TEXT-BOOK.
IT SAID THERE WERE ATTEMPTS TO BREED THEM...
...BUT IT DIDN'T MENTION YOUR NAME.
YES. IT WAS MY DUTY TO BREED THEM.
IT'S BEEN 30 YEARS SINCE I CAME HERE.
THERE USED TO BE MANY MORE OF THEM, BUT THE ENDEAVOR DIDN'T WORK OUT.
IT WAS MY HOPE TO SOMEDAY RETURN THIS CHILD'S DESCENDANTS TO THE SURFACE.
NOW SHE'S THE ONLY ONE LEFT.
SOME "KING OF AQUACULTURE," HUH?

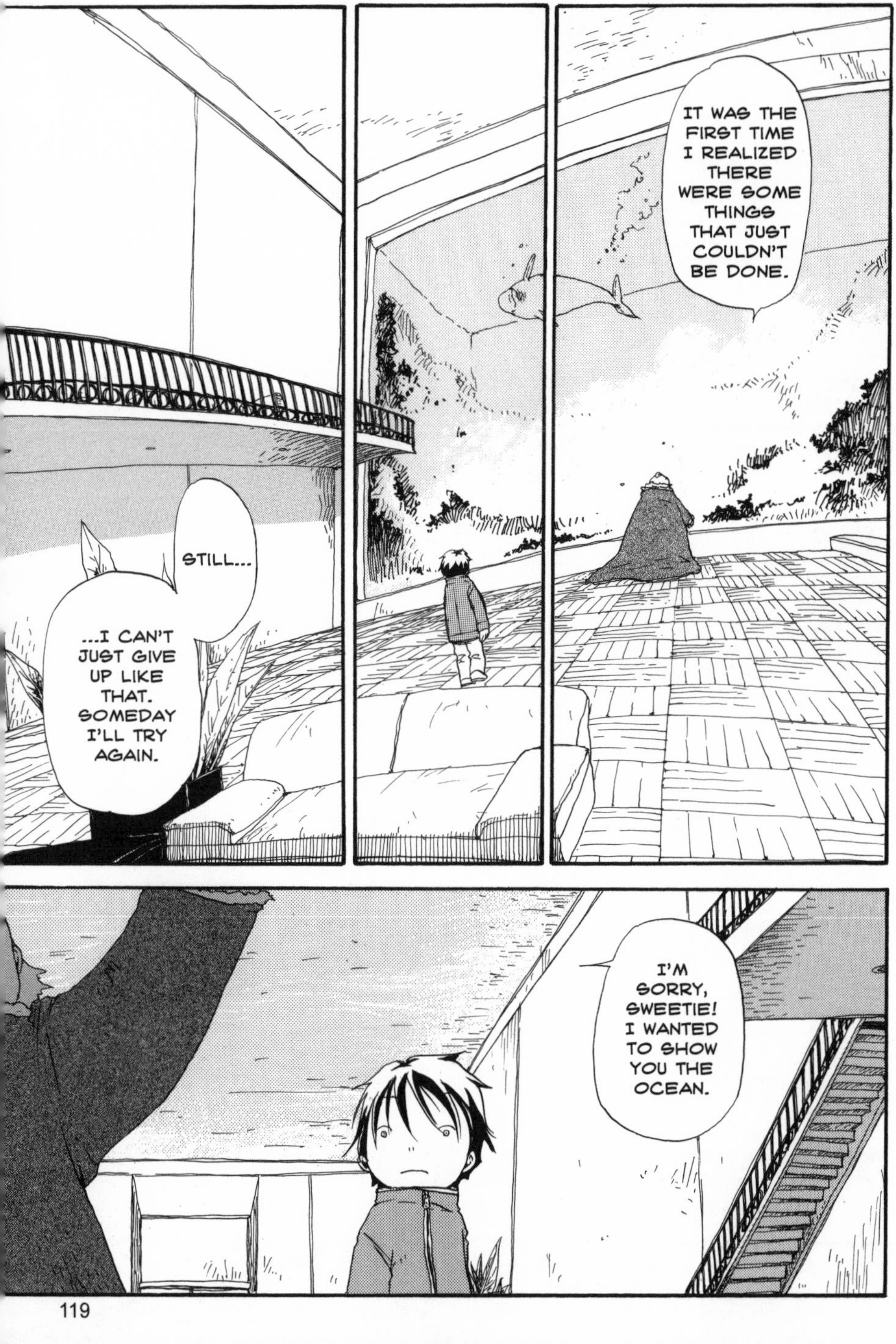
IT WAS THE FIRST TIME I REALIZED THERE WERE SOME THINGS THAT JUST COULDN'T BE DONE.
STILL...
...I CAN'T JUST GIVE UP LIKE THAT. SOMEDAY I'LL TRY AGAIN.
I'M SORRY, SWEETIE! I WANTED TO SHOW YOU THE OCEAN.

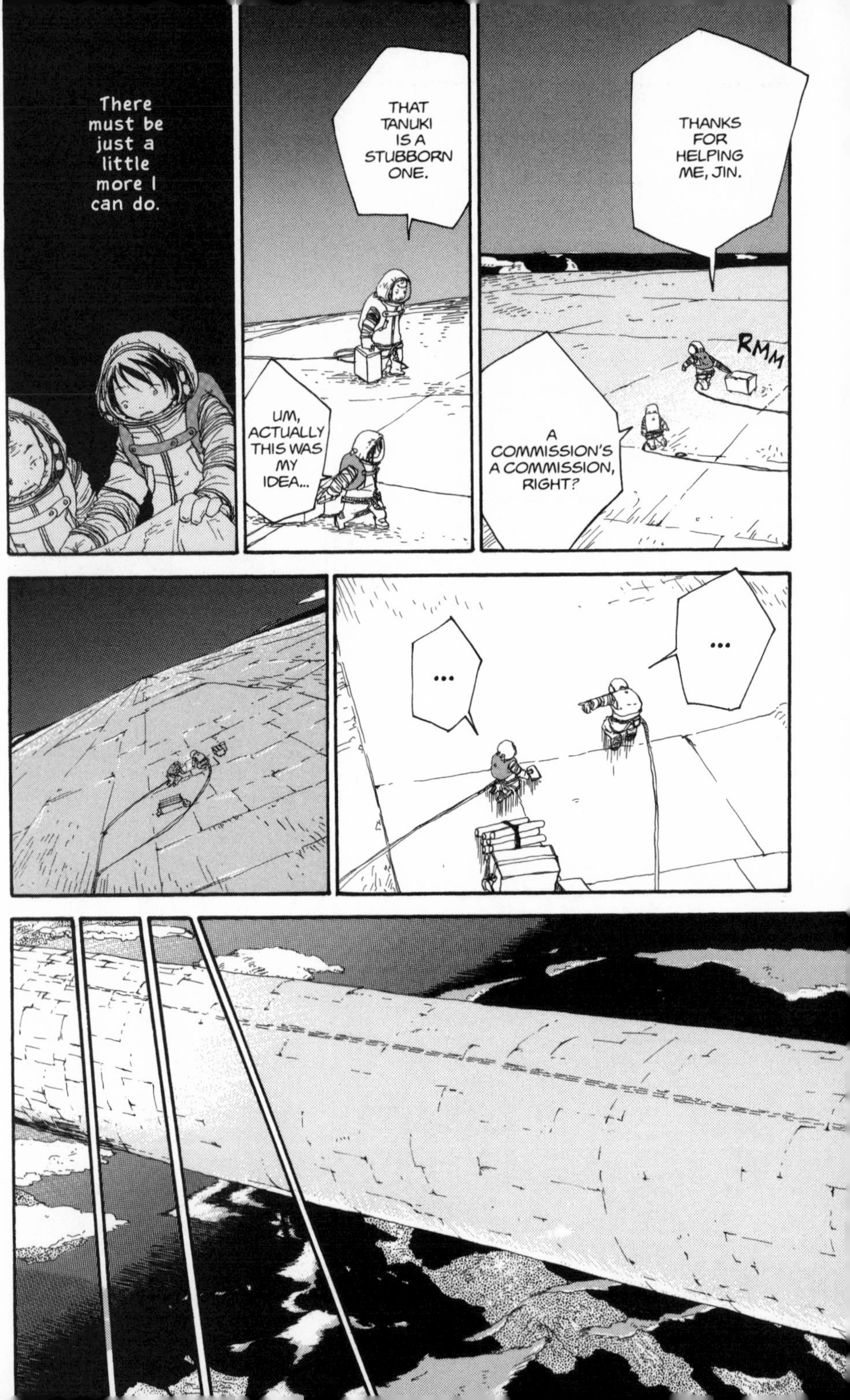
THANKS FOR HELPING ME, JIN.
RMM
A COMMISSION'S A COMMISSION, RIGHT?
THAT TANUKI IS A STUBBORN ONE.
UM, ACTUALLY THIS WAS MY IDEA...
There must be just a little more I can do.
...
...

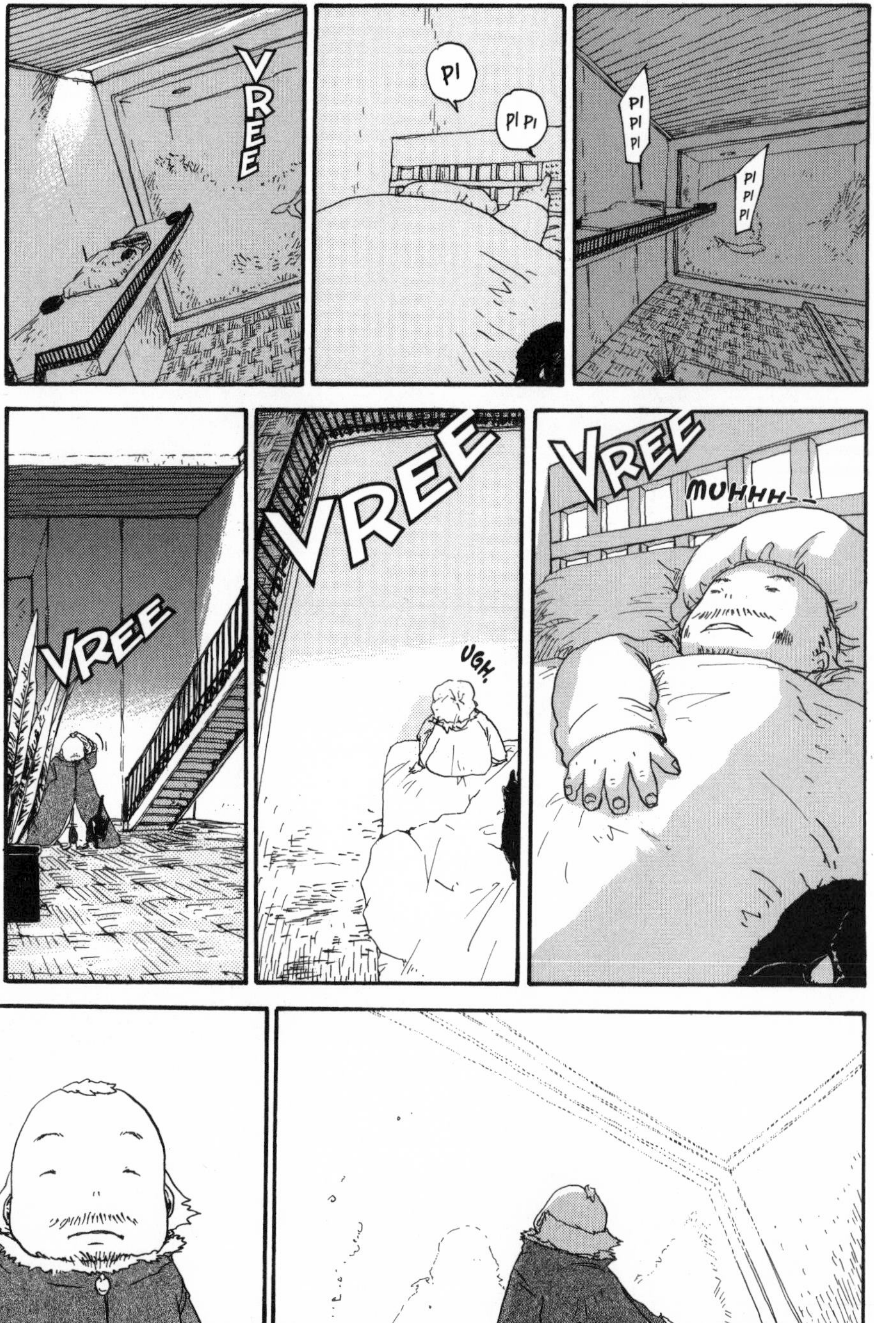
PI PI PI
PI PI PI
PI
PI PI
VREE
VREE
MUHHH...
VREE
UGH.
VREE

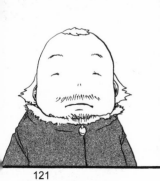

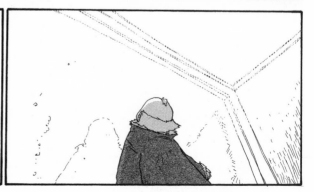

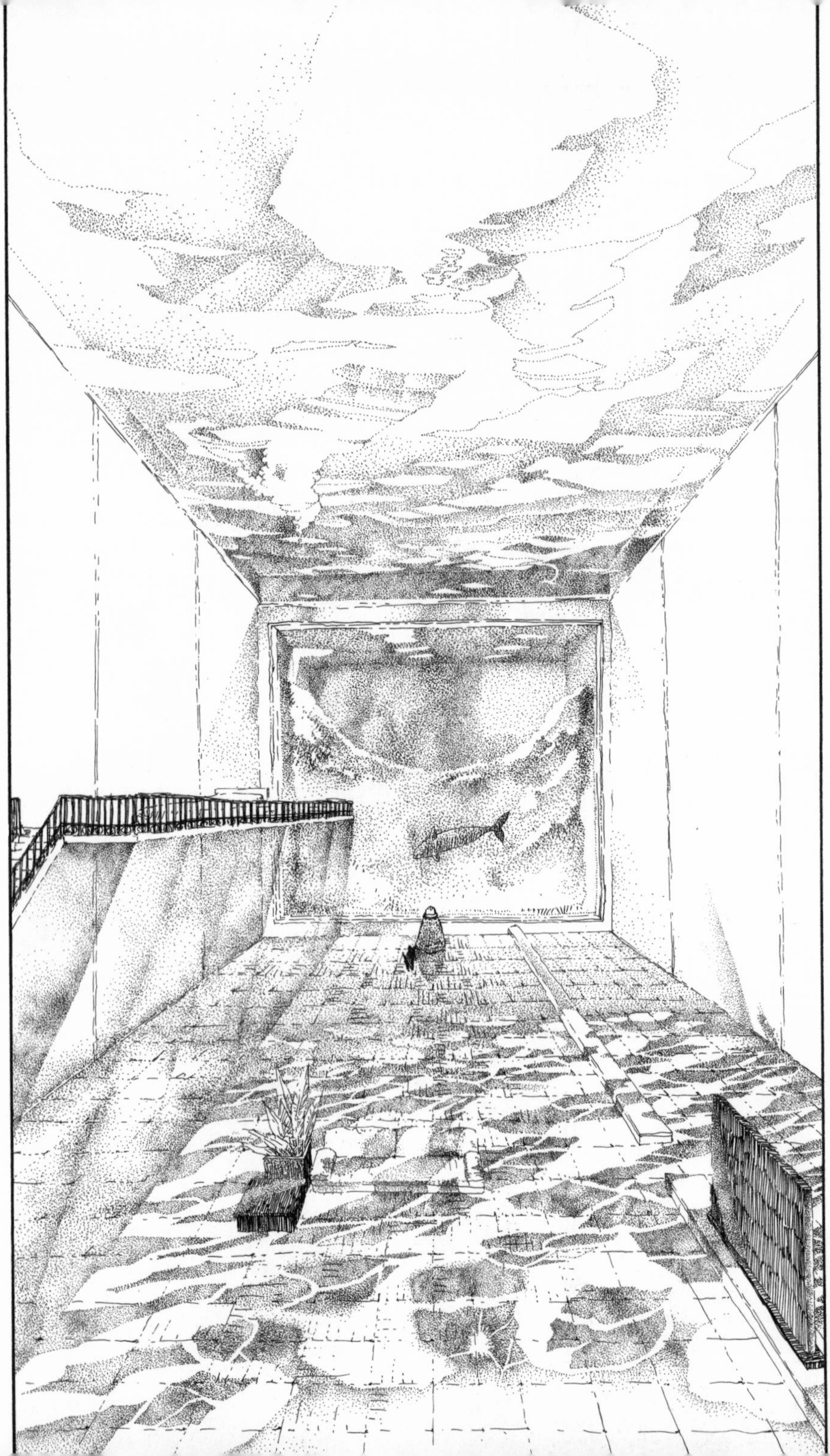

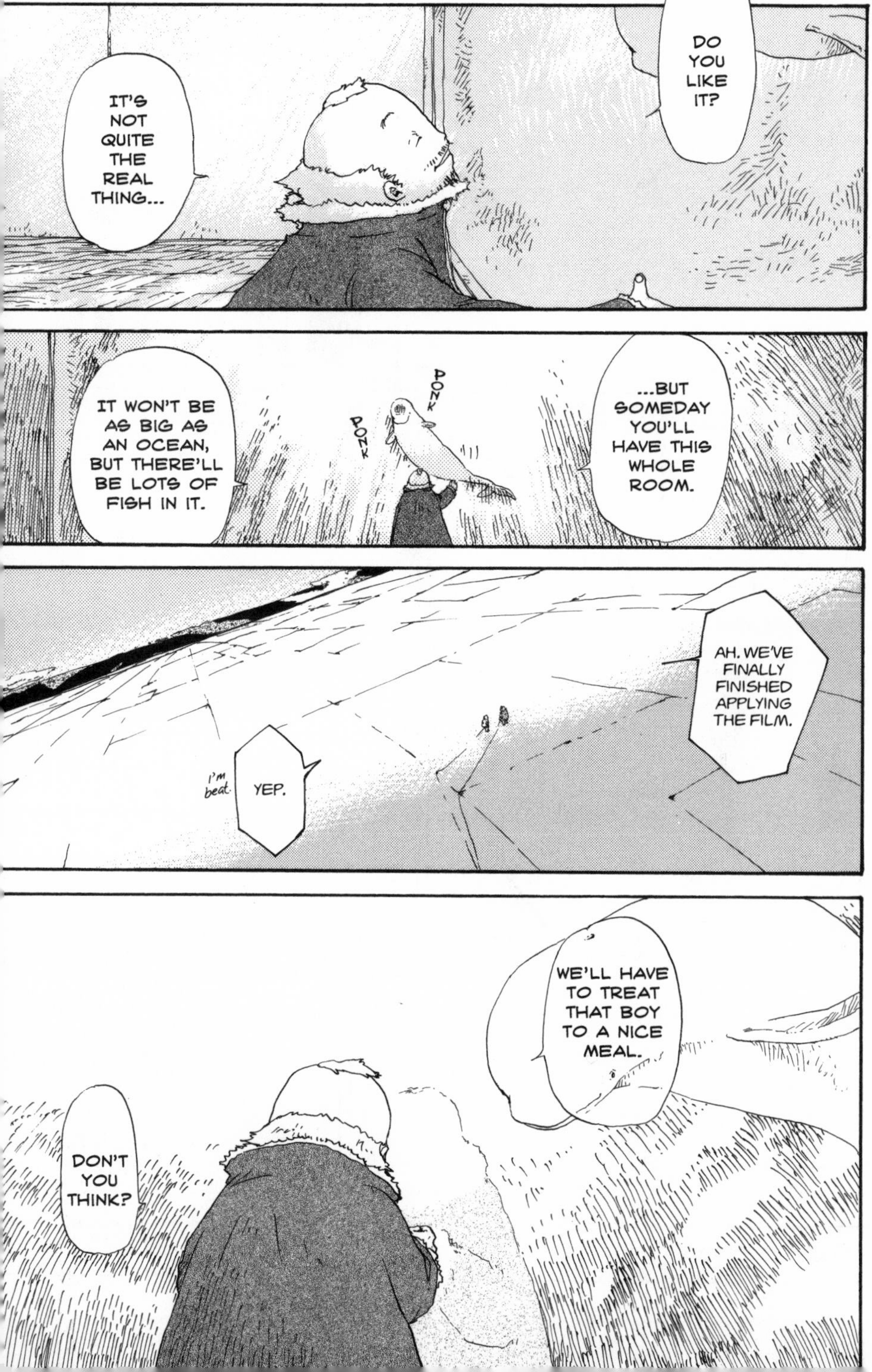
DO YOU LIKE IT?
IT'S NOT QUITE THE REAL THING...
...BUT SOMEDAY YOU'LL HAVE THIS WHOLE ROOM.
PONK
PONK
IT WON'T BE AS BIG AS AN OCEAN, BUT THERE'LL BE LOTS OF FISH IN IT.
AH. WE'VE FINALLY FINISHED APPLYING THE FILM.
YEP.
I'm beat.
WE'LL HAVE TO TREAT THAT BOY TO A NICE MEAL.
DON'T YOU THINK?

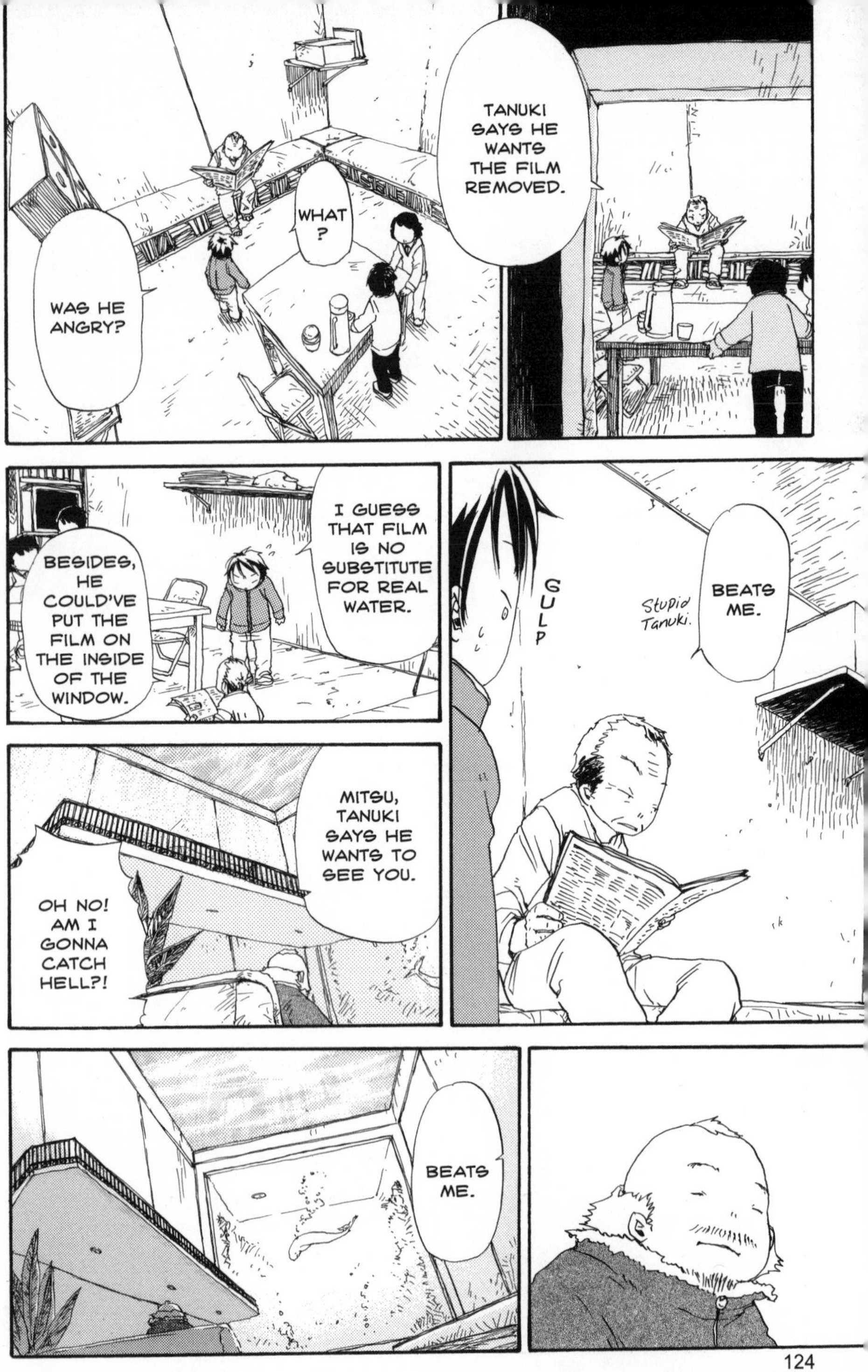
TANUKI SAYS HE WANTS THE FILM REMOVED.
WHAT?
WAS HE ANGRY?
BEATS ME.
Stupid Tanuki.
GULP
I GUESS THAT FILM IS NO SUBSTITUTE FOR REAL WATER.
BESIDES, HE COULD'VE PUT THE FILM ON THE INSIDE OF THE WINDOW.
MITSU, TANUKI SAYS HE WANTS TO SEE YOU.
OH NO! AM I GONNA CATCH HELL?!
BEATS ME.

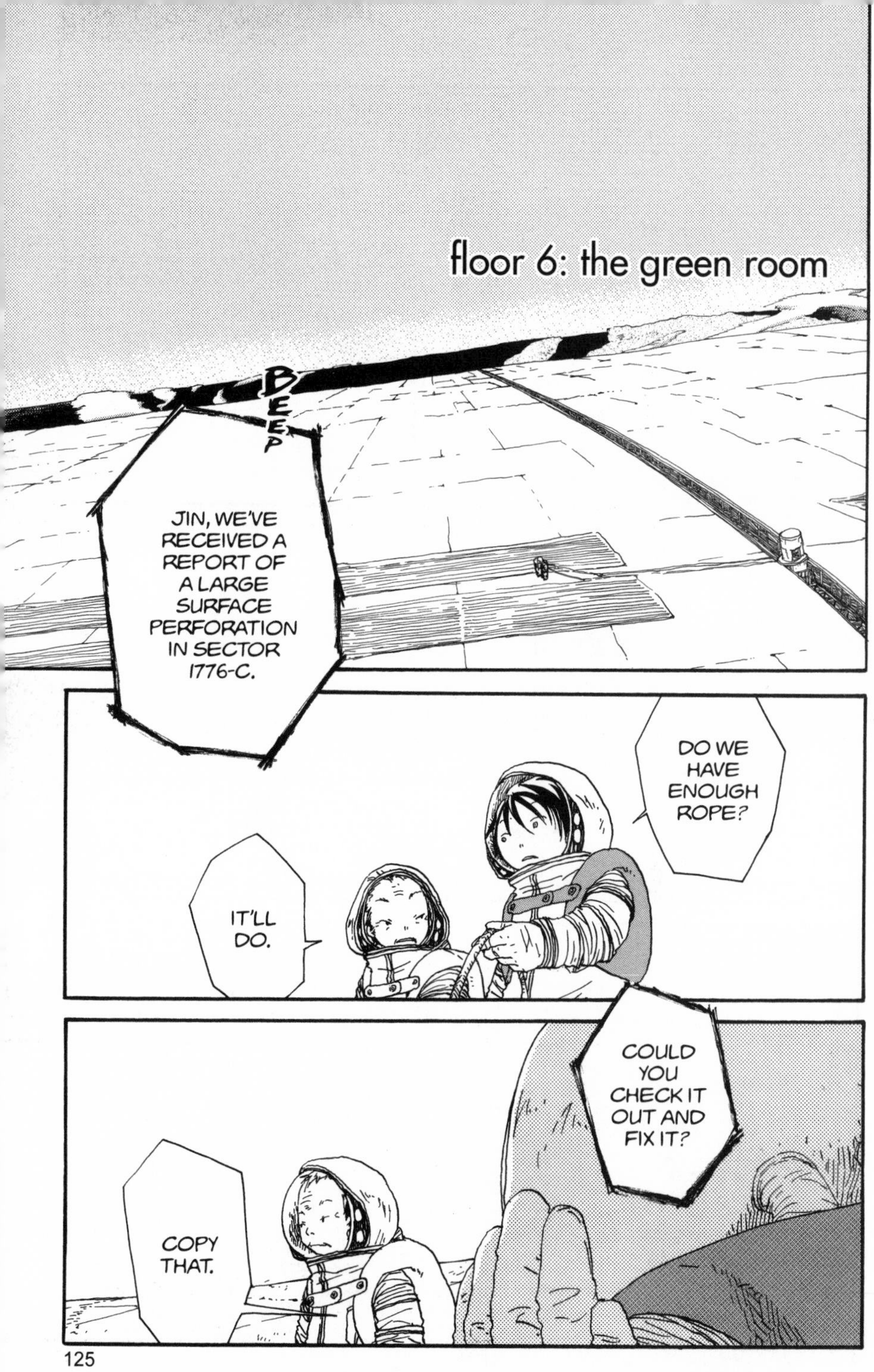
floor 6: the green room
BEEP
JIN, WE'VE RECEIVED A REPORT OF A LARGE SURFACE PERFORATION IN SECTOR 1776-C.
DO WE HAVE ENOUGH ROPE?
IT'LL DO.
COULD YOU CHECK IT OUT AND FIX IT?
COPY THAT.

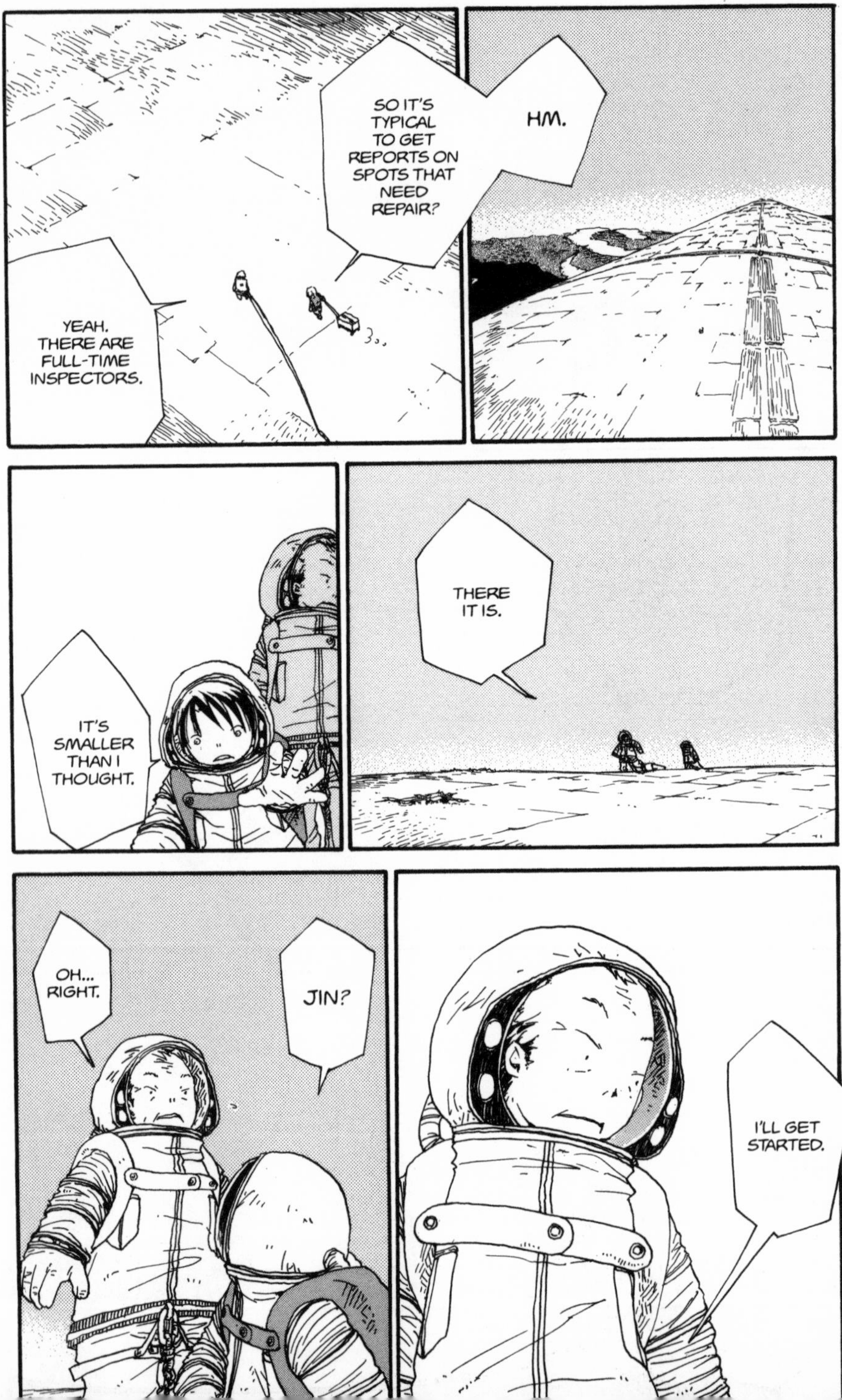
HM.
SO IT'S TYPICAL TO GET REPORTS ON SPOTS THAT NEED REPAIR?
YEAH. THERE ARE FULL-TIME INSPECTORS.
THERE IT IS.
IT'S SMALLER THAN I THOUGHT.
I'LL GET STARTED.
JIN?
OH... RIGHT.

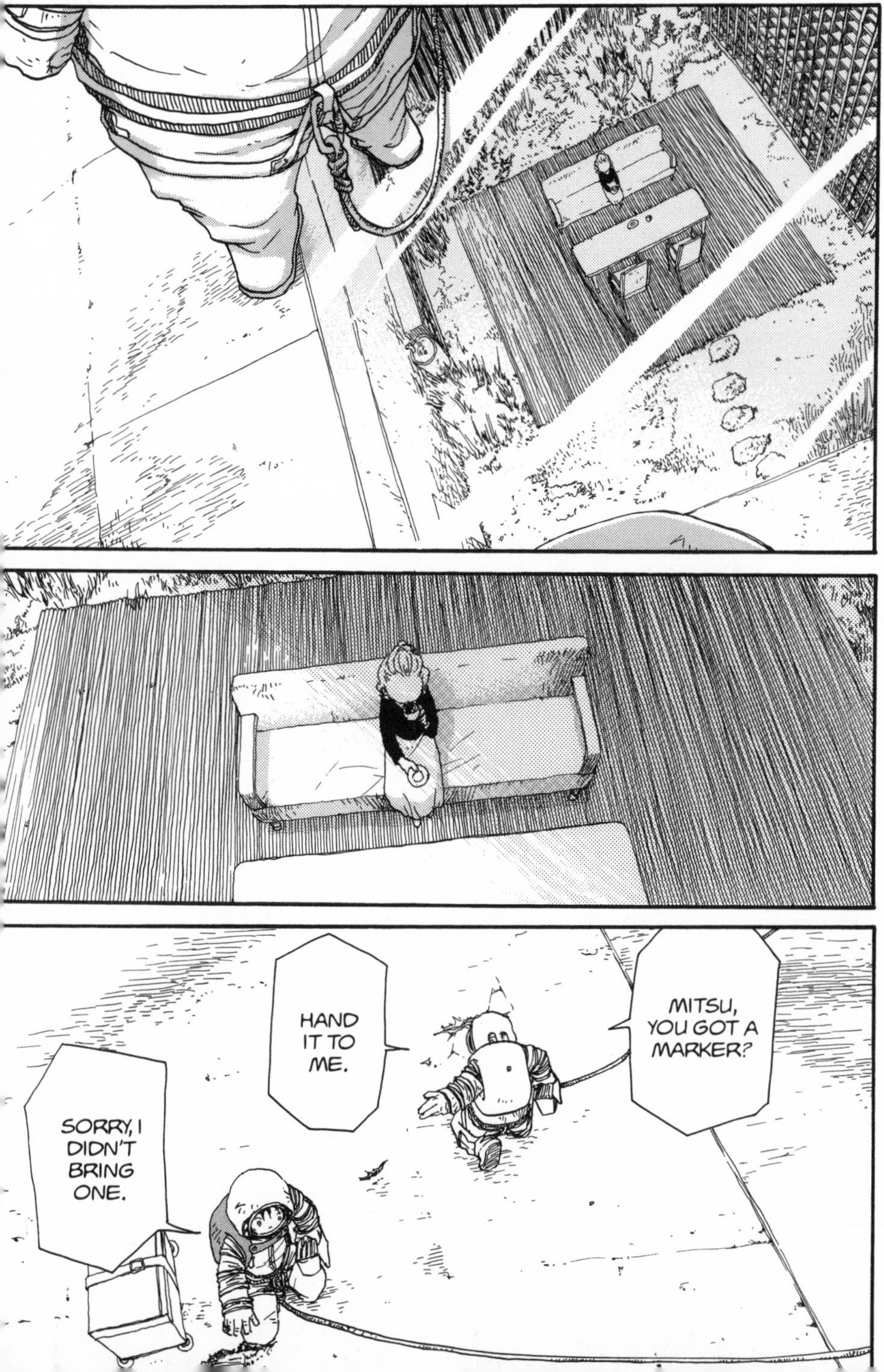
MITSU, YOU GOT A MARKER?
HAND IT TO ME.
SORRY, I DIDN'T BRING ONE.

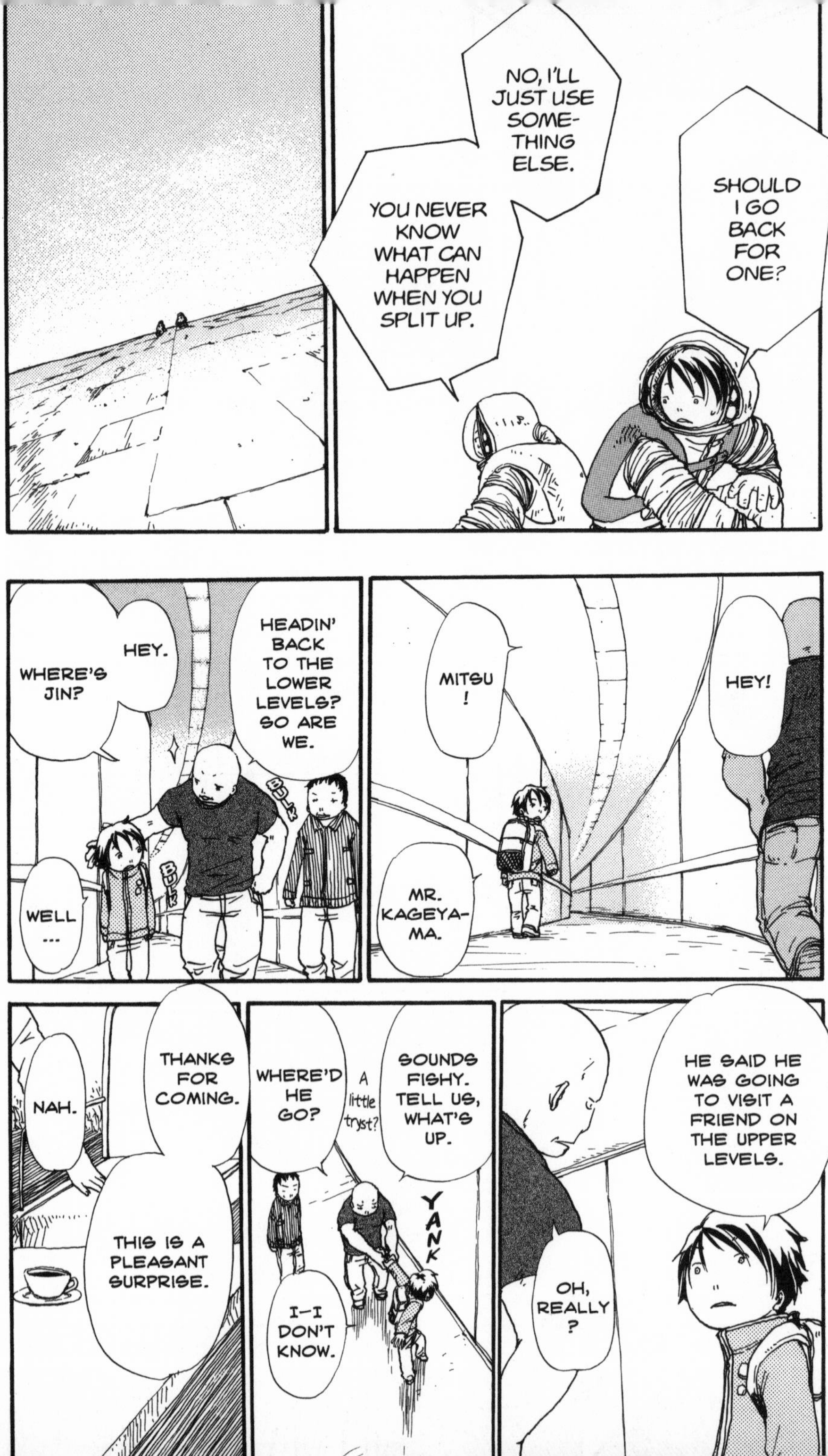
SHOULD I GO BACK FOR ONE?
NO, I'LL JUST USE SOME-THING ELSE.
YOU NEVER KNOW WHAT CAN HAPPEN WHEN YOU SPLIT UP.
HEY!
MITSU!
MR. KAGEYA-MA.
HEADIN' BACK TO THE LOWER LEVELS? SO ARE WE.
HEY. WHERE'S JIN?
BULK
WELL...
HE SAID HE WAS GOING TO VISIT A FRIEND ON THE UPPER LEVELS.
OH, REALLY?
SOUNDS FISHY. TELL US, WHAT'S UP.
A little tryst?
WHERE'D HE GO?
YANK
I-I DON'T KNOW.
THANKS FOR COMING.
NAH.
THIS IS A PLEASANT SURPRISE.

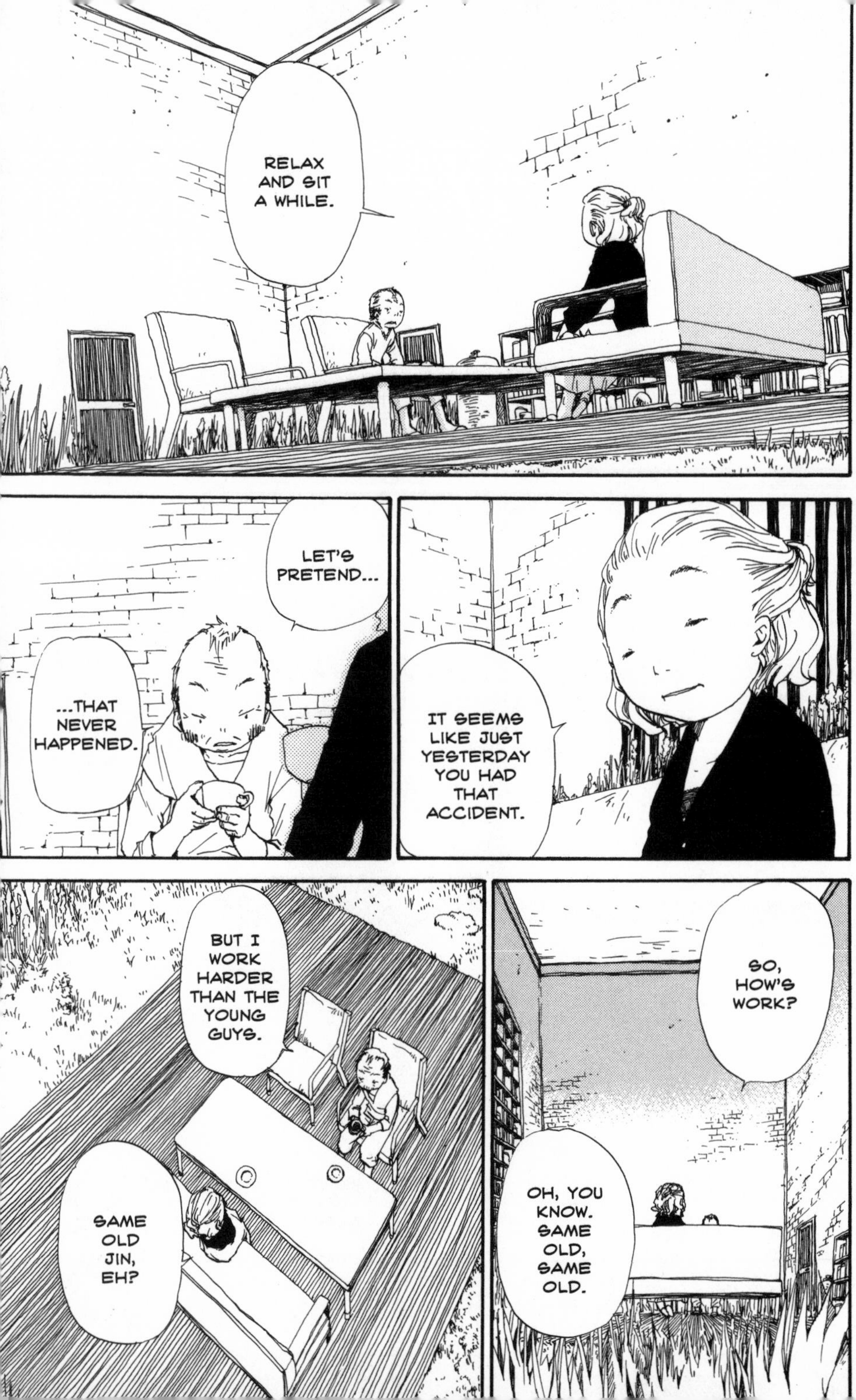
RELAX AND SIT A WHILE.
IT SEEMS LIKE JUST YESTERDAY YOU HAD THAT ACCIDENT.
LET'S PRETEND...
...THAT NEVER HAPPENED.
SO, HOW'S WORK?
OH, YOU KNOW. SAME OLD, SAME OLD.
BUT I WORK HARDER THAN THE YOUNG GUYS.
SAME OLD JIN, EH?

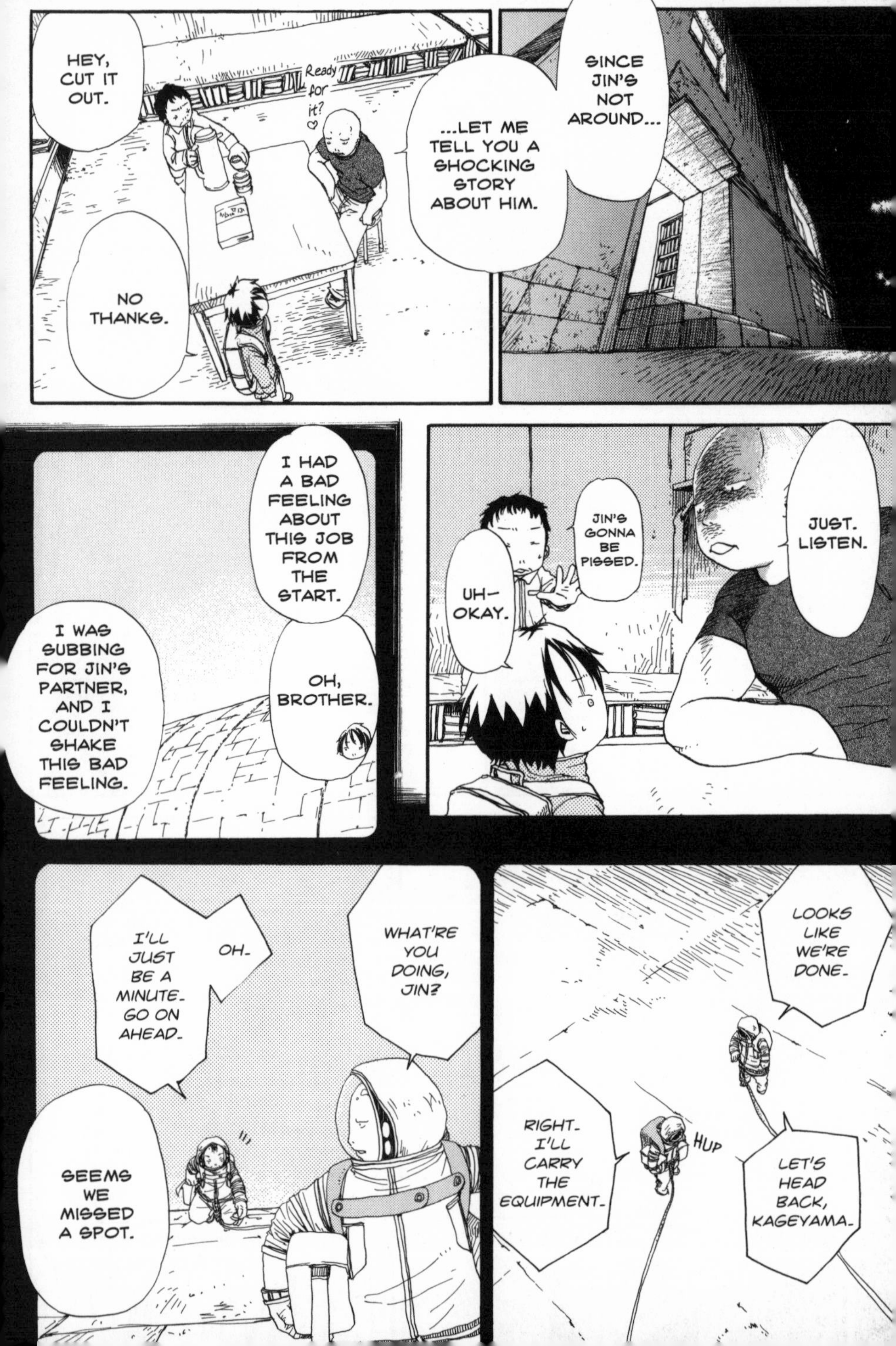
SINCE JIN'S NOT AROUND...
...LET ME TELL YOU A SHOCKING STORY ABOUT HIM.
Ready for it? ♡
HEY, CUT IT OUT.
NO THANKS.
JUST. LISTEN.
JIN'S GONNA BE PISSED.
UH— OKAY.
I HAD A BAD FEELING ABOUT THIS JOB FROM THE START.
OH, BROTHER.
I WAS SUBBING FOR JIN'S PARTNER, AND I COULDN'T SHAKE THIS BAD FEELING.
LOOKS LIKE WE'RE DONE.
LET'S HEAD BACK, KAGEYAMA.
HUP
RIGHT. I'LL CARRY THE EQUIPMENT.
WHAT'RE YOU DOING, JIN?
OH.
I'LL JUST BE A MINUTE. GO ON AHEAD.
SEEMS WE MISSED A SPOT.

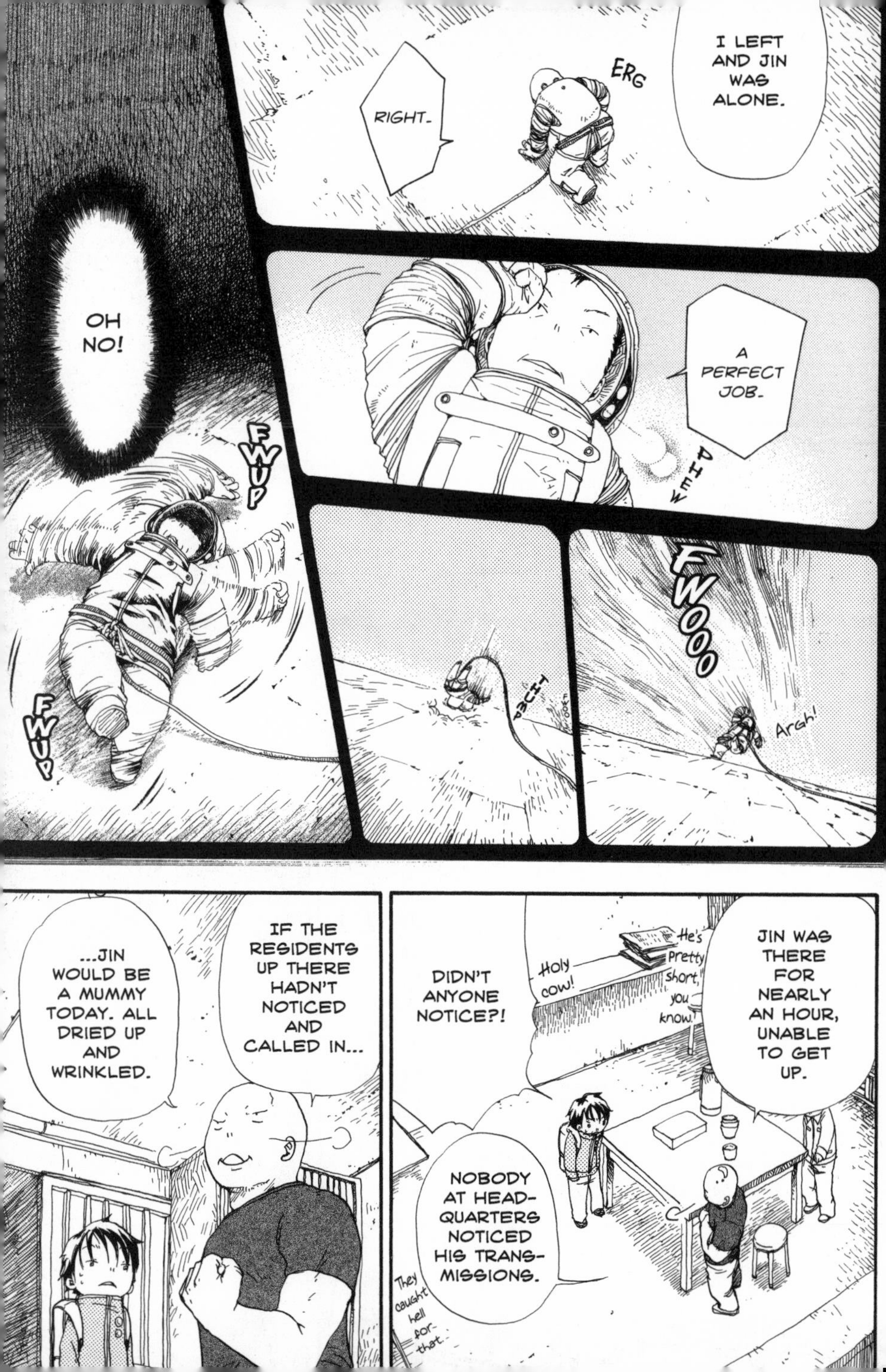
I LEFT AND JIN WAS ALONE.
ERG
RIGHT.
A PERFECT JOB.
PHEW
FWOOO
Argh!
OH NO!
FWUP
FWUP
JIN WAS THERE FOR NEARLY AN HOUR, UNABLE TO GET UP.
He's pretty short, you know.
Holy cow!
DIDN'T ANYONE NOTICE?!
NOBODY AT HEAD-QUARTERS NOTICED HIS TRANS-MISSIONS.
They caught hell for that.
IF THE RESIDENTS UP THERE HADN'T NOTICED AND CALLED IN...
...JIN WOULD BE A MUMMY TODAY. ALL DRIED UP AND WRINKLED.

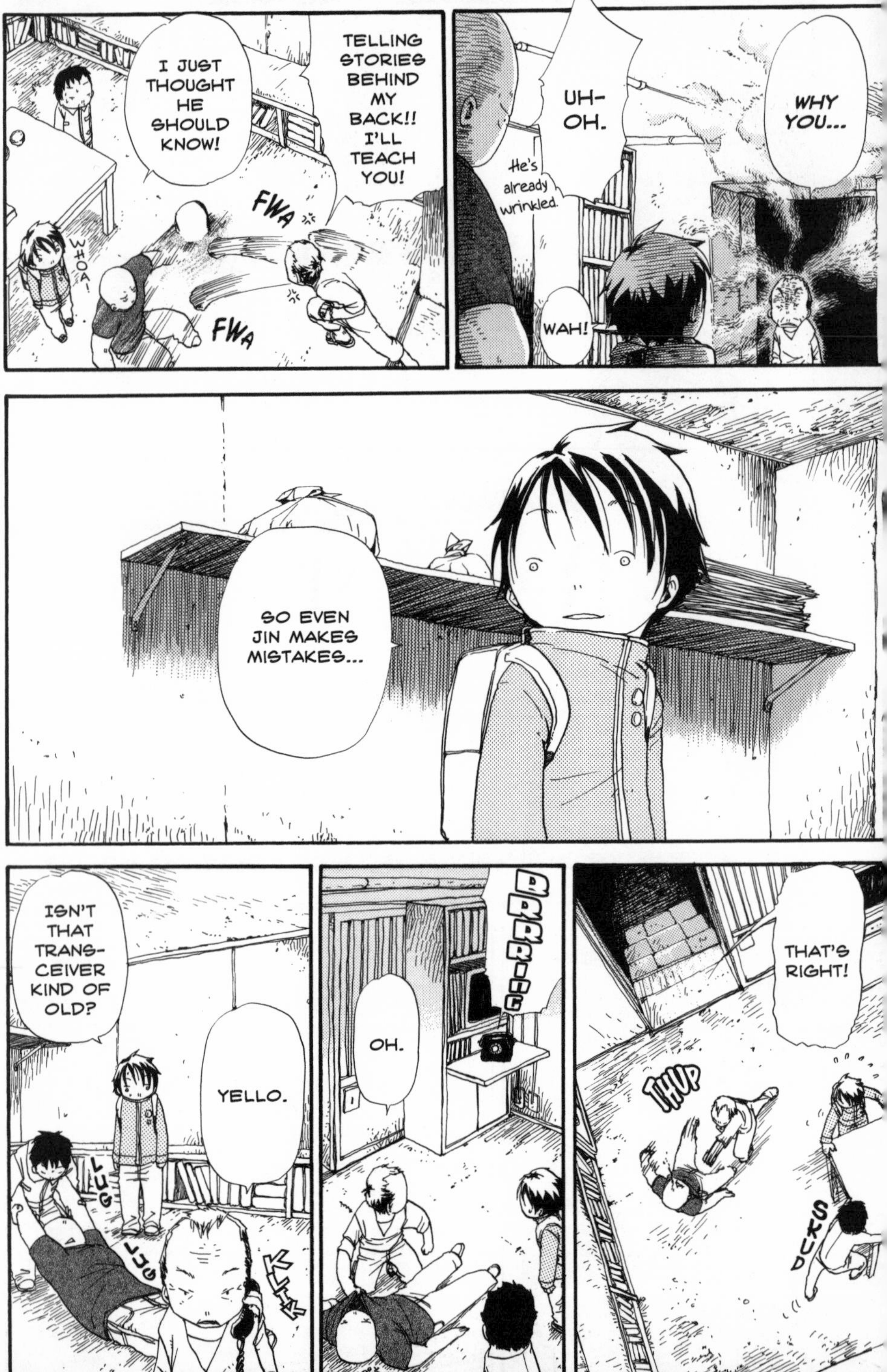
WHY YOU...
UH-OH.
He's already wrinkled.
WAH!
TELLING STORIES BEHIND MY BACK!! I'LL TEACH YOU!
I JUST THOUGHT HE SHOULD KNOW!
FWA
WHOA!
FWA
SO EVEN JIN MAKES MISTAKES...
THAT'S RIGHT!
THUP
SKUD
BRRRING
OH.
ISN'T THAT TRANS-CEIVER KIND OF OLD?
YELLO.
LUG
LUG
KLIK

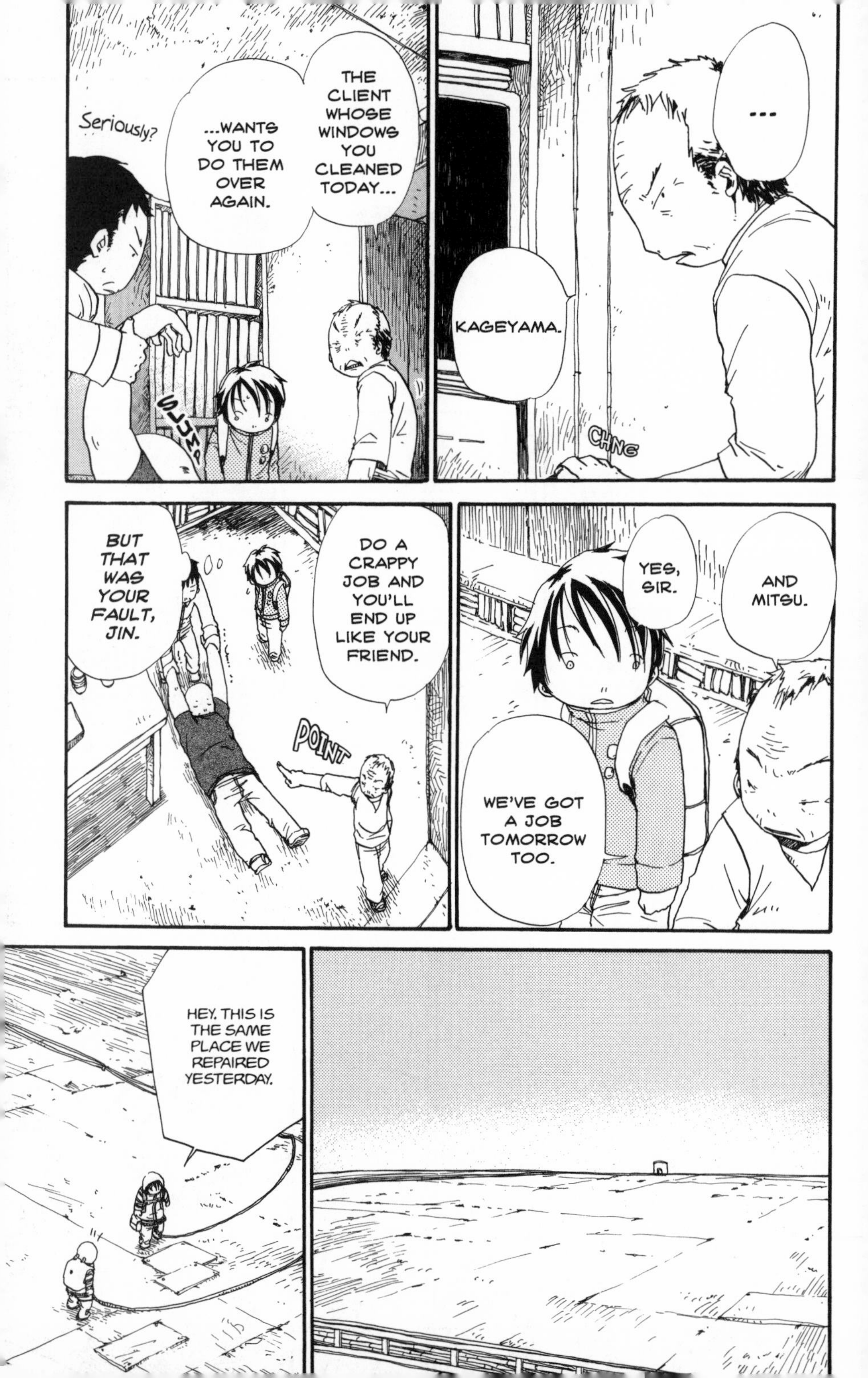
...
KAGEYAMA.
CHNG
THE CLIENT WHOSE WINDOWS YOU CLEANED TODAY...
...WANTS YOU TO DO THEM OVER AGAIN.
Seriously?
SLUMP
AND MITSU.
YES, SIR.
WE'VE GOT A JOB TOMORROW TOO.
DO A CRAPPY JOB AND YOU'LL END UP LIKE YOUR FRIEND.
POINT
BUT THAT WAS YOUR FAULT, JIN.
HEY. THIS IS THE SAME PLACE WE REPAIRED YESTERDAY.

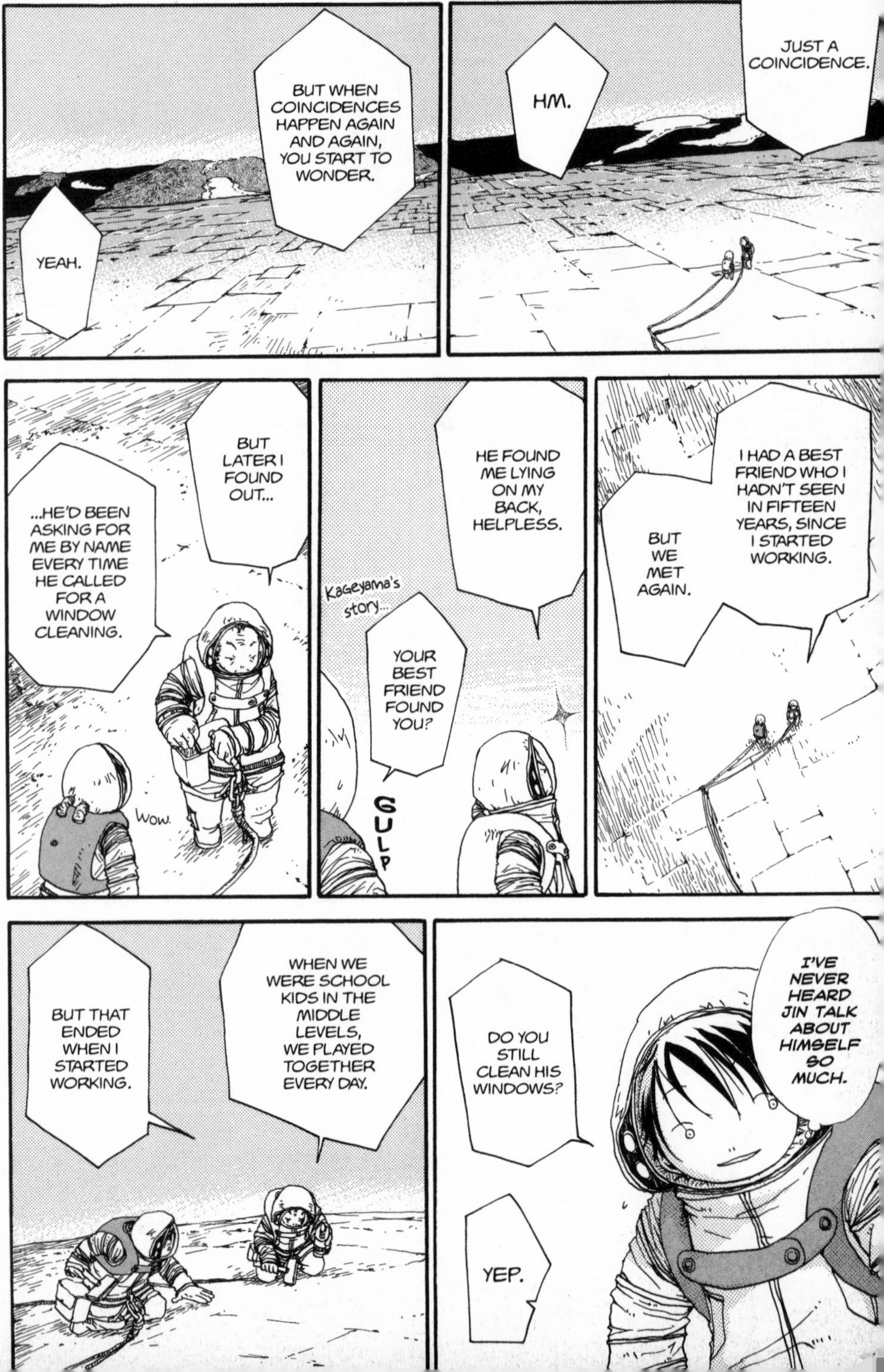
JUST A COINCIDENCE.
HM.
BUT WHEN COINCIDENCES HAPPEN AGAIN AND AGAIN, YOU START TO WONDER.
YEAH.
I HAD A BEST FRIEND WHO I HADN'T SEEN IN FIFTEEN YEARS, SINCE I STARTED WORKING.
BUT WE MET AGAIN.
HE FOUND ME LYING ON MY BACK, HELPLESS.
Kageyama's story...
YOUR BEST FRIEND FOUND YOU?
GULP
BUT LATER I FOUND OUT...
...HE'D BEEN ASKING FOR ME BY NAME EVERY TIME HE CALLED FOR A WINDOW CLEANING.
Wow.
I'VE NEVER HEARD JIN TALK ABOUT HIMSELF SO MUCH.
DO YOU STILL CLEAN HIS WINDOWS?
YEP.
WHEN WE WERE SCHOOL KIDS IN THE MIDDLE LEVELS, WE PLAYED TOGETHER EVERY DAY.
BUT THAT ENDED WHEN I STARTED WORKING.

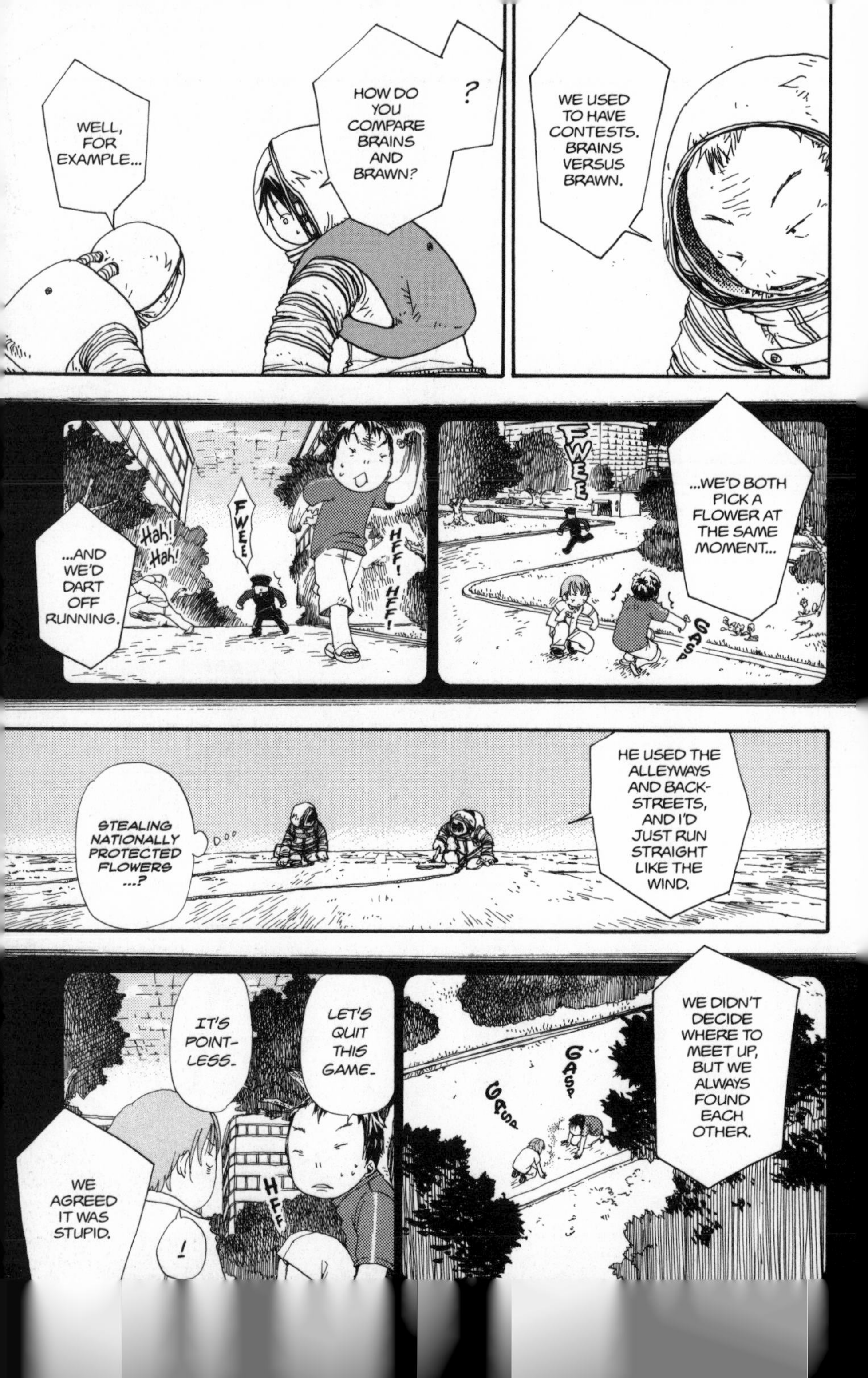
WE USED TO HAVE CONTESTS. BRAINS VERSUS BRAWN.
HOW DO YOU COMPARE BRAINS AND BRAWN?
?
WELL, FOR EXAMPLE...
FWEE
...WE'D BOTH PICK A FLOWER AT THE SAME MOMENT...
GASP
HFF! HFF!
FWEE
Hah! Hah!
...AND WE'D DART OFF RUNNING.
HE USED THE ALLEYWAYS AND BACK-STREETS, AND I'D JUST RUN STRAIGHT LIKE THE WIND.
STEALING NATIONALLY PROTECTED FLOWERS ...?
WE DIDN'T DECIDE WHERE TO MEET UP, BUT WE ALWAYS FOUND EACH OTHER.
GASP
GASP
LET'S QUIT THIS GAME.
IT'S POINTLESS.
HFF
WE AGREED IT WAS STUPID.
!

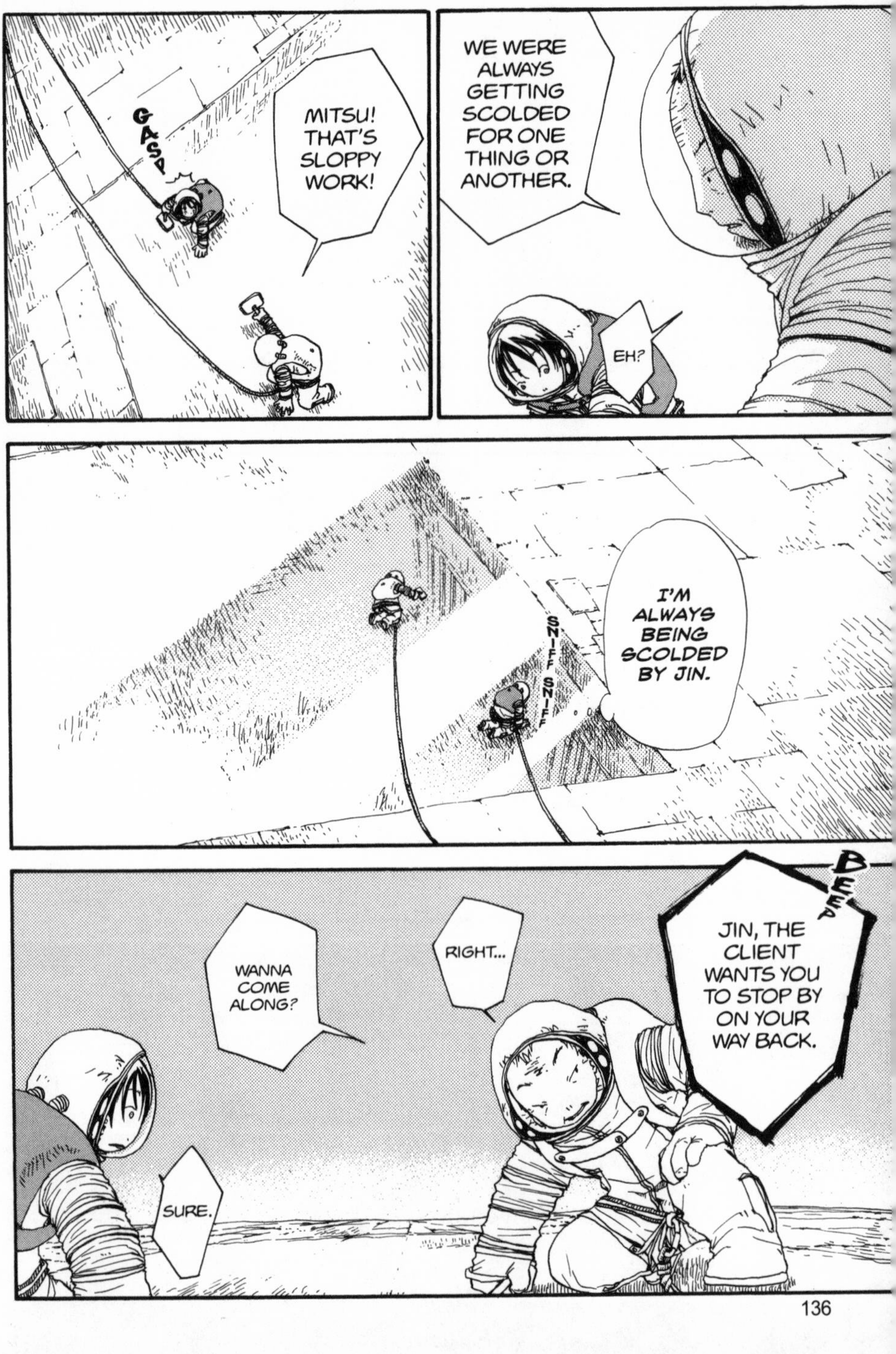
WE WERE ALWAYS GETTING SCOLDED FOR ONE THING OR ANOTHER.
EH?
GASP
MITSU! THAT'S SLOPPY WORK!
I'M ALWAYS BEING SCOLDED BY JIN.
SNIFF SNIFF
BEEP
JIN, THE CLIENT WANTS YOU TO STOP BY ON YOUR WAY BACK.
RIGHT...
WANNA COME ALONG?
SURE.

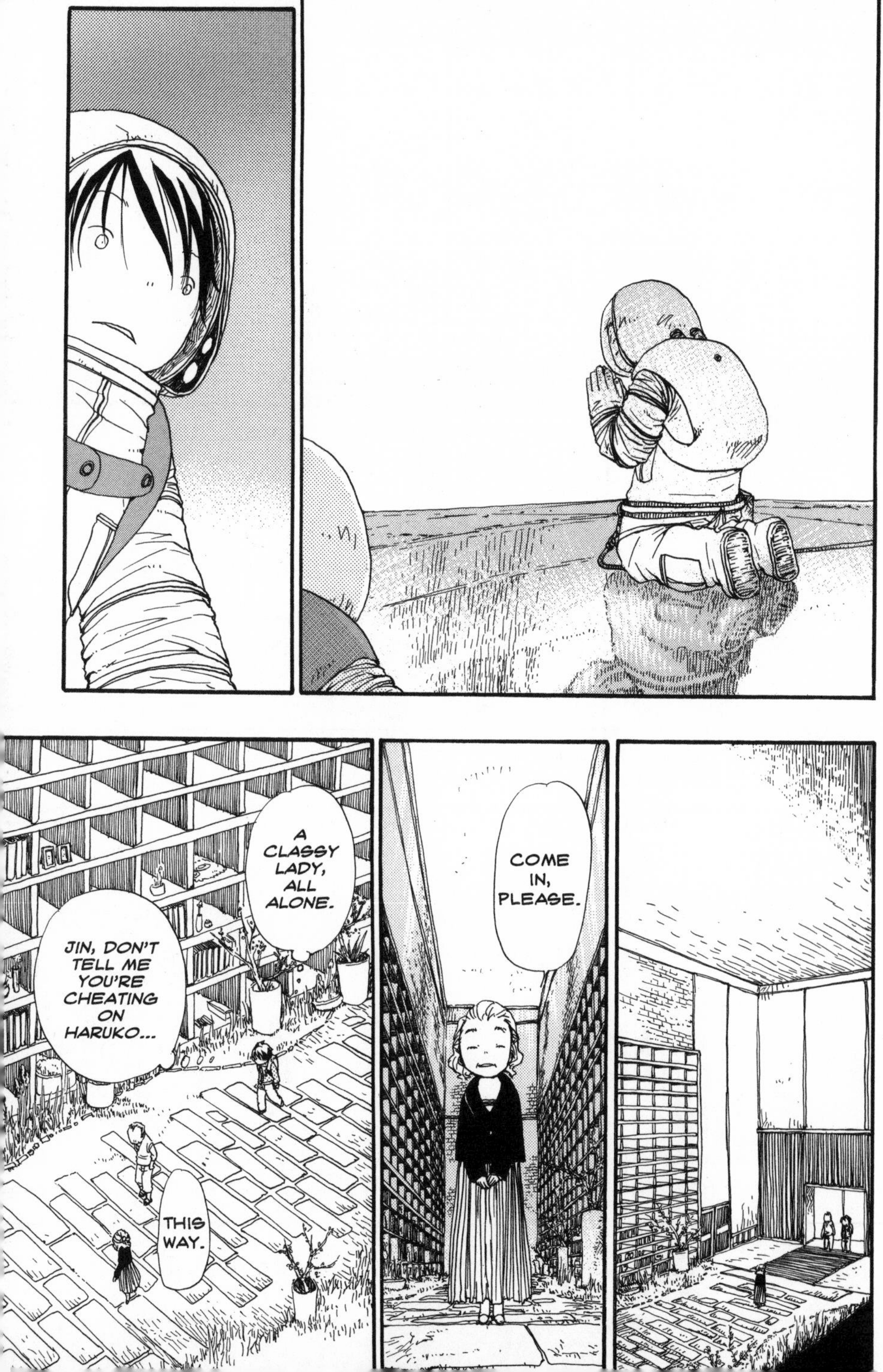
COME IN, PLEASE.
A CLASSY LADY, ALL ALONE.
JIN, DON'T TELL ME YOU'RE CHEATING ON HARUKO...
THIS WAY.

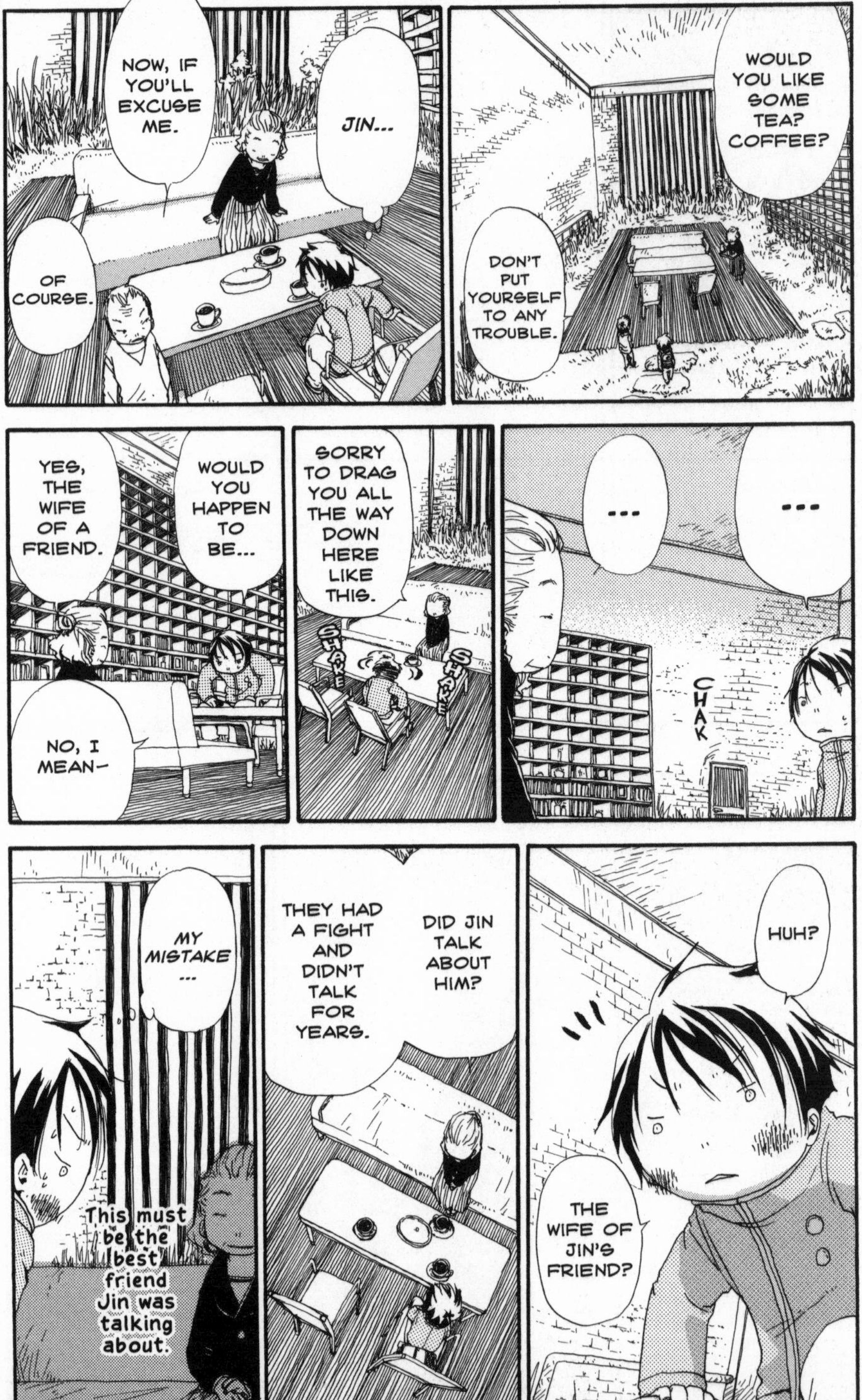
WOULD YOU LIKE SOME TEA? COFFEE?
DON'T PUT YOURSELF TO ANY TROUBLE.
JIN...
NOW, IF YOU'LL EXCUSE ME.
OF COURSE.
...
...
CHAK
SORRY TO DRAG YOU ALL THE WAY DOWN HERE LIKE THIS.
SHAKE
SHAKE
WOULD YOU HAPPEN TO BE...
YES, THE WIFE OF A FRIEND.
NO, I MEAN—
HUH?
THE WIFE OF JIN'S FRIEND?
DID JIN TALK ABOUT HIM?
THEY HAD A FIGHT AND DIDN'T TALK FOR YEARS.
MY MISTAKE...
This must be the best friend Jin was talking about.

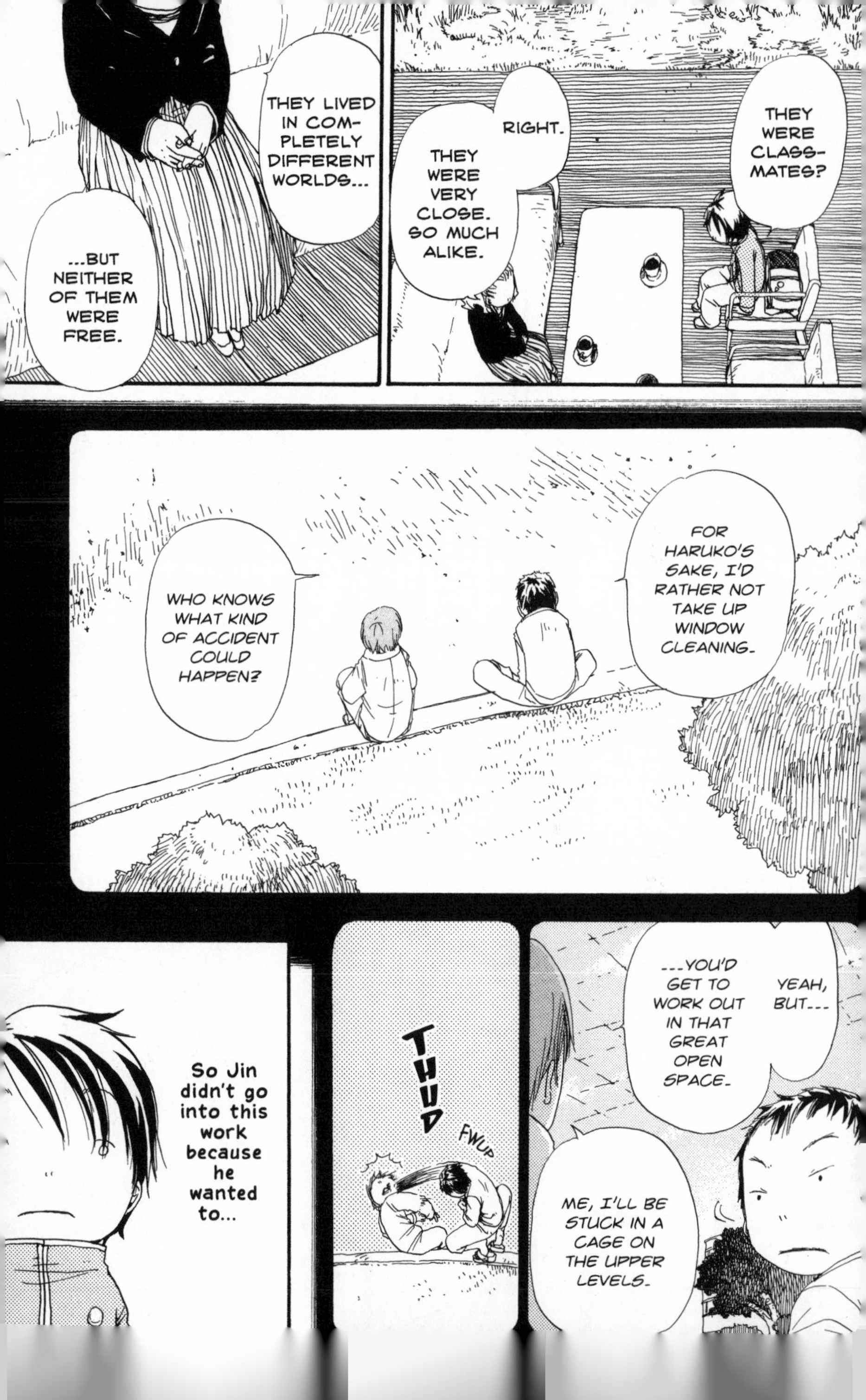
THEY WERE CLASS-MATES?
RIGHT.
THEY WERE VERY CLOSE. SO MUCH ALIKE.
THEY LIVED IN COM-PLETELY DIFFERENT WORLDS...
...BUT NEITHER OF THEM WERE FREE.
FOR HARUKO'S SAKE, I'D RATHER NOT TAKE UP WINDOW CLEANING.
WHO KNOWS WHAT KIND OF ACCIDENT COULD HAPPEN?
YEAH, BUT...
...YOU'D GET TO WORK OUT IN THAT GREAT OPEN SPACE.
ME, I'LL BE STUCK IN A CAGE ON THE UPPER LEVELS.
THUD
FWUP
So Jin didn't go into this work because he wanted to...

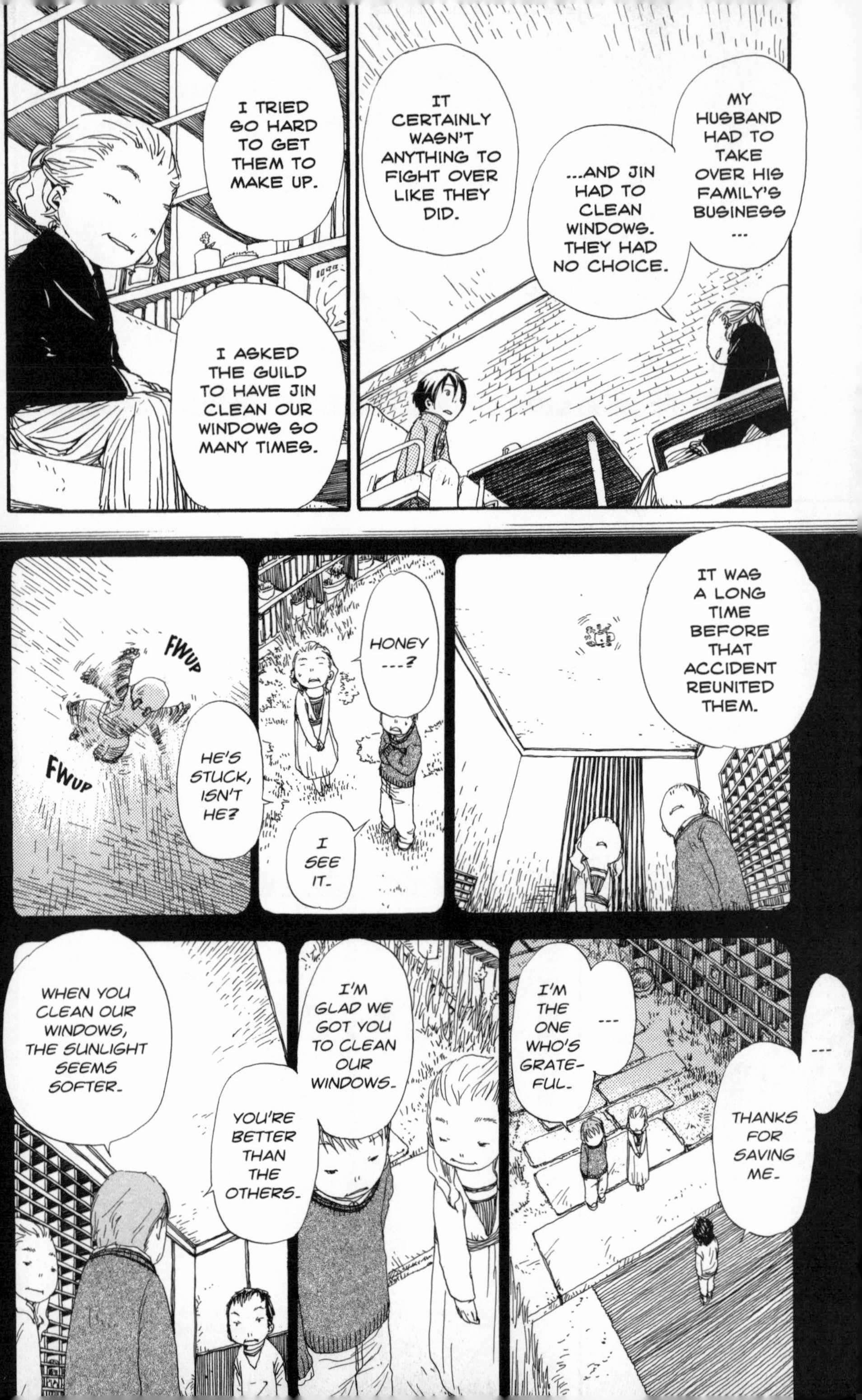
MY HUSBAND HAD TO TAKE OVER HIS FAMILY'S BUSINESS...
...AND JIN HAD TO CLEAN WINDOWS. THEY HAD NO CHOICE.
IT CERTAINLY WASN'T ANYTHING TO FIGHT OVER LIKE THEY DID.
I TRIED SO HARD TO GET THEM TO MAKE UP.
I ASKED THE GUILD TO HAVE JIN CLEAN OUR WINDOWS SO MANY TIMES.
IT WAS A LONG TIME BEFORE THAT ACCIDENT REUNITED THEM.
HONEY...?
HE'S STUCK, ISN'T HE?
I SEE IT.
FWUP
FWUP
...
THANKS FOR SAVING ME.
...
I'M THE ONE WHO'S GRATEFUL.
I'M GLAD WE GOT YOU TO CLEAN OUR WINDOWS.
YOU'RE BETTER THAN THE OTHERS.
WHEN YOU CLEAN OUR WINDOWS, THE SUNLIGHT SEEMS SOFTER.

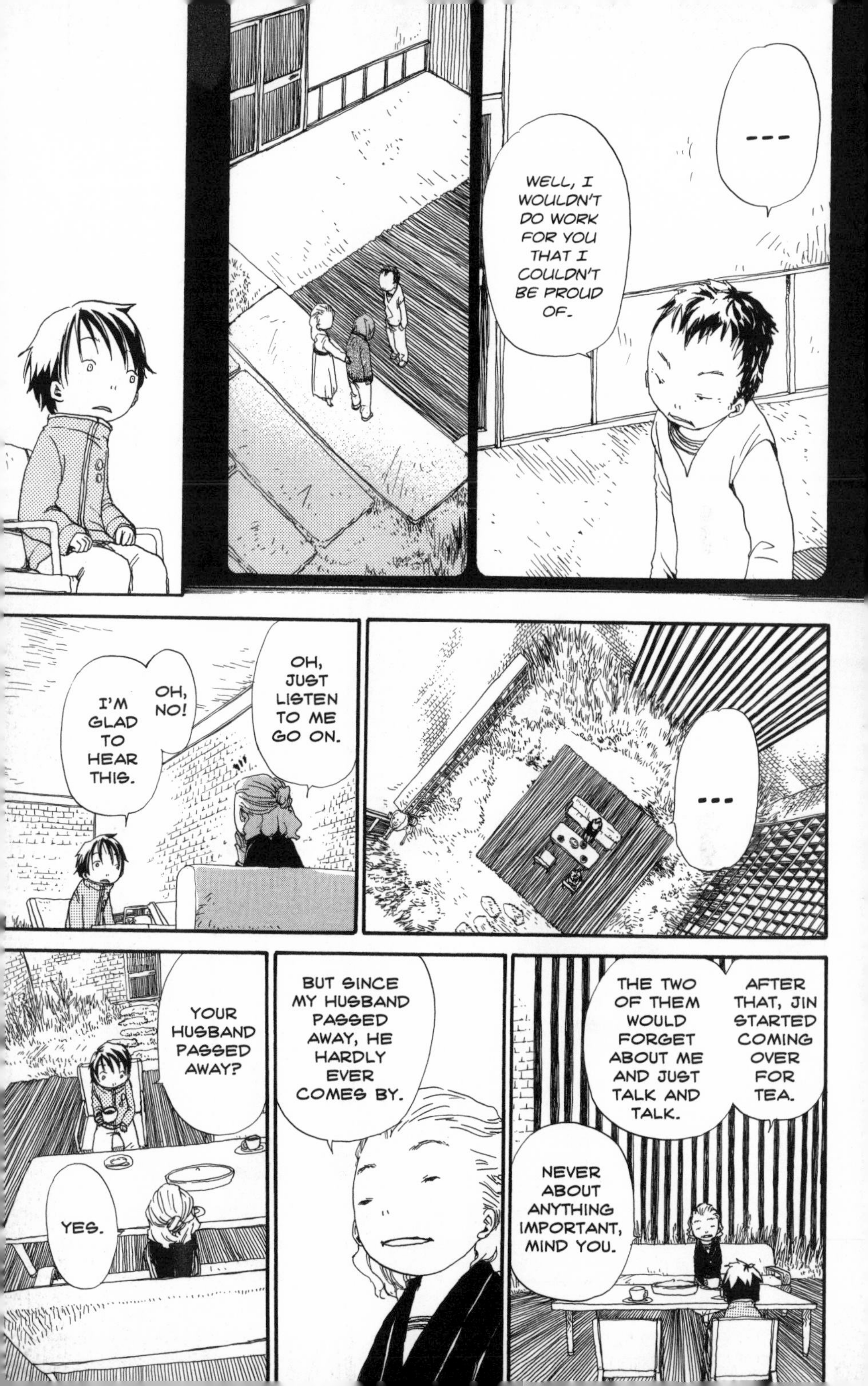
...
WELL, I WOULDN'T DO WORK FOR YOU THAT I COULDN'T BE PROUD OF.
...
OH, JUST LISTEN TO ME GO ON.
OH, NO!
I'M GLAD TO HEAR THIS.
AFTER THAT, JIN STARTED COMING OVER FOR TEA.
THE TWO OF THEM WOULD FORGET ABOUT ME AND JUST TALK AND TALK.
NEVER ABOUT ANYTHING IMPORTANT, MIND YOU.
BUT SINCE MY HUSBAND PASSED AWAY, HE HARDLY EVER COMES BY.
YOUR HUSBAND PASSED AWAY?
YES.

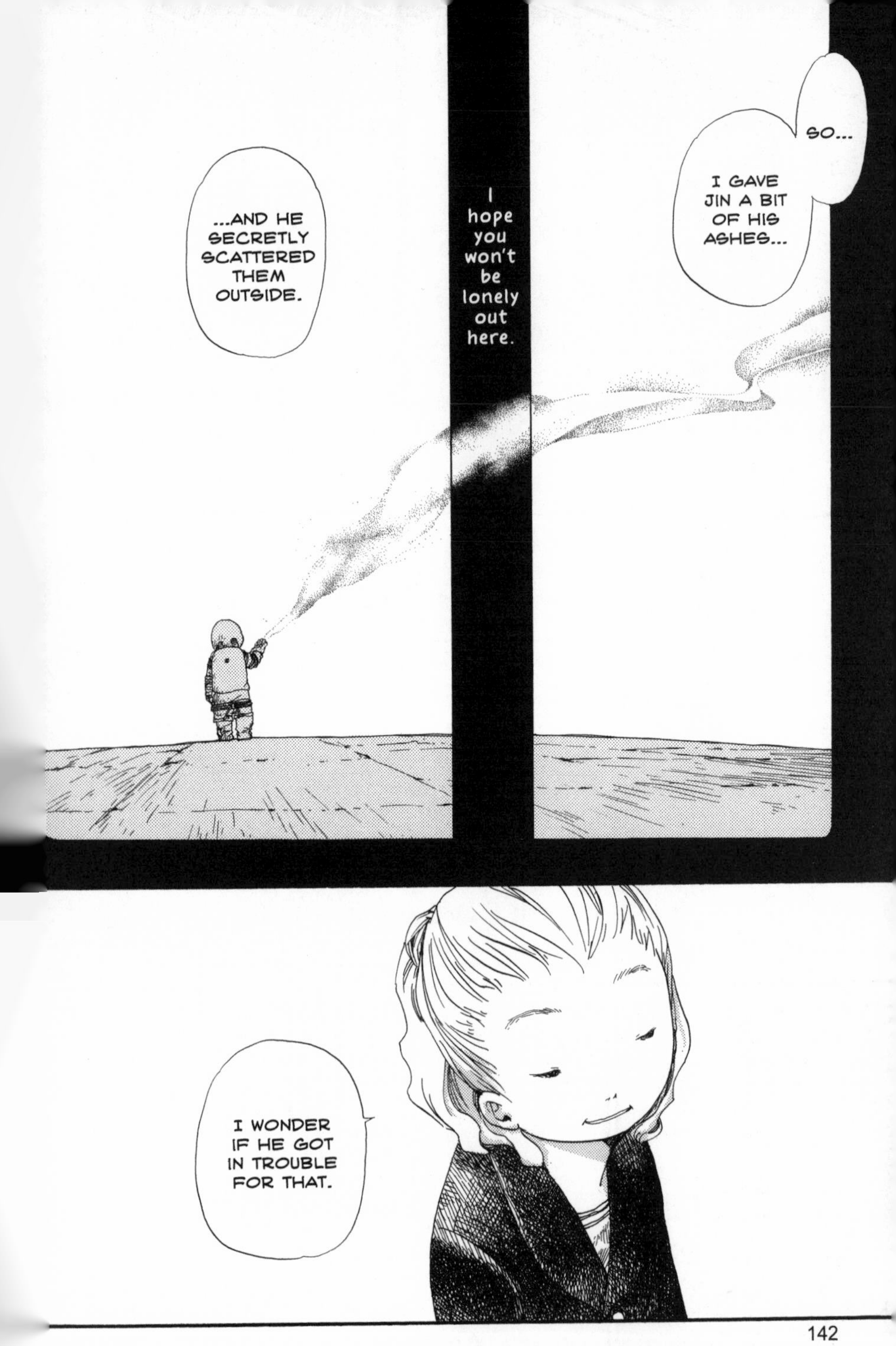
SO...
I GAVE JIN A BIT OF HIS ASHES...
I hope you won't be lonely out here.
...AND HE SECRETLY SCATTERED THEM OUTSIDE.
I WONDER IF HE GOT IN TROUBLE FOR THAT.

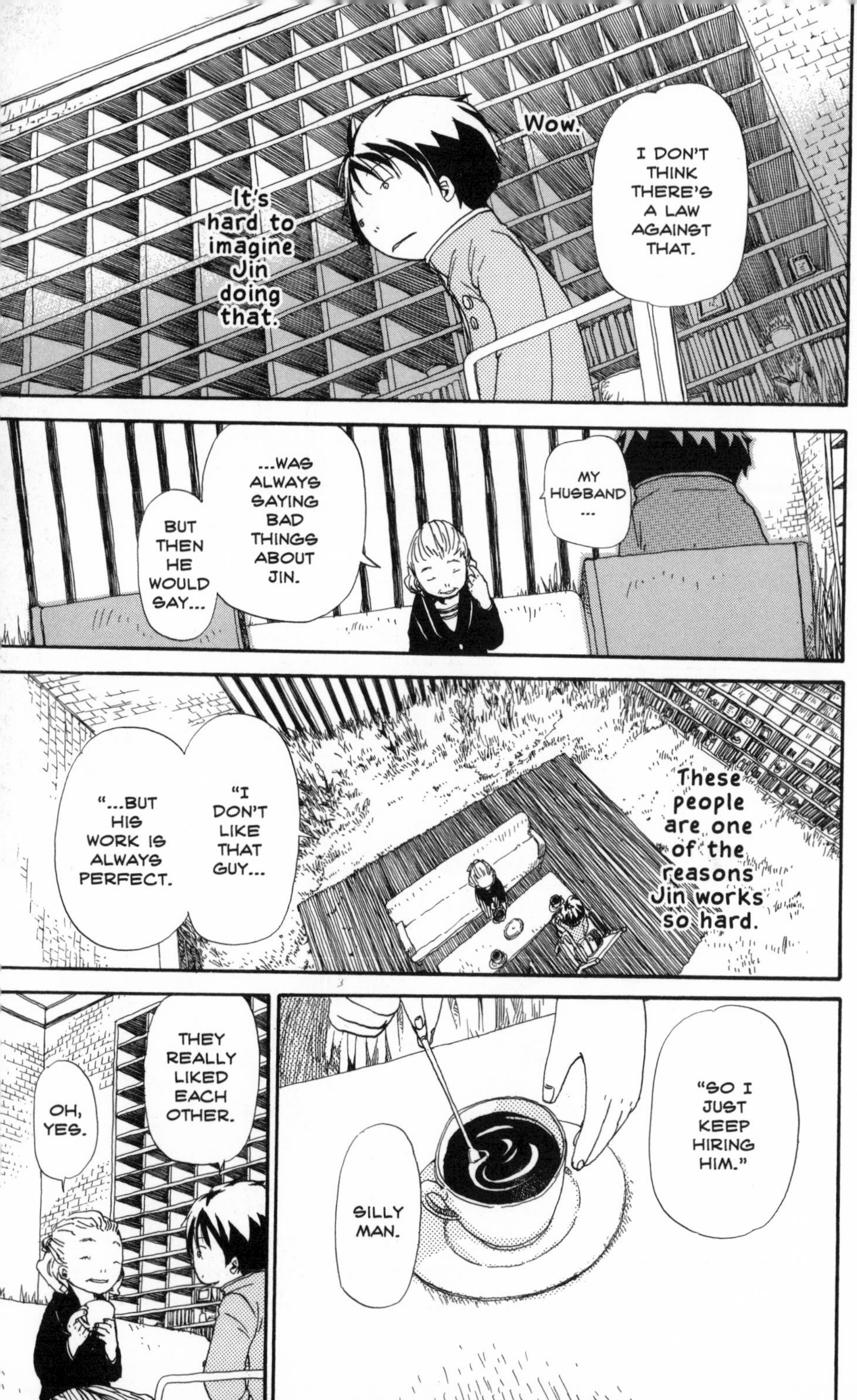
I DON'T THINK THERE'S A LAW AGAINST THAT.
Wow.
It's hard to imagine Jin doing that.
MY HUSBAND...
...WAS ALWAYS SAYING BAD THINGS ABOUT JIN.
BUT THEN HE WOULD SAY...
These people are one of the reasons Jin works so hard.
"I DON'T LIKE THAT GUY...
"...BUT HIS WORK IS ALWAYS PERFECT.
"SO I JUST KEEP HIRING HIM."
SILLY MAN.
THEY REALLY LIKED EACH OTHER.
OH, YES.

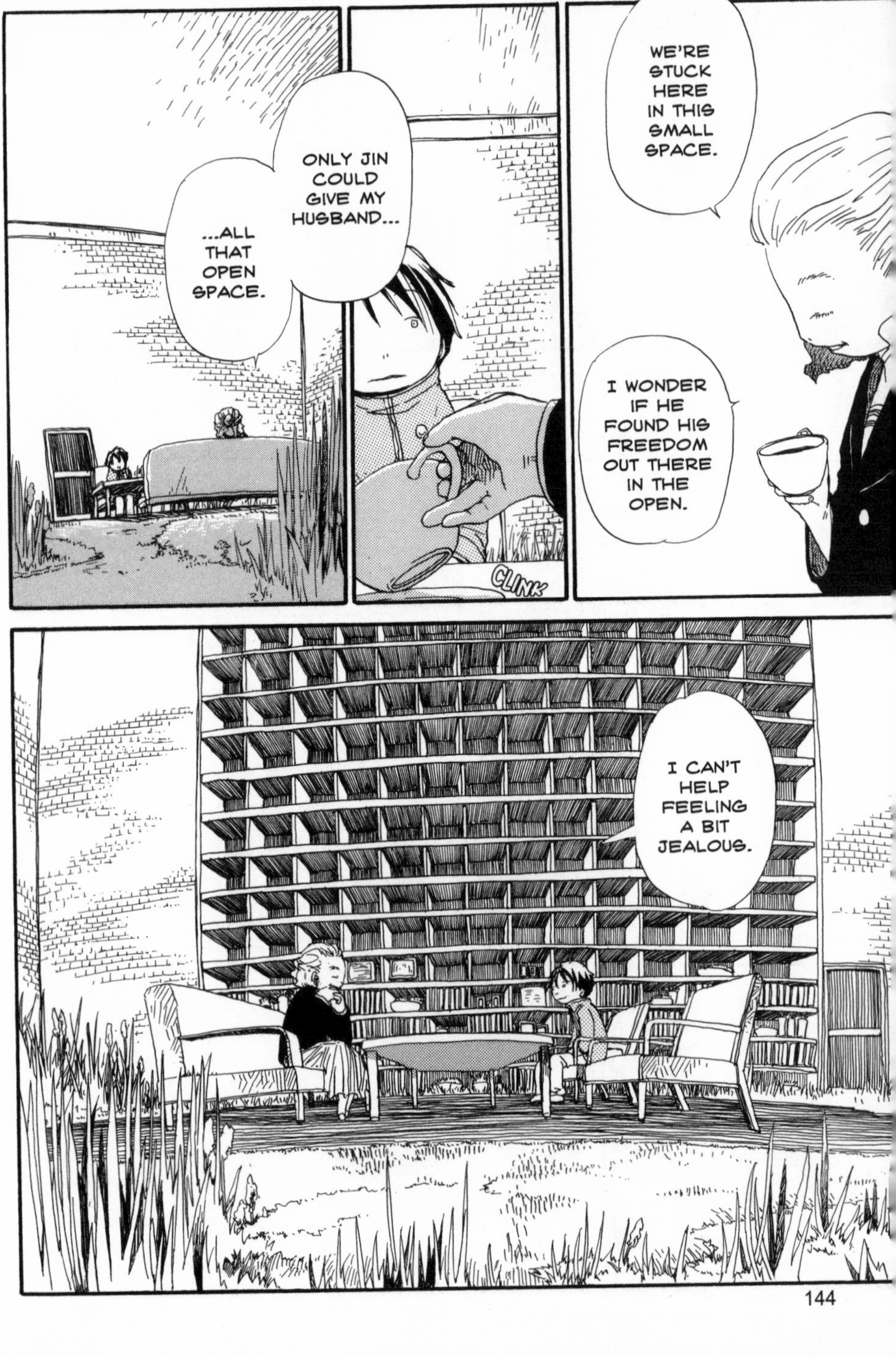
WE'RE STUCK HERE IN THIS SMALL SPACE.
I WONDER IF HE FOUND HIS FREEDOM OUT THERE IN THE OPEN.
CLINK
ONLY JIN COULD GIVE MY HUSBAND...
...ALL THAT OPEN SPACE.
I CAN'T HELP FEELING A BIT JEALOUS.

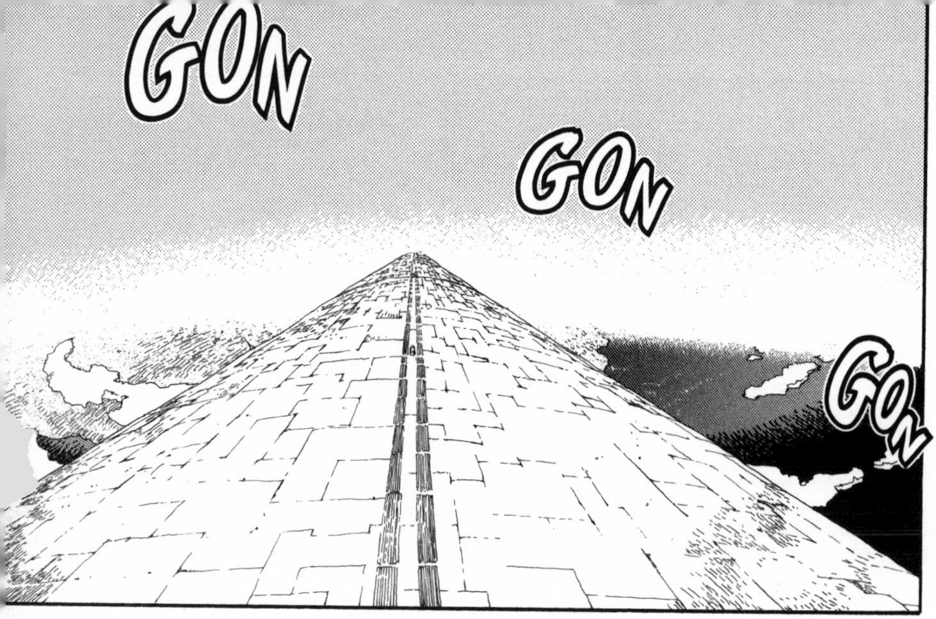
GON
GON
GON

floor 7: beneath the mask

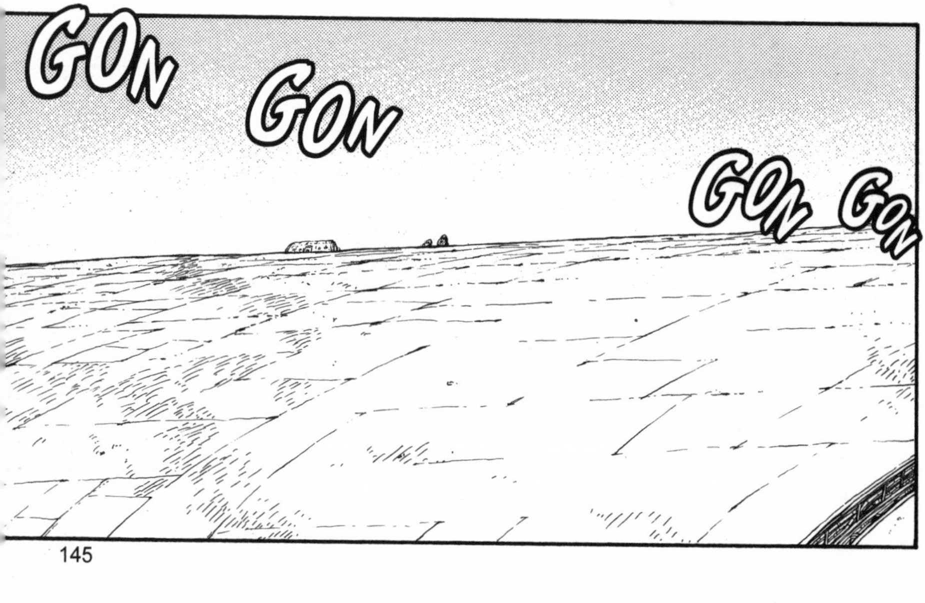
GON
GON
GON
GON

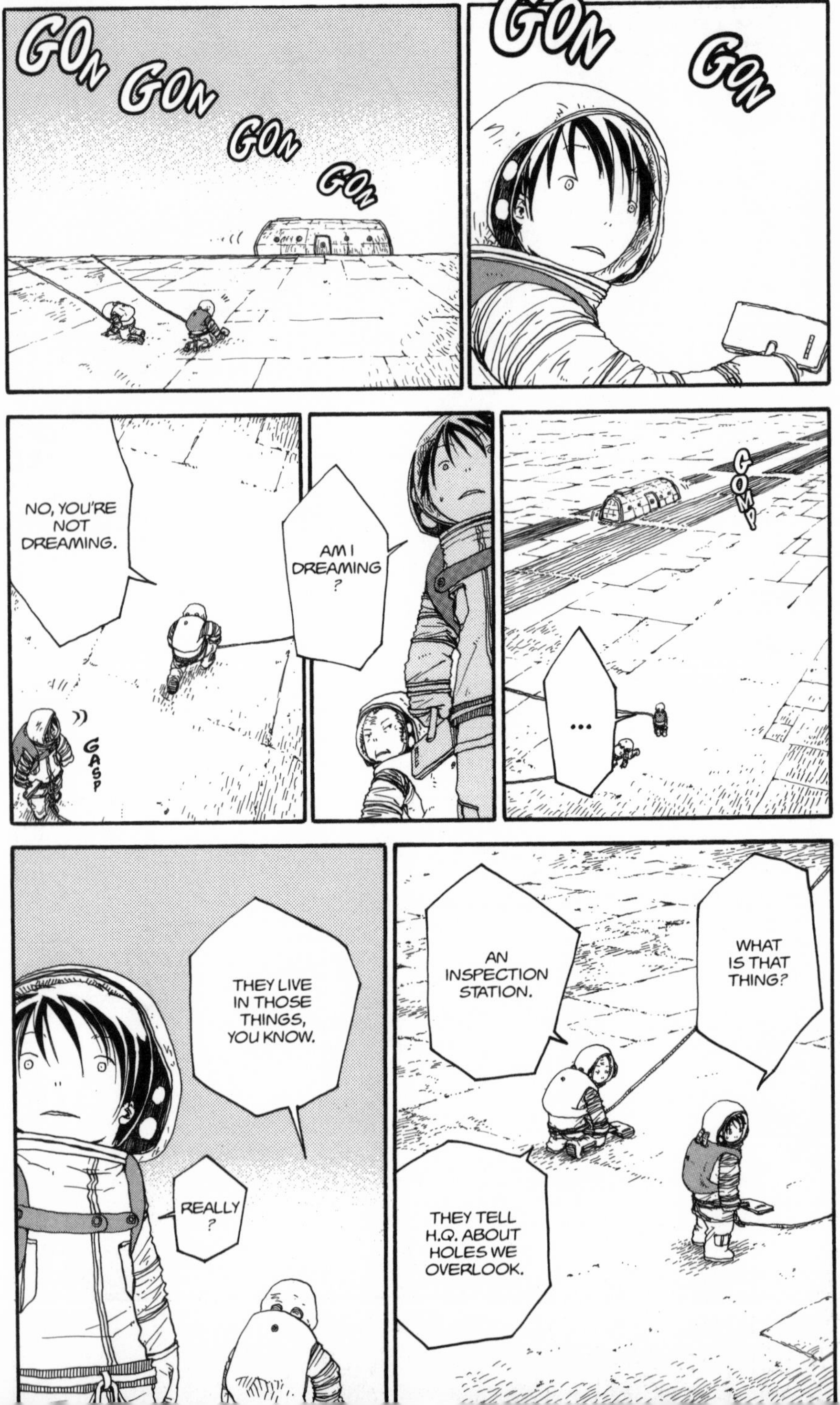
GON
GON
GON
GON
GON
GON
GOMP
...
AM I DREAMING?
NO, YOU'RE NOT DREAMING.
GASP
WHAT IS THAT THING?
AN INSPECTION STATION.
THEY TELL H.Q. ABOUT HOLES WE OVERLOOK.
THEY LIVE IN THOSE THINGS, YOU KNOW.
REALLY?

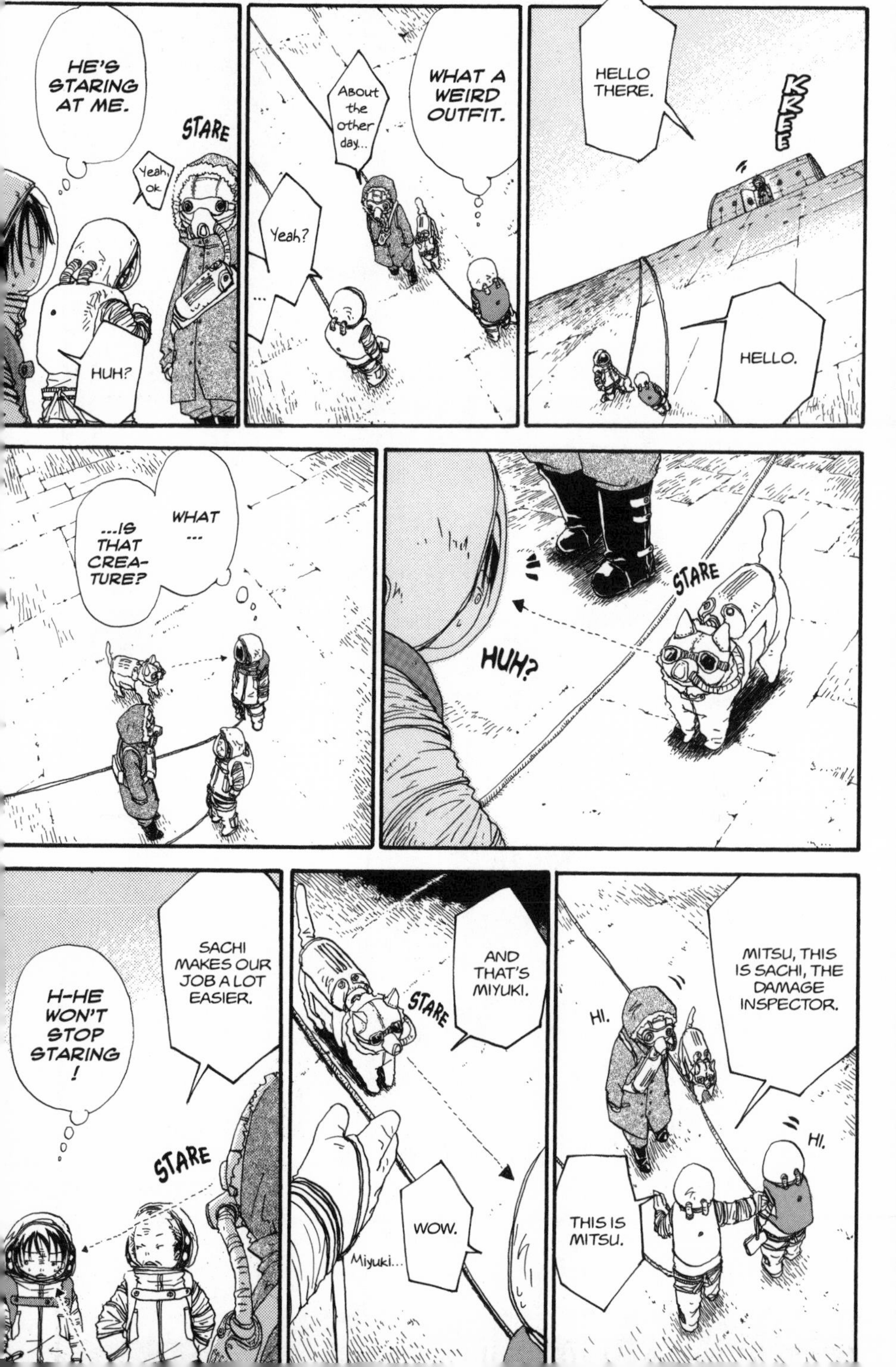
HELLO THERE.
KREE
HELLO.
WHAT A WEIRD OUTFIT.
About the other day...
Yeah?
...
HE'S STARING AT ME.
STARE
Yeah, ok
HUH?
HUH?
STARE
WHAT ---
...IS THAT CREATURE?
MITSU, THIS IS SACHI, THE DAMAGE INSPECTOR.
HI.
HI.
THIS IS MITSU.
AND THAT'S MIYUKI.
STARE
WOW.
Miyuki...
SACHI MAKES OUR JOB A LOT EASIER.
H-HE WON'T STOP STARING!
STARE

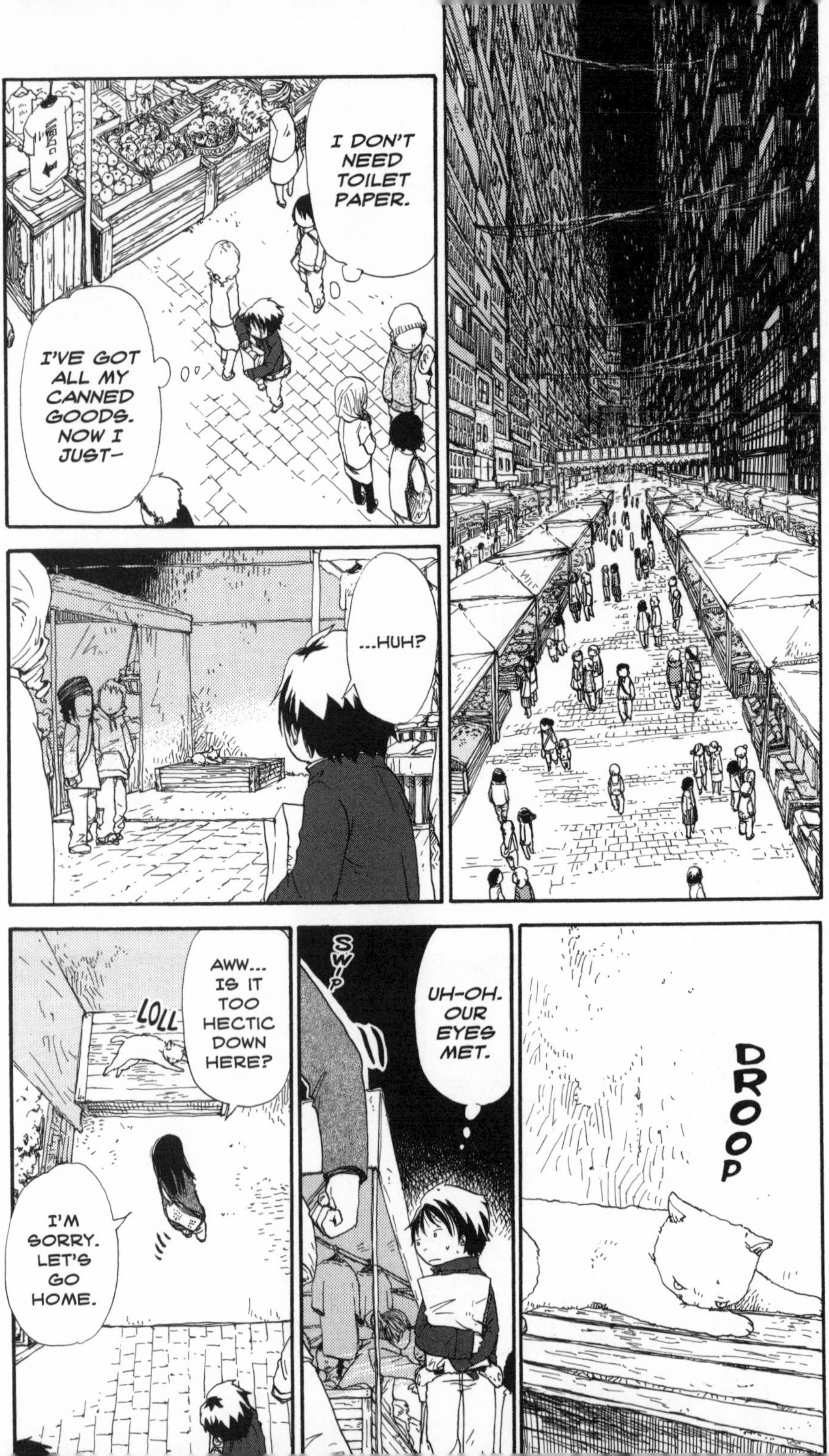
I DON'T NEED TOILET PAPER.
I'VE GOT ALL MY CANNED GOODS. NOW I JUST-
...HUH?
DROOP
SWIP
UH-OH. OUR EYES MET.
AWW... IS IT TOO HECTIC DOWN HERE?
LOLL
I'M SORRY. LET'S GO HOME.

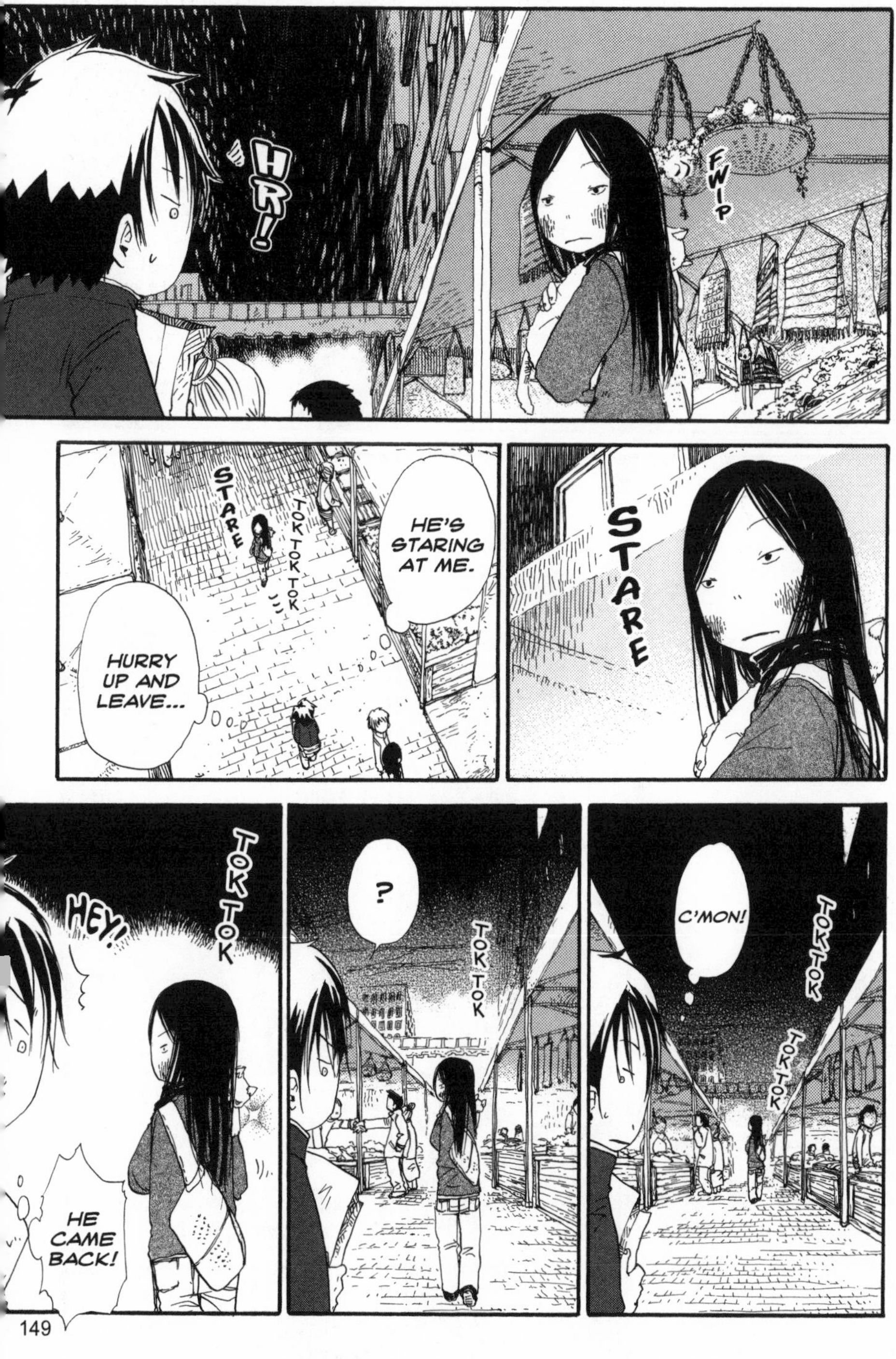
FWIP
HR!
STARE
HE'S STARING AT ME.
STARE
TOK TOK TOK
HURRY UP AND LEAVE...
C'MON!
TOK TOK
TOK TOK
?
TOK TOK
TOK TOK
HEY!!
HE CAME BACK!

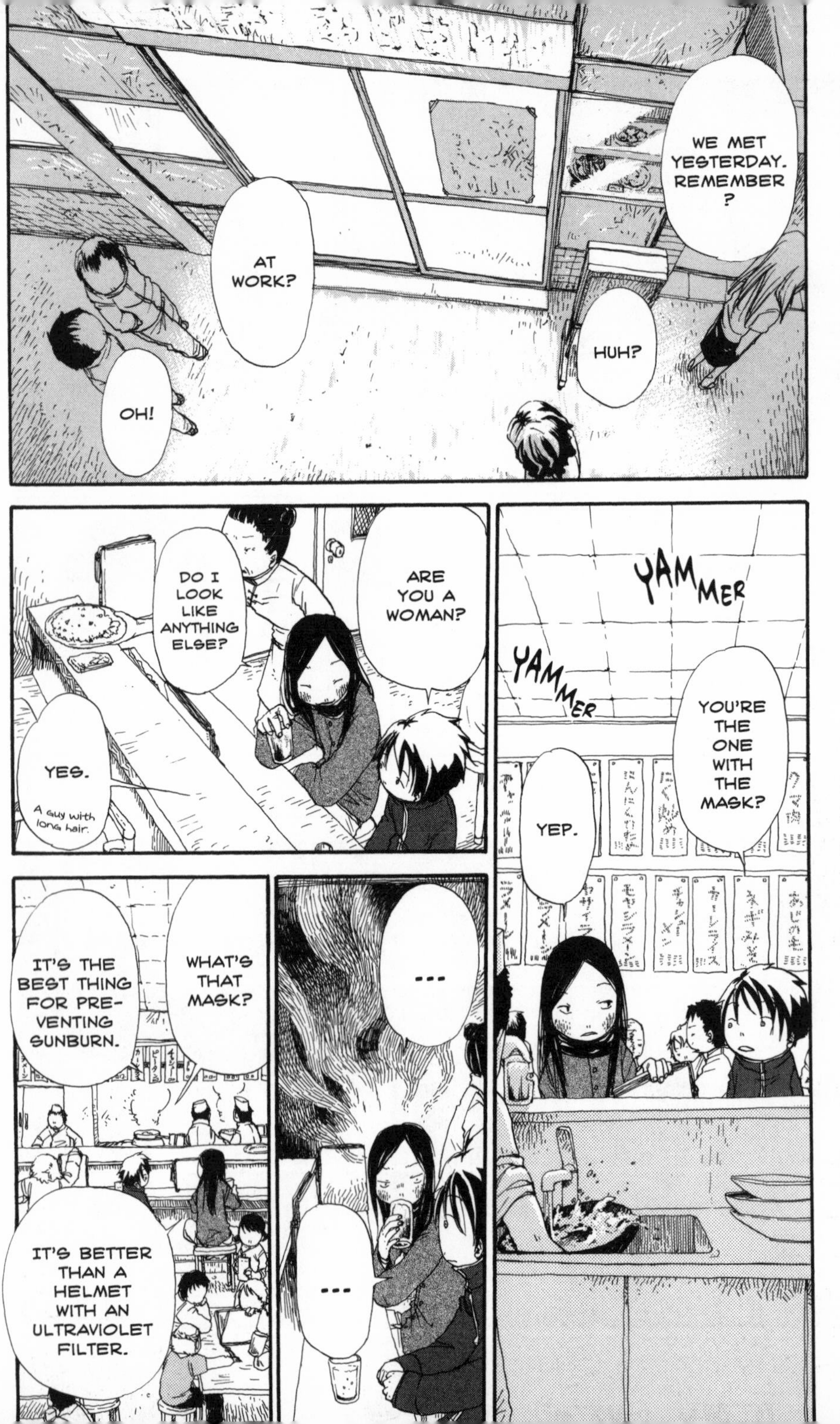
WE MET YESTERDAY. REMEMBER?
HUH?
AT WORK?
OH!
YAMMER
YAMMER
YOU'RE THE ONE WITH THE MASK?
YEP.
ARE YOU A WOMAN?
DO I LOOK LIKE ANYTHING ELSE?
YES.
A guy with long hair.
...
...
WHAT'S THAT MASK?
IT'S THE BEST THING FOR PRE-VENTING SUNBURN.
IT'S BETTER THAN A HELMET WITH AN ULTRAVIOLET FILTER.

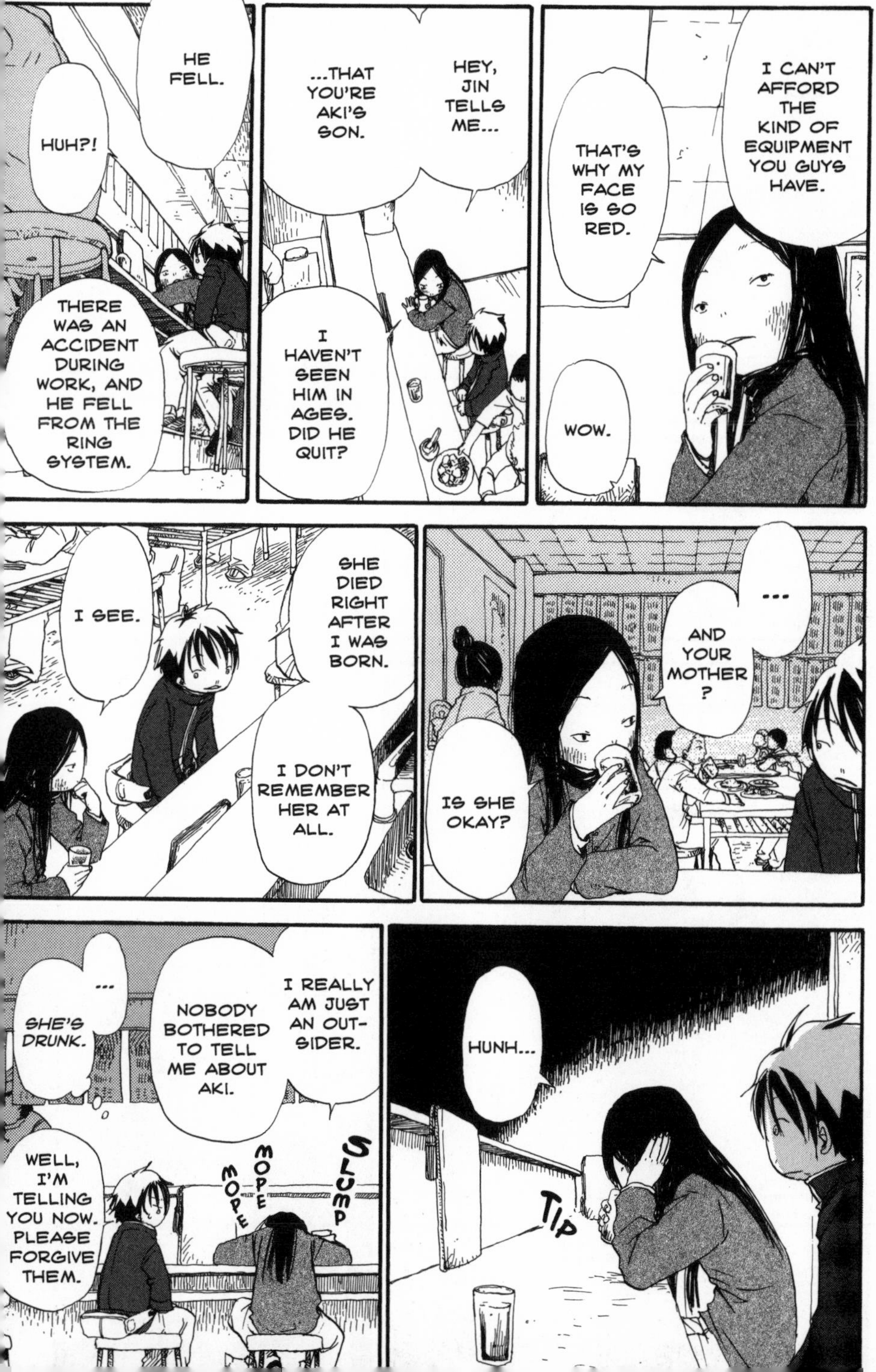
I CAN'T AFFORD THE KIND OF EQUIPMENT YOU GUYS HAVE.
THAT'S WHY MY FACE IS SO RED.
WOW.
HEY, JIN TELLS ME...
...THAT YOU'RE AKI'S SON.
I HAVEN'T SEEN HIM IN AGES. DID HE QUIT?
HE FELL.
HUH?!
THERE WAS AN ACCIDENT DURING WORK, AND HE FELL FROM THE RING SYSTEM.
...
AND YOUR MOTHER?
IS SHE OKAY?
SHE DIED RIGHT AFTER I WAS BORN.
I DON'T REMEMBER HER AT ALL.
I SEE.
HUNH...
TIP
I REALLY AM JUST AN OUT-SIDER.
NOBODY BOTHERED TO TELL ME ABOUT AKI.
...
SHE'S DRUNK.
SLUMP
MOPE MOPE
WELL, I'M TELLING YOU NOW. PLEASE FORGIVE THEM.

HAVE YOU SEEN MIYUKI?

HEY, JIN!

YOU'RE SURE YOU HAVEN'T SEEN HER?

NO, I HAVEN'T.

WHAT'S WRONG?

SHE DISAPPEARED.

THAT'S NOTHING TO PANIC ABOUT, IS IT?

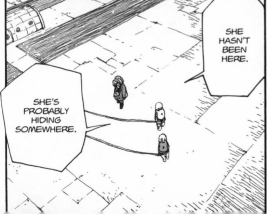

SHE HASN'T BEEN HERE.

SHE'S PROBABLY HIDING SOMEWHERE.

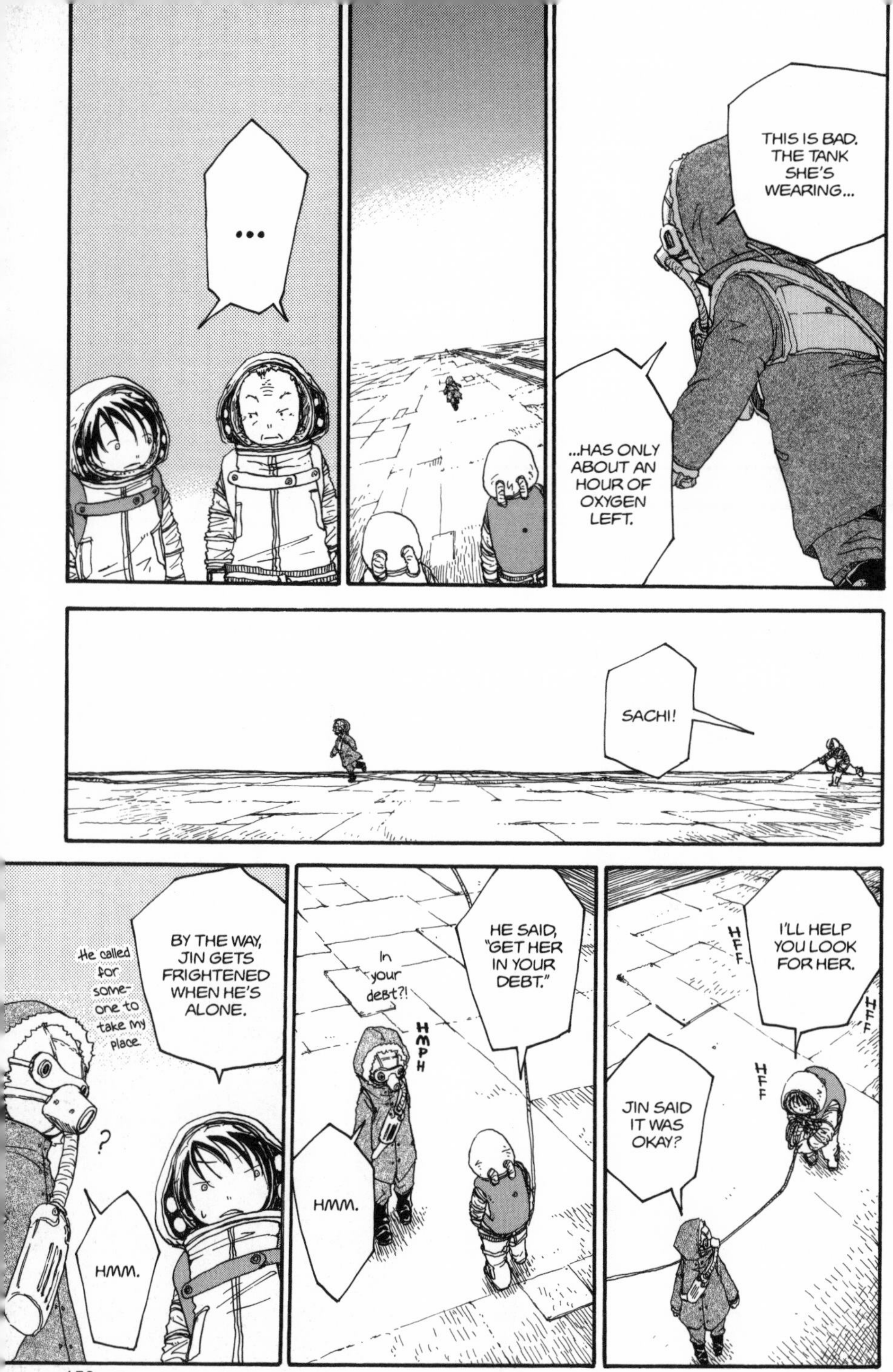
THIS IS BAD. THE TANK SHE'S WEARING...
...HAS ONLY ABOUT AN HOUR OF OXYGEN LEFT.
...
SACHI!
I'LL HELP YOU LOOK FOR HER.
HFF
HFF
HFF
JIN SAID IT WAS OKAY?
HE SAID, "GET HER IN YOUR DEBT."
In your debt?!
HMPH
HMM.
BY THE WAY, JIN GETS FRIGHTENED WHEN HE'S ALONE.
He called for some-one to take my place.
?
HMM.

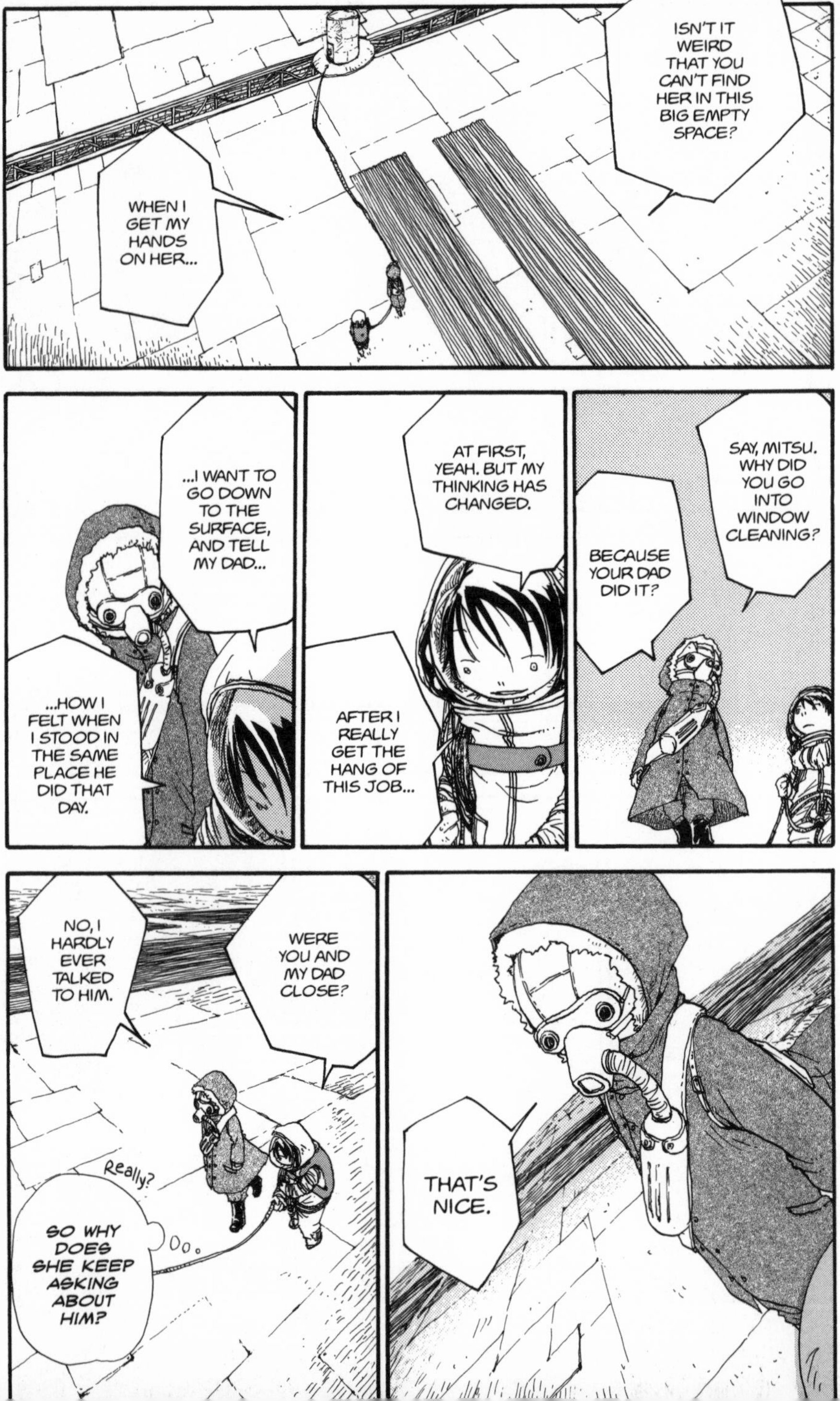
ISN'T IT WEIRD THAT YOU CAN'T FIND HER IN THIS BIG EMPTY SPACE?
WHEN I GET MY HANDS ON HER...
SAY, MITSU. WHY DID YOU GO INTO WINDOW CLEANING?
BECAUSE YOUR DAD DID IT?
AT FIRST, YEAH. BUT MY THINKING HAS CHANGED.
AFTER I REALLY GET THE HANG OF THIS JOB...
...I WANT TO GO DOWN TO THE SURFACE, AND TELL MY DAD...
...HOW I FELT WHEN I STOOD IN THE SAME PLACE HE DID THAT DAY.
THAT'S NICE.
WERE YOU AND MY DAD CLOSE?
NO, I HARDLY EVER TALKED TO HIM.
Really?
SO WHY DOES SHE KEEP ASKING ABOUT HIM?

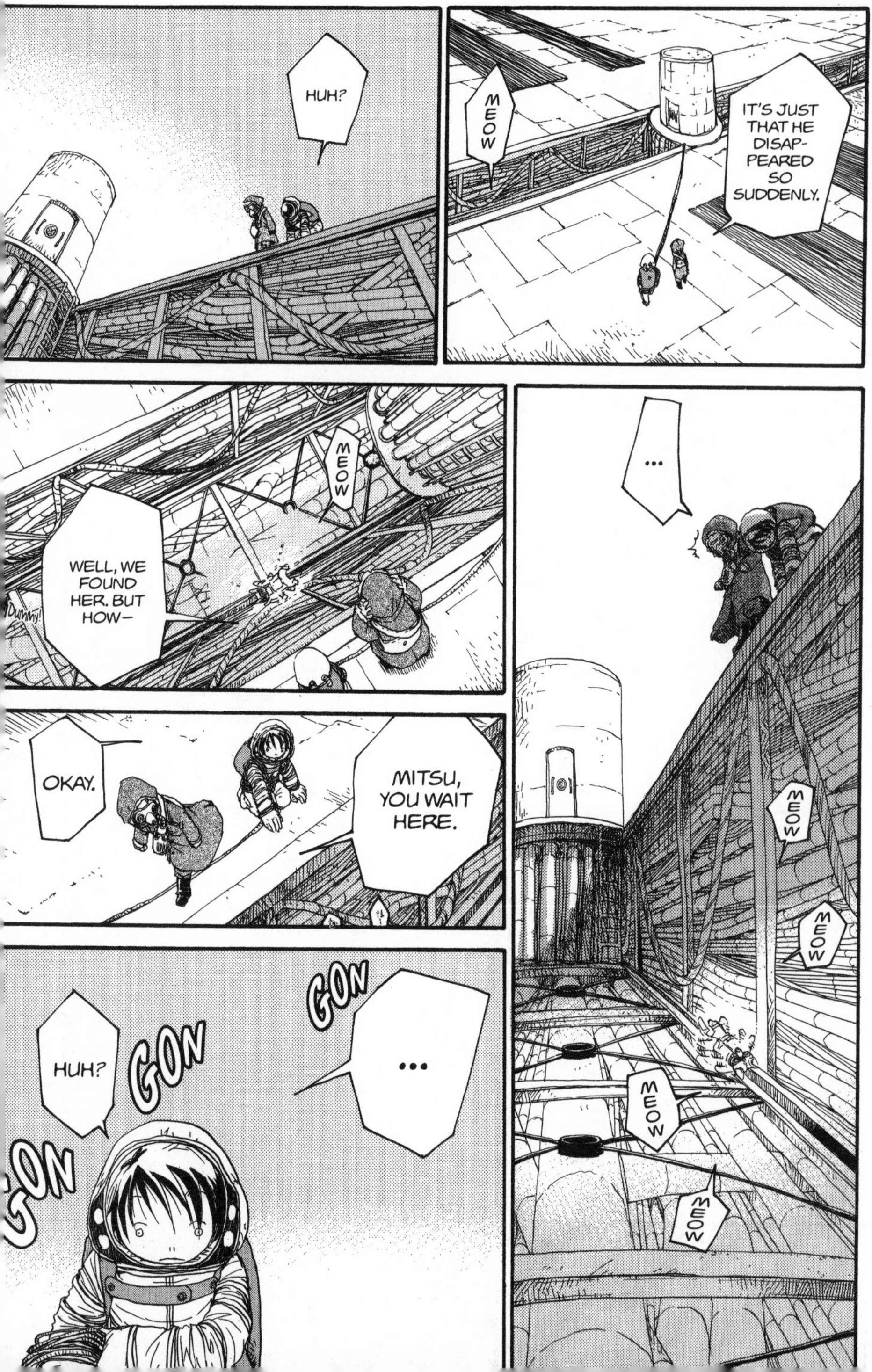
MEOW
IT'S JUST THAT HE DISAPPEARED SO SUDDENLY.
HUH?
...
MEOW
MEOW
MEOW
MEOW
MEOW
WELL, WE FOUND HER. BUT HOW—
MITSU, YOU WAIT HERE.
OKAY.
GON
...
GON
HUH?
GON

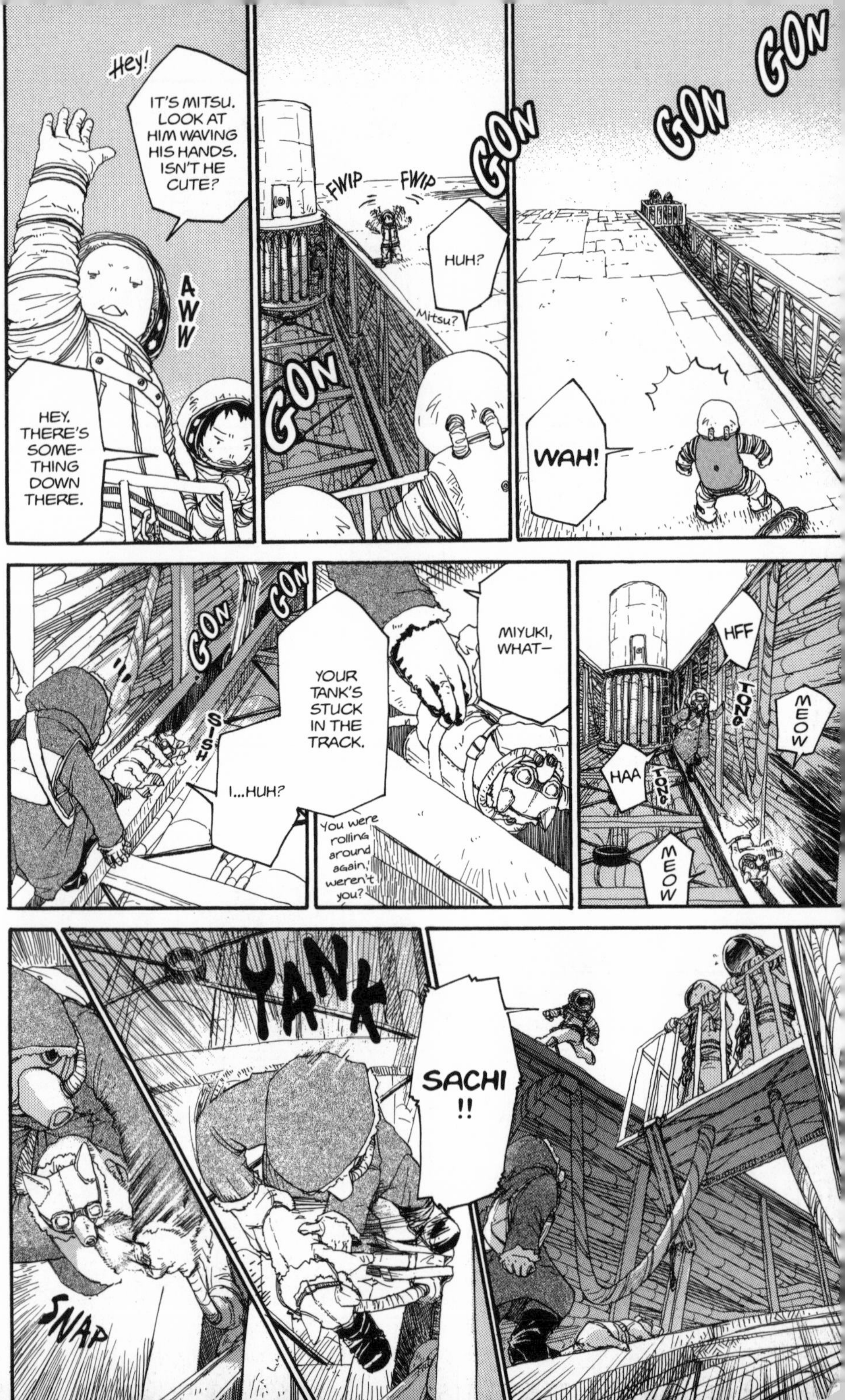
GON GON
GON
WAH!
GON
FWIP FWIP
HUH?
Mitsu?
GON
Hey!
IT'S MITSU. LOOK AT HIM WAVING HIS HANDS. ISN'T HE CUTE?
AWW
HEY. THERE'S SOME-THING DOWN THERE.
HFF
TONG
MEOW
HAA
TONG
MEOW
MIYUKI, WHAT—
YOUR TANK'S STUCK IN THE TRACK.
You were rolling around again, weren't you?
GON GON
SISH
I...HUH?
SACHI !!
YANK
SNAP

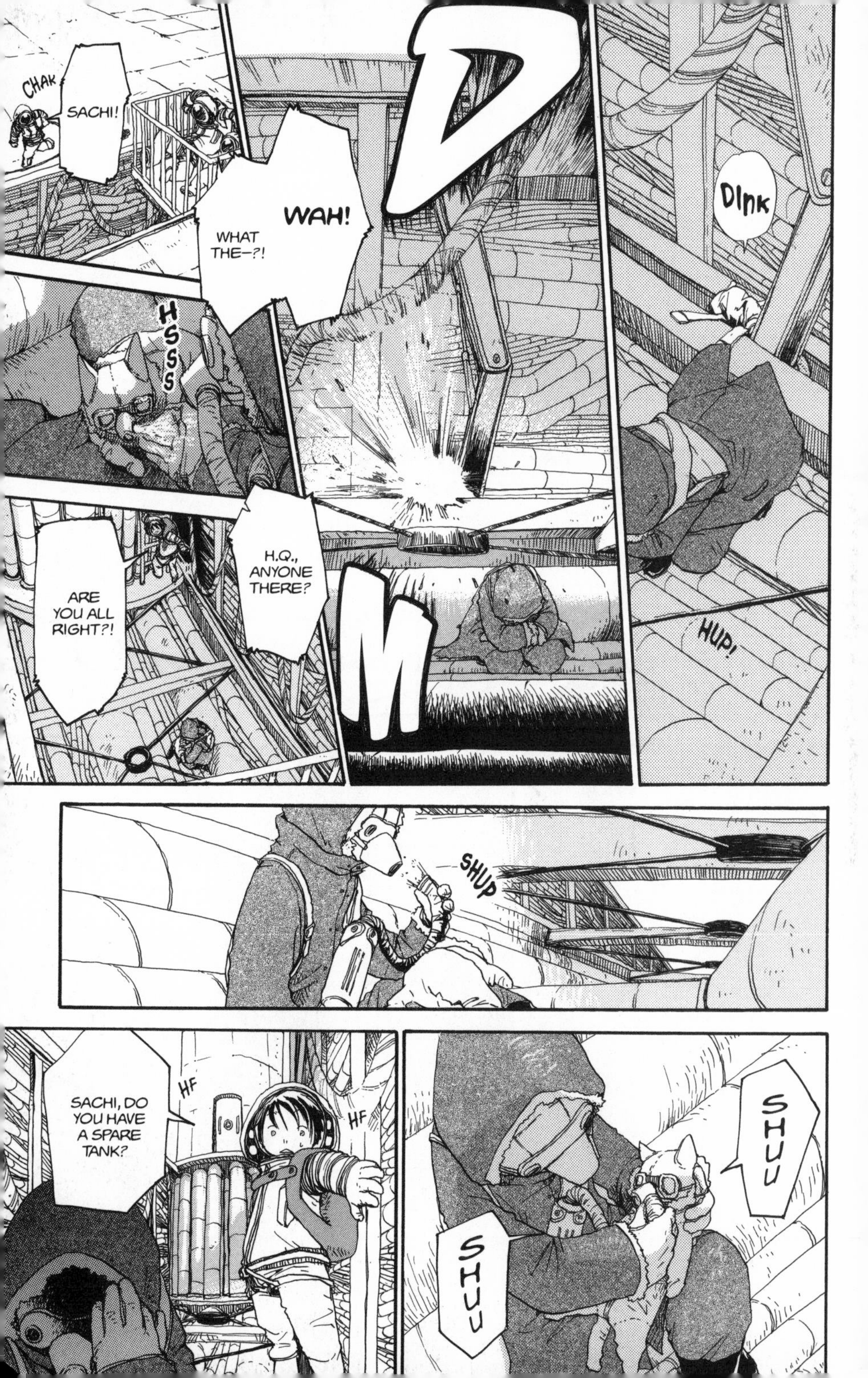
DInk
HUP!
D
M
WAH!
WHAT THE—?!
H.Q., ANYONE THERE?
CHAK
SACHI!
HSSS
ARE YOU ALL RIGHT?!
SHUP
SHUU
SHUU
SACHI, DO YOU HAVE A SPARE TANK?
HF
HF

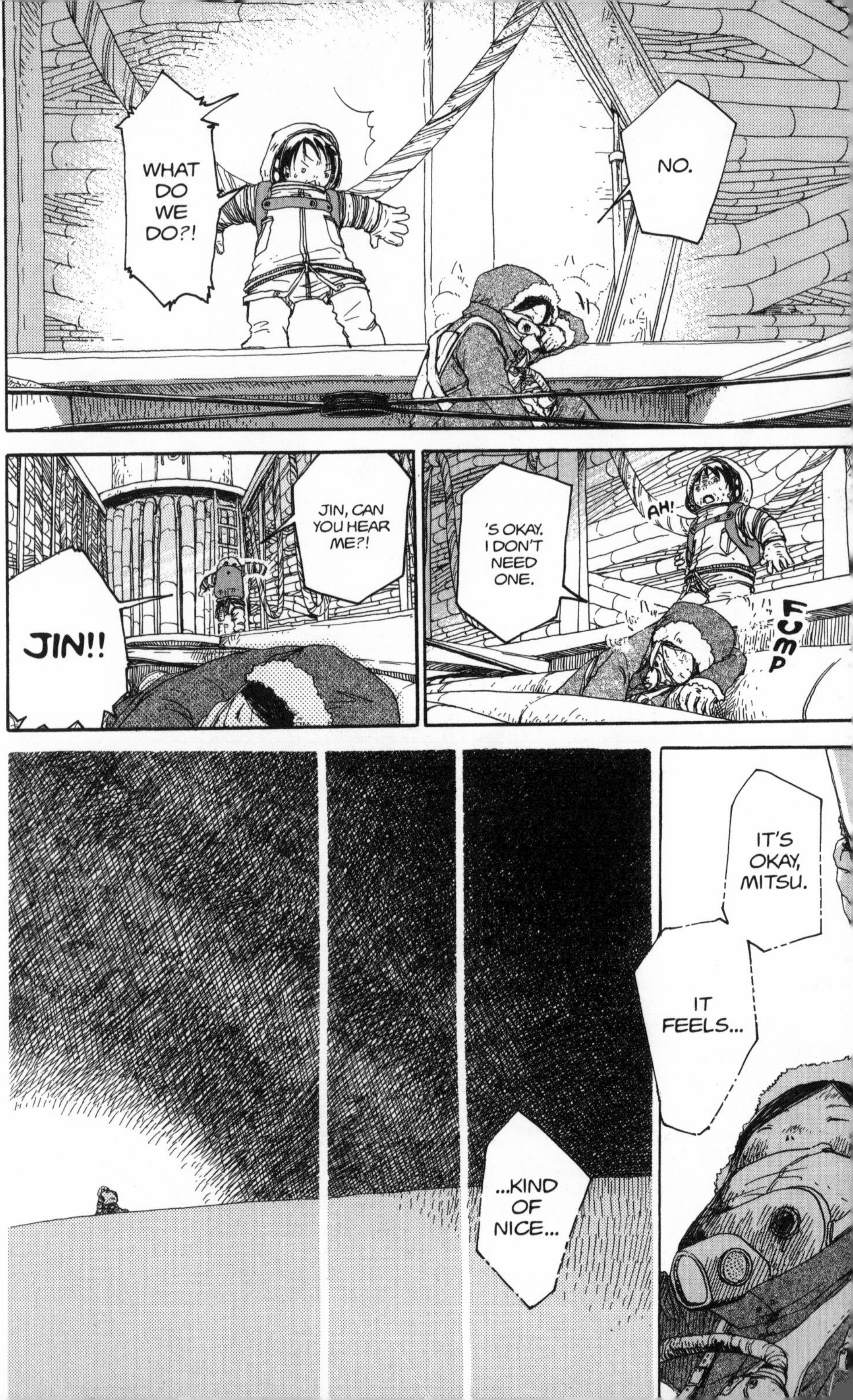
NO.
WHAT DO WE DO?!
AH!
'S OKAY. I DON'T NEED ONE.
FUMP
JIN, CAN YOU HEAR ME?!
JIN!!
IT'S OKAY, MITSU.
IT FEELS...
...KIND OF NICE...

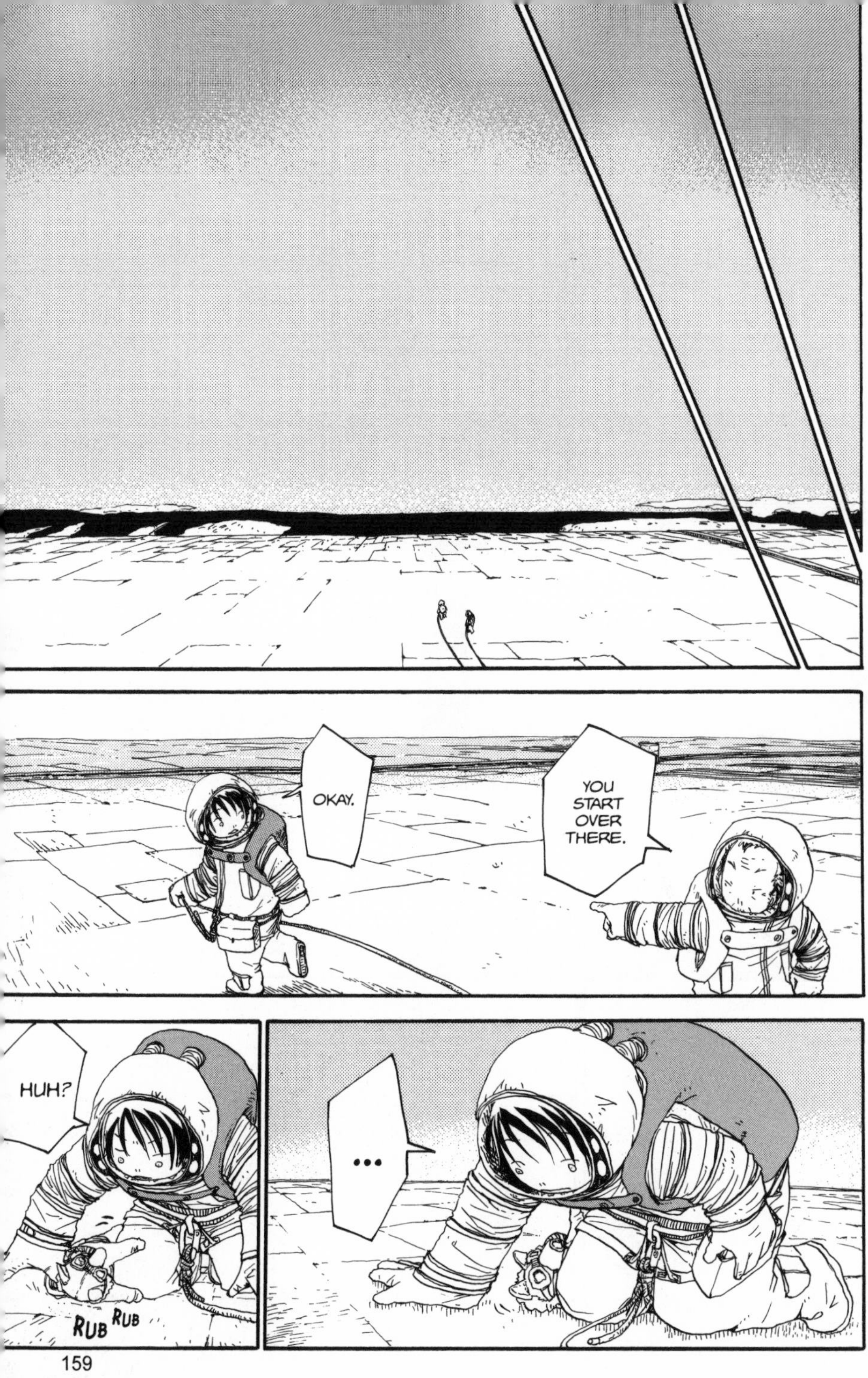
YOU START OVER THERE.
OKAY.
...
HUH?
RUB RUB

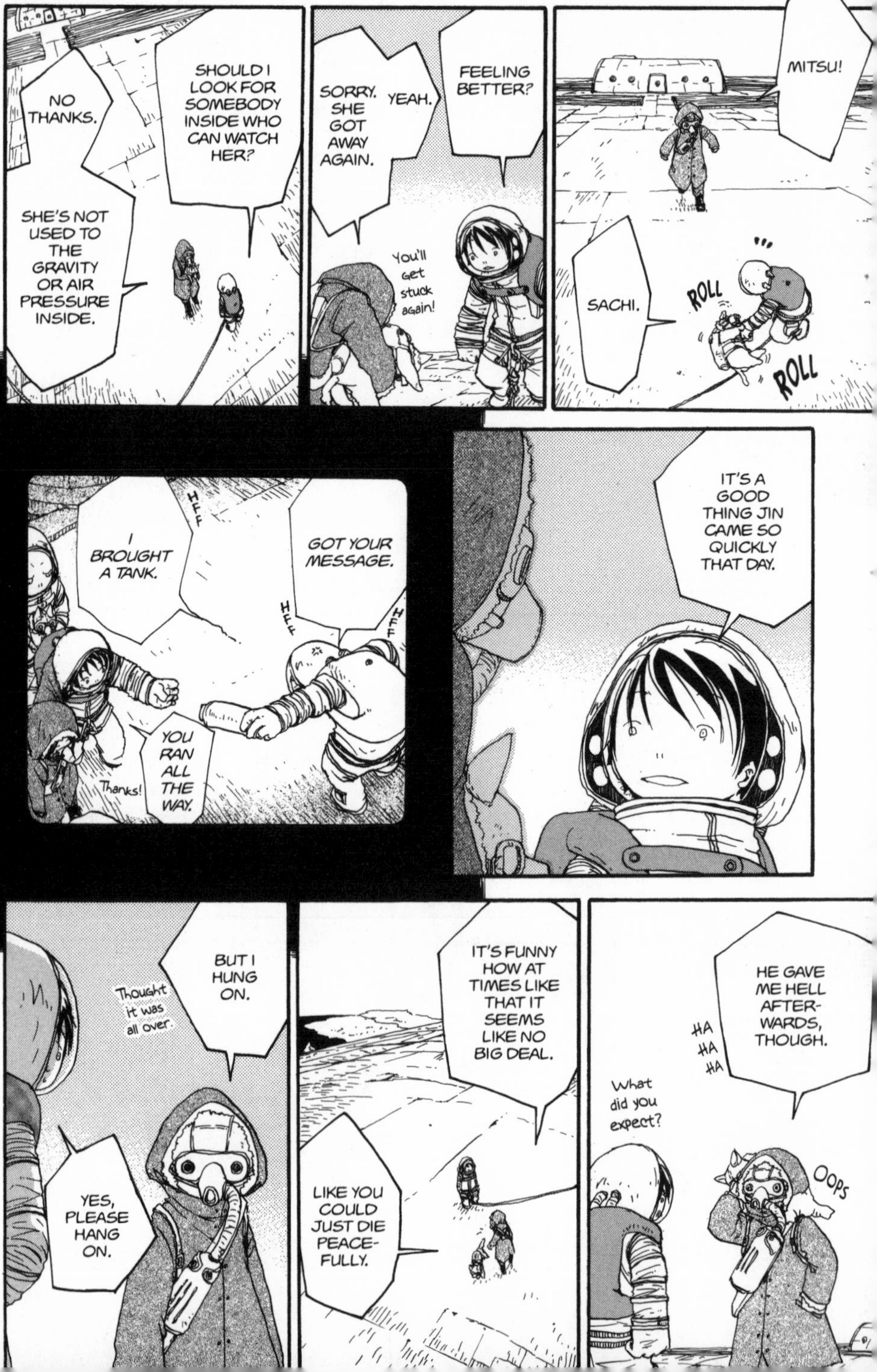
MITSU!
SACHI.
ROLL
ROLL
FEELING BETTER?
YEAH.
SORRY. SHE GOT AWAY AGAIN.
You'll get stuck again!
SHOULD I LOOK FOR SOMEBODY INSIDE WHO CAN WATCH HER?
NO THANKS.
SHE'S NOT USED TO THE GRAVITY OR AIR PRESSURE INSIDE.
IT'S A GOOD THING JIN CAME SO QUICKLY THAT DAY.
GOT YOUR MESSAGE.
HFF
HFF
I BROUGHT A TANK.
HFF
YOU RAN ALL THE WAY.
Thanks!
HE GAVE ME HELL AFTER-WARDS, THOUGH.
HA HA HA
What did you expect?
OOPS
IT'S FUNNY HOW AT TIMES LIKE THAT IT SEEMS LIKE NO BIG DEAL.
LIKE YOU COULD JUST DIE PEACE-FULLY.
BUT I HUNG ON.
Thought it was all over.
YES, PLEASE HANG ON.

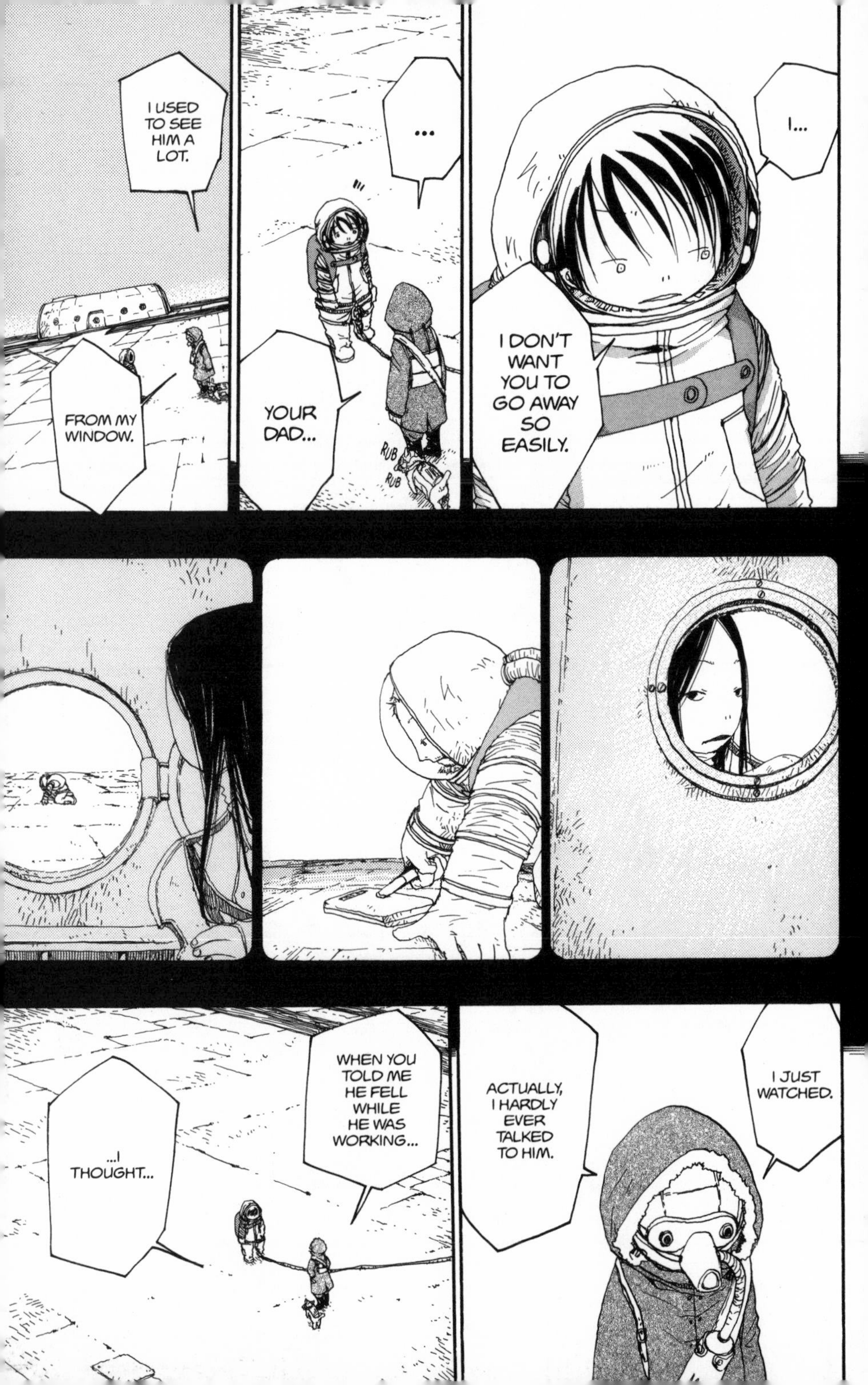
I...
I DON'T WANT YOU TO GO AWAY SO EASILY.
...
YOUR DAD...
RUB RUB
I USED TO SEE HIM A LOT.
FROM MY WINDOW.
I JUST WATCHED.
ACTUALLY, I HARDLY EVER TALKED TO HIM.
WHEN YOU TOLD ME HE FELL WHILE HE WAS WORKING...
...I THOUGHT...

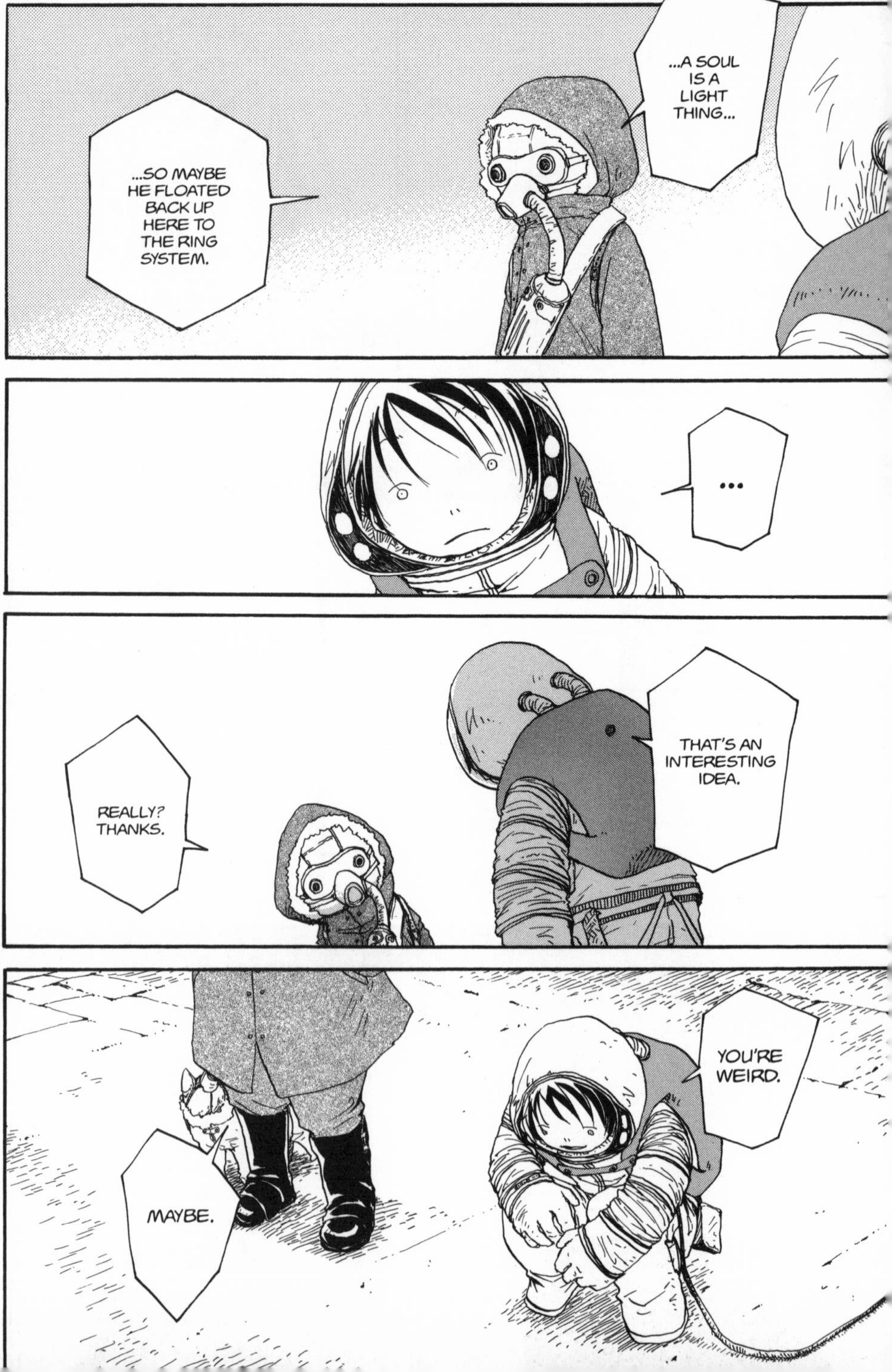
...A SOUL IS A LIGHT THING...
...SO MAYBE HE FLOATED BACK UP HERE TO THE RING SYSTEM.
...
THAT'S AN INTERESTING IDEA.
REALLY? THANKS.
YOU'RE WEIRD.
MAYBE.

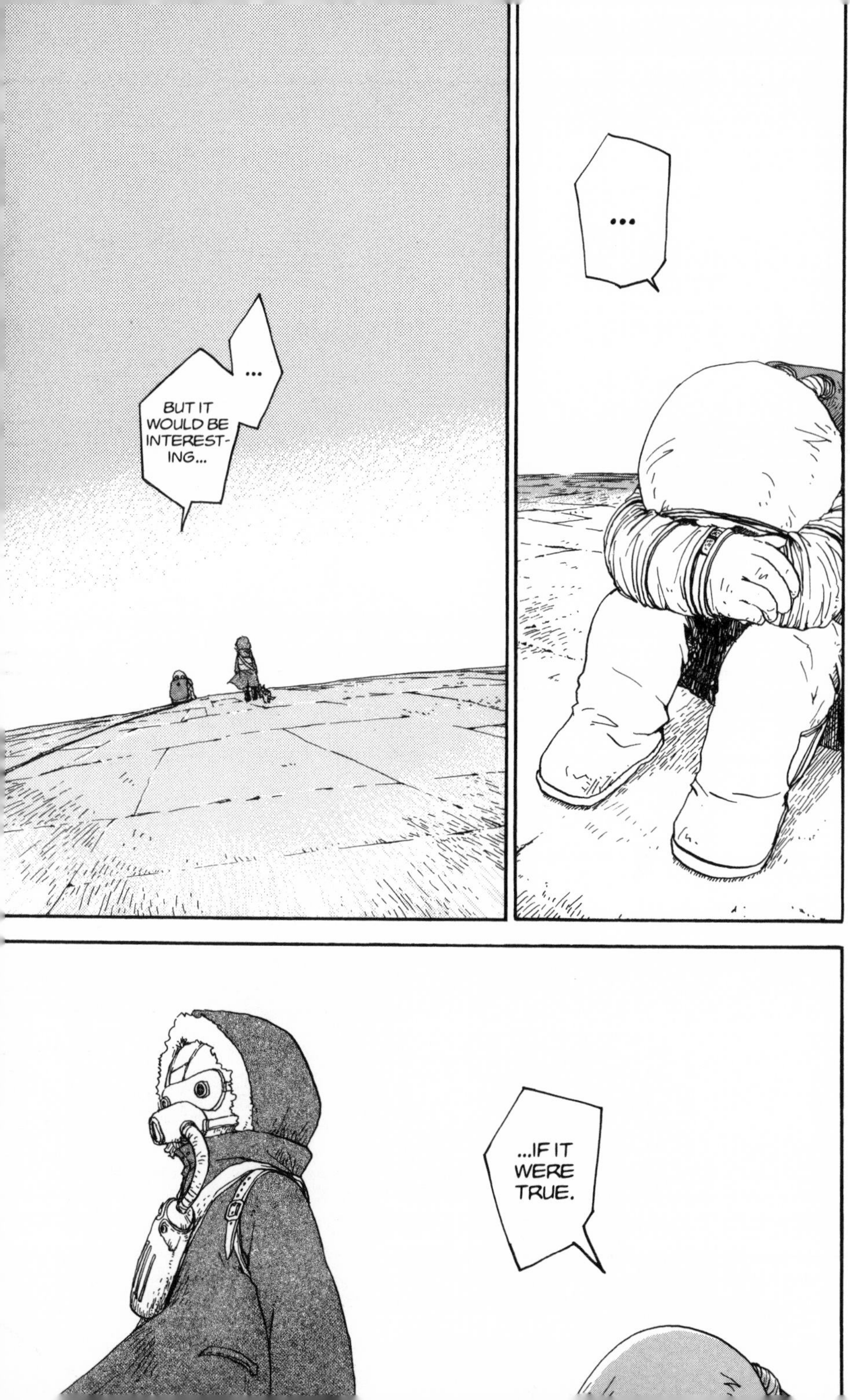
...
...
BUT IT WOULD BE INTEREST-ING...
...IF IT WERE TRUE.

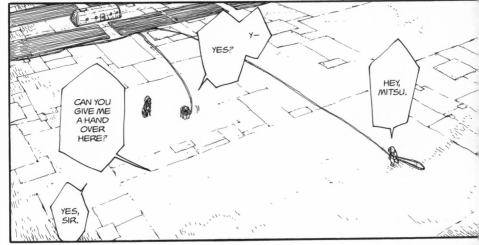

HEY, MITSU.
Y— YES?
CAN YOU GIVE ME A HAND OVER HERE?
YES, SIR.
THANKS, SACHI.
IT'S JUST WHAT I WANT TO BELIEVE.
WHAT?
NOTHING.
MITSU...
That's just what I want to believe.
YOU SHOUD GO DOWN TO THE SURFACE SOMEDAY.
I was happy just watching him.
I WILL.

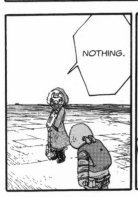

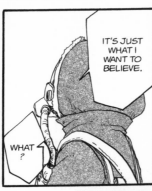

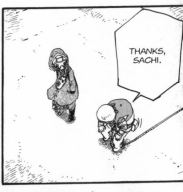

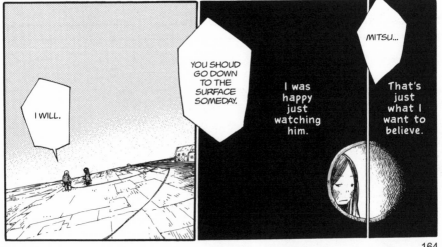

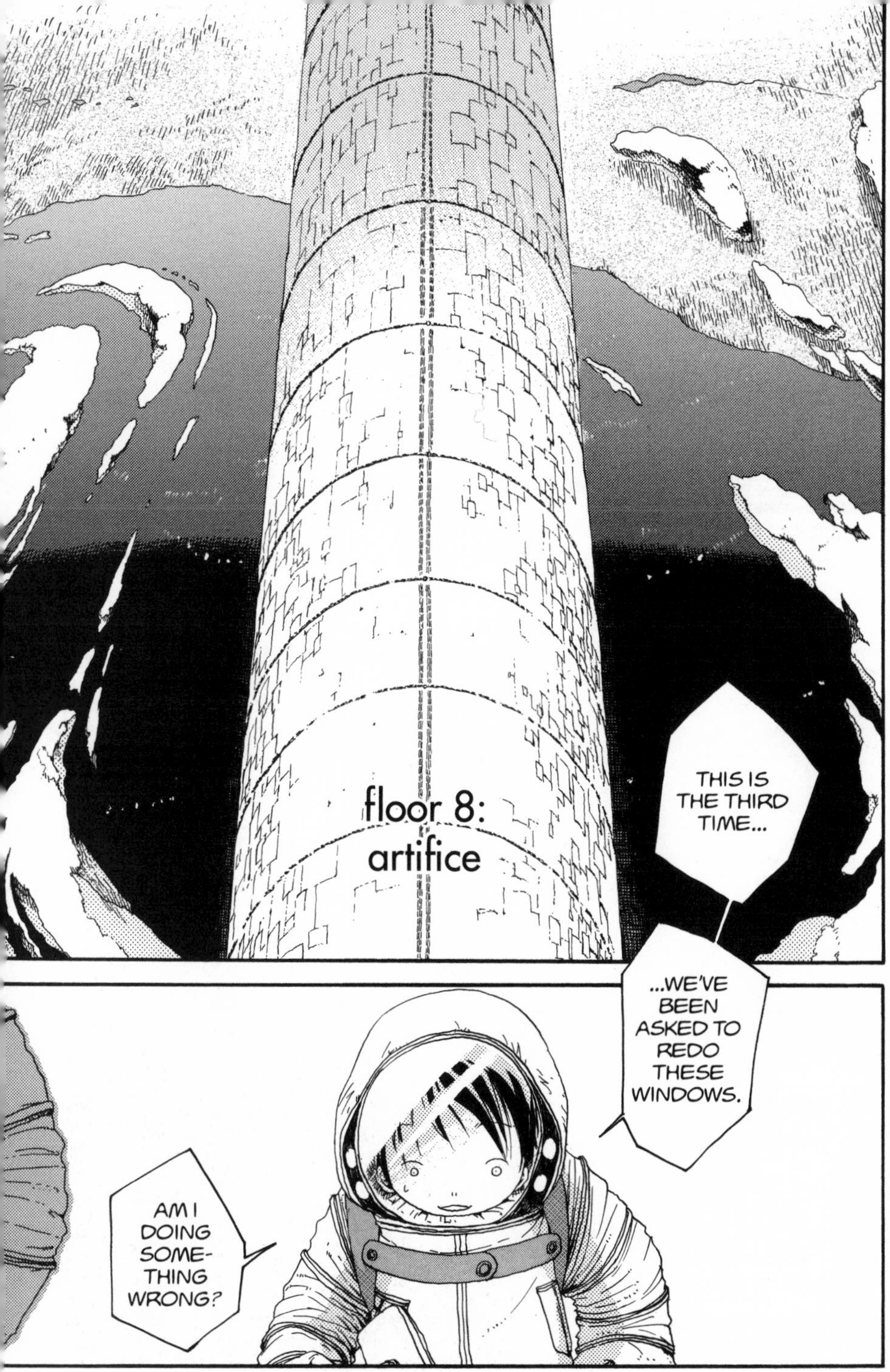
floor 8:
artifice
THIS IS THE THIRD TIME...
...WE'VE BEEN ASKED TO REDO THESE WINDOWS.
AM I DOING SOME-THING WRONG?

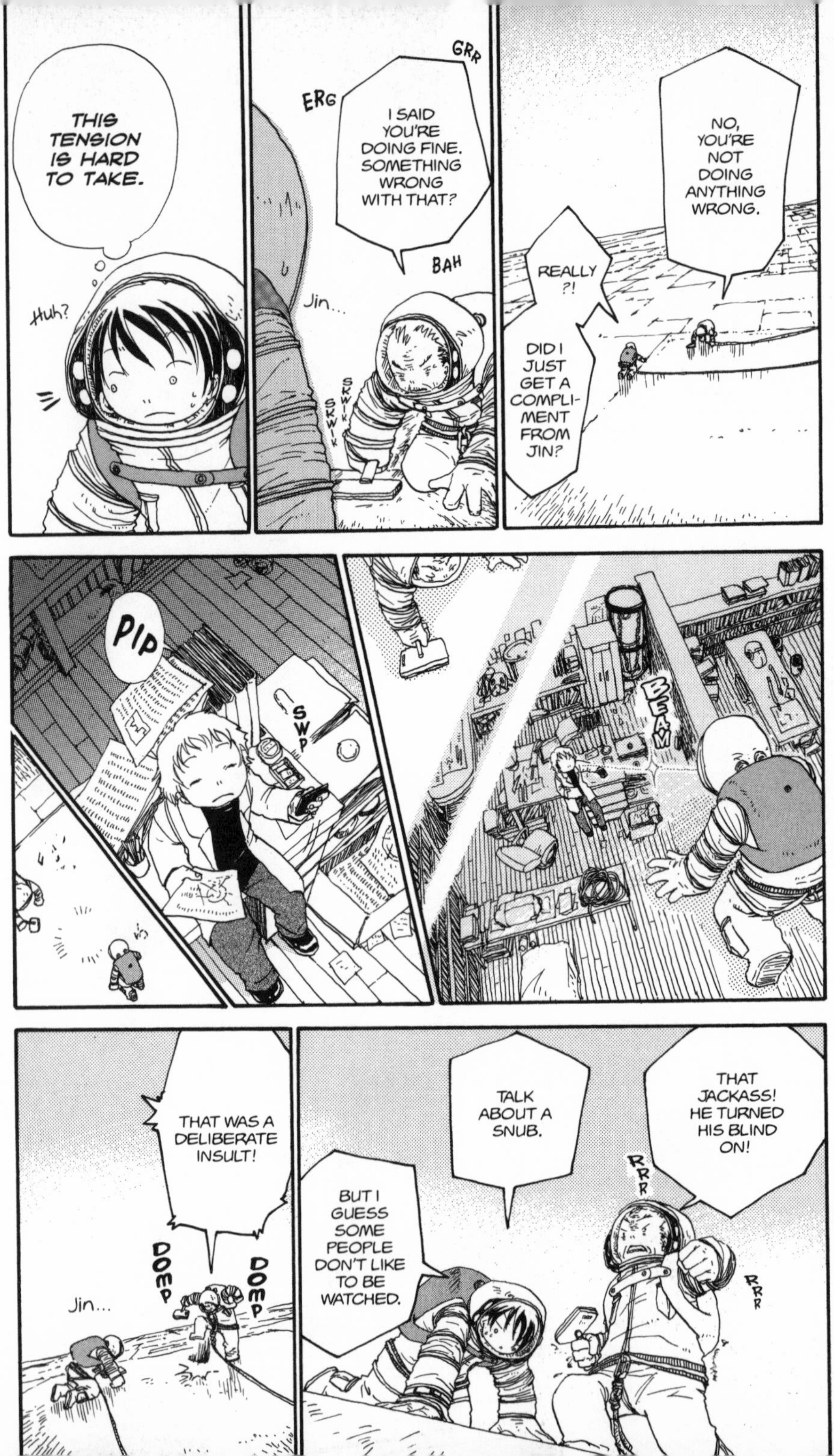
NO, YOU'RE NOT DOING ANYTHING WRONG.
REALLY ?!
DID I JUST GET A COMPLIMENT FROM JIN?
GRR
ERG
I SAID YOU'RE DOING FINE. SOMETHING WRONG WITH THAT?
BAH
Jin...
SKWIK
SKWIK
THIS TENSION IS HARD TO TAKE.
Huh?
BEAM
PIP
SWP
THAT JACKASS! HE TURNED HIS BLIND ON!
RRR
TALK ABOUT A SNUB.
BUT I GUESS SOME PEOPLE DON'T LIKE TO BE WATCHED.
RRR
THAT WAS A DELIBERATE INSULT!
DOMP
DOMP
Jin...

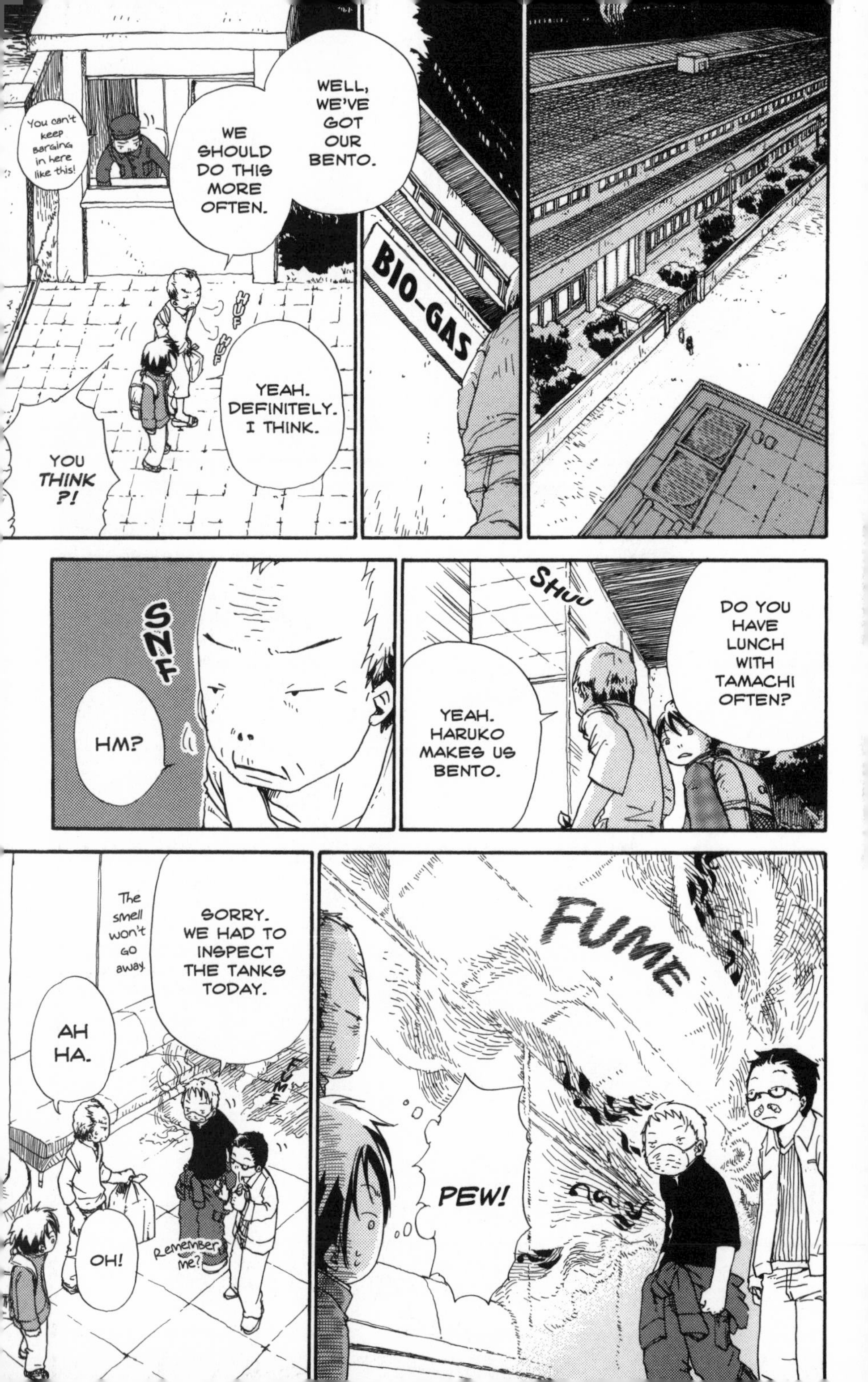
BIO-GAS
WELL, WE'VE GOT OUR BENTO.
WE SHOULD DO THIS MORE OFTEN.
You can't keep barging in here like this!
HUF HUF
YEAH. DEFINITELY. I THINK.
YOU THINK?!
SHUU
DO YOU HAVE LUNCH WITH TAMACHI OFTEN?
YEAH. HARUKO MAKES US BENTO.
SNF
HM?
FUME
PEW!
SORRY. WE HAD TO INSPECT THE TANKS TODAY.
The smell won't go away.
AH HA.
FUME
OH!
Remember me?

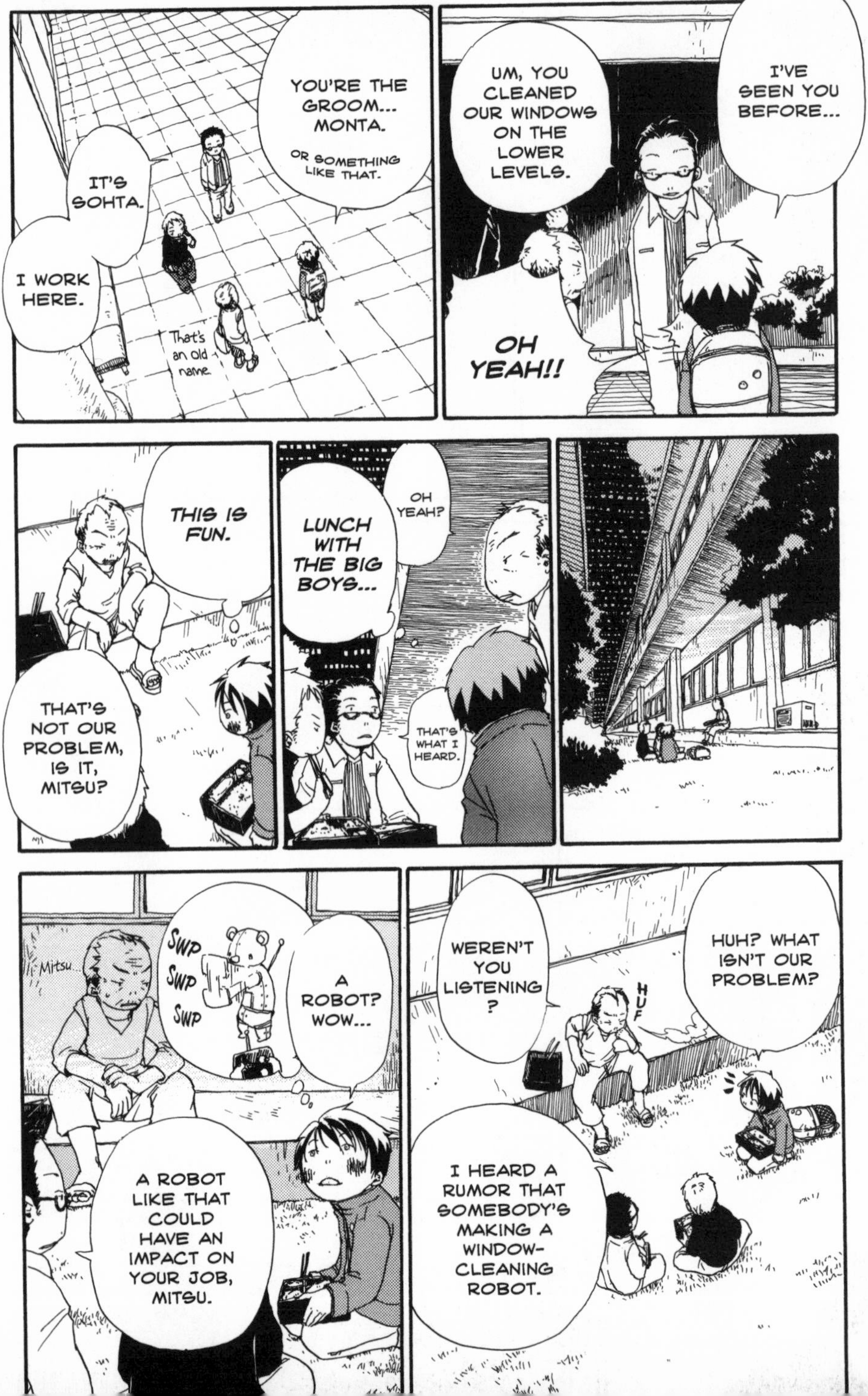
I'VE SEEN YOU BEFORE...
UM, YOU CLEANED OUR WINDOWS ON THE LOWER LEVELS.
OH YEAH!!
YOU'RE THE GROOM... MONTA.
OR SOMETHING LIKE THAT.
IT'S SOHTA.
I WORK HERE.
That's an old name.
OH YEAH?
LUNCH WITH THE BIG BOYS...
THAT'S WHAT I HEARD.
THIS IS FUN.
THAT'S NOT OUR PROBLEM, IS IT, MITSU?
HUH? WHAT ISN'T OUR PROBLEM?
WEREN'T YOU LISTENING?
HUF
I HEARD A RUMOR THAT SOMEBODY'S MAKING A WINDOW-CLEANING ROBOT.
A ROBOT? WOW...
SWP SWP SWP
Mitsu...
A ROBOT LIKE THAT COULD HAVE AN IMPACT ON YOUR JOB, MITSU.

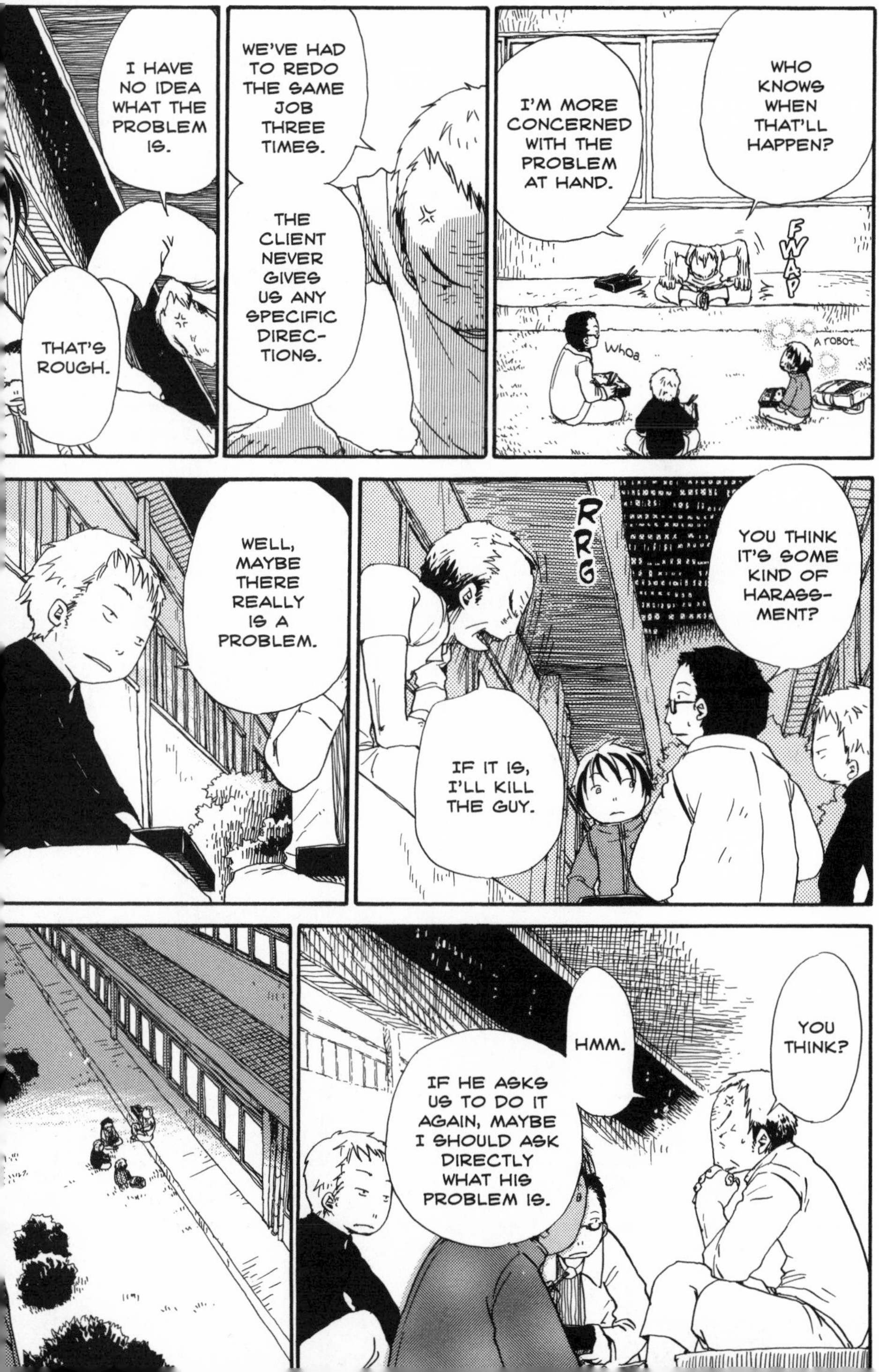
WHO KNOWS WHEN THAT'LL HAPPEN?
I'M MORE CONCERNED WITH THE PROBLEM AT HAND.
FWAP
A robot...
Whoa.
WE'VE HAD TO REDO THE SAME JOB THREE TIMES.
THE CLIENT NEVER GIVES US ANY SPECIFIC DIREC-TIONS.
I HAVE NO IDEA WHAT THE PROBLEM IS.
THAT'S ROUGH.
YOU THINK IT'S SOME KIND OF HARASS-MENT?
RRG
IF IT IS, I'LL KILL THE GUY.
WELL, MAYBE THERE REALLY IS A PROBLEM.
YOU THINK?
HMM.
IF HE ASKS US TO DO IT AGAIN, MAYBE I SHOULD ASK DIRECTLY WHAT HIS PROBLEM IS.

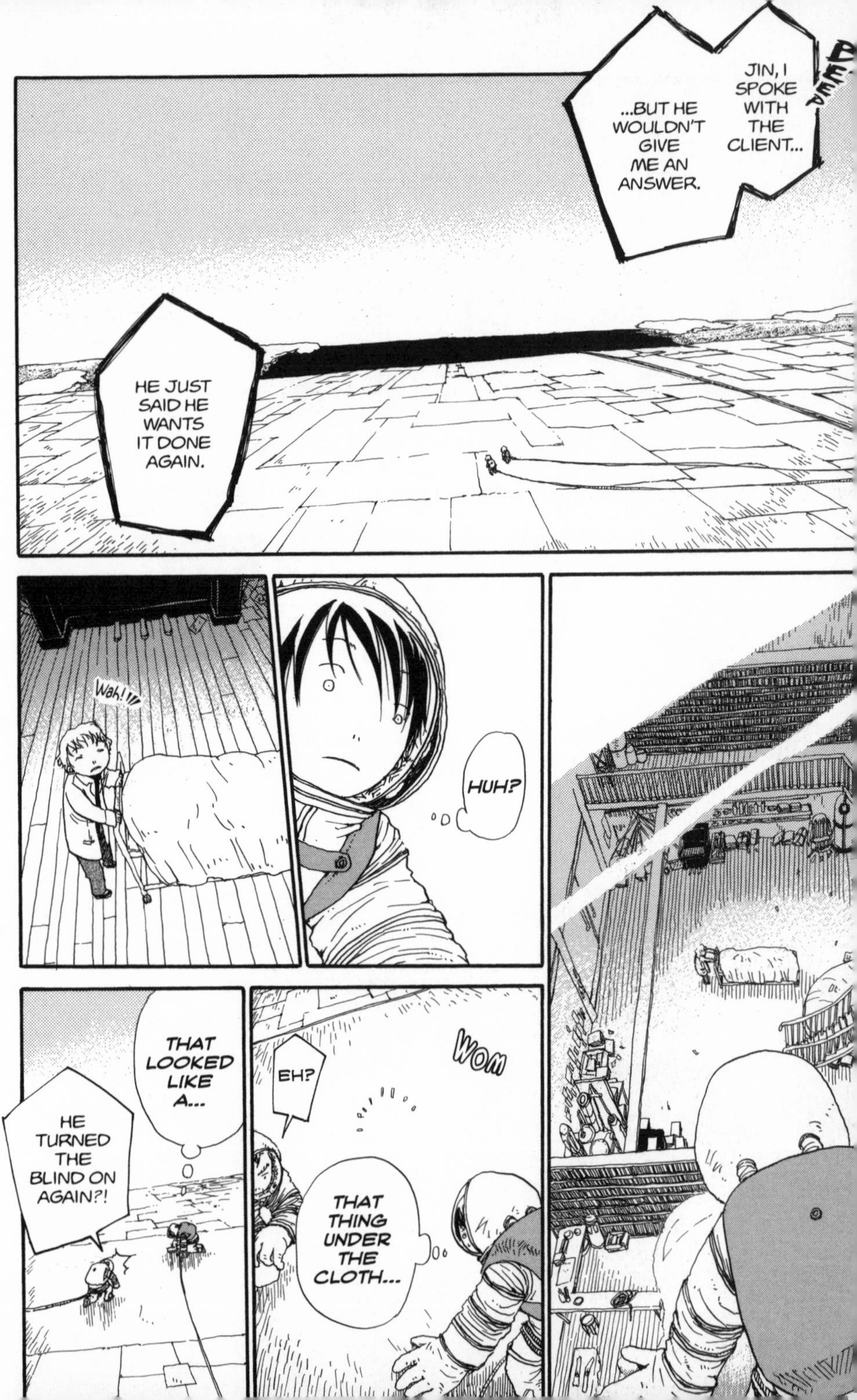
BEEP
JIN, I SPOKE WITH THE CLIENT...
...BUT HE WOULDN'T GIVE ME AN ANSWER.
HE JUST SAID HE WANTS IT DONE AGAIN.
HUH?
Wah!
WOM
EH?
THAT THING UNDER THE CLOTH...
THAT LOOKED LIKE A...
HE TURNED THE BLIND ON AGAIN?!

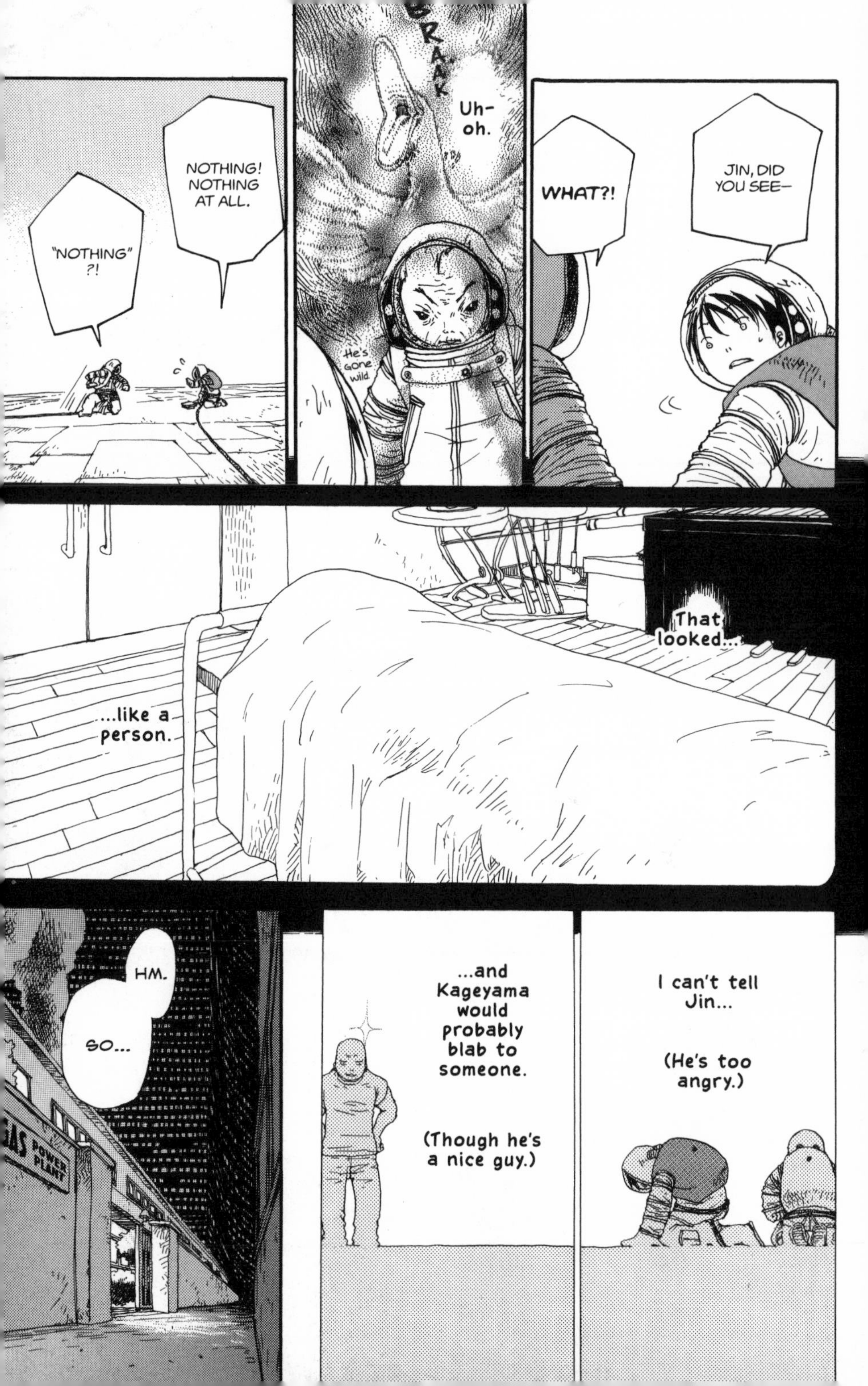
JIN, DID YOU SEE—
WHAT?!
BRAAK
Uh-oh.
He's gone wild.
NOTHING! NOTHING AT ALL.
"NOTHING"?!
That looked...
...like a person.
I can't tell Jin...
(He's too angry.)
...and Kageyama would probably blab to someone.
(Though he's a nice guy.)
HM.
SO...
POWER PLANT

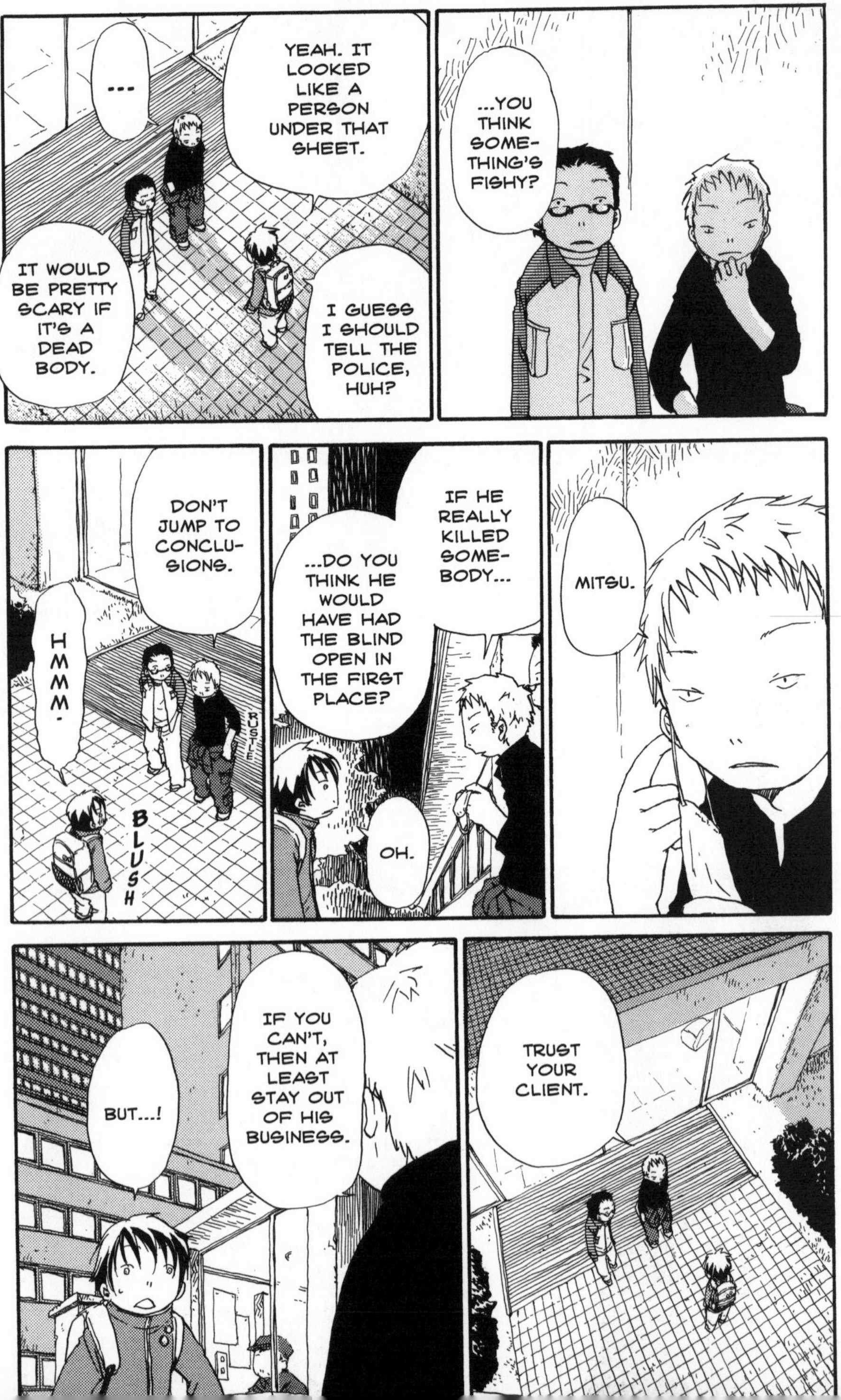
...YOU THINK SOME-THING'S FISHY?
YEAH. IT LOOKED LIKE A PERSON UNDER THAT SHEET.
...
IT WOULD BE PRETTY SCARY IF IT'S A DEAD BODY.
I GUESS I SHOULD TELL THE POLICE, HUH?
MITSU.
IF HE REALLY KILLED SOME-BODY...
...DO YOU THINK HE WOULD HAVE HAD THE BLIND OPEN IN THE FIRST PLACE?
OH.
DON'T JUMP TO CONCLU-SIONS.
HMMM.
RUSTLE
BLUSH
TRUST YOUR CLIENT.
IF YOU CAN'T, THEN AT LEAST STAY OUT OF HIS BUSINESS.
BUT...!

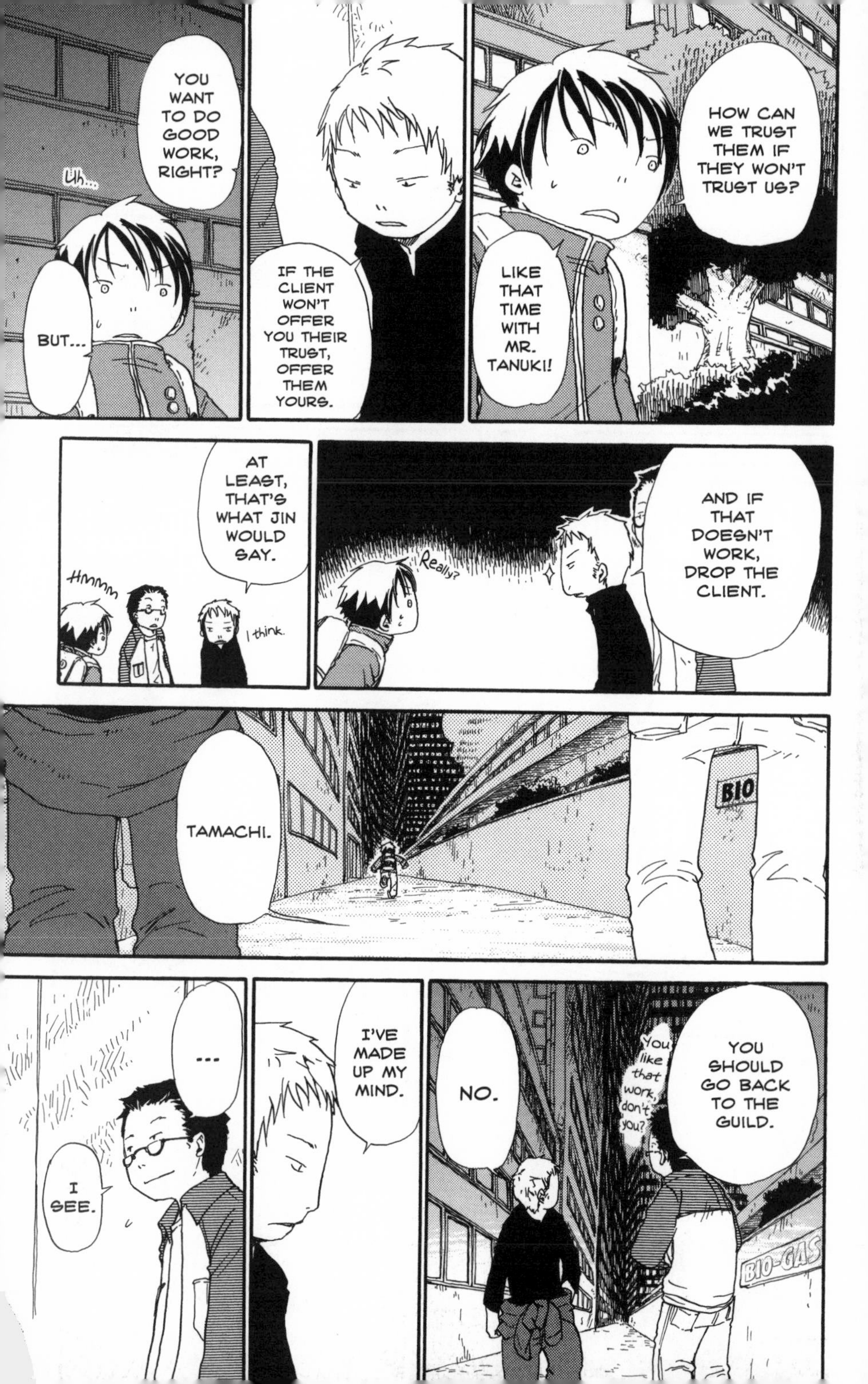
HOW CAN WE TRUST THEM IF THEY WON'T TRUST US?
LIKE THAT TIME WITH MR. TANUKI!
IF THE CLIENT WON'T OFFER YOU THEIR TRUST, OFFER THEM YOURS.
YOU WANT TO DO GOOD WORK, RIGHT?
Uh...
BUT...
AND IF THAT DOESN'T WORK, DROP THE CLIENT.
Really?
AT LEAST, THAT'S WHAT JIN WOULD SAY.
Hmmm
I think.
BIO
TAMACHI.
YOU SHOULD GO BACK TO THE GUILD.
You like that work, don't you?
NO.
BIO-GAS
I'VE MADE UP MY MIND.
...
I SEE.

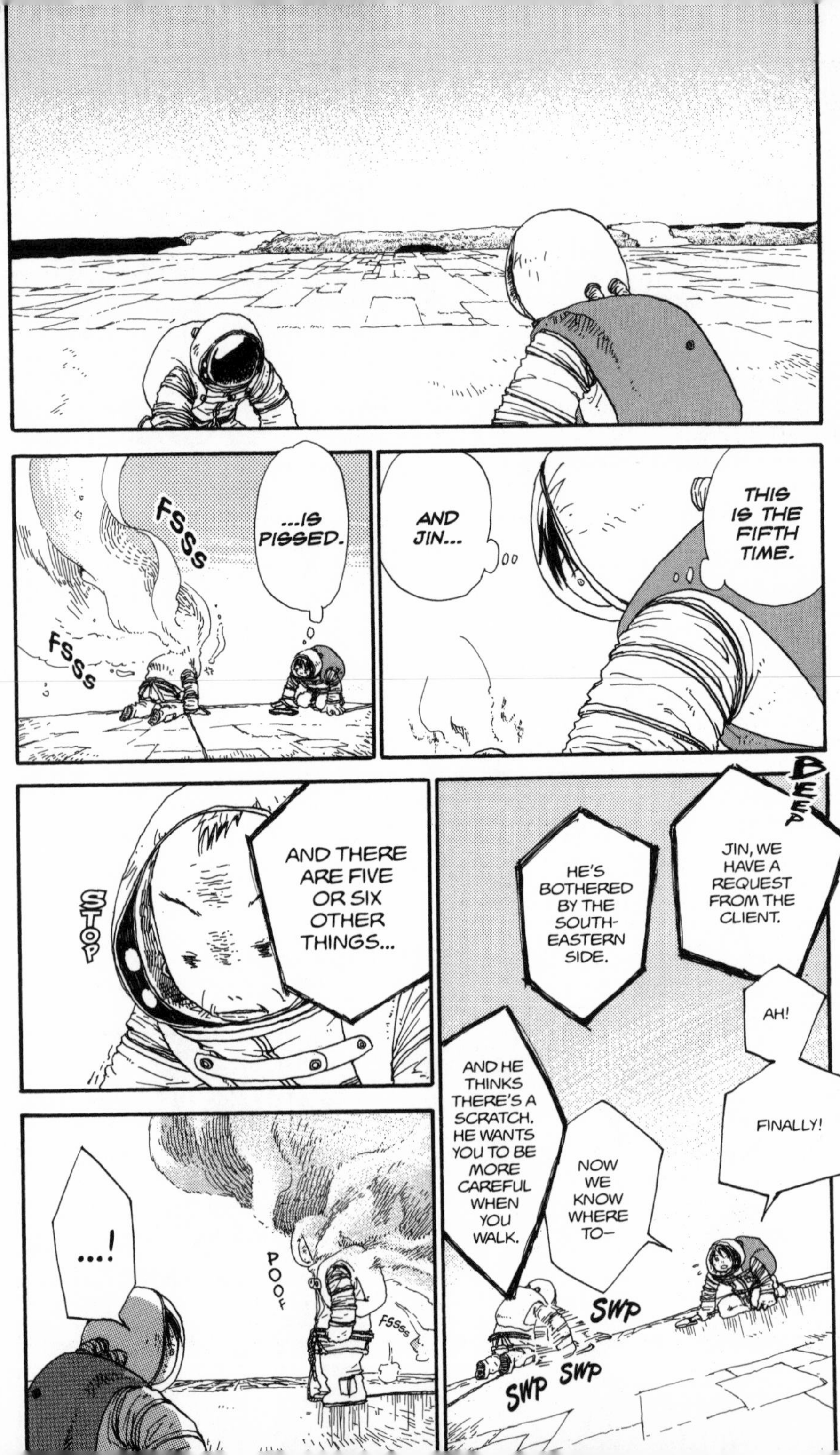
THIS IS THE FIFTH TIME.
AND JIN...
...IS PISSED.
FSSS
FSSS
BEEP
JIN, WE HAVE A REQUEST FROM THE CLIENT.
HE'S BOTHERED BY THE SOUTH-EASTERN SIDE.
AH!
FINALLY!
AND HE THINKS THERE'S A SCRATCH. HE WANTS YOU TO BE MORE CAREFUL WHEN YOU WALK.
NOW WE KNOW WHERE TO—
SWP
SWP SWP
AND THERE ARE FIVE OR SIX OTHER THINGS...
STOP
...!
POOF
FSSSS

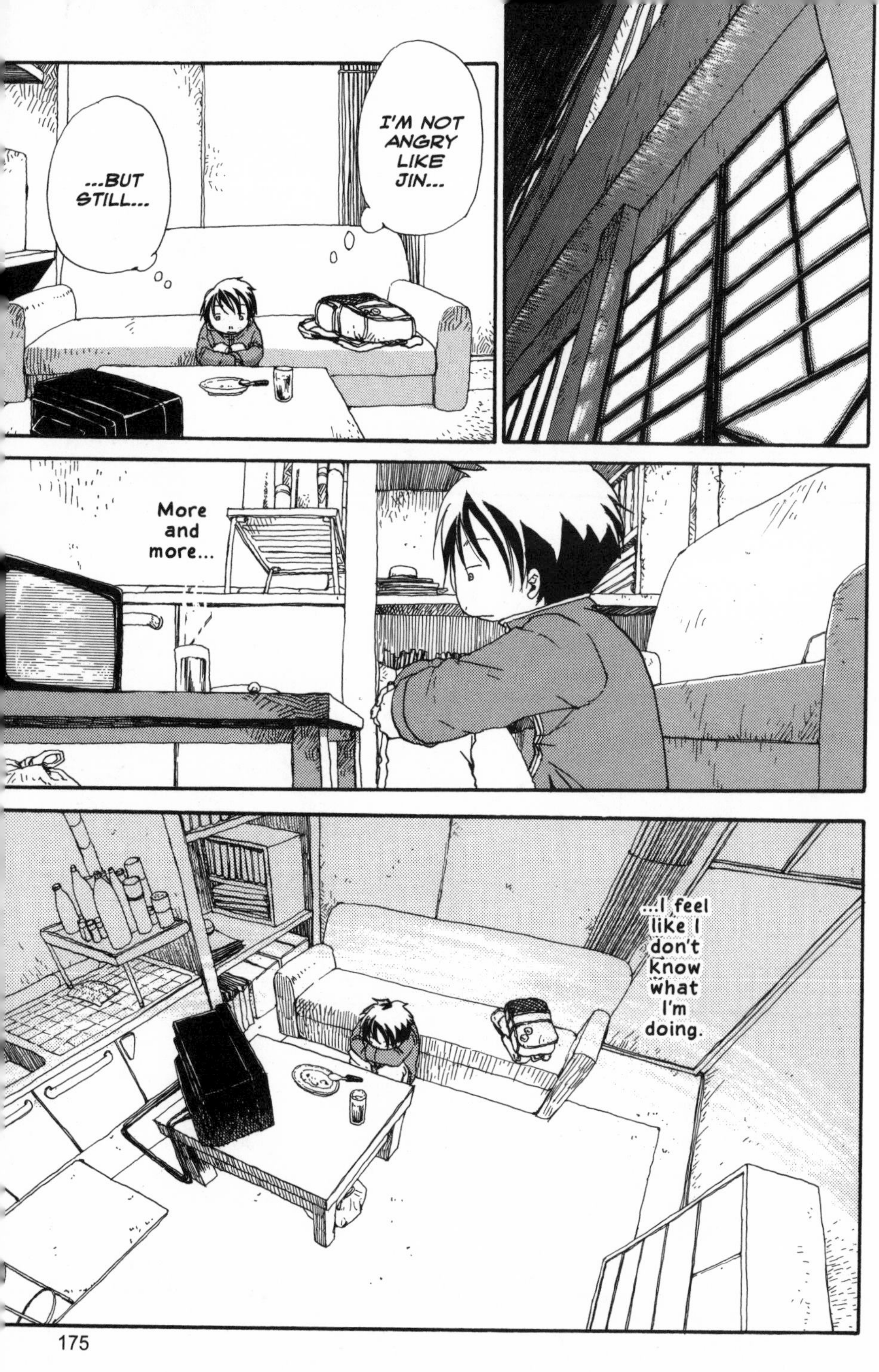
I'M NOT ANGRY LIKE JIN...
...BUT STILL...
More and more...
...I feel like I don't know what I'm doing.

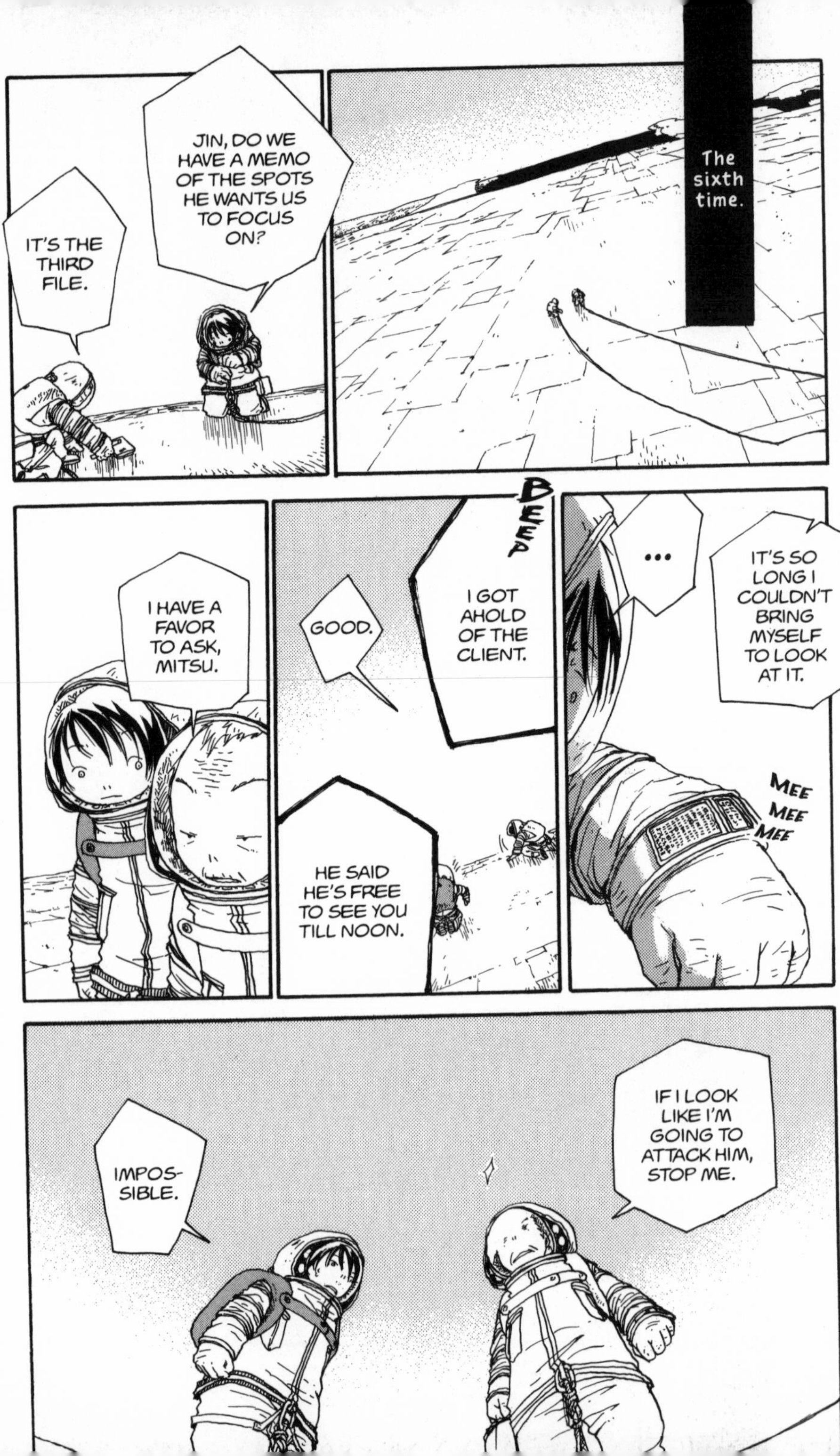
The sixth time.
JIN, DO WE HAVE A MEMO OF THE SPOTS HE WANTS US TO FOCUS ON?
IT'S THE THIRD FILE.
IT'S SO LONG I COULDN'T BRING MYSELF TO LOOK AT IT.
...
MEE MEE MEE
BEEP
I GOT AHOLD OF THE CLIENT.
GOOD.
HE SAID HE'S FREE TO SEE YOU TILL NOON.
I HAVE A FAVOR TO ASK, MITSU.
IF I LOOK LIKE I'M GOING TO ATTACK HIM, STOP ME.
IMPOS-SIBLE.

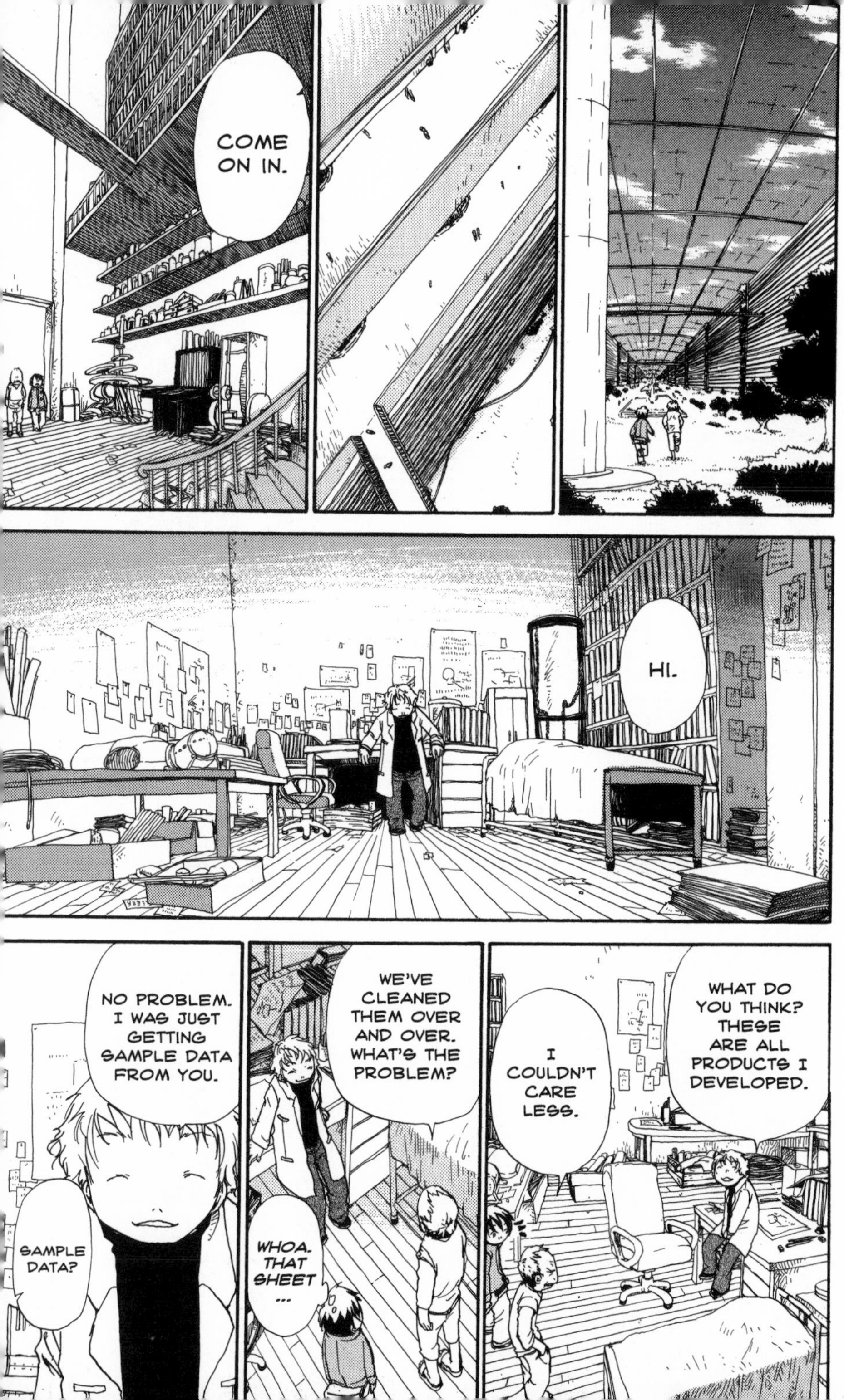
COME ON IN.
HI.
WHAT DO YOU THINK? THESE ARE ALL PRODUCTS I DEVELOPED.
I COULDN'T CARE LESS.
WE'VE CLEANED THEM OVER AND OVER. WHAT'S THE PROBLEM?
WHOA. THAT SHEET ...
NO PROBLEM. I WAS JUST GETTING SAMPLE DATA FROM YOU.
SAMPLE DATA?

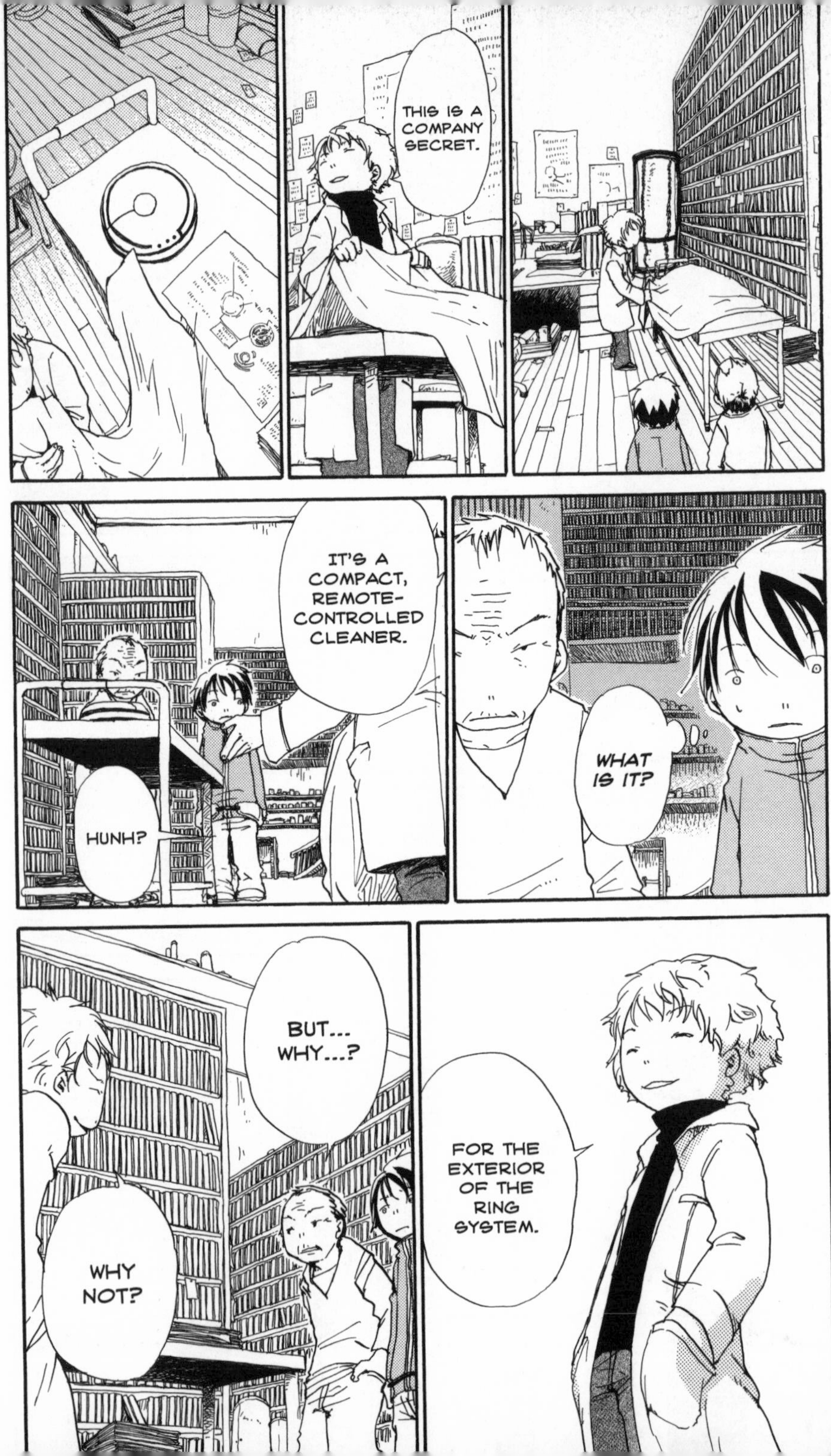
THIS IS A COMPANY SECRET.
WHAT IS IT?
IT'S A COMPACT, REMOTE-CONTROLLED CLEANER.
HUNH?
FOR THE EXTERIOR OF THE RING SYSTEM.
BUT... WHY...?
WHY NOT?

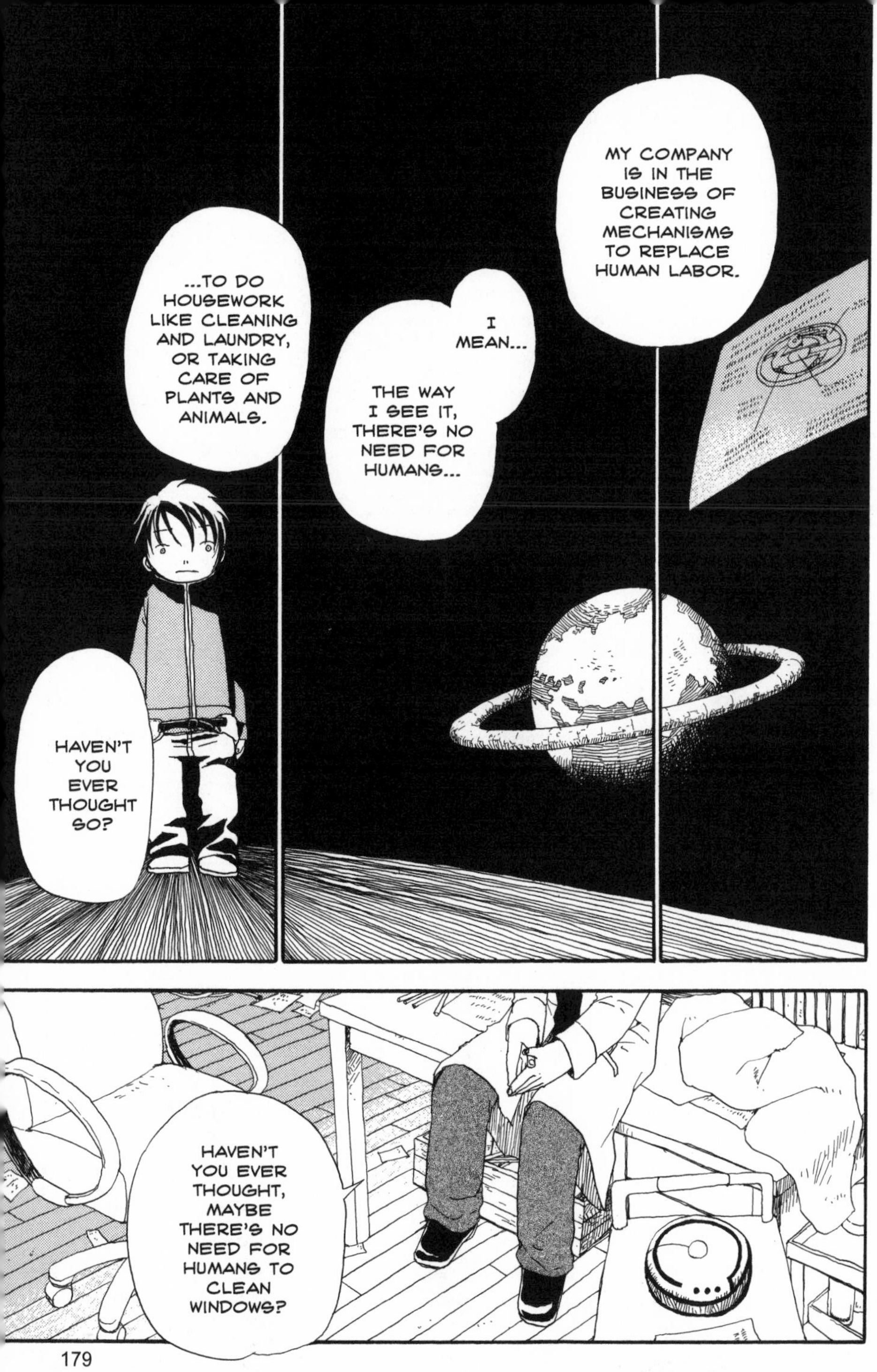
MY COMPANY IS IN THE BUSINESS OF CREATING MECHANISMS TO REPLACE HUMAN LABOR.
I MEAN...
THE WAY I SEE IT, THERE'S NO NEED FOR HUMANS...
...TO DO HOUSEWORK LIKE CLEANING AND LAUNDRY, OR TAKING CARE OF PLANTS AND ANIMALS.
HAVEN'T YOU EVER THOUGHT SO?
HAVEN'T YOU EVER THOUGHT, MAYBE THERE'S NO NEED FOR HUMANS TO CLEAN WINDOWS?

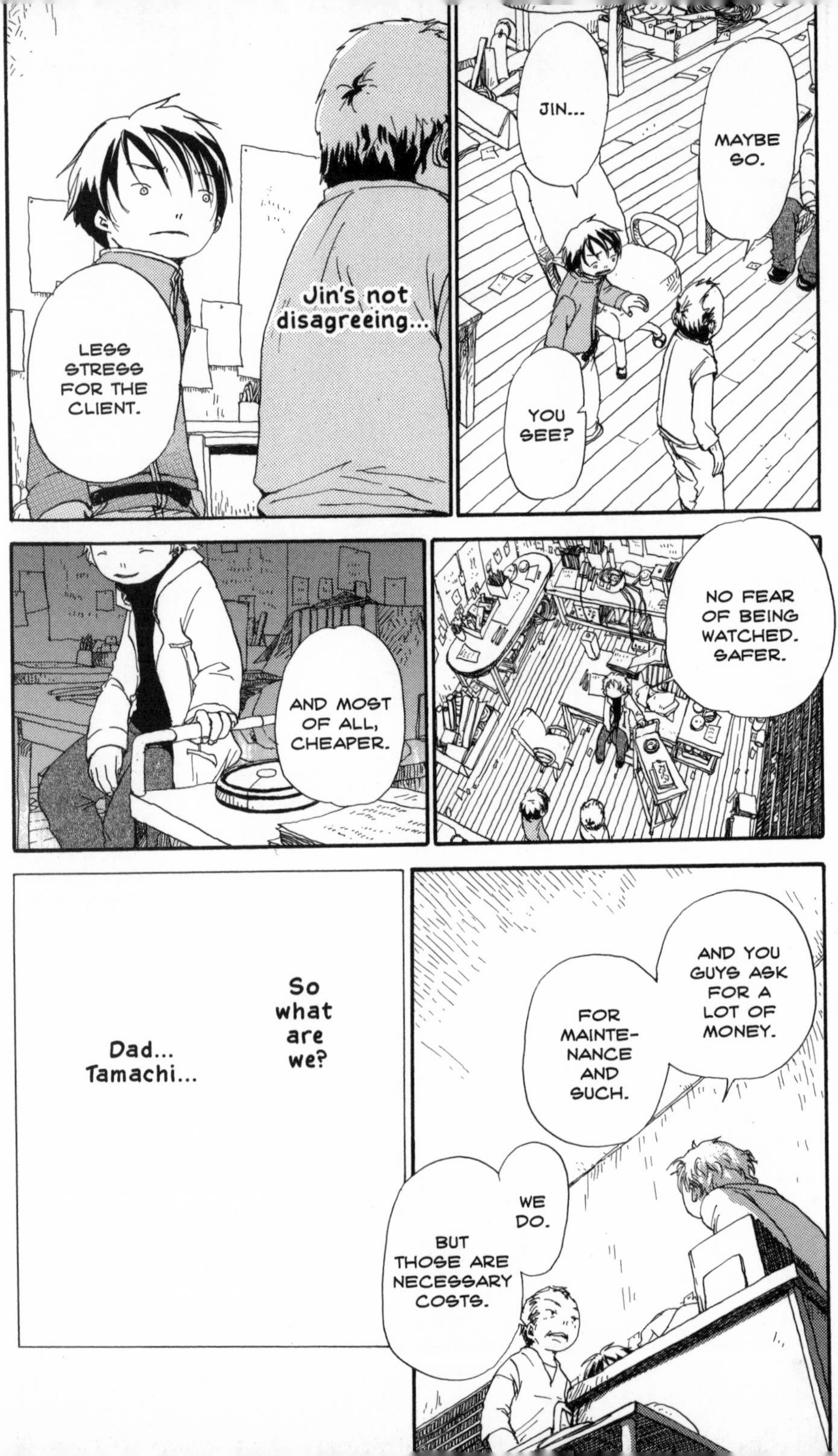
JIN...
YOU SEE?
MAYBE SO.
Jin's not disagreeing...
LESS STRESS FOR THE CLIENT.
NO FEAR OF BEING WATCHED. SAFER.
AND MOST OF ALL, CHEAPER.
AND YOU GUYS ASK FOR A LOT OF MONEY.
FOR MAINTENANCE AND SUCH.
WE DO.
BUT THOSE ARE NECESSARY COSTS.
So what are we?
Dad... Tamachi...

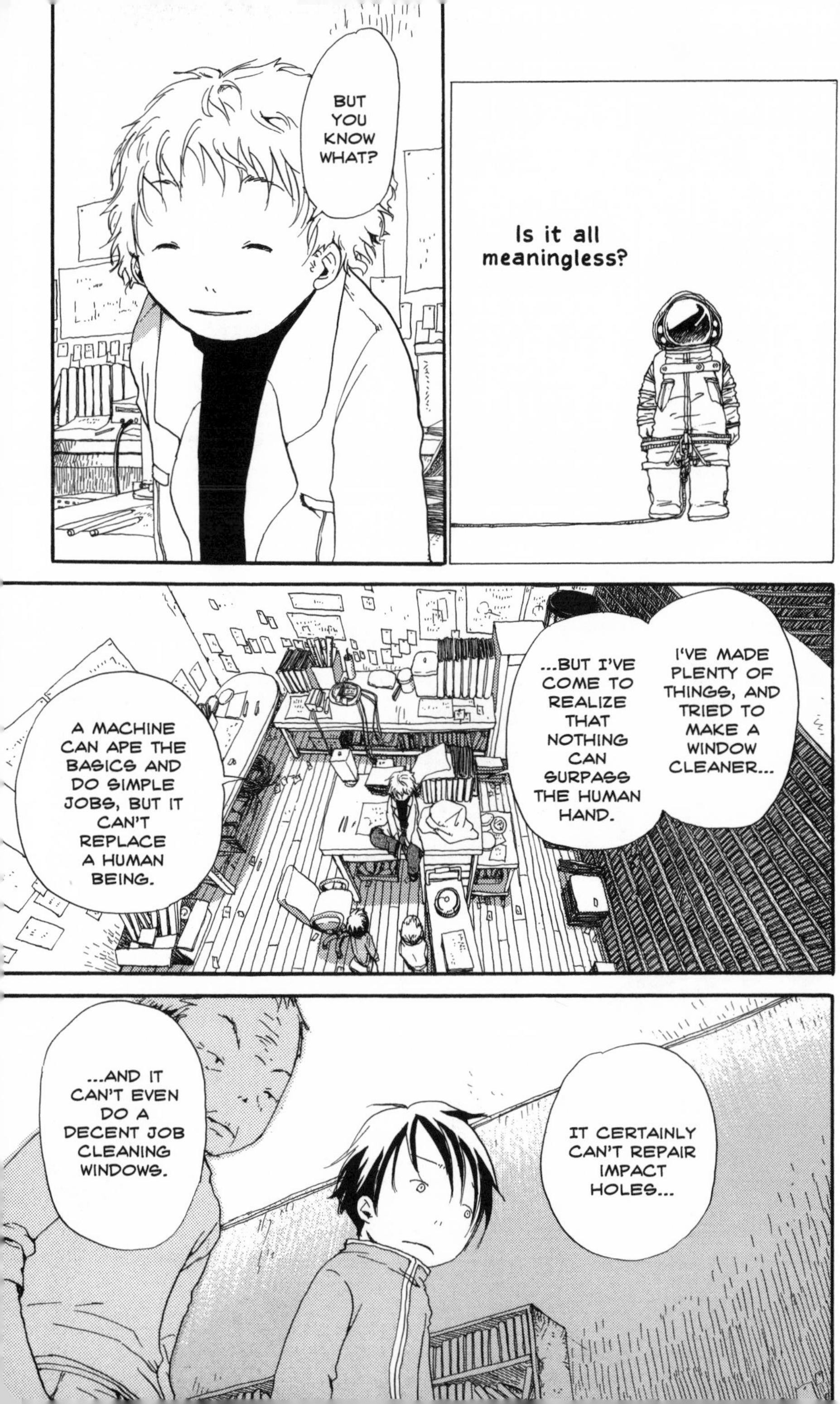
Is it all meaningless?
BUT YOU KNOW WHAT?
I'VE MADE PLENTY OF THINGS, AND TRIED TO MAKE A WINDOW CLEANER...
...BUT I'VE COME TO REALIZE THAT NOTHING CAN SURPASS THE HUMAN HAND.
A MACHINE CAN APE THE BASICS AND DO SIMPLE JOBS, BUT IT CAN'T REPLACE A HUMAN BEING.
IT CERTAINLY CAN'T REPAIR IMPACT HOLES...
...AND IT CAN'T EVEN DO A DECENT JOB CLEANING WINDOWS.

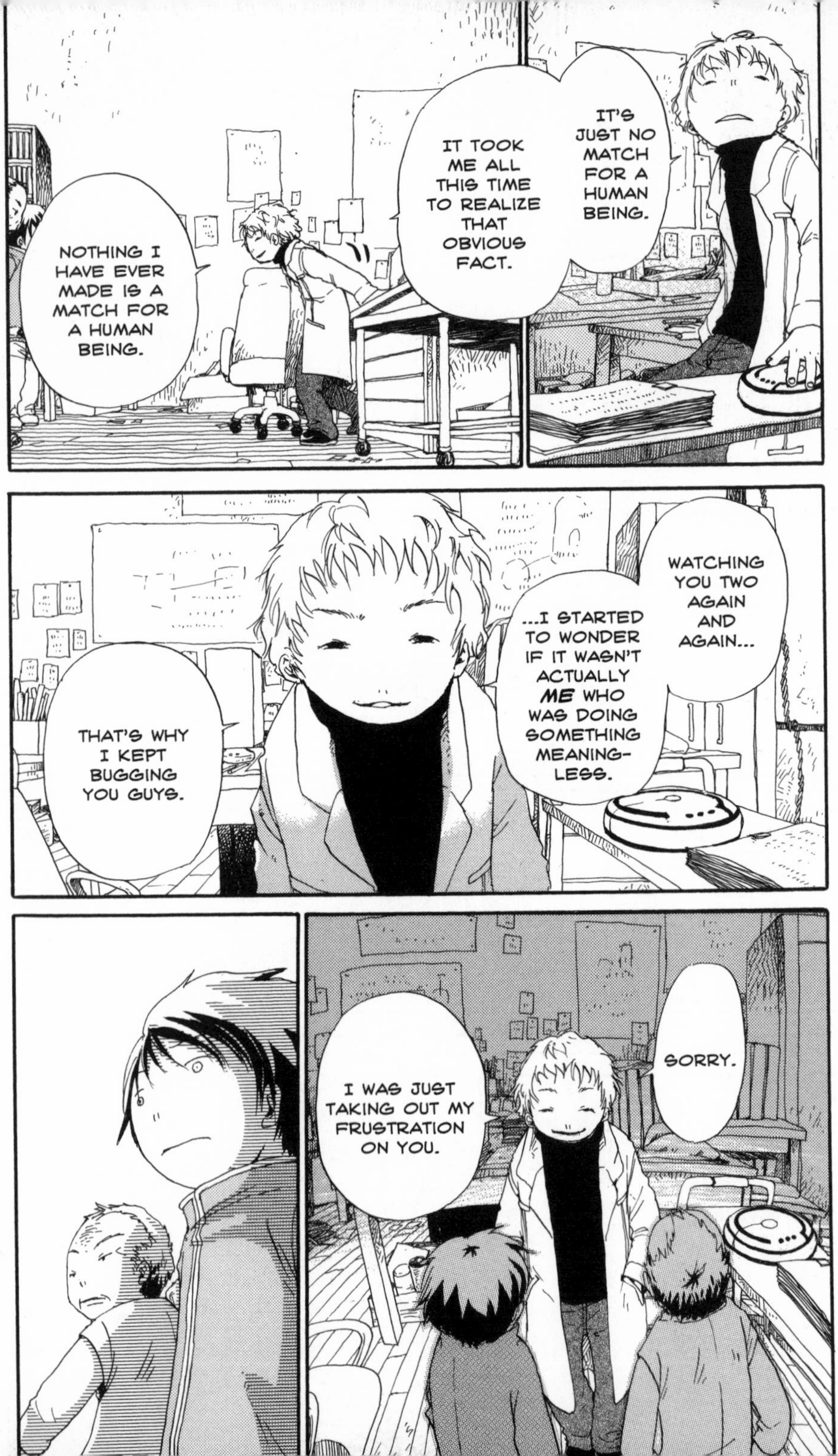
IT'S JUST NO MATCH FOR A HUMAN BEING.
IT TOOK ME ALL THIS TIME TO REALIZE THAT OBVIOUS FACT.
NOTHING I HAVE EVER MADE IS A MATCH FOR A HUMAN BEING.
WATCHING YOU TWO AGAIN AND AGAIN...
...I STARTED TO WONDER IF IT WASN'T ACTUALLY *ME* WHO WAS DOING SOMETHING MEANING-LESS.
THAT'S WHY I KEPT BUGGING YOU GUYS.
SORRY.
I WAS JUST TAKING OUT MY FRUSTRATION ON YOU.

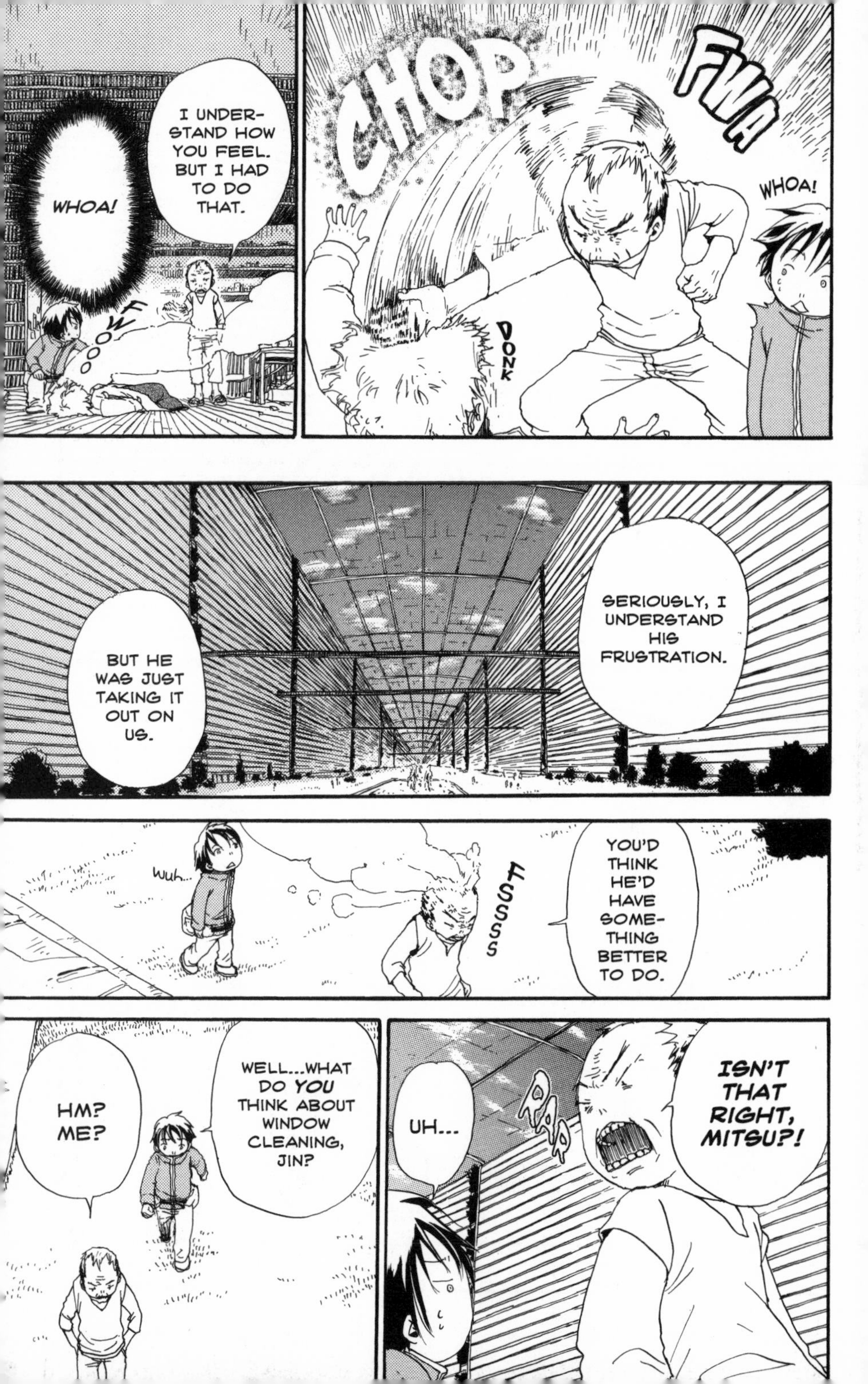
FWA
CHOP
WHOA!
DONK
I UNDERSTAND HOW YOU FEEL. BUT I HAD TO DO THAT.
WHOA!
FWOOO
SERIOUSLY, I UNDERSTAND HIS FRUSTRATION.
BUT HE WAS JUST TAKING IT OUT ON US.
YOU'D THINK HE'D HAVE SOMETHING BETTER TO DO.
FSSSSS
Wuh...
ISN'T THAT RIGHT, MITSU?!
UH...
WELL...WHAT DO *YOU* THINK ABOUT WINDOW CLEANING, JIN?
HM? ME?

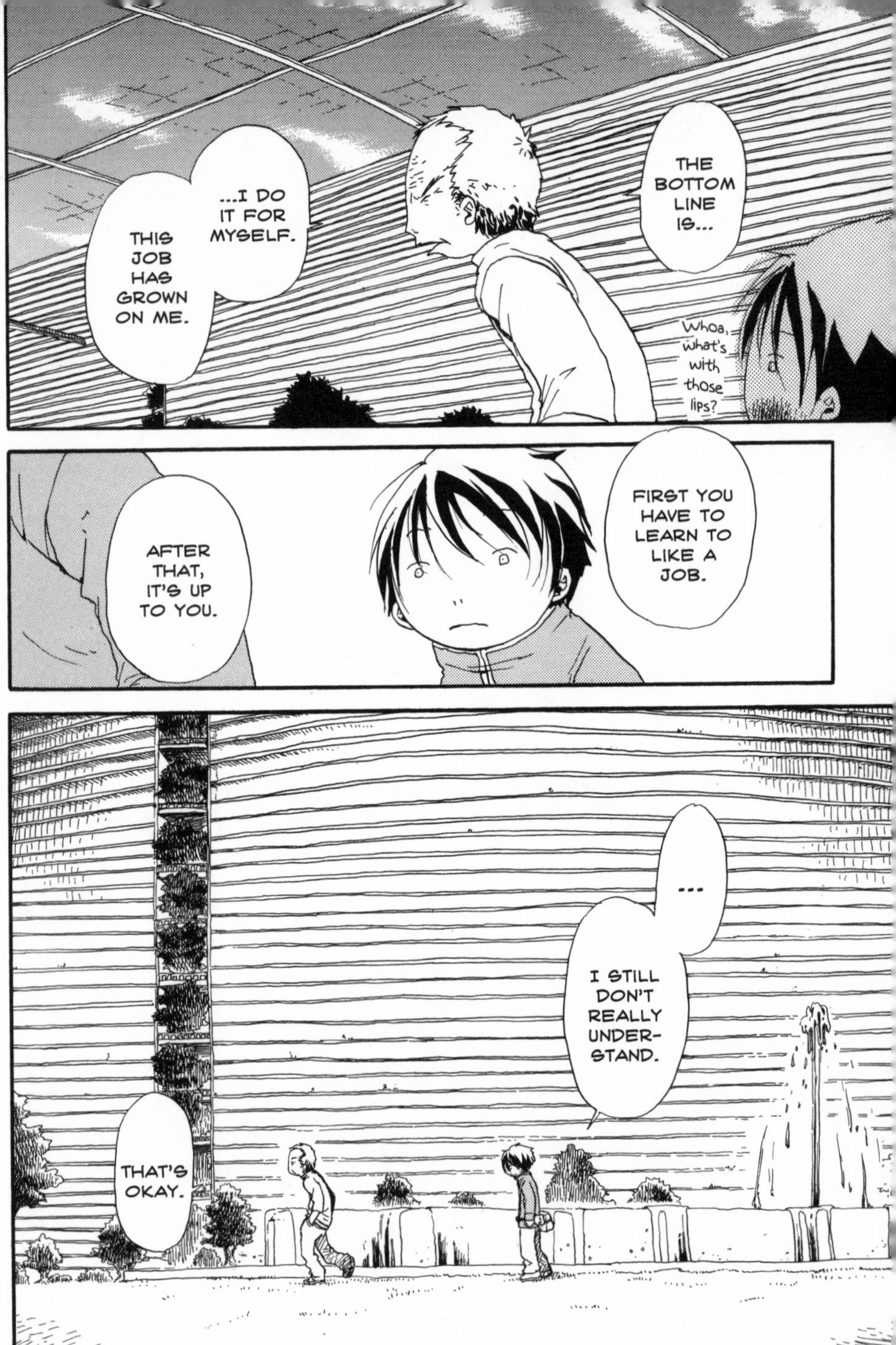
THE BOTTOM LINE IS...
Whoa, what's with those lips?
...I DO IT FOR MYSELF.
THIS JOB HAS GROWN ON ME.
FIRST YOU HAVE TO LEARN TO LIKE A JOB.
AFTER THAT, IT'S UP TO YOU.
...
I STILL DON'T REALLY UNDER-STAND.
THAT'S OKAY.

in the loft

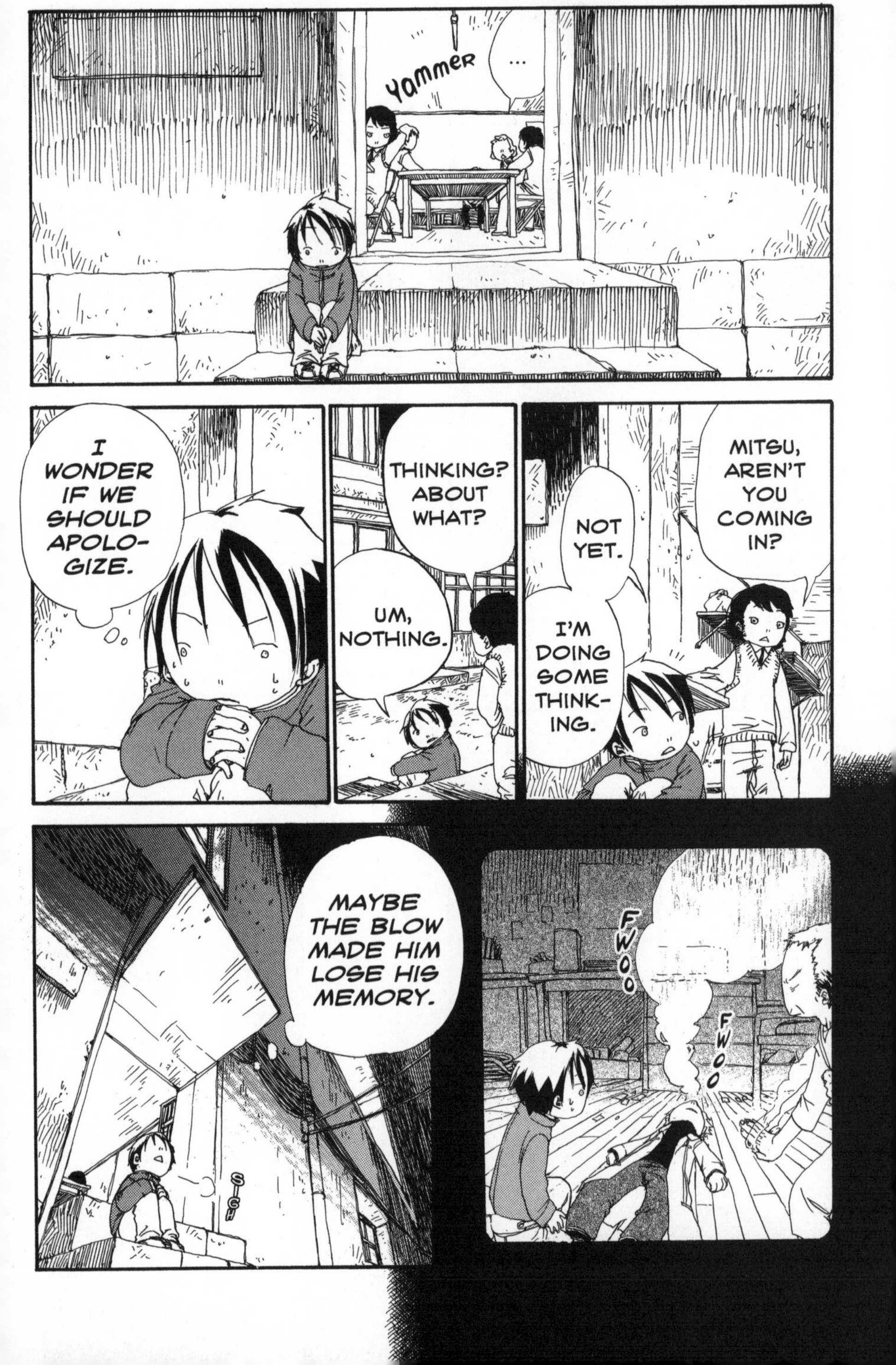
Yammer
...
MITSU, AREN'T YOU COMING IN?
NOT YET.
I'M DOING SOME THINKING.
THINKING? ABOUT WHAT?
UM, NOTHING.
I WONDER IF WE SHOULD APOLOGIZE.
FWOO
FWOO
MAYBE THE BLOW MADE HIM LOSE HIS MEMORY.
SIGH

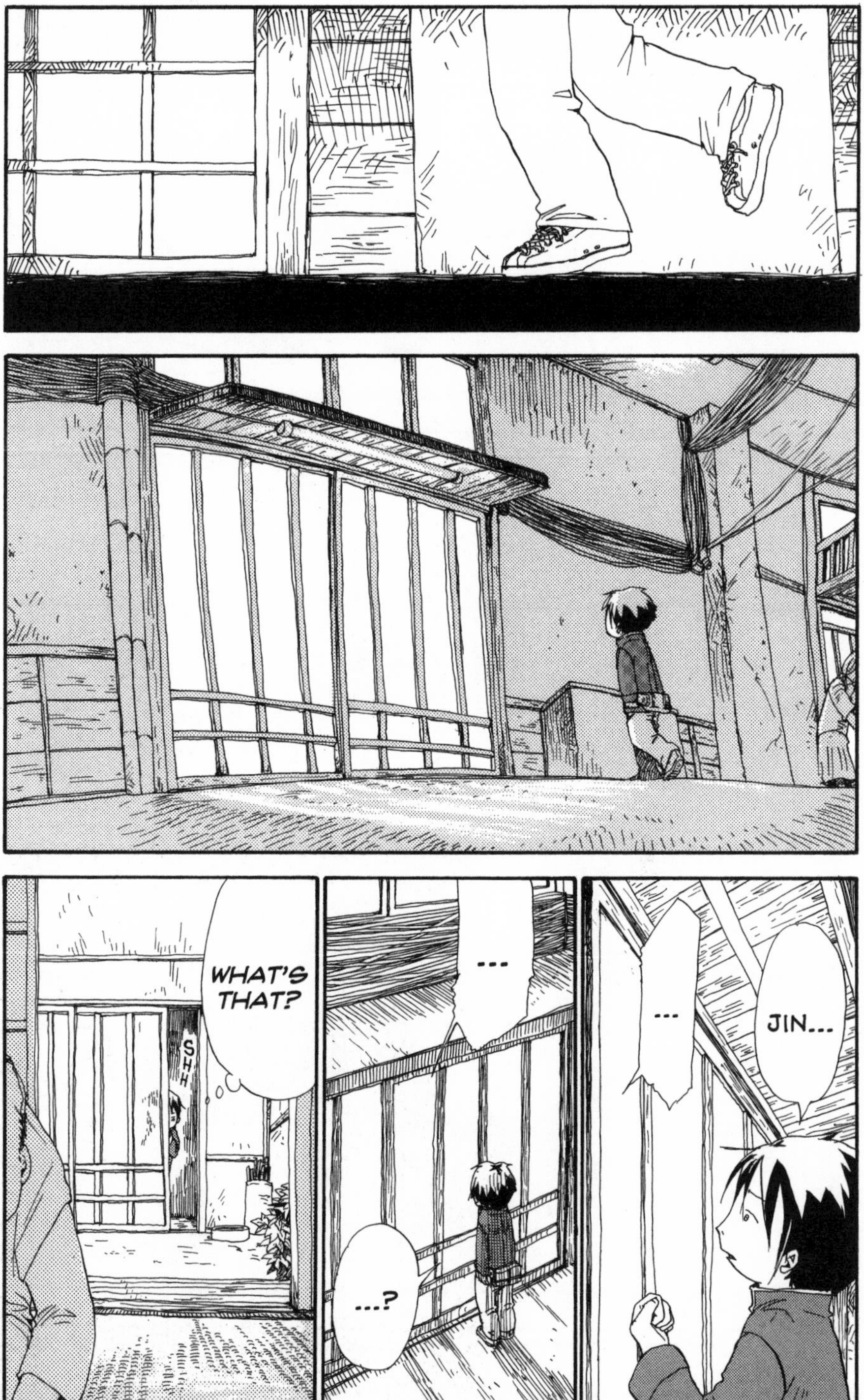
JIN...
...
...
...?
WHAT'S THAT?
SHH

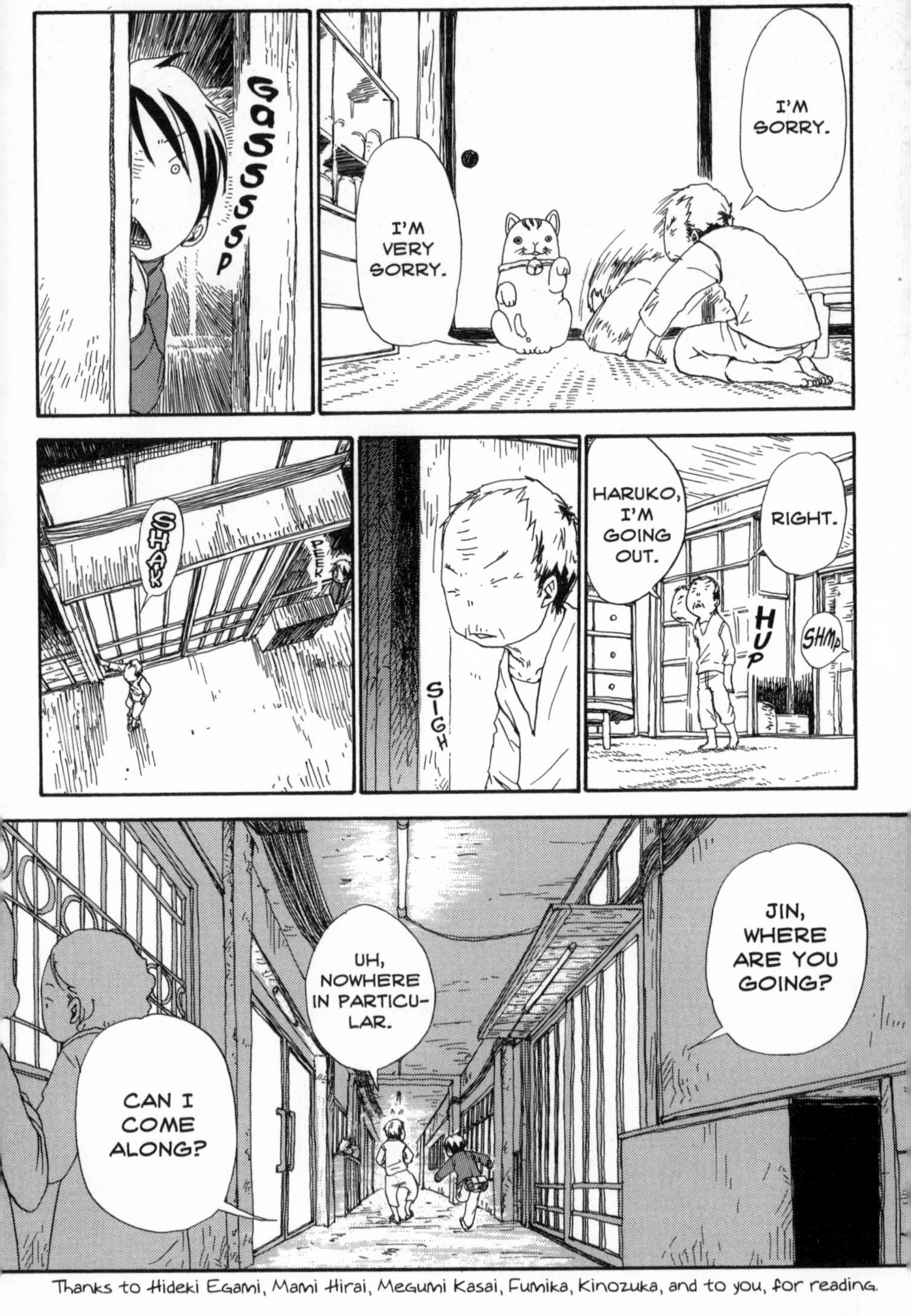
I'M SORRY.
I'M VERY SORRY.
GASSSSSP
HARUKO, I'M GOING OUT.
RIGHT.
HUP
SHMP
SIGH
SHAK
PEEK
JIN, WHERE ARE YOU GOING?
UH, NOWHERE IN PARTICU-LAR.
CAN I COME ALONG?

Thanks to Hideki Egami, Mami Hirai, Megumi Kasai, Fumika, Kinozuka, and to you, for reading.

THE END OF SATURN APARTMENTS 1

SATURN APARTMENTS
Volume 1
VIZ Signature Edition

Story and Art by **HISAE IWAOKA**

© 2006 Hisae IWAOKA/Shogakukan
All rights reserved.
Original Japanese edition "DOSEI MANSION" published by SHOGAKUKAN Inc.

Design of original Japanese edition by Kei Kasai

Translation/Matt Thorn
Touch-up Art & Lettering/Eric Erbes
Design/Yukiko Whitley
Editor/Daniel Gillespie

VP, Production/Alvin Lu
VP, Sales & Product Marketing/Gonzalo Ferreyra
VP, Creative/Linda Espinosa
Publisher/Hyoe Narita

Printed in the U.S.A.

Published by VIZ Media, LLC
P.O. Box 77010
San Francisco, CA 94107

10 9 8 7 6 5 4 3 2 1
First printing, May 2010

www.sigikki.com

www.viz.com

YOU'RE READING THE WRONG WAY

SATURN APARTMENTS IS PRINTED RIGHT TO LEFT IN ORDER TO PRESERVE THE ORIGINAL ORIENTATION OF HISAE IWAOKA'S GORGEOUS ART. PLEASE TURN THE BOOK OVER AND ENJOY.

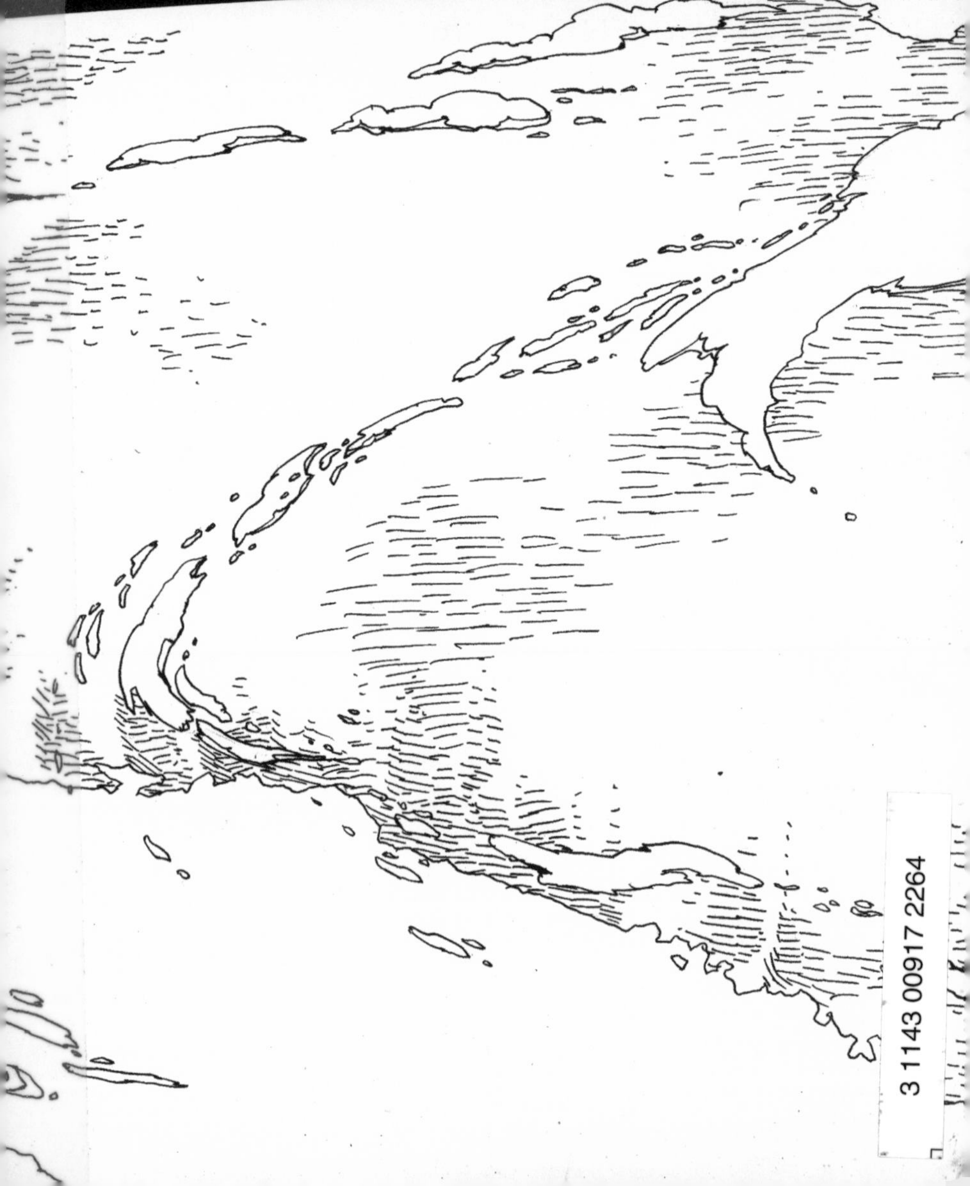